Tasks and Techniques: A Sampling of the Methodologies for the Investigation of Animal Learning, Behavior and Cognition

TASKS AND TECHNIQUES: A SAMPLING OF THE METHODOLOGIES FOR THE INVESTIGATION OF ANIMAL LEARNING, BEHAVIOR AND COGNITION

MATTHEW J. ANDERSON
EDITOR

Nova Science Publishers, Inc.
New York

For permission to use material from this book please contact us:
Telephone 631-231-7269; Fax 631-231-8175
Web Site: http://www.novapublishers.com

NOTICE TO THE READER

The Publisher has taken reasonable care in the preparation of this book, but makes no expressed or implied warranty of any kind and assumes no responsibility for any errors or omissions. No liability is assumed for incidental or consequential damages in connection with or arising out of information contained in this book. The Publisher shall not be liable for any special, consequential, or exemplary damages resulting, in whole or in part, from the readers' use of, or reliance upon, this material.

Independent verification should be sought for any data, advice or recommendations contained in this book. In addition, no responsibility is assumed by the publisher for any injury and/or damage to persons or property arising from any methods, products, instructions, ideas or otherwise contained in this publication.

This publication is designed to provide accurate and authoritative information with regard to the subject matter cover herein. It is sold with the clear understanding that the Publisher is not engaged in rendering legal or any other professional services. If legal, medical or any other expert assistance is required, the services of a competent person should be sought. FROM A DECLARATION OF PARTICIPANTS JOINTLY ADOPTED BY A COMMITTEE OF THE AMERICAN BAR ASSOCIATION AND A COMMITTEE OF PUBLISHERS.

Library of Congress Cataloging-in-Publication Data
Tasks and techniques : a sampling of the methodologies for the investigation of animal learning, behavior, and cognition / Matthew J. Anderson (editor).
     p. cm.
  Includes index.
  ISBN 1-60021-126-7
  1. Learning in animals. 2. Animal behavior. 3. Cognition in animals. I. Anderson, Matthew J.
QL785.T37   2006
591.5--dc22   2006008450

Published by Nova Science Publishers, Inc. ✛New York

CONTENTS

PREFACE

The purpose of this volume is to provide the reader with an overview of a wide sampling of research methodologies employed in the investigation of animal learning, behavior, and cognition. The subject matter of primary concern in this text are the experimental methods employed in these fields, not necessarily the findings obtained with the methodologies themselves. Each chapter was written by a researcher with extensive knowledge and experience employing a particular technique. It is my hope that after reading each chapter, the reader will be better prepared to successfully apply the technique in his or her own research. While this edited volume is intended to serve primarily as a starting point for new research projects, it may also be of use in research methods or animal learning and cognition courses.

The tasks and methods covered in the text represent what I feel to be a fair mix of classic, well-established methodologies, and several lesser-known and relatively new techniques. The reader should note however that, as the title implies, this volume contains only a relatively small sampling of the countless methods employed in these areas. Indeed, it is simply not possible to fit the enormous variety of existing methodologies into one volume.

ACKNOWLEDGEMENTS

To the many brilliant authors who have contributed to this volume I am forever indebted. I thank you for your contributions and for helping to make this project a reality. I also owe my eternal gratitude to my wife and best friend Triniti. Without her endless support and patience this project could not have been completed. I dedicate my portion of this work to my daughter Emily, who has brought more joy to my life than I ever believed possible.

M.J.Anderson (January 5, 2006)

ABOUT THE AUTHORS

Matthew J. Anderson, Ph.D., is currently an Assistant Professor of Psychology at Saint Joseph's College of Maine (Standish, ME). He earned a B.A. from Susquehanna University and pursued graduate training at Kent State University, where he obtained his M.A. and Ph.D. in Experimental Psychology. His research focuses on animal learning, memory, and cognition with a particular interest in developmental psychobiology. Additional interests include contextual influences on memory, the effects of novelty and curiosity on exploratory behaviors, and time perception. Begining in the fall of 2006 he will be at Saint Joseph's Univeristy (Philadelphia, PA).

Antonio Armario is Full Professor of Physiology at the School of Sciences of the Autonomous University of Barcelona. He earned his PhD at this University working on endocrine effects of chronic stress in rats. He has been interested in the neuroendocrinology of stress, animal models of depression and the mechanisms underlying adaptation to chronic repeated stress, with special emphasis in the role of the hypothalamus-pituitary-adrenal axis. Actually, he is studying neurobiological bases of individual differences in responsiveness to stress and the long-term consequences of exposure to stress on anxiety-like behavior and drug addiction.

Barry D. Berger BDB received his B.Sc. 1962 from the University of Maryland in Psychology and Zoology; his MA 1964 from Bryn Mawr College in Comparative Psychology; and his Ph.D. 1968 also from Bryn Mawr College in Psychopharmacology. He has been a member of the Department of Psychology, University of Haifa (Israel), from 1972 and is currently Head of the Graduate Program in Psychobiology. Research foci include: brain and behavioral mechanisms of social interaction and pathologies of social interaction (including aggression); brain and behavioral mechanisms of drug seeking behavior; brain and behavioral mechanisms and applied and theoretical aspects of taste aversion learning. Teaching foci include the courses: "Psychopharmacology for the Clinical Psychologist" and "Drugs, Society, and Behavior".

Rick Bevins, Ph.D., is an Associate Professor of Psychology at the University of Nebraska-Lincoln (UNL). He earned his B.S. from Jacksonville State University in Alabama and his Ph.D. in Neuroscience and Behavior from the University of Massachusetts, Amherst. His Ph.D. work focused on associative learning and Pavlovian fear conditioning. After postdoctoral work in behavioral pharmacology at the University of Kentucky, he took a faculty position at UNL. His research includes assessment of factors affecting learned associations between environmental cues and abused drugs, the ability of drugs to serve as conditional stimuli and occasion setters, and immunotherapy techniques against drug addiction.

James Briggs is currently a doctoral student at Kent State University studying animal learning and memory under David C. Riccio.

Elizabeth E. Caldwell is a post-doctoral fellow at Tufts University, researching the role of serotonin on alcohol-heightened aggression in rodents, with support from the National Institutes of Alcohol Abuse and Alcoholism. She received a Bachelor of Science from the University of Iowa in 1995, and completed her PhD at Kent State University in 2004. Dr. Caldwell has served as adjunct professor at Kent State University (Kent, OH) and Hiram College (Hiram, OH).

Adem Can graduated with a B.A. degree from Bogaziçi University in Istambul, Turkey, in 2000, and subsequently moved to the United States. He is currently a doctoral candidate in Behavioral Neuroscience at The University of Texas.

Amber M. Chenoweth is a graduate student at Kent State University. She earned her B.A. in Psychology in 2004 from Albion College. Current research interests include sequential learning in the rat and examining the effects of pharmacological manipulations on the various components of serial patterns, both in acquisition and retention.

Christopher Cunningham, Ph.D., is Professor of Behavioral Neuroscience at the Oregon Health and Science University. He earned an A.B. from the University of Notre Dame, an M.A. from the University of Iowa, and a Ph.D. in experimental psychology from the University of Oregon Medical School. After teaching at Indiana University and completing postdoctoral work in Pavlovian conditioning at Yale University, he returned to Oregon in a faculty position at OHSU. He has published over 120 scientific papers in the areas of animal learning, behavioral pharmacology and behavioral genetics. More than 1/3 of those papers have involved the place conditioning procedure.

Dr. Terrence Deak earned his PhD from the University of Colorado in 1999 where he specialized in the study of neuroendocrine stress responses, alterations in immune function, and long-term behavioral consequences of stressor exposure. His early work focused largely on outcomes of inescapable tailshock exposure, a well-validated animal model of learned helplessness. After a brief period of post-doctoral training in neurotoxicology, Dr. Deak joined the faculty at SUNY-Binghamton in 2001. His most recent work focuses on neural mechanisms of stress and seeks to understand how exposure to intense stressors produces protracted changes in behavior in order to better understand antecedents of human depression and anxiety.

Michael Domjan is Professor of Psychology at The University of Texas (Austin), where he has been teaching and conducting research on basic mechanisms of Pavlovian conditioning since 1973. His research on sexual conditioning has been funded by the National Institute of Mental Health for nearly 20 years and was recognized by a MERIT Award. In addition to numerous journal articles and book chapters, he is also author of *The Principles of Learning and Behavior* (now in its 5th edition) and *The Essential of Conditioning and Learning* (now in its 3rd edition).

Rosa M. Escorihuela is Associate Professor of Medical Psychology at the Autonomous University of Barcelona, where she earned her PhD. Her initial work focused on psychopharmacology of anxiety and depression as well as on the effects of postnatal handling and environmental enrichment treatments in Sprague-Dawley rats. She also studied the effects of perinatal treatments upon anxiety, learning and memory in the Roman rat lines bred in Zürich, where she developed a postdoctoral fellowship in the ETH-Zentrum. Current research includes evaluation of environmental enrichment effects in old rats, as well as the long-term consequences of several stressors upon anxiety, hippocampal function and drug addiction systems.

Michael S. Fanselow is a Professor of Psychology at U.C.L.A. He received his Ph.D. from the University of Washington and received the Edwin B Newman Award for Excellence in Research for his dissertation work there. He has also received the Early Career Distinguished Scientific Contribution Award and the D. O. Hebb Award from the American Psychological Association and the Troland Award from the National Academy of Science. He was elected President of the American Psychological Association's Division of Behavioral Neuroscience and Comparative Psychology and President of the Pavlovian Society.

Terri Finamore received a BS in psychology from Slippery Rock University. She earned her MA degree at Kent State University where she is currently working on her dissertation under the direction of David Riccio. Her research focuses on animal learning and memory. More specifically, her research interests include the effects of stress on learning and memory and PTSD.

Stephen B. Fountain, Ph.D., is a Professor of Psychology at Kent State University. He earned a B.A. in psychology from Baylor University, a Ph.D. in biopsychology from Johns Hopkins University. He then conducted research in postdoctoral positions in the Neurotoxicology Program at the School of Hygiene and Public Health of the Johns Hopkins University Medical Center and the Department of Neurobiology of the Northeastern Ohio Universities College of Medicine before taking a faculty position at Kent State University. His current research focuses on the psychological and neural processes that give animals the ability to organize complex sequences of behavior through time. The research can be described generally as "comparative cognition," though some lines of research also explore the organization of sequential behavior through psychobiological techniques and computational models of cognitive processes.

Kevin B. Freeman is a doctoral candidate in the Department of Psychology at American University. He received his undergraduate training at the University of Mississippi. Kevin's research focus is on animal models of drug abuse with particular emphasis on the characterization of the pharmacological factors underlying the motivational properties, both rewarding and aversive, of self-administered compounds.

Gordon G. Gallup, Jr. is a Professor in the Department of Psychology at the State University of New York at Albany, Albany, New York 12222. He is a former editor of the Journal of Comparative Psychology. His current research focuses on localizing self-awareness in the brain, as well as looking at schizophrenia as a self-processing deficit. He is also pursing a number of topics on the impact of evolution on human behavior. More detailed information about his recent work can be found at http://www.evolutionarypsych.com

Derek A. Hamilton is an Assistant Professor of Psychology and Neurosciences at The University of New Mexico in Albuquerque, New Mexico. He obtained Master's and Ph.D. degrees in Psychology from The University of New Mexico and received postdoctoral training at the Canadian Centre for Behavioural Neuroscience at The University of Lethbridge. Hamilton's research is focused on associative learning and memory with an emphasis on spatial learning and navigation in humans and rodents.

Gretchen Hanson Gotthard received a B.S. in Psychology from the University of North Dakota (Grand Forks, ND) before working in the laboratory of J. Bruce Overmier at the University of Minnesota (Minneapolis, MN). She earned her Ph.D. in Experimental Psychology with a concentration in Biological Psychology from Kent State University (Kent, OH) under the direction of David C. Riccio and Michael D. Bunsey. Following her graduate training, Dr. Gotthard taught at Carleton College (Northfield, MN) for two years as a Visiting Assistant Professor. She is currently an Assistant Professor in the Psychology Department at Randolph-Macon Woman's College (Lynchburg, VA).

Paulo Guilhardi received his BA (Dec, 1999) from Universidade Federal de São Carlos, Brazil, and his MS (May, 2002) and PhD (May, 2005) in Psychology from Brown University. He is currently a Research Associate in the Timing Laboratory at Brown University in the area of animal learning and behavior. Some of his recent research has focused on the description and explanation of acquisition, extinction, and choice using temporal discrimination procedures.

Yaniv Larish is currently a senior pursuing a B.S. in psychobiology at the State University of New York at Binghamton. He has been working in Dr. Terrence Deak's stress research laboratory for three years. Through his work he has developed an interest in many facets of human and animal behavior, with a particularly strong interest in the development of animal models of the human condition. Having already been accepted into medical school, Yaniv intends to pursue a career in medicine so that he can further integrate his scientific training with treatment of the human condition.

Mika MacInnis received her BA (May, 2002) and MS (May, 2004) in Psychology from Brown University. She is currently working in the Timing Laboratory at Brown University pursuing her doctoral degree in psychology, in the area of animal timing and behavior.

Paula Millin is a professor of Psychology and Neuroscience at Kenyon College in Gambier, Ohio. She received her Ph.D. from Kent State University in Kent, Ohio. Her research investigates the contribution of conditioning to the development and expression of narcotic tolerance, as well as the mechanisms underlying forgetting due to contextual changes and retrograde amnesia.

Melissa Muller is a graduate student at Kent State University where she earned her master's degree in Experimental Psychology and is finishing her doctorate in Biopsychology. She is currently teaching in the psychology department at DePauw University. Her research interests include pattern detection, timing, numerical processing, concept learning, social cognition, spatial cognition, and associative learning.

Roser Nadal, Ph.D. is Associate Professor of Psychobiology at the Autonomous University of Barcelona (Spain). She earned her B.S. in Psychology in 1988 and her Ph.D. in Psychology and Neuroscience in 1992 from the same University. Her Ph.D. focused in the effects of ethanol in anxiety behaviour in rats. She worked as an Assistant Professor from 1992 to 1998, and took a faculty position at UAB in 1998. She visited Wake Forest University in North Carolina and University of California in San Francisco, working in alcohol self-administration. After working in learning and memory, she is actually interested in the relationship between stress, drug addiction and individual differences and in the study of the long-term behavioral consequences of severe stressors.

Richard Port received his BS in psychology from Pennsylvania State University, and his PhD in experimental psychology from Ohio University. He completed postdoctoral training in behavioral neuroscience at the University of Pittsburgh and is currently a Professor of Psychology at Slippery Rock University.

Glen T. Prusky is Chair and Professor of Neuroscience at The University of Lethbridge, Alberta, Canada. Prusky obtained his Ph.D. and Master's in Psychology from Dalhousie University, and postdoctoral training in Neurobiology at Yale University. In addition he has served as faculty in Neural Systems and Behavior at the Marine Biological Laboratory. His work is focused on the neurobiology of visual system development and plasticity, visual learning and memory, and retinal degenerative disease. His work is funded by, Natural Science and Engineering Research Council of Canada, the Canadian Stroke Network, and the National Institutes of Health.

Anthony L. Riley is the chair of the Department of Psychology at American University where he is a Professor of Psychology. He received his undergraduate training at the University of North Carolina and obtained his Ph.D. from the University of Washington. He did a post-doctoral fellowship in pharmacology at Dalhousie University in Canada. He joined the faculty at American University in 1976. He is also a Research Professor in the Department of Neurosciences at Georgetown University. Dr. Riley's research interests include animal models of drug abuse, drug interactions, opioid receptor pharmacology, behavioral toxicology, immunology, chronic drug administration and the effects of prenatal cocaine exposure. He has co-authored over 130 journal articles and book chapters.

James D. Rowan, Ph.D., is a Professor of Psychology at Wesleyan College in Macon, GA. He earned his B.A. from Malone College in Canton, OH, and his M.A. and Ph.D. in Experimental Psychology from Kent State University in Kent, OH. His area of research interest is in comparative cognition, more specifically, serial-pattern learning. His research includes the examination of the effects of neurotransmitter antagonists on pattern learning, the contributions of various factors (pattern structure, phrasing, chunk length) on pattern learning, and the effects of adolescent exposure to drugs on pattern learning in adults.

Matt Sanders was born in Florissant, Missouri in 1971. He graduated from Saint Louis University in 1992 with a B.S. in Psychology. He received his Ph.D. from the University of Miami in 1998. He became a post-doctoral scholar at UCLA in 1999. He continues to investigate the neural bases of Pavlovian fear conditioning and will start an assistant professorship in the Psychology Department at Marquette University in Spring 2006. He currently lives in Milwaukee, Wisconsin with his wife Heather and their daughter Alex.

Richard Schuster: RS received a B.A. from Columbia University (1962) and Ph.D. from Harvard University (1968) in Experimental Psychology with the focus on animal learning from the Behaviorist perspective. Interest in biological bases of behavior led to a post-doctoral position at the University of Pennsylvania in Biophysics and an appointment as Lecturer in Psychology at the University of Zambia in Central Africa (1971-1977) where field research was conducted on the social behavior of an antelope – the Kafue lechwe (Kobus leche). This study was part of a larger project to develop a conservation plan submitted to the Government of Zambia for preserving the ecology and rare wildlife of the Kafue Flats following construction of hydroelectric dams. A move to Israel in 1977 led to an appointment as Lecturer in the Department of Psychology, University of Haifa, Israel (1978-pres) in the areas of animal learning and behavior. The main research focus is on a dialogue between laboratory and field studies of cooperation (dolphins and a planned study of lions and chimpanzees).

Rebecca Singer is a graduate student at the University of Kentucky. She earned her master's degree in Experimental Psychology in 2003. Current research interests include spatial cognition, episodic memory, cognitive dissonance, and the strategies used to solve duration sample conditional discriminations. In addition to her research involving pigeons and rats, Rebecca has investigated the effect of early rearing experience on future breeding success in giant pandas and personality in chimpanzees using the Five Factor Model.

Denise P. A. Smith received her master's degree from Kent State University, Kent, Ohio. Her master's research was in the biopsychology of learning and memory and specifically the hippocampal formation in serial pattern learning. She is continuing at Kent as a Ph.D. candidate investigating basal ganglia and hippocampus and their role as neurological substrates in the processes of learning and memory.

Joseph E. Steinmetz received his B.S. and M.A. degrees from Central Michigan University and his Ph.D. from Ohio University. After completing postdoctoral training at Stanford University under Richard F. Thompson, he joined the faculty at Indiana University where he is the Eleanor Cox Riggs Professor of Brain and Psychological Science. He has served as Chair of Psychology and Executive Associate Dean of Arts and Sciences at Indiana. His main research interests over they years has been exploring the neural correlates of associative learning and memory using model systems.

Robert J. Sutherland is an Alberta Heritage Medical Scientist, Director of the Canadian Centre for Behavioural Neuroscience, and a Professor of Neuroscience at The University of Lethbridge, Alberta, Canada. Sutherland obtained his Ph.D. and Master's in Psychology from Dalhousie University, as well as his postdoctoral training in Neuropsychology at The University of Lethbridge. In addition he has served as a faculty member at the University of New Mexico and University of Colorado. His work is focused on the neurobiology of learning and memory, especially the role of processes in the hippocampus in normal and pathological memory. His work is funded by the Alberta Heritage Foundation for Medical Research, Canadian Institutes of Health Research, Natural Science and Engineering Research Council of Canada, the Canadian Stroke Network, Alberta Centre for Children, Family, and Community Research, and the National Institutes of Health.

Jo Anne Tracy received her B.A. degree from the University of California at Santa Cruz in Psychology and Psychobiology. She completed her Ph.D. in 1996 in the laboratory of Richard F. Thompson at the University of Southern California. In 1999 she and her co-authors were awarded the D. G. Marquis Behavioral Neuroscience Award for their paper showing learning related plasticity in the cerebellum. Currently she is a Research Scientist at Indiana University where she continues her studies in the physiological basis of learning and collaborates on studies of eyeblink conditioning in clinical populations.

Douglas Wallace, Ph.D., is an Assistant Professor of Psychology at Northern Illinois University. He earned his B.A. from the University of Cincinnati and his Ph.D. in Experimental Psychology from Kent State University. His Ph.D. work investigated the role of spatial and proprioceptive stimuli in organizing serial pattern learning. Following a postdoctoral fellowship at the Canadian Centre for Behavioural Neuroscience in Lethbridge, Canada, he took a faculty position at Northern Illinois University where he investigates the neural basis of spatial orientation using naturally occurring behaviors (e.g., exploration, food hoarding, and food competition) and rodent models of neurodegenerative diseases.

Thomas Zentall received his PhD from the University of California at Berkeley in 1969. After serving on the faculty at the University of Pittsburgh he joined the faculty at the University of Kentucky where his now Professor of Psychology. He has been President of the Midwestern Psychological Association, President of the Comparative Cognition Society, President of Divisions 3 and 6 of the American Psychological Association, and a Member of the Governing Board of the Psychonomic Society. His research deals broadly with comparative cognition and includes the study of animal social learning, concept learning, timing, spatial learning, and memory.

PART I. ACTIVITY, EXPLORATION, AND MAZES

In: Tasks and Techniques: A Sampling of the Methodologies...   ISBN 1-60021-126-7
Editor: Matthew J. Anderson, pp. 3-18   © 2006 Nova Science Publishers, Inc.

Chapter 1

METHODS AND MOTIVES FOR USE OF THE FORCED SWIM TEST AS AN ANIMAL MODEL OF BEHAVIORAL DESPAIR/DEPRESSION

Terrence Deak and *Yaniv Larish*

Behavioral Neuroscience Program, Department of Psychology,
State University of New York at Binghamton,
Binghamton, NY 13902-6000, USA

ABSTRACT

Depression is a major psychiatric disorder affecting millions of people in America. The development and validation of effective animal models used to screen pharmacologically active anti-depressant treatments is therefore imperative. The forced swim test is one of the most commonly used behavioral tests for the screening of agents with potential anti-depressant activity, and entails placing a rat in a cylindrical container filled with water from which escape is not possible. Following several minutes of vigorous attempts to escape (swimming and climbing), the rat assumes a characteristic posture of immobility. The immobility response is thought to resemble certain features of behavioral despair/depression, though this interpretation has been somewhat controversial. Nevertheless, use of the forced swim test has increased dramatically in recent years, an effect that can be attributed at least in part to specific methodological adjustments that appear to increase sensitivity of the task without compromising its specificity. The goal of this chapter, therefore, is to provide a brief overview of the forced swim test, focusing on its uses, limitations, and specific methodology. In doing so, we seek to highlight three critical variables that must be considered by investigators who seek to employ this task: (1) individual subject characteristics; (2) parameters of the swim environment; and (3) microarchitecture of behavior during the forced swim test. Deliberate attention to these variables should promote standardization of task parameters across laboratories, optimize

---

* Address correspondence to: Terrence Deak, Ph.D. Department of Psychology, SUNY-Binghamton, Vestal Parkway East, Binghamton, NY 13902-6000, Phone: 607-777-5918, Fax: 607-777-4890, Email: tdeak@binghamton.edu

r degree of susceptibility to stimulation

sensitivity, and improve confidence in the generalizability of outcomes obtained with this commonly used behavioral task.

GENERAL OVERVIEW

Depression is a major psychiatric disorder affecting millions of people in America, with an estimated 15.1%-17.3% of the population (~35 million) affected at some point in life (Kessler *et al.*, 2003). While depression is classified as a psychiatric disorder, it is often co-morbid with a number of physiological diseases including heart-disease (Pratt *et al.*, 1996), diabetes (Anderson *et al.*, 2000) and HIV (Bing *et al.*, 2005) to name a few. The economic impact of depression on the economy is huge with an estimated $43.7 billion per year price tag in the United States. Of the $43.7 billion, $12.4 billion (28%) is attributable to direct costs of medical, psychiatric, and pharmacologic care; $7.5 billion (17%) is attributed to mortality costs arising from depression-related suicides; and $23.8 billion (55%) is attributed to morbidity costs associated with depression in the workplace. This includes the cost of excess absenteeism of depressed workers, as well as reduction in their productive capacity while at work during episodes of the illness (Greenberg *et al.*, 1990). As a result, healthcare professionals, governmental officials, and the scientific community all have a vested interest in understanding and treating depression. It is therefore of great interest to explore novel pharmacological treatments for treating human major depression, a venture that clearly must begin with the development and validation of effective animal models.

In a seminal paper by McKinney and Bunney (McKinney and Bunney, 1969), specific criteria for the use of animal models in the study of depression were proposed. These minimum criteria included four key components: (i) the model must be reasonably analogous to the human disorder in its manifestations or symptomology; (ii) monitoring of behavioral changes must be achieved objectively; (iii) treatments that work in humans must reverse depressive symptomology in the animal model; and (iv) results must be reliably reproducible between laboratories. In many regards, the forced swim test seems an appropriate fit to these criteria (see (Cryan *et al.*, 2005b) for an excellent review).

The forced swim test is perhaps one of the most commonly used animal models of behavioral despair/depression, and has been used extensively as a pre-clinical diagnostic tool for the assessment of novel anti-depressants (Armario *et al.*, 1991; Connor *et al.*, 2000; Cryan and Lucki, 2000; Einat *et al.*, 2001; Porsolt *et al.*, 1978). Porsolt and his colleagues originally developed this paradigm in the late 1970s (Porsolt et al., 1978; Porsolt *et al.*, 1977). In this simple task, rats are forced to swim in a cylinder of water from which they cannot escape on two consecutive days. The first 'priming' session is a 15 min exposure; the second 'test' period is a 5 min swim session where the impact of (putative) antidepressants administered in the 24 hr inter-exposure interval is assessed. After a short period of time the rats adopt an immobile posture and only small movements necessary to keep their heads above water is then observed. Porsolt proposed that the characteristic and easily identifiable immobility exhibited by the rats represented a state of despair analogous to depression in humans (Porsolt et al., 1977). Because the forced swim test appeared to meet all of the criteria set forth by McKinney and Bunney described above, the paradigm quickly gained favor and has become a benchmark in the industry for detecting putative antidepressant effects (Cryan *et al.*, 2002a). As a result, use of the forced swim test has increased exponentially in recent years, a trend supported by the number of studies published per year using "forced swim test" as a descriptor in a typical pubmed search (see Figure 1).

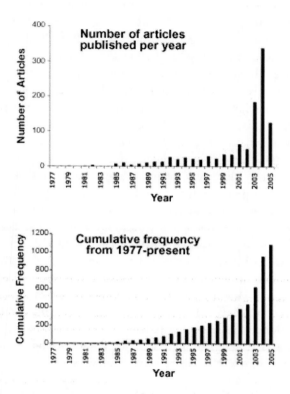

Figure 1. Prevalence of the forced swim test. Use of the forced swim test has increased dramatically as evidenced by the number of articles published per year (top graph) retrieved from a Pubmed search using the term 'forced swim test' and each year from 1977-present as descriptors. These simple criteria were not meant to be exhaustive and likely underestimate the total number of articles published on the forced swim test. Data presented in the bottom graph represent the cumulative number of articles published using the same search criteria, and illustrate the exponential increase in articles published in the last 5 years. Notably, our search revealed an increase from 51 articles published in 2002 to 186 articles in 2003, followed sharply by 339 articles in 2004 – a 6.6-fold increase in published articles in just 2 years! Data from 2005 are current as of 10/25/05.

SENSITIVITY AND USES OF THE FORCED SWIM TEST

Porsolt demonstrated that the amount of time spent immobile during the testing session was significantly reduced with the administration of common anti-depressant drugs, electroconvulsive shock, deprivation of REM sleep, and exposure to an "enriched" environment; all of which are known to alleviate symptoms associated with depression in humans (Porsolt et al., 1977). More recently, antidepressant-like activity has been observed in the forced swim test following alternative treatments for depression such as transcranial magnetic stimulation (Hargreaves *et al.*, 2005), chronic administration of zinc (Nowak *et al.*, 2003) and herbal remedies (Beijamini and Andreatini, 2003; Singewald *et al.*, 2004). One consistent problem with the forced swim test is the 'false positive' produced by psychomotor stimulants such as amphetamine. However, such nonspecific locomotor effects can be readily identified in tests of locomotor activity such as the open field test (Porsolt et al., 1978). Together, these findings support the use of the forced swim test as an effective behavioral screening test for the assessment of potential antidepressant-like activity.

It was a large conceptual inference, however, when Porsolt interpreted the immobility response during the forced swim test as 'behavioral despair'. His justification for this interpretation was based largely on the observation that many common antidepressant treatments reversed the expression of immobility. Furthermore, he observed that rats adopted the immobile posture more rapidly and for a longer duration on the second day of forced swim relative to the first, suggesting that the priming swim session on day 1 may induce a protracted state of 'hopelessness' or 'despair' in the subject. As a result, the interpretation of immobility as 'behavioral despair' came under intense scrutiny by a field entrenched in behaviorist traditions who ultimately viewed the assignment of complex emotional wherewithal such as despair/depression to rodents as gratuitously anthropomorphic. The task was further scrutinized when it was observed that rats may learn to balance precariously on their tails or by stretching a paw to the bottom/sides of the swim tank, thereby awaiting rescue by the researcher or other intervening circumstances (Borsini et al., 1989). These observations readily explained the faster transition to immobility on the second day of the task and reversed the interpretation of the immobility response from a *maladaptive* emotional state of despair to an *adaptive* strategy for surviving the situation. In response to these criticisms, researchers employed a deeper and wider swim tank so that such precarious balancing acts were no longer possible (Detke and Lucki, 1996). Even with this modification, however, some researchers still argued that the transition to immobility was simply a learned 'floating' response that had little, if anything, to do with despair.

An equally critical issue, then, is whether the forced swim test is sensitive to treatments/conditions thought to precipitate major depression in humans. Such treatments would be expected to increase immobility and would therefore be viewed as 'depressogenic' in nature. Evidence to date has been somewhat conflicted (Borsini and Meli, 1988; Borsini et al., 1986), but at least some depressogenic-like effects have been detected in the forced swim test following well-accepted antecedents of major depressive episodes in humans. For instance, exposure to intense stressors (immobilization) but not mild ones (restraint, noise, etc) has been shown to increase immobility time in the forced swim test (Armario et al., 1991) as does chronic mild stress exposure (Bielajew et al., 2003; Molina et al., 1994). Inescapable shock, but not an equivalent amount/duration of escapable shock, increased signs of behavioral depression (Weiss et al., 1981), suggesting that the traditional learned helplessness paradigm and behavioral despair models might share certain common neurobiological substrates (see (Cryan et al., 2005b; Maier and Watkins, 2005) for reviews, respectively). Social isolation of juvenile mice increased immobility (Yates et al., 1991) while older adult mice appear indifferent to even prolonged periods of social isolation (Hilakivi et al., 1989). The forced swim test successfully detects depressogenic consequences of withdrawal from chronic amphetamine exposure (Cryan et al., 2003) as well as reserpine-induced depression (Huang et al., 2004; Porsolt et al., 1977). Thus, at least some conditions associated with depression in humans appear to also increase signs of 'despair' in the forced swim test.

In contrast, olfactory bulbectomy, a well-accepted rodent model of depression (Song and Leonard, 2005), failed to alter immobility time in the forced swim test (Gorka et al., 1985). Prenatal stress also failed to produce changes in behavioral responding later in life even though the same rats exhibited other marked behavioral aberrations (eg., (Van den Hove *et al.*, 2005)). While there is evidence that the forced swim test may be sensitive to cytokine-induced depressive effects in mice (Dunn and Swiergiel, 2005; Jain *et al.*, 2001), our laboratory has failed to observe effects of immune activation on forced swim behavior in rats despite the use of rigorous controls (Deak *et al.*, 2005). With that said, it is noteworthy to mention that conflicting outcomes are often observed between rats and mice in the forced swim test, a fact that led some researchers to propose that the forced swim test may have diminished specificity, and therefore reduced face validity, in mice (Borsini and Meli, 1988).

Together, the findings described above suggest that the forced swim test appears to be sensitive to numerous conditions that seem to promote depression in humans, strengthening the view that the forced swim task is not just effective as a screening test for novel therapeutics with high predictive validity, but also maintains at least a modicum of face validity as an animal model of despair/depression. The ease of use and reliability of the task across laboratories has led to widespread use of the forced swim test for a variety of purposes. A number of investigators have systematically varied parameters of the forced swim test, yet discrepancies in the methods employed and the outcomes achieved are still widespread in the literature. As a result, it would be advantageous to provide a more detailed discussion of methodological factors that must be taken into account when designing experiments with this task to promote standardization of task parameters, to optimize sensitivity, and to improve confidence in the generalizability of outcomes. As such, we will now divert our attention to three critical areas of discussion: (1) individual subject characteristics; (2) parameters of the swim environment; and (3) microarchitecture of behavior during the forced swim test.

INDIVIDUAL SUBJECT CHARACTERISTICS

Individual subject characteristics such as age, gender, strain and species appear to be critical determinants of overall task sensitivity. For instance, gender differences in behavioral responding to antidepressants have been observed (Barros and Ferigolo, 1998; Bielajew et al., 2003), effects that may not be apparent if 'immobility' alone is measured. Differential sensitivity of the forced swim test to strains of rats and mice that differ naturally in depressive phenotypes or that have been artificially selected for depressive tendencies has also been reported (Cryan et al., 2002a; Cryan et al., 2005a; Lucki, 1997; Rittenhouse et al., 2002; Weiss *et al.*, 1998). Discrepant outcomes are often observed between rats and mice, a finding that may suggest reduced specificity (i.e., greater probability of 'false positive') of the task when mice are employed as test subjects (Borsini and Meli, 1988). Species and strain of subjects must be carefully considered, therefore, when designing experiments with the forced swim test. For instance, for researchers who seek to identify the relationship between early life stress and depressive tendencies later in life, it may be appropriate to use Wistar-Kyoto rats rather than Sprague Dawley rats (Rittenhouse et al., 2002).

Age of the test subject may also be an important variable predicting sensitivity of the forced swim test, and this issue requires special attention. Porsolt's early work employed male rats ranging from 175-200 g, a weight range that corresponds to approximately 44-48 days of age in Sprague Dawley rats (extrapolated from normative growth curves available on the Harlan website; www.harlan.com). This corresponds to the late adolescent period in rats, *interesting*

a developmental period where pharmacological sensitivity to various drugs can be dramatically exaggerated or dampened relative to young adult counterparts (70-75 days of age; (Spear, 2000). The natural propensity for scientists is to use rats at the minimum age necessary so that cost can be moderated (a single male rat weighing 175-200 g costs $19.90, while a 300-325 g counterpart costs $28.90; www.harlan.com). However, use of adolescent subjects may yield different results than use of young adults, thereby limiting generalization to the broader population. The goal here is not to make a specific recommendation for age, gender, strain, or species of subjects that may be better suited as subjects in the forced swim test, but rather to draw attention to individual subject characteristics that could (i) limit the outcome of the experiment before it is ever conducted, (ii) contradict findings from other relevant studies, or (iii) define a very specific population towards which results may be generalized.

PARAMETERS OF THE SWIM ENVIRONMENT

General Comments

One distinct advantage of the forced swim test is that successful testing depends on only a few situational variables that can be readily controlled by the researcher. Group housing of mice prior to testing has been shown to increase baseline immobility and enhance sensitivity of the task to antidepressant treatment (Karolewicz and Paul, 2001). Though some variation in behavioral responding has been observed across the circadian cycle (Kelliher et al., 2000), most researchers conduct behavioral testing during 'lights-on'. Circannual fluctuations in forced swim behavior has also been observed, with lowest immobility observed during the summer months despite a tightly controlled laboratory environment (Abel, 1995). Lighting conditions during the task also vary across labs (ambient lighting versus testing in the dark using an infrared camera), but the impact of lighting on task sensitivity is presently unclear. Camera position also varies, with some researchers video-taping from directly above the swim tank (i.e., the only direction possible if cylinders are opaque) and others taping from a side or downward angle. Testing is typically conducted in clean water since soiled water may contain alarm substances that modify behavioral outcomes (Abel and Bilitzke, 1990). The three remaining aspects of the swim session are water depth, temperature, and duration of the swim session; each of these parameters is addressed below.

Water Depth

As described above, it was noted that certain rats appeared to become immobile because they had learned to balance on their paws or tails. The obvious problem that arose, then, was that 'immobility time' became contaminated by 'balancing time,' thereby confounding the interpretation of results. Even when strict criteria for immobility were established (i.e., omitting time spent balancing), task sensitivity could suffer dramatically since the task would no longer be inescapable. The simple solution to this problem was to increase the depth of water from 15 cm to 30 cm, a change that prevents nearly all rats from supporting themselves on their tails or hind legs. Thus, water depth should be chosen for the species and age of the subject such that no active escape-oriented postures such as balancing can be effectively employed.

Water Temperature

so couldn't you say the temp is causing depress? [hypothermia]

Rats forced to swim show a rapid and robust hypothermia during even brief sessions of forced swim (Porsolt *et al.*, 1979). Several studies examining this issue have shown that immobility time varies dramatically based on temperature of the water, with less immobility observed at higher temperatures (Abel, 1993; Jefferys and Funder, 1994). Importantly, Porsolt also showed that successful antidepressant tests with the forced swim test do not depend on reversal of hypothermia, suggesting that sensitivity of the task to antidepressant treatment is independent of changes in core temperature produced by most drugs (Porsolt et al., 1979). Most researchers use water temperature in the range of 23-25°C as Porsolt did. In our laboratory, swim cylinders are submerged in a circulating water bath (Precision Water Bath, model 270) to maintain temperature of the swim water as close to 25°C as possible. We have found that maintaining the water bath at 27°C with cylinders submerged for several hours produces a steady and reliable internal temperature of the swim environment at 25°C (since the cylinders are taller than the water bath, some heat appears to be lost). An added advantage is that the pump on the water bath provides a consistent level of background noise so that extraneous noise in the laboratory does not capture attention of subjects during testing. This procedure also minimizes variability in temperature of the swim water both within and across experiments, thereby alleviating one potential source of unnecessary variance in one's data.

Duration of Session

The third and final parameter of the swim environment that is free to vary is the length of the swim session. Physiological outcomes of forced swim vary as a function of the length of the swim session (Abel, 1993), and a number of reports have suggested increased sensitivity of the task when the typical 15 min 'priming' session or the 5 min 'test' session are increased in duration (eg., (Kitada *et al.*, 1981). However, the vast majority of reports adhere strictly to Porsolt's original design.

MICROARCHITECTURE OF BEHAVIOR DURING THE FORCED SWIM TEST

Behavioral Assessments

One major limitation of the original forced swim test was it failed to reliably detect the effects of selective 5-HT re-uptake inhibitors, an effect that was interpreted as a 'false negative' (Borsini and Meli, 1988; Porsolt et al., 1977). Because SSRIs are one of the most commonly used pharmaceutical treatments for depression in humans, this seemed to be a serious limitation for a task with otherwise high predictive validity. Several researchers postulated that a more detailed examination of active behaviors during the forced swim test (climbing, struggling, swimming, diving, head shakes, etc) rather than just passive behavior (immobility) might broaden sensitivity of the task (Armario *et al.*, 1988). However, early classification of active behaviors was not well standardized, making generalization of the findings difficult. To address this issue, Detke *et al.* (1995) classified the behaviors exhibited by the rat during the forced swim test as one of three distinct categories: (1) *climbing/thrashing*, where the rat makes active movements with its forepaws in and out of the water, usually directed against the walls of the cylinder; (2) *mild swimming*, where the rat makes active swimming motions, more than what is necessary to keep its head above water; and (3) *immobility*, where the rat adopted the characteristic floating posture without overt swimming/struggling, making only the movements necessary to keep its head above water. Though these behavioral categories are readily identifiable, they are by far the most fundamental component of task sensitivity. As such, a series of photos is provided in Figures 2-4 to serve as a more comprehensive guide for classification of behavioral responses during the forced swim test.

what is

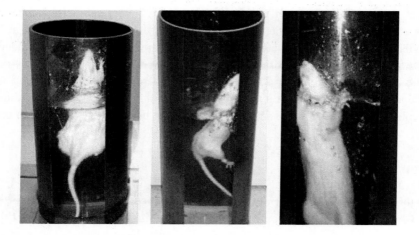

Figure 2. Climbing behavior involves active thrashing and scratching at the walls. In most cases, the vigor of swimming during this phase causes the rat to be propelled out of the water such that the rats shoulders are well above the water line (as depicted in left picture). Though the rat in the middle photo is not propelled out of the water, swimming is still quite vigorous and is represented by large amounts of water displacement (water turmoil), active use of all 4 limbs, and a flaring of toes on the hind paws. The image on the right depicts typical climbing behavior in which the rat actively scratches at the sides of the cylinder with its front paws (also with flared toes).

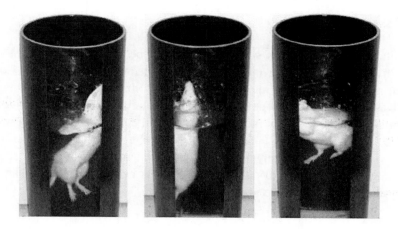

Figure 3. Mild swimming is much more difficult to capture with still images, but some key features of this period can be readily identified. Notice in all photos that water movement is substantially reduced relative to climbing and toes are distributed in a more 'cupped' manner resembling a treading of water. The left picture shows a rat swimming in circles around the perimeter of the tank, a common feature of mild swimming. The reduced vigor during the mild swimming phase rarely leads to acceleration of more than just the head above the water line. Though behavior is typically still directed towards the walls in this phase, substantially less contact is made with the wall of the cylinder. Body posture in the right photo is more horizontal, indicative of steady hind paw motion.

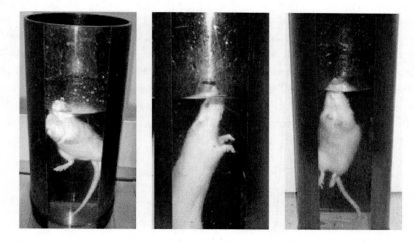

Figure 4. Immobility occurs when only movements necessary to keep the rats head above water are produced. Often times it is just the snout of the rat that rises above the water line (middle and right pictures). Notice the characteristically hunched posture in the left and right photos, often accompanied by piloerection and/or 'puffing' of the thoracic region. Notice in the right photo that the rat has begun listing to the side due to the minimal activity being produced. In many cases, the rat will remain completely immobile, begin listing to one side, then have a small burst of limb activity to reinstate a vertical position in the water.

Interval-Based Scoring

To facilitate the simultaneous scoring of multiple behaviors, Detke *et al.* (1995) also employed a five-second sampling method which enabled the investigator to score several behaviors during a single viewing much more efficiently. In this sampling technique, the rats behavior is classified as meeting one of the 3 categories described above during each 5 sec interval. A brief program can be written for any personal computer to beep every 5 sec when behavior is to be classified. In our laboratory, we have found this technique to be highly sensitive, to yield data that nicely parallel cumulative measures of time spent in each behavioral category, and yet it still allows less frequent active behaviors (head shakes and diving) to be tabulated with relative ease.

Enhanced Sensitivity

The net outcome of these modifications has been the demonstration that while both serotonergic and noradrenergic antidepressants reduced immobility, they appear to do so by differential effects on active behaviors. Specifically, noradrenergic drugs such as desipramine decreased immobility by increasing climbing, while serotonergic drugs decreased immobility by increasing mild swimming (Detke and Lucki, 1996; Detke *et al.*, 1995). Moreover, the effect of serotonergic antidepressants can be reversed by pretreatment with the selective serotonergic inhibitor para-chlorophenylalanine (PCPA; an irreversible inhibitor of tryptophan hydroxylase), while antidepressant activity of noradrenergic antidepressants is largely intact following the same treatment (Page *et al.*, 1999). In a similar vein, 6-hydroxydopamine lesions of the ventral noradrenergic bundle reversed the antidepressant-like effects produced by reboxetine, a noradrenergic reuptake inhibitor (Cryan *et al.*, 2002b). These findings provide powerful tests of both specificity and sensitivity of the modified forced swim test, and further support systematic and thorough classification of both active and passive behaviors during this task.

Microarchitecture of Behavior

Detailed analyses of the relationship among behaviors observed during the forced swim test has recently been performed, and sheds important light on the nature and development of behavioral responding during the forced swim test (Lino-de-Oliveira *et al.*, 2005). The first of these analyses was a principle components analysis which ultimately determined that behavioral patterns loaded onto two separate components that they interpreted as active and passive behaviors, respectively. In addition, sequential analysis of behavior revealed that climbing was initially high and declined rapidly across the 5 min test session, mild swimming increased initially but tended to decline towards the end, and immobility time increased dramatically across the testing session. Their report indicated that mild swimming was strongly related to immobility and head-shakes, while climbing and diving were expressed significantly less. Finally, the authors showed that climbing was only marginally related to measures of open field activity from the same rats, corroborating reports that forced swim behavior can be dissociated from more general measures of locomotor activity (eg., (Detke et al., 1995; Kitada et al., 1981). These more sophisticated approaches towards understanding the microarchitecture of behavior fits well with recent trends in the behavioral sciences, and promise to clarify past discrepancies and identify future directions for novel therapeutics. Though automated systems for the assessment of behavior during the forced swim test are available and have certain distinct advantages for screening large coffers of potential antidepressants (Crowley *et al.*, 2004; De Pablo *et al.*, 1989; Hedou *et al.*, 2001; Kurtuncu *et al.*, 2005; Shimazoe *et al.*, 1987), we believe that more refined analyses are possible with a well-trained eye.

Data Analysis

In more practical applications of the task where the impact of novel therapeutics/manipulations is being assessed, a few comments regarding data analysis are warranted. In our laboratory, all observers are trained to criteria with an experienced researcher using archived tapes with documented treatment effects. All swim sessions are scored by two investigators who are blind to experimental treatment for determination of inter-rater reliability. Data for the two observers is then averaged together and these averages are used as the final unit of analysis, a procedure that minimizes the potential for individual observer bias. Final numbers can then be analyzed using an ANOVA appropriate to the experimental design. Though most researchers typically perform a separate ANOVA for each dependent measure (climbing, mild swim and immobility analyzed independently), it should be noted that these measures are not independent of one another and ANOVA with repeated measures or MANOVA should be considered as an alternative.

The goal of this chapter was not to provide a comprehensive overview of the forced swim test as this has already been done (Cryan et al., 2005b), but instead we sought to provide a conceptual basis for investigators to make informed decisions about how to select parameters that will allow for maximum sensitivity and generalization of findings for their intended purpose. With that said, we now provide a brief protocol for use of the forced swim test as employed in our laboratory (see also (Deak *et al.*, 2003; Deak et al., 2005)).

1. Rats are handled briefly for several days prior to testing in order to acclimate them to experimental handling (3-5 min per day). Weights of animals are recorded on the final day of handling for experimental reporting and subsequent weight-based injections.
2. Prior to each swim session, cylinders (45 cm high, 20 cm diameter) are thoroughly cleaned and disinfected, filled with 30 cm of water, and equilibrated at 25°C prior to use.
3. Rats are placed swiftly and gently into the cylinder hind-paw first while the video camera is already running so as not to lose the first few intervals of recording (often rich in 'climbing', though some rats show an immediate yet transient 'immobility' response). Swim sessions may vary in duration, but the first 'priming' session is typically 15 min in duration while the subsequent 'test' session conducted 24 hr later is typically only 5 min long.
4. At the end of each swim session, the rat is quickly removed from the tank, briefly dried with a fresh towel and returned to their home cages. Some investigators use a heating pad beneath the cage or 15-30 min exposure to a warm environment. Our (unpublished)

observations indicate that hypothermia after 30 min of swim in 25°C water lasts less than 30 min after termination of the session, so use of a warming environment may not be particularly beneficial.

5. If testing for potential antidepressant action, subjects are typically injected with agents at three time points between the 'priming' and 'test' sessions: 23.5, 5, and 1 hr prior to the 5 min 'test' session. The timing of injections and/or other manipulations may vary significantly depending on the half-life of the drug and the specific hypothesis being tested.

6. Video recordings can be scored at one's leisure. We recommend use of the 5 sec interval based scoring system described by Detke *et al.* (1995). Simple cumulation of time spent in each behavioral category is equally sensitive but more laborious to perform.

ACKNOWLEDGMENTS

Generously supported by NIH grant MH65959 and a Young Investigator Award provided by the National Alliance for Research on Schizophrenia and Depression (NARSAD) to T.D.

REFERENCES

Abel, E. L. (1993). Physiological correlates of the forced swim test in rats. *Physiology and Behavior, 54*, 309-317.

Abel, E. L. (1995). Circannual changes in the duration of the immobility response of rats in the forced swim test. *Physiology and Behavior, 58*, 591-593.

Abel, E. L., and Bilitzke, P. J. (1990). A possible alarm substance in the forced swimming test. *Physiology and Behavior, 48*, 233-239.

Anderson, R. J., Lustman, P. J., and Clouse, R. E. (2000). Prevalence of depression in adults with diabetes: A systematic review. *Diabetes, 49*, A64.

Armario, A., Gavalda, A., and Marti, O. (1988). Forced-swimming test in rats: Effect of desipramine administration and the period of exposure to the test on struggling behavior, swimming, immobility and defecation rate. *European Journal of Pharmacology, 158*, 207-212.

Armario, A., Gil, M., Marti, J., Pol, O., and Balasch, J. (1991). Influence of various acute stressors on the activity of adult male rats in a holeboard and in the forced swim test. *Pharmacology, Biochemistry, and Behavior, 39*, 373-377.

Barros, H. M. T., and Ferigolo, M. (1998). Ethnopharmacology of imipramine in the forced-swimming test: Gender differences. *Neuroscience and Biobehavioral Reviews, 23*, 279-286.

Beijamini, V., and Andreatini, R. (2003). Effects of hypericum perforatum and paroxetine on rat performance in the elevated t-maze. *Pharmacological Research, 48*(2), 199-207.

Bielajew, C., Knonkle, A. T., Kentner, A. C., Baker, S. L., Stewart, A., Hutchins, A. A., et al. (2003). Strain and gender specific effects in the forced swim test: Effects of previous stress exposure. *Stress, 6*, 269-280.

Bing, E. G., Burnam, M. A., and Longshore, D. (2005). The estimated prevalence of psychiatric disorders, drug use and drug dependence among people with hiv disease in the united states: Results from the hiv cost and services utilization study. *Archives of General Psychiatry, in press.*

Borsini, F., Lecci, A., Sessarego, A., Frassine, R., and Meli, A. (1989). Discovery of antidepresant activity by forced swimming test may depend on pre-exposure of rats to a stressful situation. *Psychopharmacology, 97*, 183-188.

Borsini, F., and Meli, A. (1988). Is the forced swimming test a suitable model for revealing antidepressant activity? *Psychopharmacology, 94*(2), 147-160.

Borsini, F., Volterra, G., and Meli, A. (1986). Does the behavioral "despair" test measure "despair"? *Physiology and Behavior, 38*(3), 385-386.

Connor, T. J., Kelliher, P., Shen, Y., Harkin, A., Kelly, J. P., and Leonard, B. E. (2000). Effect of subchronic antidepressant treatments on behavioral, neurochemical, and endocrine changes in the forced-swim test. *Pharmacology, Biochemistry, and Behavior, 65*(4), 591-597.

Crowley, J. J., Jones, M. D., O'Leary, O. F., and Lucki, I. (2004). Automated tests for measuring the effects of antidepressants in mice. *Pharmacology, Biochemistry, and Behavior, 78*(2), 269-274.

Cryan, J. F., Hoyer, D., and Markou, A. (2003). Withdrawal from chronic amphetamine induces depressive-like behavioral effects in rodents. *Biological Psychiatry, 54*, 49-58.

Cryan, J. F., and Lucki, I. (2000). Antidepressant-like behavioral effects mediated by 5-hydroxytryptamine (2c) receptors. *Journal of Pharmacology and Experimental Therapeutics, 295*(3), 1120-1126.

Cryan, J. F., Markou, A., and Lucki, I. (2002a). Assessing antidepressant activity in rodents: Recent developments and future needs. *Trends in Pharmacological Sciences, 23*(5), 238-245.

Cryan, J. F., Mombereau, C., and Vassout, A. (2005a). The tail suspension test as a model for assessing antidepressant activity: Review of pharmacological and genetic studies in mice. *Neuroscience and Biobehavioral Reviews, 29*, 571-625.

Cryan, J. F., Page, M. E., and Lucki, I. (2002b). Noradrenergic lesions differentially alter the antidepressant-like effects of reboxetine in a modified forced swim test. *European Journal of Pharmacology, 436*, 197-205.

Cryan, J. F., Valentino, R. J., and Lucki, I. (2005b). Assessing substrates underlying the behavioral effects of antidepressants using the modified rat forced swimming test. *Neuroscience and Biobehavioral Reviews, 29*, 547-569.

De Pablo, J., Parra, A., Segovia, S., and Guillamon, A. (1989). Learned immobility explains the behavior of rats in the forced swimming test. *Physiology and Behavior, 46*(2), 229-237.

Deak, T., Bellamy, C., and D'Agostino, L. G. (2003). Exposure to forced swim stress does not alter central production of IL-1. *Brain Research, 972*, 53-63.

Deak, T., D'Agostino, L. G., Bellamy, C., Rosanoff, M., McElderry, N. K., and Bordner, K. A. (2005). Behavioral responses during the forced swim test are not affected by anti-inflammatory agents or acute illness induced by lipopolysaccharide. *Behavioural Brain Research, 160*, 125-134.

Detke, M. J., and Lucki, I. (1996). Detection of serotonergic and noradrenergic antidepressants in the rat forced swimming test: The effects of water depth. *Behavioural Brain Research, 73*, 43-46.

Detke, M. J., Rickles, M., and Lucki, I. (1995). Active behaviors in the rat forced swimming test differentially produced by serotonergic and noradrenergic antidepressants. *Psychopharmacology, 121*, 66-72.

Dunn, A. J., and Swiergiel, A. H. (2005). Effects of interleukin-1 and endotoxin in the forced swim and tail suspension tests in mice. *Pharmacology, Biochemistry, and Behavior, 81*(3), 688-693.

Einat, H., Clenet, F., Shaldubina, A., Belmaker, R. H., and Bourin, M. (2001). The antidepressant activity of inositol in the forced swim test involves 5-ht2 receptors. *Behavioural Brain Research, 118*, 77-83.

Gorka, Z., Earley, B., and Leonard, B. E. (1985). Effect of bilateral olfacotry bulbectomy in the rat, alone or in combination with antidepressants, on the learned immobility model of depression. *Neuropsychobiology, 13*, 26-30.

Greenberg, P. E., Stiglin, L. E., Finkelstein, S. N., and Berndt, E. R. (1990). The economic burden of depression in 1990. *Journal of Clinical Psychiatry, 54*(11), 405-418.

Hargreaves, G. A., McGregor, I. S., and Sachdev, P. S. (2005). Chronic repetitive transcranial magnetic stimulation is antidepressant but not anxiolytic in rat models of anxiety and depression. *Psychiatry Research, Epub ahead of print.*

Hedou, G., Pryce, C., Di Iorio, L., Heidbreder, C. A., and Feldon, J. (2001). An automated analysis of rat behavior in the forced swim test. *Pharmacology, Biochemistry, and Behavior, 70*, 65-76.

Hilakivi, L. A., Ota, M., and Lister, R. G. (1989). Effect of isolation on brain monoamines and the behavior of mice in tests of exploration, locomotion, anxiety and behavioral 'despair'. *Pharmacology, Biochemistry, and Behavior, 33*(2), 371-374.

Huang, Q. J., Jiang, H., Hao, X. L., and Minor, T. R. (2004). Brain il-1 beta was involved in reserpine-induced behavioral depression in rats. *Acta Pharmacologica Sin, 25*(3), 293-296.

Jain, N. K., Kulkarni, S. K., and Singh, A. (2001). Lipopolysaccharide-mediated immobility in mice: Reversal by cyclooxygenase enzyme inhibitors. *Methods and Findings in Experimental and Clinical Pharmacology, 23*, 441-444.

Jefferys, D., and Funder, J. (1994). The effect of water temperature on immobility in the forced swimming test in rats. *European Journal of Pharmacology, 253*, 91-94.

Karolewicz, B., and Paul, I. A. (2001). Group housing of mice increases immobility and antidepressant sensitivity in the forced swim and tail suspension tests. *European Journal of Pharmacology, 415*, 197-201.

Kelliher, P., Connor, T., Harkin, A., Sanchez, C., Kelly, J., and Leonard, B. (2000). Varying responses to the rat forced swim test under diurnal and nocturnal conditions. *Physiology and Behavior, 69*, 531-539.

Kessler, R. C., Berglund, P., Demler, O., Jin, R., Koretz, D., Merikangaas, K. R., et al. (2003). The epidemiology of major depressive disorder: Results from the ational comorbidity survey replication (ncs-r). *Journal of American Medical Association, 289*(3095-3105).

Kitada, Y., Miyauchi, T., Satoh, A., and Satoh, S. (1981). Effects of antidepressants in the rat forced swimming test. *European Journal of Pharmacology, 72*(145-152).

Kurtuncu, M., Luka, L. J., Dimitrijevic, N., Uz, T., and Manev, H. (2005). Reliability assessment of an automated forced swim test device using two mouse strains. *Journal of Neuroscience Methods, in press.*

Lino-de-Oliveira, C., De Lima, T. C. M., and de Padua Carobrez, A. (2005). Structure of the rat behaviour in the forced swimming test. *Behavioural Brain Research, 158,* 243-250.

Lucki, I. (1997). The forced swimming test as a model for core and component behavioral effects of antidepressant drugs. *Behavioural Pharmacology, 8,* 523-532.

Maier, S. F., and Watkins, L. R. (2005). Stressor controllability and learned helplessness: The roles of the dorsal raphe nucleus, serotonin, and corticotropin-releasing factor. *Neuroscience and Biobehavioral Reviews, 29,* 829-841.

McKinney, W. T., and Bunney, W. E. (1969). Animal model of depression. I. Review of evidence: Implications for research. *Archives of General Psychiatry, 21,* 240-248.

Molina, V. A., Heyser, C. J., and Spear, L. P. (1994). Chronic variable stress or chronic morphine facilitates immobility in a forced swim test: Reversal by naloxone. *Psychopharmacology, 114,* 433-440.

Nowak, G., Szewczyk, B., Wieronska, J. M., Branski, P., Palucha, A., Pilc, A., et al. (2003). Antidepressant-like effects of acute and chronic treatment with zinc in forced swim test and olfactory bulbectomized model in rats. *Brain Research Bulletin, 61*(2), 159-164.

Page, M. E., Detke, M. J., Dalvi, A., Kirby, L. G., and Lucki, I. (1999). Serotonergic mediation of the effects of fluoxetine, but not desipramine, in the rat forced swimming test. *Psychopharmacology, 147,* 162-167.

Porsolt, R. D., Anton, G., Blavet, N., and Jalfre, M. (1978). Behavioural despair in rats: A new model sensitive to antidepressant treatments. *European Journal of Pharmacology, 47,* 379-391.

Porsolt, R. D., Deniel, M., and Jalfre, M. (1979). Forced swimming in rats: Hypothermia, immobility and the effects of imipramine. *European Journal of Pharmacology, 57*(4), 431-436.

Porsolt, R. D., LePichon, M., and Jalfre, M. (1977). Depression: A new animal model sensitive to antidepressant treatments. *Nature, 266,* 730-732.

Pratt, L. A., Ford, D. E., and Crum, R. M. (1996). Depression, psychotropic medication, and risk of myocardial infarction. *Circulation, 94,* 3123-3129.

Rittenhouse, P. A., Lopez-Rubalcava, C., Stanwood, D., and Lucki, I. (2002). Amplified behavioral and endocrine responses to forced swim stress in the wistar-kyoto rat. *Psychoneuroendocrinology, 27,* 303-318.

Shimazoe, T., Shibata, S., and Ueki, S. (1987). A new forced swimming test for the evaluation of antidepressants in rats by recording vibration of a water tank. *Journal of Pharmacobiodynamics, 10,* 639-643.

Singewald, N., Sinner, C., Hetzenauer, A., Sartori, S. B., and Murck, H. (2004). Magnesium-deficient diet alters depression- and anxiety-related behavior in mice -- influence of desipramine and hypericum perforatum extract. *Neuropharmacology, 47*(8), 1189-1197.

Song, C., and Leonard, B. E. (2005). The olfactory bulbectomised rat as a model of depression. *Neuroscience and Biobehavioral Reviews, 29,* 627-647.

Spear, L. P. (2000). The adolescent brain and age-related behavioral manifestations. *Neuroscience and Biobehavioral Reviews, 24,* 417-463.

Van den Hove, D. L., Blanco, C. E., Aendekerk, B., Desbonnet, L., Bruschettini, M., Steinbusch, H. P., et al. (2005). Prenatal restraint stress and long term affective consequences. *Developmental Neuroscience, 27*(5), 313-320.

Weiss, J. M., Cierpial, M. A., and West, C. H. (1998). Selective breeding of rats for high and low motor activity in a swim test: Toward a new animal model of depression. *Pharmacology, Biochemistry, and Behavior, 61*(1), 49-66.

Weiss, J. M., Goodman, P., Losito, B., Corrigan, S., Charry, J., and Bailey, W. (1981). Behavioral depression produced by an uncontrollable stressor: Relationship to norepinephrine, dopamine and serotonin levels in various regions of the rat brain. *Brain Research Reviews, 3*, 167-205.

Yates, G., Panksepp, J., Ikemoto, S., Nelson, E., and Conner, R. (1991). Social isolation effects on the "behavioral despair" forced swimming test: Effect of age and duration of testing. *Physiology and Behavior, 49*(2), 347-353.

In: Tasks and Techniques: A Sampling of the Methodologies...   ISBN 1-60021-126-7
Editor: Matthew J. Anderson, pp. 19-23   © 2006 Nova Science Publishers, Inc.

Chapter 2

OPEN FIELD TESTS: MEASURING ACTIVITY LEVELS

*Matthew J. Anderson**
Saint Joseph's College of Maine
Standish, ME 04084

ABSTRACT

This chapter discusses one of the primary methods utilized by behavioral researchers to examine basic activity levels. Open field tests, while incredibly simply to employ, are essential to many investigations. While used primarily as control measures to examine the contribution of activity level alterations to some experimental outcome, open field tests also provide us with a tool to examine curiosity, exploration, and anxiety levels. Following an introduction to the task and a discussion of some basic findings, a thorough description of open field test methodologies is provided.

INTRODUCTION

Open field tests (OFT) are perhaps some of the simplest tasks employed in animal behavioral research. This ease of methodology however should not be confused with triviality. Open field tests allow the investigator to examine the effects of various experimental manipulations on freely occurring behaviors, unhampered by contingencies or reinforcement. The OFT provides a measure of activity level, curiosity, and exploratory responses. While interesting in its own right, this type of task is typically ran as one part of a series of control measures taken to ensure that an observed experimental result is not simply the byproduct of a change in the overall activity levels. ← It's ran after other experiments to ensure beh isn't caused by something else

For example, say that you are conducting research with a new drug that is believed to enhance memory formation. To test this drug you choose to employ a passive avoidance task (for review see the chapter on passive avoidance). Passive avoidance typically involves the

---
* Address Correspondence to: Matthew J. Anderson, Ph.D. Department of Psychology, Saint Joseph's University, 5600 City Avenue, Post Hall, Philadelphia, PA 19131, e-mail: mander06@sju.edu, phone: (207) 893-7924

pairing of one side of an apparatus with shock so that the static cues associated with that part of the chamber come to produce a fear response. At test in this type of situation, the animal shows us that it remembers the training experience by remaining in the "safe" side of the apparatus that has not been paired with shock. So, after training the subjects to avoid one side of the apparatus you administer the drug to half of your subjects, and find later that the experimental subjects who have received the drug do not cross into the shock paired side, while control (no drug) subjects immediately cross. Can you now conclude that the drug has in fact enhanced the memory of the training experience? The answer is no. The drug may simply have caused a decrease in overall activity resulting in behavior that only appears to be the product of learning. To examine this possibility, one should employ a task in order to measure the activity levels of experimental and control groups. This is where open field type tasks prove invaluable.

In addition to offering this type of control, the open field task allows an investigator to examine the levels of anxiety, stress, fear, and depression in groups of animals. Many have suggested that experience with some stressor prior to open field testing can result in the enhancement of activity (e.g., Roth and Katz, 1979). The animal experiences a heightened level of arousal and is more mobile when put in the open field. Similarly, prenatal malnutrition has been shown to result in hyperactivity in the OFT (Wolf, Almli, Finger, Ryan, and Morgane, 1986).

Many psychopharmacological studies examining the effects of various drugs on overall activity levels have also employed open field measures. Nicotine administration, for example, has been shown to greatly enhance the activity of rats in the open field (Slawecki, Gilder, Roth, and Ehlers, 2003). In contrast, increases in illumination have been known to decrease locomotion in the OFT (Valle, 1970). Nelson, Jordan, and Bohan (1997) have tested the effects of fluoxetine administration on motor behaviors (cell or zone entries and number of rears) in the OFT. Their findings illustrated that rats administered daily doses of fluoxetine are less fearful, displaying less arousal and, consequently, less open field behavior when compared to animals receiving water. Thus, the importance of arousal and anxiety in the enhancement OFT activity is once again highlighted.

OFT studies have involved many types of animals including rats (e.g., Valle, 1970), mice (e.g., Elias, and Redgate, 1975; Goulet, Dore, and Mirault, 2003), opossums (Wesierska, Walasek, Kilijanek, Djavadian, and Turlejski, 2003), and sheep (Hughes, Syme, and Syme, 1977), just to name a few. While many species examined in the open field initially display thigmotaxy, preferring to stay in close proximity to the boundaries of the field, and only later shift their activity to the internal and central portions (e.g., Wesierska, Walasek, Kilijanek, Djavadian, and Turlejski, 2003), numerous strain, sex, and species differences have been discovered in the OFT. For example, female Long-Evans black-hooded rats tend to be particularly mobile, displaying much more locomotion behavior than their male counterparts (Valle, 1970). The same sex difference has been observed in Sprague-Dawley rats with females entering more squares, emitting a greater number of rears, and defecating less than their male counterparts (Alonso, Castellano, Afonso, and Rodriguez, 1991). Additionally, research with Wistar Kyoto rats, a strain of rats thought to be a possible animal model for depression, has shown that animals of this strain are significantly less active than Sprague-Dawley or Wistar rats when measured in the OFT (Tejani-Butt, Kluczynski, and Pare, 2003).

Interestingly, ontogenetic studies have suggested many changes in activity levels across the lifespan. Goodwin and Yacko (2004) have demonstrated that the exploratory motive in rats does not emerge until around postnatal day 21. As a result, one should expect initial activity in the OFT to be lower for very young animals. For all animals the frequency of exploratory responses typically declines with exposure to the arena. Interestingly, it has been shown that very young animals (e.g., 15-days-of-age) habituate to the eliciting environment much slower than older ones (e.g., 21-days-of-age), and will thus explore the arena for longer periods (e.g., Bronstein, Neiman, Wolkoff, & Levine, 1974). Additional deficits can be found at the other end of the lifespan. Evidence has been put forth suggesting that locomotor and exploratory behaviors decline in older mice (Elias, and Redgate, 1975). These developmental trends are likely to be present in many other species as well.

METHODS

There are several versions of the open field task which can be distinguished in terms of whether or not the subject is forced to engage in exploration. The only major procedural difference between these two is that in forced open field tests the animal (usually a rat or mouse) is physically placed in the field and therefore has no choice in the matter. During non-forced open field studies, the animal is typically placed in a start-box at the beginning of the trial and is allowed to explore the open field if it so wishes. In these later cases, bouts of exploration (number of times leaving the start-box) or latency to begin exploration (measured in seconds) can provide interesting measures of the animal's curiosity and activity levels. In either case, activity and exploration in this task is typically measured in terms of "zone" crossings, or number of times that the animal moves from one previously defined region to another. Another common measure in this task is the number or rears (standing up on hind legs) that the animal makes during a trial. Additionally, those studies particularly interested in stress and anxiety typically count the number of fecal boluses left by each animal over the course of a trial session.

We now turn our attention to a simple demonstration of this task. Tejani-Butt, Kluczynski, and Pare (2003) ran rats in an open field task similar to that of Broadhurst (1957). On a circular, black painted, plywood floor (82 cm in diameter) three concentric circles were drawn. The diameters of the three circles were 20 cm for the inner, 50 cm for the middle, and 82 cm for the outer circle, as defined by the arena wall which was made out of 30 cm high aluminum sheeting. The three circles were further divided into 1, 6, and 12 approximately equal size areas, for the inner, middle, and outer circle respectively. A 100-W light was suspended 132 cm above the floor of the apparatus. Keep in mind that while this study relied on concentric circles, almost any zoned off surface can be used in the OFT. Typically, however, a circular arena is preferable over a square or rectangle as animals may attempt to hide in the corners. It is important that the zones are of equal size in order to ensure accurate measurement of activity. Additionally, the entire apparatus must be located in a quiet area or a masking noise should be provided in order to prevent outside noise from disturbing the subjects' behavior.

Tejani-Butt, Kluczynski and Pare (2003) started each trial by placing the rat in one of the outer segments against the arena wall. From behind a one-way observation screen, the experimenter recorded latency to leave the starting segment as well as the total number of segments visited by each animal. The subject had to fully enter the segment with all four feet to have that area counted as visited. Each trial lasted three minutes and the arena was wiped with a soapy solution after each subject. This was done in order to eliminate any scent trail left behind by the animal that may have interfered with the behavior future subjects.

In addition to the direct observation technique used by Tejani-Butt, Kluczynski and Pare (2003), researchers may choose to monitor activity with motion tracking equipment and computer analysis in order to reduce observer bias. While the computer motion analysis systems may be the ideal method one should be warned that such equipment might exceed the budgetary constraints of a smaller lab. As a more cost efficient alternative, researchers may choose to videotape sessions and later have the activity scored by multiple raters blind to the experimental condition. If employing multiple raters, one should correlate their scores to examine inter-rater reliability.

REFERENCES

Alonso, S. J., Castellano, M. A., Afonso, D., and Rodriguez, M. (1991). Sex differences in behavioral despair: Relationship between behavioral despair and open field activity. *Physiology and Behavior, 49,* 69-72

Broadhurst, P. L. (1957). Determinants of emotionality in the rat. Situational factors. *British Journal of Psychology, 48,* 1-12.

Bronstein, P. M., Neiman, H., Wolkoff, F. D., and Levine, M. J. (1974). The development of habituation in the rat. *Animal Learning & Behavior, 2,* 92-96.

Elias, P. K., and Redgate, E. (1975). Effects of immobilization stress on open field behavior and plasma corticosterone levels of aging C57BL/6J mice. *Experimental Aging Research, 1,* 127-135.

Goodwin, G. A., and Yacko, H. (2004). Emergence of the exploratory motive in rats. *Developmental Psychobiology, 45,* 34-48.

Goulet, S., Dore, F. Y., and Mirault, M. E. (2003). Neurobehavioral changes in mice chronically exposed to methylmercury during fetal and early postnatal development. *Neurotoxicology and Teratology, 25,* 335-347.

Hughes, R. N., Syme, L. A., and Syme, G. J. (1977). Open-field behaviour in sheep following treatment with the neuroleptics azaperone and acetylpromazine. *Psychopharmacology, 52,* 107-109.

Nelson, C. J., Jordan, W. P., Bohan, R. T. (1997). Daily fluoxetine administration impairs avoidance learning in the rat without altering sensory thresholds. *Progress in Neuro-Psychopharmacology and Biological Psychiatry, 21,* 1043-1057.

Roth, K. A., and Katz, R. J. (1979). Stress, behavior arousal, and open field activity: A reexamination of emotionality in the rat. *Neuroscience and Biobehavioral Reviews, 3,* 247-263.

Slawecki, C. J., Gilder, A., Roth, J., Ehlers, C. L. (2003). Increased anxiety-like behavior in adult rats exposed to nicotine as adolescents. *Pharmacology, Biochemistry and Behavior, 75,* 355-361.

Tejani-Butt, S., Kluczynski, J., and Pare, W. P. (2003). Strain-dependent modification of behavior following antidepressant treatment. *Progress in Neuro-Psychopharmacology and Biological Psychiatry, 27,* 7-14.

Valle, F. P. (1970). Effects of strain, sex, and illumination on open-field behavior of rats. *American Journal of Psychology, 83,* 103-111.

Wesierska, M., Walasek, G., Kilijanek, J., Djavadian, R. L., and Turlejski, K. (2003). Behavior of the gray short-tailed opossum (Monodelphis domestica) in the open field and in response to a new object, in comparison with the rat. *Behavioural Brain Research, 143,* 31-40.

Wolf, C., Almli, C. R., Finger, S., Ryan, S., Morgane, P. J. (1986). Behavioral effects of severe and moderate early malnutrition. *Physiology and Behavior, 38,* 725-730.

In: Tasks and Techniques: A Sampling of the Methodologies...   ISBN 1-60021-126-7
Editor: Matthew J. Anderson, pp. 25-37   © 2006 Nova Science Publishers, Inc.

Chapter 3

THE ELEVATED PLUS-MAZE TEST OF ANXIETY: METHODOLOGICAL CONSIDERATIONS

*Roser Nadal[1,2], Rosa M. Escorihuela[1,3] and Antonio Armario[*1,4]*

[1]Institute of Neuroscience, [2]Psychobiology Unit (School of Psychology),
[3]Medical Psychology Unit (School of Medicine)
[4]Animal Physiology Unit (School of Sciences),
Autonomous University of Barcelona, Spain

ABSTRACT

The elevated plus-maze (EPM) is probably the most widely used test to evaluate anxiety-like behavior in rodents. The apparatus has two open and two closed arms and the animals can freely explore the maze (usually for 5 min). Since rodents have a natural tendency to explore new environments but also to avoid unprotected areas, a conflict is generated that results in anxiety. When classical anxiolytic drugs that modulate GABA-A receptor function (e.g. diazepam) are given, the conflict is reduced and animals visit more the open arms than vehicle-treated. Similarly, it is assumed that animals displaying an anxious phenotype will visit less the open arms. Consequently, number of open arm entries, time in open arms or the ratios open arm/closed arm entries or times are the usual measures taken in the test. The use of other ethological measures can also be useful under some circumstances. Two important considerations regarding the EPM are the extent to which it can distinguish between trait and state anxiety (the latter being influenced by procedures associated to testing) and the controversial effect of non classical anxiolytics such as those related to the serotonergic system. Finally, considering that anxiety is likely to be a multidimensional construct, the use of additional tests is recommended when evaluating individual differences in fear/anxiety and the putative anxiolytic properties of drugs.

---

[*] Address Correspondence to: Antonio Armario, Unitat de Fisiologia Animal, Facultat de Ciències, Universitat Autònoma de Barcelona, 08193, Bellaterra, Barcelona, Spain, E-mail: antonio.armario@uab.es; Phone: 3493-5811840; FAX: 3493-5812390

1. WHAT IS THE ELEVATED PLUS-MAZE AND WHAT CAN WE MEASURE?

Animal models of anxiety in rodents have been grouped in two categories, depending on the type of response measured: unconditioned or conditioned. The elevated plus-maze (EPM) is in the first group and it is used to measure anxiety in rodents and to identify acute anxiolytic effects of benzodiazepines (BZs) and other drugs. In 1995, Dawson and Tricklebank already pointed out that it had widespread appeal because it is quick and simple, do not require training, food or water deprivation of the animals and the equipment is unexpensive. If the reader performs a search by using the EPM keyword in a *database*, he/she will realised that the number of papers related to the EPM test has increased about four times over the last 10 years, reflecting the high level of acceptance of this test. However, anxiety is a complex, multidimensional, phenomenon in humans and probably in animals (Ramos and Mormède, 1998), and, therefore, different models may reflect different aspects of anxiety, what makes imperative to use different animal models to allow both a better theoretical characterization of the anxiety construct and the discovery of new anxiolytic drugs.

The EPM consists of four arms at right angles to each other, connected to a central square and all the apparatus is elevated above the floor. Two of the opposite arms have high walls, whereas the other two are the open arms, that have sometimes a small ridge to provide and additional grip. The animal is gently placed in the center of the maze. Spontaneous behavior in the maze is influenced by the curiosity towards novel environments and the fear and avoidance response engendered for the open and elevated alleys as compared to closed alleys (Montgomery, 1955). The anxiety-like behavior is thus related to the approach-avoid conflict appearing in the situation.

In the initial standardization (Pellow, Chopin, File and Briley,1985; Pellow and File, 1986), the measures proposed were: number of entries into open and closed arms, percentage of open arm entries (with regard to total arm entries: closed + open), time spent in open and in closed arms and percentage of time spent in open arms. The conventional measures of anxiety in the test are the percent of open arm entries and the percent of time spent in the open arms. Some authors (Lister, 1987; File, 2001) proposed that the percentage of time spent into the open arms had to be calculated with regard to the time spent in open + closed arms (thus excluding the time spent in the center). However, in some studies, open time measures are reported with regard to the total duration of the test (5 min). Although in the initial versions of the test (Pellow et al. 1985; Pellow and File, 1986), locomotor activity was measured by total arm entries, factorial analysis studies suggested that the number of closed arm entries is a better index of general motor activity (File, 2001). Usually, the measures are reported as global data during the total duration of the test, although it has been suggested (Carobrez and Bertoglio, 2005) that min-by-min scoring could improve the validity of the EPM and help to more thoroughly interpret animal behavior. Thus, time spent in open and closed arms did not differ until the third min of the test, what suggests that avoidance of open arms is based on previous experience with them and it is maintained since the first min on a subsequent exposure to the EPM (Carobrez and Bertoglio, 2005).

In addition to conventional measures, other authors (Rodgers and Dalvi, 1997) extended in mice the measures taken in the test to incorporate more ethological defensive behaviors. Two of the most popular of these measures are the stretched attend postures and protected and unprotected head-dippings that are related to the so named "risk assessment" construct (Rodgers and Johnson, 1995; Rodgers and Dalvi, 1997; Wall and Messier, 2000). Stretched attend posture is recorded when the animal stretches forward and retracts to original position without locomotion forward. Protected head-dippings are recorded when the animal makes a head dipping from the centre of the maze around the edge of a closed arm wall and unprotected head-dippings are the dippings of the animal's head and shoulders over the sides of the open arms. Time spent in the center has also been considered as a measure of risk-assessment. Finally, other measures that could be also recorded are rearings, defecation, freezing, grooming or ambulations in each type of arm.

EPM behavior is presently used not only to detect putative anxiolytic drugs, but also to characterize genetic and environmental influences on anxiety. Interest in the EPM has dramatically increased due to the need for behavioral characterization of transgenic mice and the search for the genetic bases of psychophatology. In addition, two rats lines have been selected and bred for extreme high (HAB) and low (LAB) anxiety-related behavior in the EPM and found to show differences in other tests related to anxiety and depression as well as critical physiological variables such as the hypothalamus-pituitary-adrenal (HPA) axis functioning (Landgraf and Wigger, 2003). These data add construct validity to the EPM model.

2. PUTATIVE FACTORS UNDERLYING ANIMAL BEHAVIOUR IN THE EPM

⌐commonly regarded as such

Animal behavior in novel environments is complex and putatively influenced by factors often acting on opposite directions. Knowledge of underlying factors is important not only to understand the meaning of the different behaviors but also the pharmacological validity of the test. Principal component analyses (PCA) is an statistical tool that have been applied to identify relationships between traditional and ethological variables measured in the EPM and between variables measured in different tests such as EPM, open field, light/dark box, hole-board, social interaction or conditioned models of anxiety. It has to be taken into account that PCA is a statistical method to simplify number of variables to be considered and the results are not necessarily related to underlying psychological constructs, which have to be based on specific hypotheses regarding animal behavior in particular situations. Nevertheless, PCA allows to reduce the number of relevant variables and helps to identify putative underlying factors.

Regarding traditional EPM measures, two main independent factors consistently emerge in most PCA, which have been called anxiety and activity. Percentage of open arm entries and percentage of time spent into the open arms both strongly load on the same factor (related to anxiety), but on a different factor than number of closed arm entries (Cruz, Frei and Graeff, 1994; Rodgers and Johnson, 1995; Fernandes, Gonzalez, Wilson and File, 1999) that is interpreted as activity. Closed arm entries appear to be a better measure of activity than total arm entries (Cruz et al., 1994), likely to the contribution of low anxiety to open arm entries. However, it should be taken into account that activity is a poorly defined concept and may represent pure locomotor activity, but also more complex behaviors such as activity-prone behavioural strategies in novel situations or motivation to explore (Wall and Messier 2001).

Although an additional factor is sometimes reported which is based on behavior in the center of the EPM and it is usually interpreted as an approach/avoidance conflict-decision-making construct (Almeida, Tonkiss and Galler, 1996; Cruz et al. 1994, File, Zangrossi, Viana and Graeff, 1993; Rodgers and Johnson, 1995), the interpretation of central maze activity is difficult because this is a very small transition area. In fact, a modified elevated maze, the circular 'zero-maze', without any transition compartment between open and enclosed alleys have been proposed to measure anxiety-related behavior (Weiss, Wadsworth, Fletcher and Dourish, 1998). When ethological measures are added, PCA results in an additional number of factors, what complicates interpretation of behavior (Rodgers and Johnson, 1995). Moreover, there is no much evidence to support a third independent factor (Wall and Messier 2000) and some authors considered that the growing indices recorded in the EPM need to be reduced and re-evaluated (Wall and Messier, 2001). In any case, some of the ethological EPM variables appear to contribute to detect anxiolytic properties of drugs acting at sites other than the GABA-A receptor (Rodgers and Dalvi, 1997) and therefore can be useful.

The existence of few underlying factors in the animal behavior in the EPM, one of them being anxiety, appears to be warranted. However, the contribution of anxiety and the other putative factors to behavior in the EPM may change in function of genetic, developmental and environmental factors. PCA indicates not only the putative factors but also the percentage of variance explained by each factor, the order of factors being a function of the percentage of variance of the population that each of them explain. For instance, Fernandes et al. (1999) reported that PCA of EPM measures revealed in both male and female rats the two classical orthogonal factors, but important gender differences emerged: whereas in male 75% of variance was explained by anxiety and 24% by activity, in females anxiety explained only a 34% of the variance and activity a 57%. These data strongly suggest male behavior in the EPM was mainly driven by anxiety, whereas female behavior was by activity. In the same tongue, Boguszewski and Zagrodzka (2002) not only demonstrated that old rats (24 months) were more anxious than young rats (4 months) in the open-field and EPM tests, but also that PCA revealed a much lower contribution of anxiety than activity in the young rats, and the opposite in old animals.

3. THE PROBLEM OF FALSE NEGATIVE AND POSITIVE IN THE EPM

From the early 1960s until 1990s, benzodiazepine drugs (BZs) had been the target compounds used and investigated for the pharmacological treatment of anxiety states. Thus, pharmacological and behavioural profiles of chlordiazepoxide (Librium), diazepam (Valium) or other classical BZs were the standard against which putative anxiolytics were tested. It is now known that the main anxiolytic effects of BZs are mediated by their allosteric modulation of the GABA-A receptor-coupled chloride channel. However, due to the fact that the different categories of anxiety disorders in humans (panic attacks, phobias, obsessive-compulsive syndromes or generalized anxiety) do not respond equally to BZs and these drugs have unwanted side effects (muscle-relaxant, sedative and amnesic actions), efforts have been made to develop other drugs also having anxiolytic effects, but devoid of those pharmacological side-effects. Thus, partial agonists of 5-HT_{1A} receptors such as buspirone, full 5-HT_{1A} agonists and other ligands of 5-HT_2 or 5-HT_3 receptors have been extensively investigated, buspirone being effective and of equivalent potency as BZs in humans (Green, 1991). However, the anxiolytic effects of buspirone and the other serotoninergic compounds in the EPM are inconsistent and even anxiogenic effects have been reported (Chopin and Briley, 1987; Handley and McBlane, 1993; Hogg, 1996).

The reasons for the inconsisten effects of serotoninergic drugs in the EPM and other animal models of anxiety is unclear, but may be related to the complexity of the serotoninergic system in terms of terminal fields and type of receptors, and also with the possibility of a differential role of serotonin in generalized anxiety and panic. Thus, it has been proposed that activation of the serotoninergic system can potentiate anxiety, but at the same time inhibits panic response to unconditioned fear, acting at the level of the periaqueductal gray matter (Graeff, 2004). Alternatively, serotoninergic system may be involved in a type of anxiety different from that generated in the EPM. In this regard, it has been developed a method involving the blockade of operant behavior induced by the withdrawal of a conditioned safety signal rather than by presentation of a punishment signal, which consistently detected anxiolytic effects of 5-HT$_{1A}$ receptor ligands (Thiébot, Dangoumau, Richard and Puech, 1991).

Finally, in some cases, it is difficult to dissociate the effects of some drugs, including anxiolytics, on anxiety and activity, as some axiolytics can increase both parameters, particulary when video-tracking allowed to measure distance travelled and speed (Dawson and Tricklebank, 1995). Since it has been argued that ethological measures in the EPM can help to improve predictive value of the test, Weiss et al. (1998) studied the effects of chlordiazepoxide and amphetamine and measured classical and ethological measures. They found that both drugs increased percent of time in open arms, but also reduced stretched-attend postures, that are considered to reflect anxiolysis. Therefore, the inclusion of ethological measures do not appear to improve predictive value of the EPM under certain conditions, psychostimulants administration given false positives.

4. PRE-TESTING FACTORS AFFECTING MEASUREMENT IN THE EPM

4.1. General Aspects

The results obtained in the EPM can be influenced by several factors not related to the estrict procedure itself. These factors are the specie, age, gender, housing conditions and all procedures used to take the animal from the animal room and put them into the EPM. As commented before, female rats usually behave as less anxious in the maze than males (Johnston and File, 1991) and gender effects in mice are strain-dependent (Rodgers and Cole, 1993). In addition, age may also be important as older rats seem also to be more anxious in this test (Boguszewski and Zagrodzka, 2002). In evaluating the effect of age, the degree of familiarization of the young animals with the procedures should be maximized because otherwise the influence of procedures may affect more younger than older animals, which are less accustomed to lab routines, and this may interfere with the evaluation of actual age-dependent anxiety levels.

Housing conditions and test-asssociated procedures are particularly relevant in order to distinguish between trait and state anxiety. If some of these procedures transiently affect behavior of animals in the EPM, these changes in state anxiety can mask or potentiate trait anxiety. It should be noted that the extent to which some of these factors can alter behavior of animals in the EPM is controversial in the literature, and we therefore can only offer some guides to better known or evaluate such impact. Single or social housing is also important for practical reasons and to avoid cohort removal effects only one rat from the same home-cage should be tested in one day (or two apparatuses should be used).

Basically, most factors that can potentially influence EPM behavior are related to the stressful procedures associated to testing. These factors can include transportation of the animal cage by hand or cart (that can exert a higher influence when the distance between animal room and testing room is longer), the way of handling the rats to put them into the tests, the influence of previously taking one animal from a cage on the behavior of the remaining animals when the animals are housed in groups and, finally, the presence or not of the experimenters in the testing room. There is evidence that all these procedures are in some way stressful for rats and mice and some researchers tried to reduce their impact by repeating exposing the animals to those situations, assuming that repeated experience can result in a reduction or abolition of stress (habituation). However, it should be note that this assumption is not usually demonstrated with direct experimental evidence and reflect habituation (see Martí and Armario, 1998 for a discussion about physiological markers of stress). Nevertheless, we can tentatively assume that the influence of all procedures would dimininish if the animals become familiarized with animal facilities routines and experimenters. It is clear that it may be ideal to eliminate or minimize all aspects related to the procedure that induce (transient) changes in state anxiety if we are interested in evaluating trait anxiety.

It may be argued that if all rats are subjected to the same procedure, its influence may be similar in all animals. However, this argument does not take into account the interaction between behavioral traits (including obviously anxiety) and the details of the procedure. This is to say that procedures associated to the test may influence in a different way individuals (or strains), depending on their specific behavioral characteristics, some animals being low-sensitive to the procedures and others high-sensitive, thus resulting in apparent differences in trait anxiety than are in fact differences in state anxiety. Because handling is an important step when animals are tested, it has been studied how adult animals handled and non-handled during days/weeks differ in their response to the EPM. Although evidence has been reported for a low anxiety profile of handled versus non-handled rats (Andrews and File, 1993), the same authors comented that the results were not always reproducible within the same lab. It is likely that the effects of handling may be more marked if the amount of lab routine-associated handling of animals is low and if the way the animals are handled before testing is not gentle.

4.2. Influence of Stress

The influence of prior stress on EPM behavior is not consistent (Falter, Gower and Gobert, 1992; Grahn, Kalman, Brennan, Watkins and Maier, 1995; Korte and De Boer, 2003). However, several factors have to be considered to explain, at least in part, the inconsistencies. Firstly, the influence of stress on behavior of animals in novel environments, including the EPM, may be critically dependent on the characteristics of stressors and the time elapsed between the termination of exposure to the stressor and testing. Stressors differ in several dimensions, that include qualitative as well as quantitative (intensity and duration) aspects. It is clear that quantitative aspects are critical because previous exposure to short-lasting (several minutes) or mild to moderate intensity stressors can result in enhanced activity of animals in novel environments (Katz, Roth and Carroll, 1981), likely to be due to activational properties of exposure to such situations. On the contrary, relatively prolonged exposure to more severe stressors (high intensity footshock, some types of immobilization procedures, presence of a predator) resulted in a generalized hypoactivity as evaluated immediately after the stressor, with a progressive recovery (Lehnert, Reinstein, Strowbridge and Wurtman, 1984; Armario, Gil, Marti, Pol and Balasch, 1991). The extent to which such changes in animal behavior are specifically related to changes in fear/anxiety or are due to more generalized debilitating effects of certain stressors is not enterily clear. However, there are numerous reports suggesting that exposure to certain stressors can specifically enhance anxiety-like behavior of animals in the EPM without modifying closed arm entries or ambulation, which is more related to changes in general activity. These effects of stress have been observed 24 h (Martineja, Calvo, Volosín and Molina, 1997) or even days/weeks (Adamec, Shallow and Budgell, 1997; Richter-Levin, 1998) after initial exposure.

The failure to find effects of a single exposure to stress on the EPM may be explained by the interaction between the characteristic of stressful conditions used and the existence of a differential susceptibility of some rat strain to stress. Whereas inbred rat or mice strains are precisely characterized from a genetic point of view, this is not the case of outbred strains. In this case, genetic differences between strains (i.e. Wistar, Sprague-Dawley, Long-Evans) are not well-characterized and almost nothing is known about differences between outbred animals raised in small animal facilities. As a consequence, the same stressor can induce changes in (EPM) behavior in one lab and no change in another lab that used rats with a different genetic background. To illustrate this point, Rodgers and Cole (1993) have observed that DBA/2 male mice are less anxious than F1 males in the EPM, but, interestingly, prior exposure to novelty increased anxiety-like behavior of DBA/2 male mice in the EPM, but reduced anxiety in T1 male mice. These data raised the interesting possibility that the impact of minor stressors may be higher in high anxiety as compared to low anxiety animals, although further studies are needed considering that only two strains were compared.

Another consideration closely related to the above is the differential effect of previous treatments on the superimposed test procedures. For instance, we have observe in our lab (unpublished data) that a single previous exposure to immobilization did not modify the response of rats in the EPM under resting conditions (that is, there is no apparent change in trait anxiety), but dramatic differences emerged when a brief footshock session (3 shocks, 0.5 mA) was imposed before testing in the EPM. In this case, shock exposure did not modify the behavior of control rats in the EPM, but markedly reduced open arms time and entries in previously immobilized rats, suggesting that previous exposure to IMO did not affect anxiety of rats under non-stress conditions but strongly sensitised animals in front of minor stressful procedures.

Regardless of discrepant results, it is important to consider the putative underlying process resulting in altered behavior in the EPM. One possibility is that exposure to certain stressors results in an state of higher fear/anxiety that outlasts exposure to the stimuli and is reflected in the behavior of animals in a novel environment such as the EPM. If this is the case, it is important to consider how fear/anxiety generated during exposure to the previous stressful situations can modify the behavior of rats in another entirely different situation (the EPM), usually less stressful than the previous ones, unless we assume that enhanced anxiety induced by previous stress could be interpreted by the animals as generated by the present situation. This interpretation may be consonant with the finding that anxiogenic drugs reduce exploration of the open arms. Alternatively, exposure to stress could transiently sensitize animal response to any kind of additional stressful situation, including novel environments. This second hypothesis assumes that fear/anxiety does not in fact outlasts actual exposure to stressors, but instead previous stress induces a state of hyperresposiveness to additional superimposed stressful situations, that can last for hours or days, depending on the characteristics of the previous stressor. The first hypothesis could explain better why familiarization of animals with all procedures associated to testing resulted in animals exploring more the open arms of the EPM, whereas the second one could better explain, without resorting to permanent changes in trait anxiety, long-lasting effects of stress on behavior of animals in the EPM.

5. THE INFLUENCE OF PREVIOUS EXPERIENCE WITH THE EPM

Another important point regarding the use of the EPM to evalute anxiolytic drugs is the well-described phenomenon of one-trial tolerance. Esentially, it has been observed that previous experience of mice and rats with the EPM renders the test insensitive to the effects of anxiolytics (File, Mabbutt and Hitchcott,1990; File, Zangrossi, Viana and Graeff, 1993; Lister, 1987). In fact, it is the previous experience with the open arms the critical factor and it has been argued that a previous experience with the open arms created a phobic state in the animals that is not sensitive to classical anxiolytics (File et al., 1990; 1993). However, in these experiments the visits and time spent in the open arms was not concomitantly reduced during the second as compared to the first trial when the animals where compared in undrugged state. If a previous experience with the EPM has created some kind of phobic reaction to the open arms, it may be expected a reduction of the number of entries and time spent in open arms. Other papers did report such reduction in rats having a previous experience with the test (e.g. Almeida et al., 1996; Espejo, 1997) and therefore this hypothesis remains as the most accepted. However, there is not at present a clear explanation for the phenomenon and alternative explanations such as the interaction between fear/anxiety generated by the EPM and motivation to explore should be taken into account. In any case, the use of animals having no previous experience with the test appears to be mandatory when the test has to be used in routine procedures.

6. TESTING

6.1. Characteristics of the EPM

The elevated plus-maze consists of four arms (length: about 50 cm in rats and 30 cm in mice; width: about 10 cm in rats and 5 cm in mice) at right angles to each other, connected to a central square (about 10 x 10 cm in rats and 5 x 5 cm in mice) and all the apparatus is elevated above the floor (about 50 cm in rats and 40-60 cm in mice). Two of the opposite arms have high walls (closed arms, about 40 cm high in rats and 15 cm in mice), whereas the other two are the open arms that have sometimes a small ridge to provide and additional grip. The type of material used in the construction of the maze varies from wood (white or black), to clear or dark plexiglas (see Carobrez and Bertoglio, 2005 for a review) and this is an important variable because each material provides different illumination (Pereira, da Cunha, Neto, Paschoalini and Faria, 2005) and somatosensorial sensitivity. The usual EPM height in rats is around 50 cm although this is not probably a critical factor because rats did not have more open arm behavior if height decreases (Treit, Menard and Royan, 1993). The presence of a small raised edge in the open arms could be important because rats explored more open arms when the additional grip is provided that when flat edges are given (Treit et al. 1993).

6.2. Methodological Variables

6.2.1. Time of The Day

Circadian variations have been obtained in several studies. For instance, percent of entries and percent of time in open arms/total, and number of closed arm entries are higher during the dark phase in rats that have been tested under illumination conditions similar to the vivarium at the moment of the test session (Andrade, Tomé, Santiago, Lúcia-Santos and Andrade, 2003).

6.2.2. Illumination

Test room illumination conditions (see Carobrez and Bertoglio, 2005) range from low (< 50 lux), moderate (50-250 lux) to high (> 250 lux). Testing rats under dark conditions increases percent of entries and percent of time in open arms/total during both the nocturnal and the diurnal phase (Bertoglio and Carobrez, 2002). Also, it has been suggested that is the gradient of luminosity between closed and open arms and not the absolute levels of lux the critical factor to determine EPM behavior (Pereira et al., 2005).

6.2.3. Prior Novelty

Especially in earlier studies was usual to test firstly animals in a novel environment (normally holeboard) before exposing them to the maze in order to supposedly increase open arm behavior. Also, motor activity in the holeboard was used to control for drug-induced changes unrelated to anxiety. However, prior novelty effects are in mice strain-specific (Rodgers and Cole, 1993) and therefore can interfere with the results of the EPM in an unpredictable way.

6.3. How to Run the Test

Before describing a detailed procedure, it should be taken into account that discrepancies in the EPM data between different independent laboratories have been observed even with the same general procedure and genetically selected mice (Wahlsten et al., 2003) what highlights the importance of subtle procedural variables in this test.

It is recommended that the animals are housed very close to testing room so that transportation cart is not really needed. If this is not the case, move animals at least 2 h before testing and left them undisturbed in their animal cages in a quiet room different from the testing room. If testing group-housed animals, simultaneously test all animals from a cage in apparatuses well-separated by partitions, or, if possible, in different rooms. As an alternative, immediately after taking the animal cage put each animal in a small cage with bedding from their own cages in the adjacent quiet room and test them at least 2 h later. It should be taken into account that these procedures do not rule out a possible effect on baseline animal behaviour.

Use a room with no objects around the maze or minimize their influence surrounding the maze by a courtain. Place the animal gently in the center of the maze. The duration of the test is 5 min. Some authors face the animal to a closed arm and others to an open arm, but we recommend to face a close arm to avoid that animals enter into an open arms because of an initial flying response. The behavior of the animal is usually videotaped for off-line analysis. The maze has to be carefully cleaned between each animal, taking special attention to the edges of the open arms and the outside walls of the closed arms closest to the center area because the animal could make head-dippings in the center and the open arms (see below). Don't forget to clean the apparatus before the first animal to provide him with the same smell as the remaining ones. It should also to be mentioned that sometimes an animal could fall from the maze and it should be excluded from the experiment. This is also an important reason for testing animals in different rooms.

Regarding scoring factors, the use of manual versus automated systems has to be considered. Although automated (photocells or video tracking) systems have obvious advantages, non conventional ("ethological") measures could only be recorded by manual scoring. The criterion to define an arm entry is also very important and most of the authors use the four paws criteria. When using video tracking systems that usually track the animal by the center of gravity, this has to be considered and usually the central zone of the EPM needs to be redefined. The possible measures have been described above, but we recommend to evaluate at least open and closed arms entries, time spent in open and close arms as basic measures and if possible, distance travelled in each type of arm. Additional, non-conventional measures may be included in more thorough analysis.

ACKNOWLEDGEMENTS

This work was supported by grants G03-005 (ISCIII), SAF 2002-623 (DGICYT) and BSA2001-2574 (DGICYT)

REFERENCES

Adamec, R.E., Shallow, T. and Budgell, J. (1997). Blockade of CCKB but not CCKA receptors before and after the stress of predator exposure prevents lasting increases in anxiety-like behavior: implications for anxiety associated with posttraumatic stress disorder. *Behavioral Neuroscience, 111*, 435-449.

Almeida, S.S., Tonkiss, J. and Galler, J.R. (1996). Prenatal protein malnutrition affects exploratory behavior of female rats in the elevated plus-maze test. *Physiology and Behavior, 60*, 675-680.

Andrade, M.M.M., Tomé, M.F., Santiago, E.S., Lúcia-Santos, A., Andrade, T.G.C.S. (2003). Longitudinal study of daily variation of rats' behavior in the elevated plus-maze. *Physiology and Behavior, 78*, 125-133.

Andrews, N. and File, S.E. (1993). Handling history of rats modifies behavioural effects of drugs in the elevated plus-maze test of anxiety. *European Journal of Pharmacology, 235*, 109-112.

Armario, A., Gil, M., Martí, J., Pol, O. and Balasch, J. (1991). Influence of various acute stressors on the activity of adult male rats in a holeboard and in the forced swim test. *Pharmacology, Biochemistry and Behavior, 39*, 373-377.

Bertoglio, L.J. and Carobrez, A.P. (2002). Behavioral profile of rats submitted to session 1-session 2 in the elevated plus-maze during diurnal/nocturnal phases and under different illumination conditions. *Behavioural Brain Research, 132*, 135-143.

Boguszewski, P. and Zagrodzka, J. (2002). Emotional changes related to age in rats-a behavioral analysis. *Behavioural Brain Research, 133*, 323-332.

Carobrez, A.P. and Bertoglio, L.J. (2005). Ethological and temporal analyses of anxiety-like behavior: the elevated plus-maze model 20 years on. *Neuroscience and Biobehavioral Reviews, 29*, 1193-1205.

Chopin, P. and Briley, M. (1987). Animal models of anxiety: the effect of compounds that modify 5-HT neurotransmission. *Trends in Pharmacological Sciencies, 8*, 383-388.

Cruz, A.P.M., Frei, F. and Graeff, F.G. (1994). Ethopharmacological analysis of rat behavior on the elevated plus-maze. *Pharmacology, Biochemistry and Behavior, 49*, 171-176.

Dawson, G.R. and Tricklebank, M.D. (1995). use of the elevated plus maze in the search for novel anxiolytic agents. *Trends in Pharmacological Sciences, 16*, 33-36.

Espejo, E.F. (1997). Effects of weekly or daily exposure to the elevated plus-maze in male mice. *Behavioural Brain Research, 87*, 233-238.

Falter, U., Gower, A.J. and Gobert, J. (1992). Resistance of baseline activity in the elevated plus-maze to exogenous influences. *Behavioural Pharmacology, 3*, 123-128.

Fernandes, C., Gonzalez, M.I., Wilson, C.A. and File, S.E. (1999). Factor analysis shows that female rat behaviour is characterized primarily by activity, male rats are driven by sex and anxiety. *Pharmacology, Biochemistry and Behavior, 64*, 731-738.

File, S.E. (2001). Factors controlling measures of anxiety and responses to novelty in the mouse. *Behavioural Brain Research, 125*, 151-157.

File, S.E., Mabbutt, P.S. and Hitchcott, P.K. (1990). Characterisation of the phenomenon of "one-trial tolerance" to the anxiolytic effect of chlordiazepoxide in the elevated plus-maze. *Psychopharmacology, 102*, 98-101.

File, S.E., Zangrossi, H., Viana, M. and Graeff, F.G. (1993). Trial 2 in the elevated plus-maze: A different form of fear? *Psychopharmacology, 111*, 491-494.

Graeff, F.G. (2004). Serotonin, the periaqueductal gray and panic. *Neuroscience and Biobehavioral Reviews, 28*, 239-259.

Grahn, R.E., Kalman, B.A., Brennan, F.X., Watkins, L.R. and Maier, S.F. (1995). The elevated plus-maze is not sensitive to the effect of stressor controllability in rats. . *Pharmacology, Biochemistry and Behavior, 52*, 565-570.

Green, S. (1991). Benzodiazepines, putative anxiolytics and animal models if anxiety. *Trends in Neurosciences, 14*, 101-104.

Handley, S.L. and McBlane, J.W. (1993). 5HT drugs in animal models of anxiety. *Psychopharmacology, 112*, 13-20.

Hogg, S. (1996). A review of the validity and variability of the elevated plus-maze as an animal model of anxiety. *Pharmacology, Biochemistry and Behavior, 54*, 21-30.

Johnston, A.L. and File, S.E. (1991). Sex differences in animal tests of anxiety. *Physiology and Behavior, 49*, 245-250.

Katz, R.J., Roth, K.A. and Carroll, B.J. (1981). Acute and chronic stress effects on open field activity in the rat: implications for a model of depression. *Neuroscience and Biobehavioral Reviews, 5*, 247-251.

Korte, S.M. and De Boer, S.F. (2003). A robust animal model of state anxiety: fear-potentiated behaviour in the elevated plus-maze. *European Journal of Pharmacology, 463*, 163-175.

Landgraf, R. and Wigger, A. (2003) Born to be anxious: neuroendocrine and genetics correlates of trait anxiety in HAB rats. *Stress, 6*, 111-119.

Lehnert, H., Reinstein, D.K., Strowbridge, B.W. and Wurtman, R.J. (1984). Neurochemical and behavioral consequences of acute, uncontrollable stress: effects of dietary tyrosine. *Brain Research, 303*, 215-223.

Lister, R.G. (1987). The use of a plus-maze to measure anxiety in the mouse. *Psychopharmacology, 92*, 180-185.

Martí, O. and Armario, A. (1998). Anterior pituitary response to stress: time-related changes and adaptation. *International Journal of Developmental Neuroscience, 16*, 241-260.

Martijena, I.D., Calvo, N., Volosin, M. and Molina, V.A. (1997). Prior exposure to a brief restraint session facilitates the occurrence of fear in response to a conflict situation: behavioral and neurochemical correlates. *Brain Research, 752*, 136-142.

Montgomery, K.C. (1955). The relation between fear induced by novel stimulation and exploratory behaviour. *Journal of Comparative and Physiological Psychology, 48*, 254-260.

Pellow, S., Chopin, P., File, S.E. and Briley, M. (1985). Validation of open:close arm entries in an elevated plus-maze as a measure of anxiety in the rat. *Journal of Neuroscience Methods, 14*, 149-167.

Pellow, S. and File, S.E. (1986). Anxiolytic and anxiogenic drug effects on exploratory activity in an elevated plus-maze: a novel test of anxiety in the rat. *Pharmacology, Biochemistry and Behavior, 24*, 525-529.

Pereira, L.O., da Cunha, I.S., Neto, J.M., Paschoalini, M.A and Faria, M.S. (2005). The gradient of luminosity between open/enclosed arms, and not the absolute level of lux, predicts the behaviour of rats in the plus-maze. *Behavioural Brain Research, 159*, 55-61.

Ramos, A. and Mormède, P. (1998). Stress and emotionality: a multidimensional and genetic approach. *Neuroscience and Biobehavioral Reviews, 22*, 33-57.

Richer-Levin, G. (1998). Acute and long-term behavioral correlates of underwater trauma-potential relevance to stress and post-stress syndromes. *Psychiatric Research, 79*, 73-83.

Rodgers, R.J. and Cole, J.C. (1993). Influence of social isolation, gender, strain and prior novelty on plus-maze behaviour in mice. *Physiology and Behavior, 54*, 729-736.

Rodgers, R.J. and Dalvi, A. (1997). Anxiety, defence and the elevated plus-maze. *Neuroscience and Biobehavioral Reviews, 21*, 801-810.

Rodgers, R.J. and Johnson, N.J.T. (1995). Factor analysis of spatiotemporal and ethological measures in the murine elevated plus-maze test of anxiety. *Pharmacology, Biochemistry and Behavior, 52*, 297-303.

Thiébot, M.H., Dangoumau, L., Richard, G., and Puech, A.J. (1991). Safety signal withdrawal: a behavioural paradigm sensitive to both 'anxiolytic' and 'anxiogenic' drugs under identical experimental conditions. *Psychopharmacology, 101*, 415-424.

Treit, D., Menard, J. and Royan, C. (1993). Anxiogenic stimuli in the elevated plus-maze. *Pharmacology, Biochemistry and Behavior, 44*, 463-469.

Whalsten, D., Metten, P., Phillips, T.J., Boehm II, S.L., Burkhart-Kasch, S., Dorow, J., Doerksen, S., Downing, C., Fogarty, J., Rodd-Henricks, K., Hen, R., McKinnon, C.S., Merrill, C.M., Nolte, C., Schalomon, M., Schlumbohm, J.P., Sibert, J.R., Wenger, C.D., Dudek, B.C. and Crabbe, J.C. (2003). Different data from different labs: lessons from studies of gene-environment interaction. *Journal of Neurobiology, 54*, 283-311.

Wall, P.M. and Messier, C. (2000). Ethological confirmatory factor analysis of anxiety-like behaviour in the murine elevated plus-maze. *Behavioural Brain Research, 114*, 199-212.

Wall, P.M. and Messier, C. (2001). Methodological and conceptual issues in the use of the elevated plus-maze as a psychological measurement instrument of animal anxiety-like behavior. *Neuroscience and Biobehavioral Reviews, 25*, 275-286.

Weiss, S.M., Wadsworth, G., Fletcher, A., and Dourish, C.T. (1998). Utility of ethological analysis to overcome locomotor confounds in elevated maze models of anxiety. *Neuroscience and Biobehavioral Reviews, 23*, 265-271.

In: Tasks and Techniques: A Sampling of the Methodologies...   ISBN 1-60021-126-7
Editor: Matthew J. Anderson, pp. 39-48   © 2006 Nova Science Publishers, Inc.

Chapter 4

NOVEL OBJECT RECOGNITION: ASSESSING MEMORY THROUGH EXPLORATORY RESPONSES

Matthew J. Anderson[*]
Saint Joseph's College of Maine
Standish, ME 04084

ABSTRACT

Novel object recognition (NOR) is used to examine the effects of novelty and curiosity on exploratory behaviors. Through slight procedural modifications, variants of this habituation driven task can be used to investigate learning and memory for previously encountered objects and environments, or memory of an object's spatial location. As all versions of the task are essentially innocuous and avoid noxious stimulation, NOR has become a favorite of many researchers. This chapter briefly highlights some of the general findings obtained with NOR tasks and provides a detailed description of how to implement NOR in the investigation of object memory.

INTRODUCTION

Berlyne (1950) first developed the novel object recognition (NOR) task and used it to call attention to the factors of novelty and curiosity as determinants of exploratory behavior. At the start of this pivotal study, rats were placed in an empty experimental box for a period of twenty minutes in order to pre-expose them to the testing conditions and habituate any curiosity about the box itself. The animals next underwent several 5-minute object-training sessions in which they were returned to the experimental box, this time containing three identical stimuli, and exploration of the stimuli were recorded. Finally, after a 10-minute rest period, animals were again returned to the box and encountered two of the initial objects from

---

[*] Address Correspondence to: Matthew J. Anderson, Ph.D. Department of Psychology, Saint Joseph's University, 5600 City Avenue, Post Hall, Philadelphia, PA 19131, e-mail: mander06@sju.edu, phone: (207) 893-7924

the previous sessions, and a third novel object that had previously not been explored. Upon completion of the training/testing sessions, Berlyne compared the time spent exploring the novel and initial objects and found that the animals spent significantly more time exploring objects with which they had had no previous experience. The animals had habituated to the original objects and later spent more time exploring the novel stimuli.

More recently, Ennanceur and Delacour (1988) conducted a series of investigations, bringing the habituation-driven NOR task into the modern literature, and reconfirming Berlyne's original findings that rats will spend more time exploring novel objects than familiar ones when given equal access to both. Moreover, they greatly expanded on the original design by including multiple intervals between the training and test exposures, thus using object recognition to assess retention across time. Their findings, as well as the results of many subsequent studies (e.g., Ennaceur, Cavoy, Costa, and Delacour, 1989; Puma, Baudoin, and Bizot, 1998; Puma, Deschaux, Molimard, and Bizot, 1999; Anderson, Karash, Ashton, and Riccio, 2003), demonstrate that an animal's ability to discriminate between novel and familiar objects fades quickly, typically returning to baseline performance within twenty-four hours. It is essential to remember, however, that a failure to discriminate between the objects at test, decreases in training object exploration and habituation (Lukaszewska and Radulska, 1994), and impairments in an animal's ability to familiarize with the training environment (Sheldon, 1969) must all be ruled out as possible explanations in order to convincingly demonstrate an initial training object memory deficit (Besheer and Bevins, 2000).

While the task has recently been used primarily in psychopharmacological investiagtions (e.g. Ennaceur, et al., 1989; Besheer, Jensen, and Bevins, 1999; Bevins, Koznarova, and Armiger, 2001; de Lima, Laranja, Bromberg, Roesler, and Schroder, 2005), several researchers have also employed NOR in the examination of basic learning and memory phenomena. It has been shown, for example, that while the performance of adult rats stays fairly high at a 2-hour retention-interval, 18-day-old pups show a significant decrement at this long delay when compared to those tested one minute after the training exposure (Anderson, Barnes, Briggs, Ashton, Moody, Joynes, and Riccio, 2004a), suggesting that retention capabilities in the NOR task increases as the animals age. Other investigators employing NOR tasks have demonstrated similar deficits in old age animals (e.g., Dellu, Mayo, Cherkaoui, Le Moal, and Simon, 1992; Liu, Smith, Appleton, Darlington, and Bilkey, 2004). Many researchers with human subjects have employed similar visual paired comparison (VPC) tasks to investigate learning and memory for visual stimuli (e.g., Fantz, 1964). Like those obtained with NOR, findings of VPC studies have shown that older infants are capable of remembering a visual training stimulus, as measured by a later preference for novel stimuli, over longer intervals than younger ones (e.g., Fagan, 1973). These similarities have led some to propose that NOR may serve as a small animal model of the VPC task (Anderson, et al., 2004a).

In addition to examinations of ontogeny, the effects of various pre-test cuing treatments have been examined in the NOR task. It has been shown that brief reminders with the training objects and context can alleviate forgetting in both adult (Anderson, et al., 2003) and infant rats (Anderson, Karash, and Riccio, 2004b), restoring a preference for the novel object that would otherwise not be seen at longer intervals. This suggests that the forgetting demonstrated in the NOR task is likely the result of a retrieval failure (Spear, 1973). For a more thorough review of previous studies that have employed NOR, the interested reader is referred to another volume (Anderson, 2006).

In addition to examining memory for objects, through slight methodological variations NOR-like tasks can be used for other purposes. For instance, variants of the task can be used as a measure of memory for environmental familiarization (e.g., Bevins, et al., 2001). Bevins and colleagues, capitalizing on the finding that increased context familiarity enhances object exploration at test (Sheldon, 1969; Besheer and Bevins, 2000), have promoted simple, single object exploration as a measure of environmental familiarization and context memory. Indeed, they have illustrated that the stronger a rat's memory for the training environment is, the greater the amount of time it will spend in exploring an object (Herrman, Wilkinson, Palmatier, and Bevins, 2004). They have also demonstrated that novelty can be rewarding, and that access to a novel object can instill a preference for the environment where that object was encountered (Bevins, Besheer, Palmatier, Jensen, Pickett, and Eurek, 2002). With another slight variation to the procedures discussed to this point, researchers can use object exploration to measure memory for an object's spatial location (e.g., Dix and Aggleton, 1999). Beck and Luine (2002) have employed a procedure in which rats were given a 3-minute training session with two identical objects followed later by a test session in which one of the two original objects is moved to a new location within the apparatus. Their results demonstrate that at short retention intervals (2.5 hours) rats remember the original spatial arrangement and spend significantly more time exploring the moved object than the one remaining unmoved. In other words, there appears to be a novel location preference. As with object recognition memory, such spatial memory is lost rather quickly and appears to be forgotten by four hours (Beck and Luine, 2002). In addition to these variations, by simply documenting a subject's interaction times with objects of various shapes and sizes, the task can be used to measure aesthetic preferences. Many of these variants are reviewed more fully elsewhere (Anderson, 2006).

METHODS

NOR methods are essentially innoculus, not involving any noxious stimulation, and take advantage of the exploratory responses found naturally in an animal's behavioral reportoire. Moreover, the methods involved in the NOR task are exceptionally simple and easy to employ. Thus it has become a favorite task of many researchers.

Training and testing in the NOR task can occur in any open container. For example, many of the studies mentioned above employed a 40 x 60 cm, 40 cm deep, blue, plastic Sterilite® storage container (Figure 1). The training and testing apparatus must be located in a quiet area or a masking noise should be provided in order to prevent outside noise from disturbing the subjects' behavior. Moreover, lighting should be kept to a minimum as increases in illumination have been shown to decrease locomotion (Valle, 1970) and would likely hinder object exploration.

Figure 1. An example of a NOR training/testing apparatus.

If you wish to employ NOR in the assessment of object learning and memory, prior to beginning the actual experiment it is essential to collect data ensuring that the subjects do not have some natural preference for any of your selected objects. This can be done by simply placing all of the objects in the chamber and observing the exploration of each object in a small number of animals that are not part of the experiment proper. If testing only two objects, a simple *t*-test is all that is needed to detect differences in object preference. If testing more than two items an ANOVA comparing mean explorations (in seconds) of each object followed by post hoc analysis should tell you if any objects are inherently preferred. If you were only interested in studying which types of objects animals aesthetically prefer, this is all the further you would need to go. Virtually any type of object can be employed in an NOR study (Figure 2). When possible NOR researchers should employ object sets containing at least three identical objects (e.g., Dix and Aggleton, 1999). This allows the animal to experience two of the objects from the set during initial object training and the third object from the set at test, reducing the likelihood that the animal will rely on scent cues.

In NOR studies of object learning and memory, (e.g., Anderson, Karash, Ashton, and Riccio, 2003) subjects typically undergo a minimum of two days of 3-minute handling sessions prior to the beginning of the study in order to reduce any anxiety that may interfere with overall activity levels. As Besheer and Bevins (2000) and others (Sheldon, 1969) have illustrated that environmental familiarization increases interaction with the objects, handling is usually followed by a minimum of two days of training/testing context pre-exposure during which each subject is individually placed in the empty chamber for 3-minute/day (Figure 3). This essentially habituates the animals to the chamber and ensures that they will spend a sufficient amount of time exploring the objects at training and test.

Figure 2. A sampling of objects that have been employed in NOR studies.

One should note that rat strain differences have been found in NOR tasks. In a slightly simplified paradigm involving significantly less handling and context pre-exposure, Long-Evans rats have been shown to far out-perform Wistar and Sprague-Dawley derived animals, which show no significant preferences for novelty at even the shortest delays (Andrew, Jansen, Linders, Princen, and Broekkamp, 1995). Interestingly however, while employing the technique described above we have failed to obtain any difference between the Long-Evans and Sprague-Dawley strains (Yellen, Williams, Asthon, Anderson, and Riccio, 2002; See also Anderson, 2006). While it is yet unclear whether the performance of Wistar derived animals would similarly benefit from increased amounts of handling and context pre-exposure prior to test, I think it safe to say that regardless of strain at least two days of handling and context pre-exposure, respectively, are necessary if optimal performance is desired.

Approximately twenty-four hours after the last pre-exposure session, each animal is returned to the chamber for a training session, which consists of three minutes in the box with a matching set of two identical objects (Figure 4). As at least two object sets are needed to conduct an NOR experiment, it is important that the object set encountered by each subject is counterbalanced within each experimental group. After the 3-minute training session, the animal is removed and returned to its home cage, and the chamber and objects are cleaned in order to dilute any potential scent trail that the animal may have left behind (Astur, Klein, Mumby, Protz, Sutherland, and Martin, 2002).

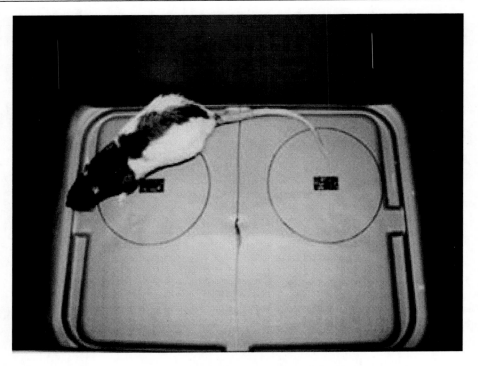

Figure 3. During context pre-exposure the subject habituates to the training/testing apparatus.

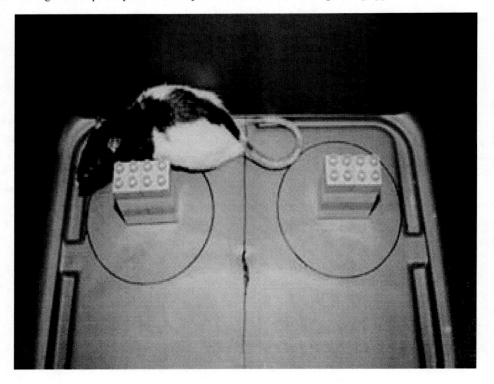

Figure 4. During the initial exposure, the subject encounters two identical objects.

A retention interval of at least twenty-four hours should be employed if you wish to ensure that the subjects will forget the original object (Ennanceur and Delacour, 1988). However, it may also be necessary to include a group of subjects trained and tested at a shorter interval (1-min, for example) in order to verify that initial object learning has actually occurred and that the subject can tell the objects apart. After the passing of the desired retention-interval, each animal is returned to the testing chamber for a 3-minute test session and encounters one of the initial objects and an object with which it has had no previous experience (Figure 5). It is worth noting that Besheer and Bevins (2000) have demonstrated that a minimum of three minutes interaction time, both at training with initial objects, and testing with novel and familiar objects, is necessesary to produce significant interaction differences with a 1-hour train-to-test interval. The items serving as novel objects, as well as the side on which the novel object appeared, should again be counterbalanced within each group. After the 3-minute session, each animal is returned to its home cage.

Figure 5. At test, the subject encounters one of the original items and a new object with which it has had no previous experience.

All training and test sessions should be videotaped, and scored for exploration of each object by at least two independent scorers blind to the experimental conditions. Later, inter-rater reliability should be established by correlating their scorers. Exploration can be defined however you like. We have defined exploration as the animal having contact or having its snout within an inch of the object. It is sometimes advisable to establish an exclusion criterion, whereby animals can be excluded from the experiment if their total exploration of both objects at training is not a satisfactory amount (e.g., 5-sec). This is done in order to eliminate variability and ensure that animals are actually receiving object training (Anderson, et al., 2004a). While scoring test sessions, explorations of the novel and initial objects for each animal are again recorded. At this point, one can choose between two measures of novelty preference. One may either calculate an absolute mean preference for novelty score for each group (seconds spent exploring the novel object minus seconds spent exploring initial object), or a relative percent preference score that takes into consideration each individual animal's total exploration ([time with novel object / total exploration of both objects] X 100). It is perhaps most advisable to calculate and report both measures (e.g., Anderson, et al., 2004b). Exclusion criteria based on minimum amounts of exploration at test may also be established to ensure the accurate measurement of object preferences. If at any time an object becomes mobile, that animal should be excluded from the experiment. Informal observations reveal that rats seem to prefer mobile objects regardless of an object's novelty. We have employed Velcro in order hold the objects fast to the base of the training/testing chamber.

In addition to the video recording technique just described, researchers have employed automated variations of the task in order to further reduce variability and the likelihood of scoring bias (e.g., Dellu, et al., 1992). One may also employ computer motion analysis systems to study object exploration. As long as the objects under investigation remain immobile such systems can provide a remarkably unbiased tool. However, such equipment can be costly and might exceed the budgetary constraints of a smaller lab.

REFERENCES

Anderson, M. J. (2006). Object Exploration: A non-aversive measure of object recognition, spatial memory, and context familiarity. In S. N. Hogan (Ed.), *Progress in Learning Research* (pp. 35-47). Hauppauge, NY: Nova Science Publishers, Inc.

Anderson, M. J., Barnes, G. W., Briggs, J. F., Ashton, K. M., Moody, E. W., Joynes, R. L., and Riccio, D. C. (2004a). The effects of ontogeny on the performance of rats in a novel object recognition task. *Psychological Reports, 94,* 437-443.

Anderson, M. J., Karash, D. L., and Riccio, D. C. (2004b). The alleviation of ontogenetic forgetting in a novel object recognition task. *Journal of Behavioral and Neuroscience Research, 2,* 1-5.

Anderson, M. J., Karash, D. L., Ashton, K. M., and Riccio, D. C. (2003). The effects of a target-stimulus reminder on performance in a novel object recognition task. *Learning and Motivation, 34,* 341-353

Andrews, J. S., Jansen, J. H. M., Linders, S., Princen, A., and Broekkamp, C. L. E. (1995). Performance of four different rat strains in the autoshaping, two-object discrimination, and swim maze test of learning and memory. *Physiology and Behavior, 57,* 785-790.

Astur, R. S., Klein, R. L., Mumby, D. G., Protz, D. K., Sutherland, R. J., and Martin, G. M. (2002). A role for olfaction in object recognition by normal and hippocampal-damaged rats. *Neurobiology of Learning and Memory, 78,* 186-191.

Beck, K. D., Luine, V. N. (2002). Sex differences in behavioral and neurochemical profiles after chronic stress: Role of housing conditions. *Physiology and Behavior, 75,* 661-673.

Berlyne, D. E. (1950). Novelty and curiosity as determinants of exploratory behaviour. *British Journal of Psychology, 41,* 68-80.

Besheer, J., and Bevins, R. A. (2000). The role of environmental familiarization in novel-object preference. *Behavioural Processes,* 50, 19-29.

Besheer, J., Jensen, H. C., and Bevins, R. A. (1999). Dopamine antagonism in a novel-object recognition and a novel-object place conditioning preparation with rats. *Behavioural Brain Research,* 103, 35-44.

Bevins, R. A., Besheer, J., Palmatier, M. I., Jensen, H. C., Pickett, K. S., and Eurek, S. (2002). Novel-object place conditioning: Behavioral and dopaminergic processes in expression of novelty reward. *Behavioural Brain Research, 129,* 41-50.

Bevins, R. A., Koznarova, J., and Armiger, T. J. (2001). Environmental familiarization in rats: Differential effects of acute and chronic nicotine. *Neurobiology of Learning and Memory,* 75, 63-76.

de Lima, M. N. M., Laranja, D. C., Bromberg, E., Roesler, R., Schroder, N. (2005). Pre- or post-training administration of the NMDA receptor blocker MK-801 impairs object recognition memory in rats. *Behavioural Brain Research, 156,* 139-143.

Dellu, F., Mayo, W., Cherkaoui, J., Le Moal, M., and Simon, H. (1992). A two-trial memory task with automated recording : Study in young and aged rats. *Brain Research, 588,* 132-139.

Dix, S. L., and Aggleton, J. P. (1999). Extending the spontaneous preference test of recognition : evidence of object-location and object-context recognition. *Behavioural Brain Research, 99,* 191-200.

Ennaceur, A., Cavoy, A., Costa, J., and Delacour, J. (1989). A new one-trial test for neurobiological studies of memory in rats. II: Effects of piracetam and pramiracetam. *Behavioural Brain Research,* 33, 197-207.

Ennaceur, A., and Delacour, J. (1988). A new one-trial test for neurobiological studies of memory in rats. 1: Behavioral data. *Behavioural Brain Research,* 31, 47-59.

Fagan, J. F. (1973). Infants' delayed recognition memory and forgetting. *Journal of Experimental Child Psychology, 16,* 424-450.

Fantz, R. L. (1964). Visual experience in infants: Decreased attention familiar patterns relative to novel ones. *Science, 146,* 668-670.

Herrman, L. E., Wilkinson, J. L., Palmatier, M. I., and Bevins, R. A. (2004). Factors affecting environmental familiarization in rats. Poster presented at the annual meeting of the Midwestern Psychological Association, Chicago, Il (May).

Liu, P, Smith, P. F., Appleton, I., Darlington, C. L., and Bilkey, D. K. (2004). Potential involvement of NOS and arginase in age-related behavioural impairments. *Experimental Gerontology, 39,* 1207-1222.

Lukaszewska, I., and Radulska, A. (1994). Object recognition is not impaired in old rats. *Acta Neurobiologiae Experimentalis, 54,* 143-150.

Puma, C., Baudoin, C., and Bizot, J.-C., (1998). Effects of intraseptal infusions of *N*-methyl-D-aspartate receptor ligands on memory in an object recognition task in rats. *Neuroscience Letters, 244,* 97-100.

Puma, C., Deschaux, O., Molimard, R., and Bizot, J.-C. (1999). Nicotine improves memory in an object recognition task in rats, *European Neuropsychopharmacology, 9,* 323-327.

Sheldon, A. B. (1969). Preference for familiar versus novel stimuli as a function of the familiarity of the environment. *Journal of Comparative and Physiological Psychology, 67,* 173-180.

Spear, N. E. (1973). Retrieval of memory in animals. *Psychological Review, 80,* 163-194.

Valle, F. P. (1970). Effects of strain, sex, and illumination on open-field behavior of rats. *American Journal of Psychology, 83,* 103-111.

Yellen, K., Williams, J., Ashton, K. M., Anderson, M. J., and Riccio, D. C. (2002). Strain differences in novel object recognition. Poster presented at the 31st Annual Western Pennsylvania Undergraduate Psychology Conference, Mercyhurst College, Erie, PA (April).

In: Tasks and Techniques: A Sampling of the Methodologies...   ISBN 1-60021-126-7
Editor: Matthew J. Anderson, pp. 49-54   © 2006 Nova Science Publishers, Inc.

Chapter 5

BASIC PROCEDURES FOR UTILIZING THE T-MAZE AS AN APPETITIVE TASK FOR THE RAT

James F. Briggs[*]
Kent State University
Kent, OH 44242

ABSTRACT

Maze use has a long history in the study of animal learning and behavior. The maze task utilizes the innate tendencies for the rat to burrow and use tunnels. One of the simplest types of maze is the T-maze. As the name implies, this maze is shaped like the letter "T". The T-maze paradigm takes advantage of natural behaviors of the rat to study a number of behaviors including discrimination of spatial and sensory cues, habit formation, place and response learning, alternation, and memory, just to name a few. This chapter describes the basic function of the T-maze procedure, describes a sample of findings using this task, and provides a description of the procedures for using the T-maze as an appetitive task with rats.

INTRODUCTION

Maze use has a long history in the study of animal learning and behavior. Early in the twentieth century, Small (1901) introduced the use of mazes into the examination of animal intelligence. Small's investigations focused on the mental processes of the rat using a Hampton Court maze, which is a complex maze with many blocked paths and one correct pathway. Small took advantage of the rat's evolutionarily acquired tendencies of burrowing and living in underground tunnels. Thus, the maze paradigm uses the natural behaviors of the rat to study a number of behaviors, including discrimination of spatial and sensory cues, habit formation, place and response learning, alternation, and memory, just to name a few (for

---

[*] Address Correspondence to: James F. Briggs, Department of Psychology, Kent State University, Kent, OH 44242, Phone: 330-672-2166, E-mail: jbriggs@kent.edu

review of early maze use see Munn, 1950). In this chapter the T-maze paradigm as an appetitive task is reviewed starting with a sample of findings using this paradigm and focusing on the procedures to employ the technique.

Besides the straight runway, one of the simplest mazes used is the T-maze. As the name implies, this maze resembles the letter "T" (see Figure 1). The rat is placed in the start box (a) and a door separating the start box from the stem (b) is opened. The rat moves up the stem to a choice point. The rat must turn left or right into an arm (c) where a reinforcer (e.g., food) is placed in a goal box (d). Doors separating the goal boxes can be closed after the rat enters so the rat can be removed before being placed back in the start box. This creates a discrete trial. This paradigm has been used to investigate a variety of behaviors, all of which are too extensive for this chapter. A sample of findings will provide an introduction to some uses of the T-maze.

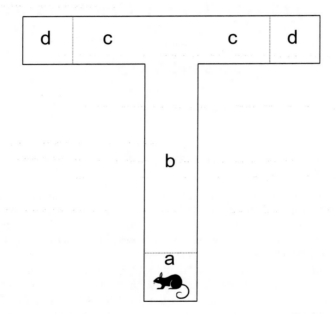

Figure 1. Top view of a T-maze. Dashed lines represent removable doors separating the start box (a) from the stem (b) and the goal boxes (d) from the arms (c).

There is little doubt that when an animal is exposed to a T-maze and finds the reward, the stimuli present (i.e., extramaze cues, intramaze cues, and the internal state of the organism) are encoded to be used for finding the reward in the future. Exactly what cues are used depends on the cues that are available. It should be noted that it is impossible to determine the exact cues used for memory retrieval. Despite this fact, the T-maze has been used to test for discrimination using a variety of cues.

In an early study, Zentall (1970) used the T-maze to demonstrate that training of competing responses in distinctively different contexts compartmentalizes memories of two competing tasks. Zentall found that if rats were trained to turn left for food reward in one particular T-maze, and later trained to turn right in a different T-maze, retrieval depended on the T-maze where testing occurred. If tested in the first T-maze the rats turned left and if tested in the second T-maze the rats turned right. Thus, the contextual cues of each particular T-maze served as instructions for the animal on how to perform in each setting. *reminds me of what we learned in class*

The T-maze has also been used to demonstrate that spatial cues are important for memory retrieval. Hamberg and Spear (1978) revealed a cueing procedure that alleviated forgetting over time using a spatial discrimination task with a T-maze. When tested 28 days following learning the spatial discrimination task, the rats showed substantial forgetting. However, if prior to testing the rats received a cueing treatment that consisted of running in a runway for food reward, the forgetting of the discrimination task was reduced producing an increase in the probability of a correct choice in the T-maze at test. — cool

The T-maze paradigm has also been used to investigate the importance of internal cues. In one of the first demonstrations of state-dependent retention, Overton (1964) trained rats to escape an electric shock by turning left or right in a T-maze. One group was injected with the drug pentobarbital (a short-acting barbiturate) just before training, while another group was injected with saline. Following training, the rats were given a series of test trials while in the drug state (pentobarbital) or the non-drug state (saline). A disassociation effect was observed – subjects made very few errors when tested in the same state as training, and were at chance performance when in the state that differed from training. These results suggest that the rats in one state are unable to retrieve what was learned in a different state (see Spear and Riccio, 1994). *isn't that obvious?*

Besides being used in the study of discrimination and memory, the T-maze task has been used to study a number of different psychological phenomena. Brown, Pagani, and Stanton (2005) have recently used the T-maze paradigm to establish a procedure to study spatial discrimination learning in the developing rat. Olton (1979) describes the use of the T-maze to study spontaneous alternation and exploration behaviors. Spontaneous alternation is a behavior where animals prefer not to repeat their previous choice. Thus, in a T-maze the rat tends to alternate its preference between the left and right goal boxes. The T-maze has also been used with the study of cognitive maps, which is an internal schematic image of the maze (see Mazur, 2006). The T-maze can be utilized to study many naturalistic behaviors in rodents. *why. novelty.*

METHOD

Food Deprivation

When using the T-maze paradigm as an appetitive task, a hungry rat is typically employed with a highly desirable reinforcement for reward. Although rats, like humans, find sweet flavors highly desirable, some mild food deprivation is needed to motivate them and maintain steady responding. The standard weight restriction for rats is 85% of their free feeding weight (National Institute of Mental Health, 2002). Although this may appear to be somewhat severe food deprivation, it is only mild and has no detrimental effects. In fact, studies have shown that wild animals can be 15% below their free feeding weight when in their natural environment (Poling, Nickel, and Alling, 1990), and this reduced diet can be beneficial to the animals health (Hubert, Laroque, Gillet, and Keenan, 2000; see also National Institute of Mental Health, 2002).

Before restricting the rat's weight one must first record its free feeding weight. This should be done at the same time each day for approximately three consecutive days. This provides an average free feeding weight. Food can then be reduced to approximately 50% until the rat reaches 85% of its *ad libitum* weight. Once the target weight is achieved, daily feeding should be adjusted to maintain the target weight.

Another way to food deprive is to restrict the amount of food intake by allowing the rat to eat for only a short period of time each day. With this method the rat is allowed to consume food for a set amount of time each day (e.g., 2 hours of free food access per day). This procedure has the drawback of lacking consistency. Each animal consumes different amounts of chow, thus preventing a consistent weight. However, this procedure has been used with positive results.

Maze Acclimation

Once the target weight is obtained the rats should be acclimated to the maze. Before training begins, the animals should be allowed to become familiar with the environment and to discover the reinforcers. Acclimation involves placing the rat in the T-maze for a set period of time (e.g., 7 min per session) to freely explore the entire maze. Reinforcers should be placed throughout the T-maze: one in each goal box (Figure 1 d) and another in the stem (Figure 1 b) of the maze. A highly desirable reinforcer often used is a piece of Froot Loops cereal (Kelloggs', Battle Creek, MI).

haha

Training

Once acclimated, the rats are ready to begin training. The arm designated to be the correct choice should be determined prior to training. There are three ways to determine which arm is the correct choice. For one method the correct choice is chosen by the experimenter either the left arm being correct or the right arm being the correct choice. This is probably the most commonly used method. If the direction is chosen by the investigator the correct response should be counterbalanced within each group (i.e., randomly assign half of each group to be trained right arm correct and the other half trained left arm correct). Other methods include allowing the rat to choose which arm is the correct response by placing a reinforcer in both goal boxes or in neither goal box. By placing the reward in both goal boxes the rat will be correct on its first choice regardless of the response being left or right. If the rat chooses the left arm on the first response all subsequent responses will be correct for the left goal box and vice versa for the right goal box. Alternatively, by not placing a reinforcer in either goal box on the first trial the rat makes an incorrect choice. Following the first trial the goal box not chosen becomes the correct response. Having the rat choose the correct or incorrect response on the first trial can either take advantage of or alleviate any directional preference, respectively. *doesn't the rat change up his course?*

Once the correct direction is chosen, training consists of placing a rat in the start box with the door closed to confine the animal, making sure there is reinforcement placed in the correct goal box. Confining the rat to the start box is beneficial if recording latencies (see below). After a brief period (e.g., 15 sec) the door is opened allowing the animal to enter the stem of the T-maze. If after the start box door is opened and the rat does not exit the box, it is not uncommon for the experimenter to gently nudge the rat to initiate movement into the stem

(Holden, Overmier, Cowan, and Matthews, 2004). Once the rat leaves the start box, the door should be shut forcing a choice into a goal box.

Upon the rat entering the stem, the doors should be opened to both goal boxes to allow access. Once the rat makes a choice and moves into a goal box, the doors should be lowered. This prevents the rat from retracing to the other goal box or the start box (a non-correction procedure). Leeper (1932) has found higher reliability of the T-maze with doors over mazes without. Confining the rat to the goal box also provides a discrete trial by removing the animal before the next trial. Doors also serve practical purposes of holding the rat in the goal box until it consumes the reward if it chooses the correct response, or allowing the rat to learn it made an incorrect response by exploring the goal box without finding a food reward. Doors also make it easier to remove the rat from the maze so you are not chasing the animal through the maze.

Once a choice is made, the rat should remain in the goal box for enough time to consume the reward. If an incorrect response is made, the rat should be left in the empty goal box for approximately as long as one takes to consume the reward. When the reward is consumed or enough time has passed, the rat is removed and returned to its home cage or into the start box for another trial. The T-maze should be wiped down manually using a disinfectant to clean the maze and to remove any olfactory cues that could assist the rat in finding the reinforcement on later trials.

Scoring

How do we know when or if the rat has learned the appropriate response? The trials should be repeated until the rat demonstrates learning of the maze or fails to master the task within a set number of trials.

There are three commonly used measures that can be taken as evidence of maze learning. Running speed, or latency, can be recorded as an indication of learning. Latency provides a measure of how long it takes the rat to traverse the maze from the start box to the goal box. Typically, over successive trials the running speed should become shorter if learning is occurring. Trials to criterion can also be recorded as a measure of learning. The criterion is set by the experimenter and must be a reliable indication that learning has taken place. Exactly what criterion used depends on some sense of how well learning should be established. Very strict trials to criterion may be ten consecutive errorless trials. A less severe criterion might be set at some percent of correct trials to criterion. For example, an 80% criterion signifies eight out of ten correct trials; whereas four correct trials out of eight represents a 50% criterion. Finally, errors to criterion can be obtained as a measure. This measure is very similar to trials to criterion, but is based on a criterion of allowing only a certain number of wrong responses. Errors to criterion are also set by the experimenter and can be very strict (i.e., only allowing one error for ten consecutive trials, or 10%) to a more lenient criterion (i.e., allowing four errors in a block of ten trials, or 40%). Because of the similarity between trials to criterion and errors to criterion, both measures can be used. However, the decision of which criterion will be used should be determined before training has started.

The T-maze paradigm has been used for some time as a technique for investigating a variety of animal behaviors. As noted above, because of its simplistic design, the T-maze is very suitable for studying phenomena like discrimination and alternation. There are a number of behaviors that can be assessed by using this maze. There are also numerous studies in the animal literature describing how the T-maze paradigm has been and could be employed. This chapter provided the basic procedures for using the T-maze as an appetitive task with rats.

REFERENCES

Brown, K. L., Pagani, J. H., and Stanton, M. E. (2005). Spatial conditional discrimination learning in developing rats. *Developmental Psychobiology, 46*, 97-110.

Hamberg, J. M., and Spear, N. E. (1978). Alleviation of forgetting of discrimination learning. *Learning and Motivation, 9*, 466-476.

Holden, J. M., Overmier, J. B., Cowan, E. T., and Matthews, L. (2004). Effects of lipopolysaccharide on consolidation of partial learning in the Y-maze. *Integrative Physiological and Behavioral Science, 39*, 334-340.

Hubert, M. F., Laroque, P., Gillet J. P., and Keenan, K. P. (2000). The effects of diet, ad libitum feeding, and moderate and severe dietary restriction on body weight, survival, clinical pathology parameters, and cause of death in control Sprague-Dawley rats. *Toxicological Science, 58*, 195-207.

Leeper, R. (1932). The reliability and validity of maze experiments with white rats. *Genetic Psychology Monographs, 11*, 137-245.

Mazur, J. E. (2006). *Learning and Behavior* (6th ed.). Upper Saddle River, NJ: Pearson Prentice Hall.

Munn, N. L. (1950). *Handbook of psychological research on the rat: An introduction to animal psychology*. Boston: Houghton Mifflin Company.

National Institute of Mental Health (2002). *Methods and welfare considerations in behavioral research with animals: Report of a national institutes of health workshop*. Morrison, A. R., Evans, H. L., Ator, N. A., Nakamura, R. K. (Eds). (NIH Publication No. 02-5083). Washington, DC: U.S. Government Printing Office.

Olton, D. S. (1979). Mazes, maps, and memory. *American Psychologist, 34*, 583-596.

Overton, D. A. (1964). State-dependent or "dissociated" learning produced with pentobarbital. *Journal of Comparative and Physiological Psychology, 57*, 3-12.

Poling, A., Nickel, M., and Alling, K. (1990). Free birds aren't fat: Weight gain in captured wild pigeons maintained under laboratory conditions. *Journal of the Experimental Analysis of Behavior, 53*, 423-424.

Small, W. S. (1901). Experimental study of the mental processes of the rat. II. *American Journal of Psychology, 12*, 206-239.

Spear, N. E., and Riccio, D. C. (1994). *Memory: Phenomena and principles*. Boston: Allyn and Bacon.

Zentall, T. R. (1970). Effects of context change on forgetting in rats. *Journal of Experimental Psychology, 86*, 440-448.

In: Tasks and Techniques: A Sampling of the Methodologies...   ISBN 1-60021-126-7
Editor: Matthew J. Anderson, pp. 55-61   © 2006 Nova Science Publishers, Inc.

Chapter 6

RADIAL ARM MAZE

Terri L. Finamore[*1] *and Richard L. Port*[2]

[1] Department of Psychology, Kent State University, Kent, OH 44242
[2] Department of Psychology, Slippery Rock University, Slippery Rock, PA 16057

ABSTRACT

Mazes have played an important role in the study of memory processes in animals. Maze testing has a long standing history in psychological research investigating spatial memory, cognitive maps, foraging strategies and particular characteristics of memory. Many present day conceptualizations about cognition were developed historically, and continue to be postulated from the empirical observations of rats in mazes. Spatial memory, or the memory for places and locations in space, has been extensively studied using radial arm mazes. The radial arm maze task provides a spatial analogue of an operant procedure with the capacity to assess and provide information about the characteristics of working and reference memory in animals. Maze testing takes full advantage of the natural predisposition of rats, and other animals, to follow spatial strategies and uses their inherent abilities to further our understanding of spatial cognition. Research utilizing radial arm mazes suggests that in spatial tasks subjects demonstrate the ability to remember information, and to use that information in a flexible and adaptive fashion. This chapter illustrates the fundamental rationale and utility of maze testing and highlights significant findings derived from research using the radial arm maze. Basic maze methodology is discussed.

INTRODUCTION

In order to adapt and survive in their natural habitats, animals must be able to maintain a specific memory for particular places within the context of their environmental surroundings that bear critical relevance to their survival needs. For example, foraging animals must remember the specific location where they last found food. Revisiting depleted food source

---

[*] Corresponding author: Terri L. Finamore, e-mail: tfinamor@kent.edu

locations would not be an efficient survival strategy and lapses in memory for the spatial layout of their natural habitat could prove costly in terms of individual survival and the survival of dependent offspring.

A particularly well suited and widely used technique for studying spatial memory in rodents utilizes the radial arm maze task to assess what animals are capable of learning and remembering about their spatial environment. (Olton, 1979; Olton and Samuelson, 1976). In this task, memory is inferred from improvements in performance observed across days of training in a radial arm maze (Dubreuil, Tixier, Dutrieux and Edeline, 2003). The relative ease with which rats are able to learn the maze task may be due to preexisting genetic tendencies. It is well documented that rats explore their spatial surroundings in an exhaustive fashion (Small, 1901), with great efficiency (Uster, Bättig and Nageli, 1976) and in both the natural and maze environments do not often revisit previously encountered locations (Gaffan and Davies, 1981). Tolman (1948) initially postulated that rats learn more than direct stimulus response associations, suggesting instead that spatial maps are constructed based on exposure to a particular environment. Rats appear to have a systematic technique of exploration and maze data supports the contention that rodents form spatial representations of their environment and efficiently execute organized foraging paths (Olton, 1979).

The radial arm maze (RAM) consists of a center platform with a number of identical arms (e.g., eight) radiating away from the central area (see figure). Maze designs are variable in that the center area can be circular or hexagonal and arms can be of varying heights, widths and lengths with either rounded or squared ends. Located at the furthest extremity of each arm is a goal box. Food rewards are baited in specific arms during the task, depending upon the nature of each particular investigation. Basically, a food deprived animal is placed in the center of the maze and allowed a specific amount of time to explore the maze and retrieve the food rewards. Optimal performance would require that animals enter each baited arm only once without revisiting previously entered arms as they navigate the maze and arm choices.

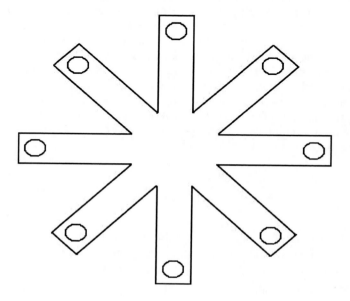

8 arm radial maze

Working and reference memory are two distinct memory processes that can be simultaneously assessed in the radial arm maze (He, Yamada, Nakajima, Kamei and Nabeshima, 2002). Working memory is the short-term trial dependent retention of information necessary for successful responding on a current task and only retained long enough to complete the given task. Reference memory is the long-term trial independent retention of background information relevant and necessary for the successful use of recently acquired information. Reference memory allows working memory to be useful. In the wild, or in the maze, food sources may be located across many natural environmental caches, or baited in several goal boxes. It is useful and adaptive to remember which places have been visited in search of food and efficiency relies on working memory. However, in order to forage successfully an animal also needs to remember the background information about the task at hand, such as the environmental habitat, maze or foraging procedure, and is dependent upon reference memory to provide that necessary informational framework.

In their original maze experiment, Olton and Samuelson (1976) used a fully baited maze and required an animal to visit each arm only once per trial to locate food reward. Rats quickly learned where food was located and accurately remembered not to re-enter arms previously visited. Their findings demonstrated that rats employed the most efficient foraging strategies and did not rely on intramaze (internal) cues, such as food or scent cues to navigate the maze. This spatial task was found to be dependent on the spatial locations of extramaze (external) cues (Olton and Samuelson, 1976). Subsequent research further negated the use of odor cues or specific response sequence chains in maze exploration strategies (Olton, Collison and Werz, 1977; Zoladek and Roberts, 1978). Instead, the location of each arm was specified by extramaze visual cues positioned outside of the maze. These findings suggest that rats formed a "list" of the arms visited during each trial by using the room layout, lab apparatus or visual cues as landmarks identifying particular arms when the cues were positioned in consistent locations relative to the arms of the maze. Suzuki, Augerinos and Black (1980) found that altering the spatial landmark cues resulted in rats exploring the arms as new locations and the subsequent disruption of performance. Therefore, spatial locations within the maze appear to be identified by distal cues located outside of the maze and not by stimuli inside of the maze environment (Morris, 1981). Finamore, Riccio, Vaskova and Port (in preparation) found further evidence supporting previous findings demonstrating the salience of extramaze cues in maze navigation. Rats trained in a particular maze (A) and subsequently tested in either the original training maze (A) or an altered maze (B) showed no performance differences or a context shift effect when tested across two delay intervals (one and seven days after training). Rats tested in the altered maze were able to navigate as efficiently as rats tested in the original training context maze presumably due to the fact that both mazes were positioned in the same location within a testing room in which all extramaze spatial cues were held constant.

More elaborate versions of the classic task were developed to assess particular aspects of memory processing (Olton and Collison, 1979; Packard and White, 1990) but the basic version is widely used in research investigations. The radial arm maze has been used extensively to assess hippocampal lesions (Gisquet-Verrier and Schenk, 1994). The hippocampus plays an important role in learning and memory processes and is critical in the processing of spatial information (Nadel, 1991). Hippocampal lesions have produced working memory impairments in radial arm maze tasks (Olton, 1979). Complete lesions of the hippocampus resulted in increased error rates for both working and reference memory in maze testing (Jarrard, 1995). Both working and reference memory were found to be impaired when the spatial locations of the extramaze cues were altered in a fixed position reward task (FPRT), while performance in a variable position reward task (VPRT) was not affected (He et al, 2002). Spatial learning deficits were observed in unilaterally lesioned rats and damage to either hemisphere resulted in inferior reference memory across radial maze training and a tendency of lesioned animals to commit more working memory errors than control animals (Port, Finamore, Noble and Seybold, 2000). An investigation into the effect of stress on maze performance revealed impaired working memory in stressed rats but no observed impairment in reference memory (Sandstrom and Hart, 2005). Radial maze performance of aged animals was evaluated and age-related deficits of both working and reference memory were observed (Ward, Stoelzel and Markus, 1999). Radial arm maze testing has been used to determine the involvement of particular genes and proteins in memory traces (Davis, Rodger, Hicks, Mallet and Laroche, 1996 and 1998; Nogues, Micheau and Jaffard, 1994) and potential memory deficits resulting from electromagnetic emissions related to cell phone usage have also been investigated (Dubreuil, Jay and Edeline, 2002).

Radial arm maze performance has revealed specific characteristics of working memory capacity and duration. Rats have successfully navigated radial mazes with up to 17 arms (Olton, Collison and Werz, 1977; Wilkie and Slobin, 1983) and spatial memory has been shown to last for several hours (Wilson and Wilkie, 1991; Spetch, 1990). Beatty and Shavalia (1980a and b) demonstrated the durability of working memory and the resistance of spatial memory to interference. In one study rats were interrupted half-way through maze exploration but were found to successfully and accurately continue the exploration after delays of up to 6 hours (Beatty and Shavalia, 1980a). Kesner and Novak (1982) documented serial position effects in rodents observed learning a modified radial arm maze task.

For humans, the ability to navigate our world largely depends on spatial learning and memory (Astur, Taylor, Mamelak, Philpott and Sutherland, 2002). Analogous to working memory in rodents (Olton, 1979), spatial working memory in humans also retains information long enough for the completion of the current task (Baddeley, 1990). The hippocampus is critically important in human spatial learning and hippocampal lesions have resulted in performance deficits in the radial maze task (Feigenbaum, Polkey and Morris, 1996). Various studies have implicated the right temporal lobes in spatial memory (Smith and Milner, 1981; Smith and Milner, 1989; Pigott and Milner, 1993). Feigenbaum, Polkey and Morris (1996) investigated spatial memory in surgical patients after unilateral temporal lobectomy for the treatment of intractable epilepsy using a computerized analogue of Olton's radial maze, thereby enabling them to draw parallels between the animal literature and human studies. Results suggest the need for further investigation into specific brain structures, the neural system involved in the processing of spatial information and the formation of cognitive maps. Assessment of spatial memory using the radial arm maze has helped elucidate the biological foundations of memory and continues to contribute to our understanding of cognitive processes.

METHODS

Maze methodology varies according to the specific interests of each investigation. In a basic maze task, approximately two weeks prior to maze training animals are placed on modestly restricted diets to achieve body weights of approximately 85% of their free feeding weights. Subjects are adapted to the radial arm maze by allowing them to explore the maze for a predetermined number of minutes (e.g. 10) on specified number of consecutive days (e.g. 3) Food reinforcers (Froot Loops or Noyes pellets) are placed in the central platform area during adaptation and each animal is placed in the central area and allowed to freely explore the maze for the allotted time period. Spatial learning may be assessed over a specified period of time (weeks) or animals may be trained to a specific criteria (a certain number of error free days) during which time randomly predetermined arms are baited. Each animal is placed in the center area and permitted a specified amount of time (minutes) to retrieve all food rewards. Arm entries are recorded based on full body entry into each arm (all four paws cross from central area). Upon retrieval of all reinforcers, subjects are removed from the maze and returned to the home cage. Entry into an unbaited arm is scored as a reference memory error. Reentry into a previously baited arm is scored as a working memory error.

REFERENCES

Astur, R. S., Taylor, L. B., Mamelak, A. N., Philpott, L., and Sutherland, R. J. (2002). Humans with hippocampus damage display severe spatial memory impairments in a virtual Morris water task. *Behavioural Brain Research, 132,* 77-84.

Baddeley, A. D. (1990). *Human Memory: Theory and Practice.* Needham Heights, MA: Allyn and Bacon

Beatty, W. W., and Shavalia, D. A. (1980a). Rat spatial memory: resistance to retroactive interference at long retention intervals. *Animal Learning and Behavior, 8,* 550-552.

Beatty, W. W., and Shavalia, D. A. (1980b). Spatial memory in rats: time course of working memory and effects of anesthetics. *Behavioral and Neural Biology, 28,* 454-462.

Davis, S., Rodger, J., Hicks, A., Mallet, J., and Laroche, S. (1996). Brain structure and task-specific increase in expression of the gene encoding syntaxin 1b during learning in rat: A potential molecular marker for learning-induced synaptic plasticity in neural networks. *The European Journal of Neuroscience, 8,* 2068-2074.

Davis, S., Rodger, J., Hicks, A., Mallet, J., and Laroche, S. (1998). Increase in syntaxin 1b mRNA in hippocampal and cortical circuits during spatial learning reflects a mechanism of transynaptic plasticity involved in establishing a memory trace. *Learning and Memory, 5,* 375-390.

Dubreuil, D., Jay, T., and Edeline, J. M. (2002). Does head-only exposure to GSM-900 electromagnetic fields affect the performance of rats in spatial learning tasks. *Behavioural Brain Research, 129,* 203-210.

Dubreuil, D., Tixier, C., Dutrieux, G., and Edeline, J. M. (2003). Does the radial arm maze necessarily test spatial memory? *Neurobiology of Learning and Memory, 79,* 109-117.

Feigenbaum, J. D., Polkey, C. E., and Morris, R. G. (1996). Deficits in spatial working memory after unilateral temporal lobectomy in man. *Neuropsychologia, 34,* 163-176.

Finamore, T. L., Riccio, D. C., Vaskova, L., and Port, R. L. (2005). *The effect of contextual manipulations on radial arm maze performance.* Unpublished manuscript.

Gaffan, E. A., and Davies, J. (1981). The role of exploration in win-shift and win-stay performance on a radial maze. *Learning and Motivation, 12,* 282-299.

Gisquet-Verrier, P., and Schenk, F. (1994). Selective hippocampal lesions in rats do not affect retrieval processes promoted by prior cuing with the conditioned stimulus or the context. *Psychobiology, 22,* 289-303.

He, J., Yamada, K., Nakajima, A., Kamei, H.., and Nabeshima, T. (2002). Learning and memory in two different reward tasks in a radial arm maze in rats. *Behavioural Brain Research, 134,* 139-148.

Jarrard, L. E. (1995). What does the hippocampus really do? *Behavioural Brain Research, 71,* 1-10.

Kesner, R. P., and Novak, J. M. (1982). Serial position curve in rats: Role of the dorsal hippocampus. *Science, 218,* 173-175.

Morris, R. G. M. (1981). Spatial localization does not require the presence of local cues. *Learning and Motivation, 12,* 239-260.

Nadel, L. (1991). The hippocampus and space revisited. *Hippocampus. 1,* 221-229.

Nogues, X., Micheau, J., and Jaffard, R. (1994). Protein kinase c activity in the hippocampus following spatial learning tasks in mice. *Hippocampus, 4,* 71-77.

Olton, D. S. (1979). Mazes, maps, and memory. *American Psychologist, 34,* 583-596.

Olton, D. S., and Collison, C. (1979). Intramaze cues and "odor trails" fail to direct choice behavior on an elevated maze. *Animal Learning and Behavior, 7,* 221-223.

Olton, D. S., Collison, C., and Werz, M. A. (1977). Spatial memory and radial arm maze performance of rats. *Learning and Motivation, 8,* 289-314.

Olton, D. S., and Samuelson, R. J. (1976). Remembrance of places passed: Spatial memory in rats. Journal of Experimental Psychology. *Animal Behavior Processes, 2,* 97-116.

Packard, M. G., and White, N. M. (1990). Lesions of the caudate nucleus selectively impair "reference memory" acquisition in the radial maze. *Behavioral and Neural Biology, 53,* 39-50.

Pigott, S., and Milner, B. (1993). Memory for different aspects of complex visual scenes after unilateral temporal- or frontal-lobe resection. *Neuropsychologia, 31,* 1-15.

Port, R. L., Finamore, T. L., Noble, M. M., and Seybold, K. S. (2000). Unilateral hippocampal damage impairs spatial cognition in rats. *International Journal of Neuroscience, 103,* 25-32.

Sandstrom, N. J., and Hart, S. R. (2005). Isolation stress during the third postnatal week alters radial arm maze performance and corticosterone levels in adulthood. *Behavioural Brain Research, 156,* 289-296.

Small, W. S. (1901). Experimental study of the mental processes of the rat. *American Journal of Psychology, 12,* 206-239.

Smith, M. L., and Milner, B. (1981). The role of the right hippocampus in the recall of spatial location. *Neuropsychologia, 19,* 781-793.

Smith, M. L., and Milner, B. (1989). Right hippocampal impairment in the recall of spatial location: Encoding deficit or rapid forgetting? *Neuropsychologia, 27,* 71-81.

Spetch, M. L. (1990). Further studies of pigeons' spatial working memory in the open-field task. *Animal Learning and Behavior, 18*, 332-340.

Suzuki, S., Augerinos, G., and Black, A. H. (1980). Stimulus control of spatial behavior on the eight-arm maze in rats. *Learning and Motivation, 11*, 1-18.

Tolman, E. C. (1948). Cognitive maps in rats and men. *Psychological Review, 55*, 189-208.

Uster, H. J., Bättig, K., and Nageli, H. H. (1976). Effects of maze geometry and experience on exploratory behavior in the rat. *Animal Learning and Behavior, 4*, 84-88.

Ward, M. T., Stoelzel, C. R., and Markus, E. J. (1999). Hippocampal sysfunction during aging II: Deficits on the radial-arm maze. *Neurobiology of Aging, 20*, 373-380.

Wilkie, D. M., and Slobin, P. (1983). Gerbils in space: Performance on the 17-arm radial maze. *Journal of the Experimental Analysis of Behavior, 40*, 301-312.

Wilson, R. J., and Wilkie, D. M. (1991). Discrimination training facilitates pigeons' performance on one-trial-per day delayed matching of key location. *Journal of the Experimental Analysis of Behavior, 55*, 201-212.

Zoladek, L., and Roberts, W. A. (1978). The sensory basis of spatial memory in the rat. *Animal Learning and Behavior, 6*, 77-81.

In: Tasks and Techniques: A Sampling of the Methodologies…   ISBN 1-60021-126-7
Editor: Matthew J. Anderson, pp. 63-86   © 2006 Nova Science Publishers, Inc.

Chapter 7

THE MORRIS WATER TASK AND RELATED METHODS

Derek A. Hamilton[1], Glen T. Prusky[2] and Robert J. Sutherland[*3]

[1] Departments of Psychology and Neurosciences,
The University of New Mexico Albuquerque, New Mexico, USA
[2] Department of Neuroscience, Canadian Centre for Behavioural Neuroscience
The University of Lethbridge Lethbridge, Alberta, Canada
[3] Department of Neuroscience, Canadian Centre for Behavioural Neuroscience
The University of Lethbridge Lethbridge, Alberta, Canada

ABSTRACT

We describe here the essential apparatus for the Morris water task and discuss some of the learning and memory phenomena typically observed in rodents. The commonly used behavioural procedures are outlined, along with some procedural variants that have been shown to be important in revealing the nature of processes underlying performance. In addition, we describe methods that are direct extensions using a virtual (computerized) Morris water task with humans and a computerized visual discrimination task for rodents.

INTRODUCTION

It is difficult to overestimate the invigorating effect that the invention of the Morris water task (Morris, 1981) exerted within the community of scientists interested in learning, memory, and cognition in rodents over the past two decades. This simple, but extraordinarily useful, task reliably provides an opportunity for animals to demonstrate their ability to navigate to a place within an environment. A cursory scan of scientific literature reveals that in terms of number of papers reporting use of this task, it has been the most popular

---

[*] Primary author contact information: R. J. Sutherland, Department of Neuroscience, Canadian Centre for Behavioural Neuroscience, The University of Lethbridge, Lethbridge, Alberta, Canada T1K 3M4, Email: robert.sutherland@uleth.ca

behavioural task for rodents for decades and its popularity appears to be increasing. Why? Three reasons seem obvious; conceptual preparedness, relative reliability and flexibility, and solid linkage to underlying neurobiological processes.

By the late 1970s the application of cognitive concepts, even those linked to neuroscience, had become much more widely accepted within the animal learning field. There was an accumulated appreciation within this field that learning and memory were based upon processes that were constrained by neurobiological mechanisms acquired through the evolutionary history of species. The notion, common among animal learning investigators for decades, that learning proceeds along the same lines, regardless of which type of stimulus or type of response was arbitrarily selected by the experimenter, had lost favour. There were descriptions of situations in which learning did not proceed very well at all, even though the learning episode was properly organized, and of situations in which animals seemed to be especially well-prepared to learn even complex information surprisingly quickly (conditioned taste aversion learning was an early example). Furthermore, O'Keefe and Nadel's book (1978; http://www.cognitivemap.net) successfully presented a cognitive theory, well-integrated with behavioural and neurobiological considerations. It had as its centrepiece the brain's spatial mapping system. This system quickly acquires a representation of explored environments, including information about places, their spatial relationships, and objects in specific places. The first Morris water task experiments were conducted and the results were presented in this context. Clearly, there were many other contemporary mazes and tasks that allowed rodents to demonstrate that they could acquire information about specific spatial locations. The radial arm maze was one. It was used very effectively, especially by Olton and his co-workers, but this task appeared to be more complex. It required more training and appeared to have more ambiguity for interpreting the nature of the processes underlying performance. The fact that on a given trial rodents need to keep track of which of several goal locations they have already visited prompted the idea that a special memory process was engaged, which Olton termed working memory. Olton and co-workers believed that processing in the hippocampus had a necessary and specific role in working memory (Olton, Becker, and Handelmann, 1979). In contrast, O'Keefe and Nadel (1978) had identified the hippocampus as the central structure in their cognitive mapping system. The Morris water task offered a way to measure place learning and memory in a behavioural context that did not require Olton's type of working memory. In the first years of use of the Morris water task there was a nice opportunity to examine behaviour after damage to the hippocampus to test a strong inference from the cognitive mapping theory. Place navigation was unambiguously disrupted (Morris, Garrud, Rawlins, and O'Keefe, 1982; Sutherland, Kolb, and Whishaw, 1982). This added to the reputation of the task as being exceptionally useful. Together with observations that nonspatial versions of the radial arm maze were unaffected by damage to the hippocampus, these findings led Olton to recant his working memory theory of hippocampal function.

Compared to many behavioural tasks, the Morris water task generates very reliable performance that is flexibly expressed over a wide range of parameters. It is especially compelling when, at any time, one can take a colleague to the pool room and without fail demonstrate in a straight-forward manner almost any phenomenon of interest. This is very difficult or impossible with most other behavioural tasks. Essentially, every rat shows clear place learning after only a small number of trials and good long-term retention if training continues after the point that performance reaches asymptote. There has never been a comprehensive evaluation of many of the basic task factors, for example, the effect of the diameter of the circular pool of water. One experiment with mice showed that performance is similar regardless of pool diameter (Staay, 2000). We have used pools in the range of .8 to 2 m in diameter and learning proceeds similarly. The basic phenomena are still observed. In a practical way a larger diameter pool is preferable because it enhances the ability to detect a preference for searching for the platform in the correct region. Likewise, performance is similar over a wide range of intertrial intervals from around 1 minute to an hour. Learning proceeds more effectively with longer intertrial intervals over a wide range. Learning can also proceed well over a range of water temperatures within a few degrees of room temperature. A major consideration is that rats will not be sufficiently motivated to escape if the temperature is warm; They spend long intervals floating and only sporadically show bursts of slow swimming. Another concern is hypothermia if the water is too cold. Hypothermia disrupts learning (Panakhova, Buresova, and Bures, 1984) and obviously this interacts with the amount of time spent in the pool. Some experimenters remove water from the rodents by toweling and provide some additional warming during the intertrial interval.

In its most frequently used version, rodents are released at the edge of the pool from the four cardinal compass points. This increases the likelihood that subjects sample swimming in all parts of the pool and sample views of the room from all sectors. Learning is robust in the face of departures from this procedure. With normal subjects, releasing them from a subset, even just one, of these start locations still produces clear place learning with enough trials such that, if they are released from other start locations, they can swim directly to the goal (Morris, 1981). This does not mean that subjects are able to navigate accurately from completely novel locations. We have shown that accurate navigation requires that the subject has previously visited the vicinity of the novel start location as part of a swim trajectory leading to the goal location (Sutherland, Chew, Baker, and Linggard, 1987). Sutherland et al. (1987) also showed that nearly all of the information necessary for place navigation performance is acquired during swimming. Once rats have boarded the platform they clearly do look at the cues around the room, rearing and rotating often during initial learning and less during later trials. Information obtained while on the platform can contribute modestly to later performance (Sutherland and Linggard, 1982), but it is not essential to learning.

A key feature of the Morris water task that generates reliable and robust performance is the use of water to motivate escape. This form of motivation does not require food or water deprivation, nor controlled cutaneous shock. The water provides more or less continuous aversive stimulation until successful escape and it generates activation of movement, producing few persistent behaviours that are incompatible with the normal escape behaviour. Conceptually similar dry-land spatial tasks do not generate such reliable and direct place navigation in open fields or on tables. Immersion in water had been used effectively in tasks going back many years before the development of the Morris water task. These included a water-based Hebb-Williams maze (Raffner, 1974), t-mazes, and even a swimming pool escape task developed by Irwin and colleagues (Barraco, Klauenberg, and Irwin, 1978) in which escape was afforded by a hanging rope that the rodents could swim to and climb on. Irwin and colleagues noted that rats showed surprisingly fast learning in the swim escape task and that navigation appeared to be controlled by the location of the rope rather by seeing the rope. It required the development of the fixed, hidden goal that could not be seen or heard or smelled by Richard Morris to produce an unambiguous demonstration of place navigation in the pool. Another important feature of the Morris water task is that one can make the goal platform plainly visible. If rats have drastic vision loss or motivational deficits, not only will they fail to learn to navigate directly to the location of the hidden goal platform, but they will fail to learn to navigate directly to a visible one. This approach has been used with some success to study lesion, drug, and genetic effects. A good version of visible platform testing uses two visible but discriminably different platforms where the goal platform is rigid, affording the rodent escape from the water and the other platform tips the rat off as it attempts to board. One consideration on the use of visible platform procedures as a way of eliminating visual problems as an explanation for poor place navigation is that the required visual acuity to accurately solve the hidden platform version is nearly always unmeasured. How many degrees of visual angle are subtended by the controlling distal visual cues in place navigation? No one is sure. It this context, in our method section we provide a description of a newer, modified water task, the visual water task, that allows for explicit control over visual cues presented on two computer monitors (McGill, Douglas, Lund, and Prusky, 2004; Prusky and Douglas, 2004; Prusky, Harker, Douglas, and Whishaw, 2002; Prusky and Douglas, 2003). One can measure visual acuity reliably using this method thereby eliminating ambiguity about whether lesion, drug, or genetic manipulations alter vision in rodents. This task has been used successfully to measure not only acuity, but visual discrimination learning in the absence of a place navigation requirement (Prusky, Douglas, Nelson, Shabanpoor, and Sutherland, 2004; Driscoll, Sutherland, Prusky, and Rudy, 2004; Driscoll, Howard, Prusky, Rudy, and Sutherland, 2005).

Finally, with the development of electronics to handle digitized video images and affordable powerful laboratory microcomputers it became possible to collect all of the behavioural measures that had been shown to be useful automatically and to have a representation of the animal's performance immediately (Morris, 1984). HVS Image, Inc. first made these systems commercially available and through regular hardware and software upgrading, they still offer a state-of-the-art product. This development dramatically enhanced the reliability of the task outcomes. The opportunity to have multiple measures of swim time, swim distance, directionality of the swim path, proportion of swim path in different parts of the pool, and number of entries into specific parts of the pool generates powerful converging evidence allowing inferences about spatial abilities.

A last reason for the popularity of the task is the impressive set of experiments linking place navigation performance to underlying neurobiology (see Table 1). Initial lesion experiments showed deficits in place navigation (Morris et al., 1982; Sutherland, Kolb, and Whishaw, 1982), even when the damage to the hippocampus occurred after learning was complete (Sutherland, 1985). All hippocampal subfields are known to be involved (Auer, Jensen, and Whishaw, 1989; Sutherland, Whishaw, and Kolb, 1983). There is also a very distributed set of structures connected with the hippocampus that have been shown to play keys roles in performance, from visual and parietal cortices to retrosplenial and rhinal cortices. There is an undisclosed but likely role of connections out of the hippocampus back to these structures. Lesion studies have also shown the importance in place navigation of subiculum, fornix, medial frontal cortex, septum, anterior thalamus, nucleus accumbens, neostriatum, mammillary bodies, and ascending monoaminergic and cholinergic forebrain projections. Using more selective physiological and neuropharmacological techniques, it is known that the NMDA dependent processes that underlie long-term synaptic enhancement (LTP) at some hippocampal synapses are necessary for place navigation learning but not expression (Morris, Anderson, Lynch, and Baudry, 1986; McNaughton, Barnes, Rao, Baldwin, and Rasmussen, 1986). This particular chain of necessity has been explored to the level of single genes expressed in hippocampus through mutant mouse experiments (Silva, Stevens, Tonegawa, and Wang, 1992). There is fortuitous consilience of evidence surrounding the Morris water task from cognitive theory to neural systems to synaptic physiology to the receptor/gene level. Thus, it provided a rich empirical and theoretical background in which to explore deficits in animal models associated with conditions such as Alzheimer's disease, aging, epilepsy, teratogenic effects of drugs or alcohol, etc. or to examine pathological processes in humans. With the development of a computerized Morris water task for humans (Astur, Ortiz, and Sutherland, 1998), the demonstration that place learning in this version of the task depends upon hippocampal integrity (Astur, Taylor, Mamelak, Philpott, and Sutherland, 2002), and the established similarities in task performance characteristics between people and rodents (Driscoll et al., 2003; Driscoll, Hamilton, Yeo, Brooks, and Sutherland, 2005; Hamilton, Driscoll, and Sutherland, 2002), there is a rich set of possibilities to extend the range of consilience into human cognitive and clinical neuroscience to the mutual benefit of human and nonhuman work.

Table 1. Publications linking place learning and navigation in the Morris water task to underlying neurobiology. Complete references are provided in the References section

Finding	Publication(s)
Hippocampus (anterograde)	Morris et al., 1982; Sutherland, Kolb, and Whishaw, 1982
Hippocampus (retrograde)	Sutherland, 1985
Fornix	Morris, Garrud, and Woodhouse, 1981
Entorhinal cortex	Schenk and Morris, 1985
Frontal cortex	Sutherland, Kolb, and Whishaw, 1982
Parietal cortex	Kolb, Sutherland, and Whishaw, 1983
Striatum	Whishaw, Mittelman, Bunch, and Dunnett, 1987
Retrosplenial/cingulate cortex	Sutherland, Whishaw, and Kolb, 1988
Nucleus accumbens	Sutherland and Rodriguez, 1989
Anterior Thalamus	Sutherland and Rodriguez, 1989
Development	Rudy, Stadlermorris, and Albert, 1987; Schenk, 1985
Aging	Gage, Dunnett, and Bjorklund, 1984
Hypothermia	Panakhova et al., 1984; Rauch et al., 1989
Neurogenesis	Gould, Tanapat, Hastings, and Shors, 1999
LTP saturation	McNaughton et al., 1986
Ischemia/Stroke	Auer et al., 1989
Traumatic Brain Injury	Hamm et al., 1992
Genetic Mutant (Mice)	Silva et al., 1992
Cholinergic sensitivity	Sutherland, Whishaw, and Regehr, 1982
NMDA receptor sensitivity	Morris et al., 1986
Dopaminergic sensitivity	Hagan, Alpert, Morris, and Iversen, 1982
Benzodiazepines	Mcnamara and Skelton, 1991
Latent Learning	Sutherland and Linggard, 1982
Platform vertical movement	Buresova et al., 1985
Auditory cue control	Sutherland and Dyck, 1984
Virtual Morris water task	Astur et al., 1998; Hamilton and Sutherland, 1999

METHODOLOGY

Rat Methods

Morris Water Task

The pool utilized in the Morris water task is typically 1.5m to 2m in diameter and .5m to .7m in height. The pool is filled with water to a depth sufficient to require swimming (i.e., the rat is not able to stand on the bottom of the pool) and for the top of the platform to be submerged by approximately 1cm in tasks that utilize a hidden platform. The inner surface of the pool is generally white which aids in tracking dark animals (see below). For optimal performance and motivation the temperature of the water should be 20deg -23deg C. If the water is too warm motivation can decrease and if the water is too cool stress and other adverse physical consequences can interfere with learning and memory as well as basic performance. Hypothermia in rats is associated with a transient impairment in performance in the water task (Rauch, Welch, and Gallego, 1989). Although rats are resistant to hypothermia in standard water task procedures, smaller rodents such as mice display large decreases in body temperature to a point of hypothermia when standard water task methods are used (Iivonen, Nurminen, Harri, Tanila, and Puolivali, 2003). If hypothermia is suspected in rats the task parameters can be modified (e.g., use longer intertrial intervals) and supplemental heating can be used.

Initially the exposure to the water without a history of training associated with successful escape from the water is associated with stress. Indeed, stressors such as these may complicate other goals of the research, however, it is virtually impossible to eliminate this component of the animal's response without altering the basic procedures and data obtained from the water task. In observing the behaviour of many rats in the Morris water task, particularly those that indicate stress, the overt signs of stress subside quickly, generally within the first or second session, which coincides nicely with the trajectory of learning in the task. One way to decrease the influence of initial exposure stress on place learning as well as factors related to procedural learning (i.e., non-specific learning) is to train animals in one environment and then subsequently measure place learning in a new environment with novel distal cues (Keith and Mcvety, 1988).

Typically the water is made opaque by adding powdered milk so that the platform cannot be detected by the animal when swimming. Approximately 6 cups of powdered milk are needed for a pool 1.5m diameter filled to a depth of 30cm. A less expensive solution is to add a small amount (approximately 2 oz. for a 1.5m diameter pool filled to a depth of 30cm) of powdered, white tempura paint (e.g., Crayola) which is non-toxic and is effective at rendering the water opaque even when highly diluted. Animals will ingest some water (and its contents) when swimming and grooming so it is important that the paint be non-toxic. Additional benefits of using powdered paint rather than milk include the elimination of proteins to which the animal is exposed and easier pool clean-up.

Figure 1. Typical set-up for the Morris water task. In the left foreground is a laptop-based data collection and analysis system (HVS 2020+ system) and underlying VCR connected by cable to a video camera fixed over the centre of the pool.

The pool should be placed at least .5m from any walls in the environment to allow sufficient room for the experimenter to walk around the pool. The pool can be placed on a stand to raise it off the floor which makes release and retrieval of the rat easier. The pool should also be located sufficiently close to a source of water and drainage.

The escape platform can be constructed from a variety of materials, but clear Plexiglass or white PVC pipe are among the most common. The bottom (base) of the platform should be sturdy enough to support the rat firmly and may need to be weighted down in order for it to stay in a fixed location in the pool. The top surface of the platform should be large enough for the animal to easily mount and sit atop the platform. Typically the top surface of the escape platform is square (10cm-15cm) or round (10cm-15cm diameter). For the visible platform task or discrimination learning tasks (see below) an additional platform top can be constructed and placed on the submerged platform so that it is visible and extends above the water surface by 3cm-4cm. Specialized, "on-demand" platforms that can be controlled by the experimenter, and can be made available when certain criteria are met (e.g., after a specific amount of time has been spent in a region of the pool) have also been developed (Buresova, Krekule, Zahalka, and Bures, 1985).

It is generally agreed that rats solve the Morris water task by using the available visual cues in the environment outside of the pool. Thus, there should be a sufficient number of cues to disambiguate the location of the platform. At least two cues appear to be necessary for rats to solve the task (Prados and Trobalon, 1998), although environments in most studies where the distal cue environment is "uncontrolled" contain a large number of visual cues (see Devan et al., 2002 for potential problems with uncontrolled distal cue environments).

Most behavioural measures used in water task research can be obtained by tracking the animal's location in the pool for multiple time-points during the swim path from the release point to the platform. The resulting path (a sequence of points in a Cartesian coordinate system) can be used to determine a number of behavioural measures, either using commercial software that accompanies the tracking system or with custom software. Tracking systems require an overhead camera that is centered above the pool. There are several tracking systems available from commercial vendors that provide software and hardware specialized for tracking rats in the Morris water task.

General Procedures

In this section we describe procedures common to most Morris water task protocols. Procedures for specific behavioural protocols are described in detail below in Procedures for Specific Protocols.

During an experimental session rats are generally placed individually in holding cages in the test environment where they remain between trials. For a given trial a rat is retrieved from its cage by the experimenter and carried to the release location in the pool. The animal should be placed into the pool gently, facing the wall of the pool. If placed against the wall of the pool most rats will push off of the wall in a trajectory perpendicular to the pool wall. If this behaviour is not desired the rat can be placed about 10cm from the pool wall upon release rather than immediately against the pool wall. Once the animal is released the experimenter can either stand still or may walk to a predetermined place in the room. One problem with the latter is that rats will often "track" the experimenter (i.e., they may swim toward the experimenter rather than the platform) and this tracking behaviour will differ depending upon where the animal is released and where the platform is located relative to where the experimenter is moving. If the experimenter stands still at the release location then the experimenter becomes an irrelevant cue for determining where the platform is (as tracking is virtually eliminated and the experimenter will be in a different location on each trial). Nonetheless, rats will often return to the release point, presumably based in part on the presence of the experimenter, after a failed attempt to find the platform. If elimination of the experimenter as a cue is desired one can place a curtain around the pool which affords the opportunity to release the rat and then disappear from the rat's view. If this method is adopted, one must be sure that the environment contains sufficient information to support place navigation.

what would you put there?

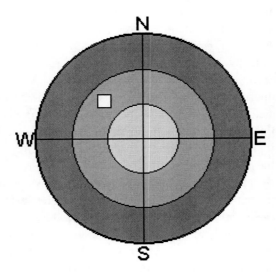

Figure 2. This figure shows the layout of a circular pool used in the Morris water task. The platform (white square) is centered in one quadrant of the pool (NW). Quadrants are demarcated by lines and are commonly used in the analysis of spatial navigation in this task, particularly for calculating measures of preference for probe trial analyses. The cardinal compass points marked along the outer perimeter of the pool are used as release points. The concentric circular regions (annuli) that are shaded in this figure are sometimes used in measures of navigation, for example, to determine whether an animal prefers to spend time in the center or outer (perimeter) regions of the pool.

Once released, the rat swims until it mounts the platform or until a previously determined maximum amount of time has elapsed since release (e.g., 60-90 sec). If the rat fails to find the platform in the allotted time it is retrieved by the experimenter and placed on the platform. The rat is usually left on the escape platform for a period of 5-10 sec during which time the animal will engage in behaviours such as rearing (perhaps to sample visual stimuli) and grooming. The rat is then retrieved by the experimenter and placed back into the holding cage until its next trial. In a typical experiment an intertrial interval of about 5 min is used during which other rats are trained. Depending upon the age of the animal it is sometimes necessary to dry the animal between trials (e.g., with very young or old animals) and a heater can be kept near the holding cages.

Behavioural Measures

This section covers the basic behavioural measures one can obtain from observation of behaviour in the Morris water task. A discussion of common measures is provided and references are provided for more specialized measures.

The most commonly-used behavioural measures in water task research are the latency and path length to navigate to the escape platform. The beginning and endpoints of these measurements are typically when the animal is able to move freely in the pool (i.e, is no longer in the grasp of the experimenter) and when the forelimbs make contact with the escape platform respectively.

Latencies can be taken either using a stopwatch or can be determined by the video tracking system. Path length measurement requires that a representation of the animals path be available in a form suitable for precise measurement. Tracking systems usually provide this measurement automatically. Alternatively, a videotaped record can be used to trace the path onto a piece of paper for analysis.

Path length is an important measure because it is not dependent upon how quickly the animal navigates to the platform. A group difference in latency to navigate to the platform but not in the path length to navigate to the platform suggests a difference in swim speed rather than navigation accuracy. Thus, it is important to utilize both latency and path length when drawing conclusions about spatial learning.

Although path length and latency are commonly-used measures, they sometimes lack sufficient sensitivity to distinguish between rats that have learned to solve the task based upon spatial cues and rats that take indirect paths that are not guided by spatial cues. For example, two swims from individual animals may yield comparable path length and latency measures despite drastically different patterns of behaviour. Gallagher, Burwell, and Burchinal (1993) developed a measure in which the cumulative proximity to the goal is measured for the entire trial. This measure provides unique information that is not contained in the latency and path length data that can be useful for analysis of training trials as well as probe trials.

Several other measures are commonly used to measure spatial navigation. Heading error is the angular deviation from a direct path to the platform and, thus, provides a measure of navigation accuracy. To compute this angular deviation the release point and platform location are used together, with one point taken along the swim path of the animal to form a triangle: If S is the location of the rat, R is the release point and P is the platform location, then the heading error is determined by find the angle SRP. One could compute the heading error for each point in the swim path or pick a particular point, for example, when the animal first travels a distance equal to the pool's radius from the release point as a single measure of heading error. Heading error is informative because it provides information about the trajectory the animal took on the way to the platform. A related measure called Whishaw's error (Whishaw, 1985) involves measuring the percentage of time an animal travels in a corridor from the release point to the platform location, which provides an index of "average directionality".

For measures that are taken on each trial, such as those described above, the average value for a particular group is computed for each trial, or sometimes the average is computed for an entire session (trial block). Averaging at the level of the session increases statistical power, however, as with any type of averaging, information about potential group differences on particular trials is lost. In some cases, averaging at the level of the session can mask group differences that are present on only one or two trials.

Another behavioural measure that can be used is the number of trials (or sessions) that it takes to abandon the inefficient strategies that rats initially engage in to solve the task. For example, when a rat is first placed in the pool and has no history of reinforcement for swimming to the escape platform, the animal will engage in "thigmotaxic" behaviour which consists of swimming around the perimeter of the pool at the wall and searching for an escape from the water. After a trial or two most, rats abandon this ineffective behaviour and begin to swim into the center of the pool where they eventually find the platform and escape from the water (see Figure 3).

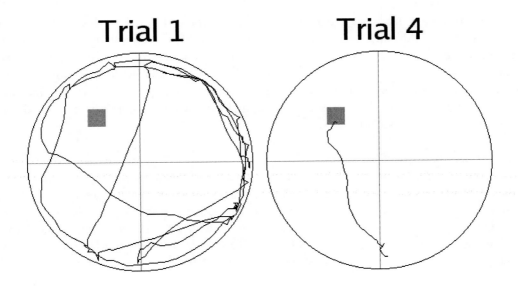

Figure 3. Example swim paths from a single rat in the Morris water task. Paths are shown for trials 1 and 4 for the first day of training in the task. Initially the animal swam around the perimeter of the pool and had to be retrieved by the experimenter because the allotted time of 60 sec to find the platform had elapsed. By trial 4 the animal no longer swims around the perimeter of the pool and finds the platform quickly (5 sec).

More detailed behavioural measures may be utilized for testing specific hypotheses about spatial behaviour or when more sensitive measures are needed in order to detect an effect of a manipulation on performance and/or learning. For example, Hamilton, Rosenfelt, and Whishaw (2004) utilized a video record from each trial in the MWT to track each individual rat's swim path from a release point to the platform approximately every 17 msec. From this record, they computed the moment-to-moment speed and trajectory of the swim path in order to test hypotheses regarding when shifts in strategy occurred. These methods revealed data in support of hypotheses that would have been lost using standard trial-level measures such as latency, path length, and quadrant preference during a probe trial (see below).

Procedures for Specific Protocols

The Fixed Hidden Platform Task

In the fixed hidden platform water task, also referred to as the reference memory version of the water task, the platform occupies a fixed spatial location in the circular pool throughout training and testing. The location of the platform is usually near the center of one of the four quadrants of the pool (see Figure 2) and four release points corresponding to the cardinal compass points are used. Trials are conducted in blocks of four with each of the four release points being used once within the block. The order of release points is randomized either via a computer program or by tracking system software. Typically, four trials are given each day (or session) although trial numbers can be increased (most easily by a multiple of four or however many release points are used).

Rats will usually learn to navigate to the platform efficiently (more or less directly) in a few trials and should reach asymptotic levels of performance within at least twelve trials. Figure 3 shows swim paths for a single animal on the first and fourth trials of training in the fixed platform task. In many water task studies, five to twelve daily sessions of four trials are used. These ranges can be modified depending upon the research questions, however, the data should be monitored daily to ensure that control and experimental animals have reached and maintained asymptotic performance[1].

Random Location

In Morris' initial report (Morris, 1981), a comparison condition was used in which the platform occupied a different spatial location during each trial. With this method the animal cannot learn to place navigate to the platform because the platform location is not reliably predicted by the platform's fixed spatial relationship to the distal cues. This method can provide a useful comparison condition if basic differences in the capacity to swim or process visual information in a group are suspected.

Probe Trial

"Probe trials" are test trials that are conducted with the hidden platform removed from the pool. Probe trials are usually conducted at the end of a daily training session and most frequently after the final training session. The animal is released from one of the release points furthest from the platform location (in Figure 2 the release points would be either S or E) and swims for a pre-determined amount of time, generally between 20 and 45 sec but probe trials as long as 90 sec are not uncommon. The primary dependent measure used for probe trial data is the percentage of time spent in the platform quadrant (see Figure 4). For example, if an animal spends 40% of the probe in the platform quadrant and 20% of the probe in each of the other three quadrants then one can conclude that the animal had a preference for the platform quadrant. It is sometimes useful to analyze probe data using only the first 15 sec of data, or to analyze 15 sec blocks of data. Often the first 15-20 sec of the probe trial are the most useful in discriminating between groups of rats that have received different treatments. Rats that have learned to navigate to the platform location will show persistence in searching with mean values around 40%-50% for the probe trial. A representative probe trial swim path for an animal that learned to place navigate is shown in Figure 4. Animals that do not learn to navigate to the platform location efficiently usually yield values of 25%. Measures of heading error and the number of times that the animal crosses the location where the platform had been as well as several of the individual trial measures for the hidden platform described above are often used as behavioural measures for the probe trial.

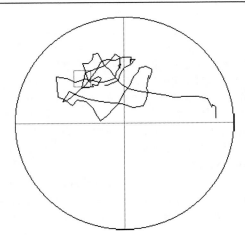

Figure 4. A swim path for a single animal during a no-platform probe trial. The path shows that the rat crossed the platform location several times and spent the majority of the probe trial in the platform quadrant.

The Moving Hidden Platform Task

The moving platform task is similar to the Random Location condition used by Morris (1981), however, the platform remains in the same location for several trials or sessions (Whishaw, 1985). Rats can learn to navigate to a new platform location in one or two trials, thus, this version of the task is excellent for repeated measurements of learning and provides a more sensitive measure of spatial learning and memory than the fixed platform task (Steele and Morris, 1999; Sutherland, McDonald, and Savage, 1997; Whishaw, 1985).

In a typical moving platform study the platform location is different for each daily training session (usually 4-8 trials). The spatial location of the platform is sampled without replacement and some constraints are usually included to ensure that the platform is always located in a unique region of the pool and is not close to the location used on the immediately prior day. Figure 5 shows a sequence of eight platform locations that have been used in our research using the moving platform version of the water task. Because the animal must learn to return to the location that was reinforced during the first trial of the session this task is sometimes referred to as the matching-to-place task or the working memory version of the Morris water task.

After finding the platform on the first trial of the session, animals typically navigate more or less directly to the platform and reach asymptotic levels of approximately 5 sec for escape latencies. Because the platform location routinely changes, probe trials may not be as informative as in the fixed platform task, however, measures of latency and path length are commonly used. In addition, the video-tape record of the trials (particularly the first trial on each day) can be analyzed to determine if the rat navigates to and persists in searching at the old location first. As mentioned, one trial is typically sufficient for the rat to cease navigating to the old location and to begin reliably navigating to the new location (Whishaw, 1985).

The moving platform task can be further modified such that the platform remains in the same place for multiple sessions which is useful for repeated assessment of long-term memory in this task.

The Visible Platform Task

The visible platform task is also referred to as a cued navigation task or a taxon navigation task. In most methodological respects the visible platform water task is similar to the hidden platform tasks, with the primary difference being that the platform is raised above the surface of the water by a few centimeters so that it is visible, or a conspicuous cue is placed at the platform location. In either case, the result is that the animal can navigate to the platform by approaching a single visual cue located at the platform. Because this task does not require the animal to navigate based upon the distal visual cues, the visible platform task is often used as a control or comparison condition when the MWT is used to evaluate effects of some manipulation on spatial learning and performance. Depending upon the hypothesis under investigation, the visible platform task may not be an appropriate control or may need to be conducted along with other comparison conditions.

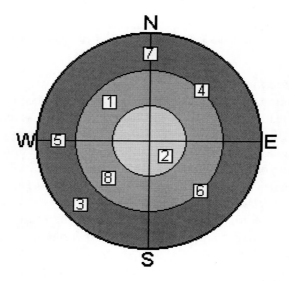

Figure 5. A sequence of 8 platform locations used in the moving platform water task. Numbers correspond to the session in which the location was used. Note that the platform location for a particular session is always in a different quadrant and annulus of the pool than the prior platform location. The goal is to avoid a bias toward a particular region of the pool while also ensuring that each platform location is not too similar to the previous location.

Visual Discrimination Learning

One variant of the visible platform task involves training the animal to discriminate between two visible platforms. For example, Sutherland et al. (2001) trained rats to navigate to one of two discriminable visible platforms: one platform allowed escape from the water whereas the other was a "false" platform that would tip over when mounted by the animal. For this purpose, the platform can be constructed of Plexiglass and packed with styrofoam so that the platform floats at the same height as the escape platform but loses stability when the rat attempts to mount it. The false platform can be attached to weights by string in order to keep it in place. In the Sutherland et al. (2001) study the two platforms were placed in adjacent quadrants of the pool which varied from trial to trial and the rats were released from the opposing cardinal compass point. Rats can quickly learn to navigate to the escape platform and to avoid the false platform. The benefit of using the water task for this type of training is that the water provides excellent motivation to escape without utilizing other techniques such as food or water restriction.

In some cases, the use of two platforms that differ with respect to whether they provide escape from the water can be useful for testing hypotheses regarding spatial navigation and learning. For example, Redhead, Roberts, Good, and Pearce (1997) first tested the hypothesis that the visible platform would interfere with learning to place navigate using distal cues. They trained rats to swim to a visible platform in the presence of distal cues and then removed the visible platform for a probe trial. If rats learned to navigate using distal cues in addition to the visible platform, then removing the visible platform should leave the ability to navigate to the platform's spatial location intact. Redhead et al., however, observed a significant disruption in performance compared to a control gourp trained with a hidden platform. Importantly, the experimental group experienced a change in their environment (removal of the platform) that was not present in the control condition. To eliminate this confound, Redhead et al. trained rats to navigate to one of two platforms, one of which provided escape from the pool. In the experimental condition the escape platform and the false platform were in opposite quadrants of the pool and remained in the same location throughout training. The platforms were visually distinguishable so the animal could navigate directly to the escape platform based on the cue at the platform location. In the control condition the platforms were not distinguishable, thus, in order to navigate directly to the escape platform the distal cues were the only features of the environment that disambiguated the location of the escape platform. Using this method, Redhead et al. found that animals in the control condition performed better on a probe trial where both platforms were removed, further suggesting that rats did not learn to place navigate when a simple taxon strategy was available (see also Hamilton et al., 2004).

The Visual Water Task

This task also takes advantage of the fact that rats and mice are innate swimmers that have a natural inclination to use distant visual cues to predict the location of an escape route. The Visual Water Task (see Figure 6) is a two-alternative visual discrimination task that takes advantage of these traits by using large, computer-generated visual stimuli, wthat animals view from a distance to demarcate the location of a submerged exit platform. The task was originally developed to measure visual thresholds (Prusky, West, and Douglas, 2000); however, the task has been modified to facilitate the measurement of picture discriminations (Driscoll et al., 2004) and visual recognition memory (Prusky et al., 2004).

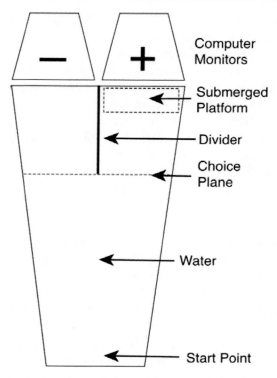

Figure 6. An overhead layout of the apparatus used in the Visual Water Task.

In its original form, the apparatus consists of a trapezoidal tank (125 cm L x 76 cm W x 26 cm W x 55 cm H) made into a Y-maze, with two computer monitors facing into the wide end, which is made of glass. A midline divider (usually 46 cm) extends into the pool from between the monitors. The tank is filled with water and an escape platform is placed just below the surface directly under one of the monitors. The platform is always located below the positive (+) stimulus. Visual stimuli are generated by, and the experiments are controlled with computer software (e.g.Vista; www.cerebralmechanics.com). Animals are released into the pool from the wall opposite the monitors, and the end of the divider within the pool sets a choice point that is as close as the animals can get to the visual stimuli without entering one of the two arms. The length of the divider, therefore, sets the effective spatial frequency of the visual stimuli.

Grating acuity is typically measured by first training animals to distinguish a low spatial frequency vertical sine wave grating (+ stimulus), from uniform gray of the same mean luminance that is displayed on the other, with high reliability. The left (L)-right (R) spatial location of the grating and platform are exchanged using a LRLLRLRR sequence, a pattern the animals cannot memorize. On any trial, animals are obligated to swim until they locate the platform. If the animals swim to the platform without entering the arm that displays gray, the trial is considered correct; if they swim into the arm of the maze that contains the gray stimulus, the trial is recorded as an error. Most animals spontaneously learn to stop at the end of the divider and inspect both screens before making a choice. Once animals achieve near-perfect performance, testing of a grating threshold is initiated. A method-of-limits procedure is used to test the threshold for animals to distinguish the stimuli, in which incremental changes in the spatial frequency of the sine wave grating are made within blocks of trials until the accuracy of animals to distinguish the stimuli falls below a predetermined criterion (i.e., 70%). This procedure is repeated at least three times, the performance at each spatial frequency is averaged for each animal, and a frequency-of-seeing curve is constructed. Typically, the point at which the curve intersects 70% accuracy is recorded as the grating acuity. Contrast sensitivity, orientation sensitivity, motion sensitivity, motion coherence, or any other visual threshold can be measured using procedures that incrementally reduce the difference between + and stimuli.

The Visual Water Task can be modified to measure the ability of rodents to learn and remember pictures. In a delayed matching-to-sample (DMTS) configuration of the task, for example, black-and-white pictures are displayed on the monitors as visual stimuli, and rats are reinforced for swimming to a correct (+) picture. The animals are first trained to make a simple visual discrimination reliably, and then in four stages, are gradually shifted to the DMTS task. In the final stage, during each trial, rats view a single picture (selected at random from a large set) in a sample phase by swimming to a faux barrier and viewing a monitor at the end of a single arm, and then in a choice phase, discriminate the sample from a novel picture, selected at random from the same set, with high accuracy (by choosing between pictures in the Y-shaped maze). The left/right position of the correct picture is varied randomly to make the task nonspatial. The delay dependence of memory for the sample picture is measured by systematically varying the delay between the sample and choice phases. Rats are not random in their choices until at least a two hour delay is placed between the sample and match phases of the trial.

Human Methods

Over the last decade a number of laboratories have begun to measure spatial learning and navigation in humans through the use of virtual, computerized environments. The precise control over the environment and behaviour of participants and the ease with which such tests can be conducted has made the use of such environments increasingly popular and this methodology has proven useful for a variety of research problems including basic hypothesis testing with respect to behavioural and psychological processes and evaluation of spatial learning and navigation in patient and other special populations. Many of the specific protocols described above for rats have been adopted for human research. Here, we describe the basic similarities and differences in approaching studies of spatial learning in humans with virtual tasks with an emphasis on a virtual Morris water task (VMWT) developed in our laboratory (Astur et al., 1998; Hamilton and Sutherland, 1999; Hamilton et al., 2002; Driscoll et al., 2003; Hamilton, Kodituwakku, Sutherland, and Savage, 2003; Driscoll, Hamilton, et al., 2005; Brandt et al., 2005; Schautzer, Hamilton, Kalla, Strupp, and Brandt, 2003).

The Environment

The virtual environment is viewed from a first-person perspective and the participant can move through the environment using keyboard keys or a joystick (see "Navigation" below). A representative view from within the virtual pool and a layout of a virtual environment used in the VMWT is shown in Figure 7. The virtual room consists of a circular pool and a collection of distal walls and cues. The platform is placed within the circular pool and can be either hidden or visible and in a fixed location or moving. Because the environment is completely controlled via a computer program it is possible to manipulate the environment in ways that are difficult or impossible to do with real environments. Further, because participants do not physically change location as they do in real navigation the major source of stimulus control is limited to the visual domain.

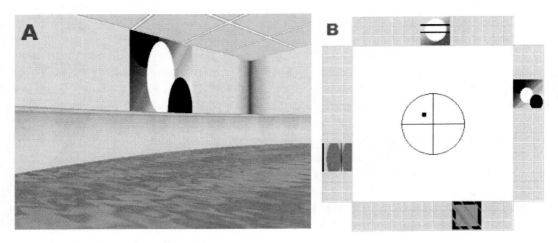

Figure 7. A) A first-person view from the circular pool showing the water, pool wall, distal walls, and a single distal cue. B) A layout of the virtual environment showing the four distal walls and cues (layed flat), the pool and platform. The pool is divided into four quadrants for analysis purposes and for determining release points.

Task Instructions

With human participants it is necessary to provide at least a minimal set of instructions regarding the goal of the task. For example, in our previously published experiments we inform participants that they 1) will be in a virtual environment, 2) will be searching for a hidden escape platform, 3) will have 60 sec to find the platform, 4) will be doing multiple trials, 5) should try to escape from the pool as quickly as possible, and 6) can navigate using the arrow keys or joystick. In studies with college-aged individuals we have not provided any information regarding the location of the platform, that it is in a fixed spatial location, or any information regarding potentially useful strategies for solving the task. In studies with special populations including individuals with neurological disorders we have found that informing participants that the platform is in a fixed location and that distal cues can be used to find the platform does not lead to accurate place navigation (Hamilton et al., 2003). That is not to say that instructions do not have an impact on performance in normal individuals, but the minimal instructions we provide are sufficient for the majority of normal participants to solve the task by navigating directly to the platform from all 4 release points (see Hamilton et al., 2003).

Navigation

In most of our published studies participants have navigated using three keyboard arrow keys (UP, LEFT, and RIGHT). The UP arrow key moves the participant forward in the environment while the LEFT and RIGHT arrow keys control rotation. In order to more closely resemble rodent navigation backward movement is not possible. Further, to increase the similarity in rodent and human behaviour in their respective tasks the rate of movement and size of the pool is set so that it takes about 4 sec to navigate from one side of the pool to another. In preliminary work we found that navigation using keyboard keys or a joystick did not differ in normal, college-aged individuals, however, some patient populations may perform better with one of the devices.

Behavioural Measures

The behavioural measures utilized in virtual navigation research are similar to those used in rodent research in the Morris water task. Latency and path length to navigate to the platform as well as heading error are standard dependent measures for training trial and percent time spent in the platform quadrant and heading error are used for probe trials. Figure 8 shows "swim" paths for a single participant in the VMWT on the first, fourth, and probe trials. Unlike rats in the Morris water task, humans often do not begin to navigate immediately when a trial begins and may take several sec to begin navigating. Thus, the initial latent period can be subtracted from the overall escape latency to reduce the influence of differences in the time to begin navigating. Because units such as screen pixels are not meaningful to readers, the path length can expressed as a percentage of some aspect of the environment, such as the diameter of the pool.

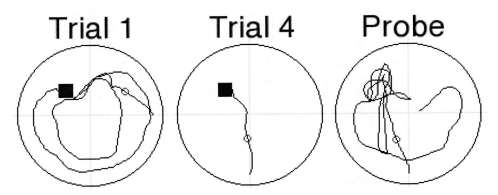

Figure 8. "Swim" paths for a single human participant in the VMWT. Paths are shown for trials 1 and 4 from fixed hidden platform training and for a single no-platform probe trial. The circle overlayed on the path indicates the point at which heading error was measured.

Basic Procedures

For standard assessments of spatial learning and navigation we have adopted a set of methods which involve first training participants in the fixed hidden platform task for 20 - 28 trials (in blocks of 4) followed by a single no-platform probe trial of 45 sec and 8 visible platform trials. Visible platform trials are conducted at the end because previous research has indicated that the visible platform may interfere with learning to use spatial cues to navigate. This particular preparation has proven useful for evaluating spatial learning and memory in a variety of normal and patient populations. More specialized procedures can be found in the papers cited above.

Self Report

Information regarding the pre-experimental history of the participant as well as information about the strategy that participant used and what was learned during the task can be obtained through post-experiment questionnaires or interviews. In our research we have found it useful to request several pieces of information. For example, we assess the degree of experience individual participants have with computers and video games. A common and reasonable expectation is that virtual navigation performance can be largely explained by knowing a person's history of experience with computers and video games. Over the course of many experiments we have observed that such measures account for only a small amount of variance (4%) in standard performance measures. Participants are also asked to describe the strategy they employed and any cues that they used to navigate. Participants who learn to place navigate are more likely to report using several distal cues. It is also informative to ask whether participants believe that the platform was fixed or moving and whether the start location was fixed or variable. Participants who fail to learn the task are more likely than learners to report that the platform moved and the start location was fixed.

REFERENCES

Astur, R. S., Ortiz, M., and Sutherland, R. J. (1998). A characterization of performance by men and women in a virtual Morris water task. *Behavioural Brain Research, 93*, 185-190.

Astur, R. S., Taylor, L. B., Mamelak, A. N., Philpott, L., and Sutherland, R. J. (2002). Humans with hippocampus damage display severe spatial memory impairments in a virtual Morris water task. *Behavioural Brain Research, 132*, 77-84.

Auer, R. N., Jensen, M. L., and Whishaw, I. Q. (1989). Neuro-behavioral deficit due to ischemic brain-damage limited to half of the CA1 sector of the hippocampus. *Journal of Neuroscience, 9*, 1641-1647.

Barraco, R. A., Klauenberg, B. J., and Irwin, L. N. (1978). Swim escape multicomponent, one-trial learning-task. *Behavioral Biology, 22*, 114-121.

Brandt, T., Schautzer, F., Hamilton, D. A., Bruning, R., Markowitsch, H. J., Kalla, R., et al. (2005). Vestibular loss causes hippocampal atrophy and impaired spatial memory in humans. *Brain, 128*, 2732-2741.

Buresova, O., Krekule, I., Zahalka, A., and Bures, J. (1985). On-demand platform improves accuracy of the Morris water maze procedure. *Journal of Neuroscience Methods, 15*, 63-72.

Devan, B. D., Petri, H. L., Mishkin, M., Stouffer, E. M., Bowker, J. L., Yin, P.-B., et al. (2002). A room with a view and a polarizing cue: individual differences in the stimulus control of place navigation and passive latent learning in the water maze. *Neurobiology of Learning and Memory, 78*, 79-99.

Driscoll, I., Hamilton, D. A., Petropoulos, H., Yeo, R. A., Brooks, W. M., Baumgartner, R. N., et al. (2003). The aging hippocampus: cognitive, biochemical and structural findings. *Cerebral Cortex, 13*, 1344-1351.

Driscoll, I., Hamilton, D. A., Yeo, R. A., Brooks, W. M., and Sutherland, R. J. (2005). Virtual navigation in humans: the impact of age, sex, and hormones on place learning. *Hormones and Behavior, 47*, 326-335.

Driscoll, I., Howard, S. R., Prusky, G. T., Rudy, J. W., and Sutherland, R. J. (2005). Seahorse wins all races: hippocampus participates in both linear and non-linear visual discrimination learning. *Behavioural Brain Research, 164*, 29-35.

Driscoll, I., Sutherland, R. J., Prusky, G. T., and Rudy, J. W. (2004). Damage to the hippocampal formation does not disrupt representational flexibility as measured by a novelty transfer test. *Behavioral Neuroscience, 118*, 1427-1432.

Gage, F. H., Dunnett, S. B., and Bjorklund, A. (1984). Spatial-learning and motor deficits in aged rats. *Neurobiology of Aging, 5*, 43-48.

Gallagher, M., Burwell, R., and Burchinal, M. (1993). Severity of spatial-learning impairment in aging - development of a learning index for performance in the Morris water maze. *Behavioral Neuroscience, 107*, 618-626.

Gould, E., Tanapat, P., Hastings, N. B., and Shors, T. J. (1999). Neurogenesis in adulthood: a possible role in learning. *Trends in Cognitive Sciences, 3*, 186-192.

Hagan, J. J., Alpert, J., Morris, R. G. M., and Iversen, S. D. (1982). Effects of neostriatal and mesocorticolimbic dopamine depletions on learning in a water maze. *Behavioural Brain Research, 5*, 103-103.

Hamilton, D. A., Driscoll, I., and Sutherland, R. J. (2002). Human place learning in a virtual Morris water task: some important constraints on the flexibility of place navigation. *Behavioural Brain Research, 129*, 159-170.

Hamilton, D. A., Kodituwakku, P., Sutherland, R. J., and Savage, D. D. (2003). Children with Fetal Alcohol Syndrome are impaired at place learning but not cued-navigation in a virtual Morris water task. *Behavioural Brain Research, 143*, 85-94.

Hamilton, D. A., Rosenfelt, C. S., and Whishaw, I. Q. (2004). Sequential control of navigation by locale and taxon cues in the Morris water task. *Behavioural Brain Research, 154*, 385-397.

Hamilton, D. A., and Sutherland, R. J. (1999). Blocking in human place learning: Evidence from virtual navigation. *Psychobiology, 27*, 453-461.

Hamm, R. J., Dixon, C. E., Gbadebo, D. M., Singha, A. K., Jenkins, L. W., Lyeth, B. G., et al. (1992). cognitive deficits following traumatic brain injury produced by controlled cortical impact. *Journal of Neurotrauma, 9*, 11-20.

Iivonen, H., Nurminen, L., Harri, M., Tanila, H., and Puolivali, J. (2003). Hypothermia in mice tested in Morris water maze. *Behavioural Brain Research, 141*, 207-213.

Keith, J. R., and Mcvety, K. M. (1988). Latent place learning in a novel environment and the influences of prior training in rats. *Psychobiology, 16*, 146-151.

Kolb, B., Sutherland, R. J., and Whishaw, I. Q. (1983). A comparison of the contribution of frontal and parietal association cortex to spatial localization in rats. *Behavioral Neuroscience, 97*, 13-27.

McGill, T. J., Douglas, R. M., Lund, R. D., and Prusky, G. T. (2004). Quantification of spatial vision in the Royal College of Surgeons rat. *Investigative Ophthalmology and Visual Science, 45*, 932-936.

Mcnamara, R. K., and Skelton, R. W. (1991). Diazepam impairs acquisition but not performance in the Morris water maze. *Pharmacology Biochemistry and Behavior, 38*, 651-658.

McNaughton, B. L., Barnes, C. A., Rao, G., Baldwin, J., and Rasmussen, M. (1986). Long-term enhancement of hippocampal synaptic transmission and the acquisition of spatial information. *Journal of Neuroscience, 6*, 563-571.

Morris, R. G. M. (1981). Spatial localisation does not require the presence of local cues. *Learning and Motivation, 12*, 239-260.

Morris, R. G. M. (1984). Developments of a water-maze procedure for studying spatial-learning in the rat. *Journal of Neuroscience Methods, 11*, 47-60.

Morris, R. G. M., Anderson, E., Lynch, G. S., and Baudry, M. (1986). Selective impairment of learning and blockade of long-term potentiation by an n-methyl-d-aspartate receptor antagonist, AP5. *Nature, 319*, 774-776.

Morris, R. G. M., Garrud, P., Rawlins, J. N. P., and O'Keefe, J. (1982). Place navigation impaired in rats with hippocampal damage. *Nature, 297*, 681-683.

Morris, R. G. M., Garrud, P., and Woodhouse, I. Q. (1981). Fornix lesions disrupt location learning by the rat. *Behavioural Brain Research, 2*, 266-267.

Olton, D. S., Becker, J. T., and Handelmann, G. E. (1979). Hippocampus, space, and memory. *Behavioral and Brain Sciences, 2*, 313-322.

Panakhova, E., Buresova, O., and Bures, J. (1984). The effect of hypothermia on the rats spatial memory in the water tank task. *Behavioral and Neural Biology, 42*, 191-196.

Prados, J., and Trobalon, J. B. (1998). Locating an invisible goal in a water maze requires at least two landmarks. *Psychobiology, 26*, 42-48.

Prusky, G. T., and Douglas, R. M. (2003). Developmental plasticity of mouse visual acuity. *European Journal of Neuroscience, 17*, 167-173.

Prusky, G. T., and Douglas, R. M. (2004). Characterization of mouse cortical spatial vision. *Vision Research, 44*, 3411-3418.

Prusky, G. T., Douglas, R. M., Nelson, L., Shabanpoor, A., and Sutherland, R. J. (2004). Visual memory task for rats reveals an essential role for hippocampus and perirhinal cortex. *Proceedings of the National Academy of Sciences, USA*, 101, 5064-5068.

Prusky, G. T., Harker, K. T., Douglas, R. M., and Whishaw, I. Q. (2002). Variation in visual acuity within pigmented, and between pigmented and albino rat strains. *Behavioural Brain Research, 136*, 339-348.

Prusky, G. T., West, P. W. R., and Douglas, R. M. (2000). Behavioral assessment of visual acuity in mice and rats. *Vision Research, 40*, 2201-2209.

Raffner, F. J. (1974). Performance on Hebb-Williams water-maze as a function of water temperature. *South African Journal of Science, 70*, 347-348.

Rauch, T. M., Welch, D. I., and Gallego, L. (1989). Hypothermia impairs performance in the Morris water maze. *Physiology and Behavior, 46*, 315-320.

Redhead, E. S., Roberts, A., Good, M., and Pearce, J. M. (1997). Interaction between piloting and beacon homing by rats in a swimming pool. *Journal of Experimental Psychology: Animal Behavioral Processes, 23*, 340-350.

Rudy, J. W., Stadlermorris, S., and Albert, P. (1987). Ontogeny of spatial navigation behaviors in the rat - dissociation of proximal-cue and distal-cue-based behaviors. *Behavioral Neuroscience, 101*, 62-73.

Schautzer, F., Hamilton, D., Kalla, R., Strupp, M., and Brandt, T. (2003). Spatial memory deficits in patients with chronic bilateral vestibular failure. *Annals of the New York Academy of Science, 1004*, 316-324.

Schenk, F. (1985). Development of place navigation in rats from weaning to puberty. *Behavioral and Neural Biology, 43*, 69-85.

Schenk, F., and Morris, R. G. M. (1985). Dissociation between components of spatial memory in rats after recovery from the effects of retrohippocampal lesions. *Experimental Brain Research, 58,* 11-28.

Silva, A. J., Stevens, C. F., Tonegawa, S., and Wang, Y. Y. (1992). Deficient hippocampal long-term potentiation in alpha-calcium-calmodulin kinase-ii mutant mice. *Science, 257,* 201-206.

Staay, F. J. van der. (2000). Effects of the size of the Morris water tank on spatial discrimination learning in the CFW1 mouse. *Physiology and Behavior, 68,* 599-602.

Steele, R. J., and Morris, R. G. M. (1999). Delay-dependent impairment of a matching-to-place task with chronic and intrahippocampal infusion of the NMDA-antagonist D-AP5. *Hippocampus, 9,* 118-136.

Sutherland, R. J. (1985). The navigating hippocampus: an individual medley of movement, space, and memory. In G. Buzsáki and C. H. Vanderwolf (Eds.), a Electrophysiology of the archicortex (p. 255-279). Budapest: Akadémiai Kiadó.

Sutherland, R. J., Chew, G. L., Baker, J. C., and Linggard, R. C. (1987). Some limitations on the use of distal cues in place navigation by rats. *Psychobiology, 15,* 48-57.

Sutherland, R. J., and Dyck, R. H. (1984). Place navigation by rats in a swimming pool. *Canadian Journal of Psychology, 38,* 322-347.

Sutherland, R. J., Kolb, B., and Whishaw, I. Q. (1982). Spatial mapping: Definitive disruption by hippocampal or frontal cortical damage in the rat. *Neuroscience Letters, 31,* 271-276.

Sutherland, R. J., and Linggard, R. (1982). Being there - a novel demonstration of latent spatial-learning in the rat. *Behavioral and Neural Biology, 36,* 103-107.

Sutherland, R. J., McDonald, R. J., and Savage, D. D. (1997). Prenatal exposure to moderate levels of ethanol can have long-lasting effects on hippocampal synaptic plasticity in adult offspring. *Hippocampus, 7,* 232-238.

Sutherland, R. J., and Rodriguez, A. J. (1989). The role of the fornix/fimbria and some related subcortical structures in place learning and memory. *Behavioural Brain Research, 32,* 265-277.

Sutherland, R. J., Weisend, M. P., Mumby, D., Astur, R. S., Hanlon, F. M., Koerner, A., et al. (2001). Retrograde amnesia after hippocampal damage: Recent vs. remote memories in two tasks. *Hippocampus, 11,* 27 - 42.

Sutherland, R. J., Whishaw, I. Q., and Kolb, B. (1983). A behavioral-analysis of spatial localization following electrolytic, kainite-induced or colchicine-induced damage to the hippocampal formation in the rat. *Behavioural Brain Research, 7,* 133-153.

Sutherland, R. J., Whishaw, I. Q., and Kolb, B. (1988). Contribution of cingulate cortex to two forms of spatial learning and memory. *Journal of Neuroscience, 8,* 1863-1872.

Sutherland, R. J., Whishaw, I. Q., and Regehr, J. C. (1982). Cholinergic receptor blockade impairs spatial localization by use of distal cues in the rat. *Journal of Comparative and Physiological Psychology, 96,* 563-573.

Whishaw, I. Q. (1985). Formation of a place learning-set by the rat: a new paradigm for neurobehavioral studies. *Physiology and Behavior, 35,* 139-143.

Whishaw, I. Q., Mittelman, G., Bunch, S. T., and Dunnett, S. B. (1987). Impairments in the acquisition, retention and selection of spatial navigation strategies after medial caudate-putamen lesions in rats. *Behavioural Brain Research, 24,* 125-138.

In: Tasks and Techniques: A Sampling of the Methodologies...   ISBN 1-60021-126-7
Editor: Matthew J. Anderson, pp. 87-95   © 2006 Nova Science Publishers, Inc.

Chapter 8

THE SAND MAZE

*Gretchen Hanson Gotthard**

Randolph-Macon Woman's College
Lynchburg, VA 24503

ABSTRACT

This chapter introduces an appetitive spatial task, called the sand maze. The sand maze is essentially identical to the Morris water maze, except it requires a rat to dig in a pool of sand to retrieve buried cereal rewards, rather than find a hidden platform in a pool of water. The sand maze has been used to examine a number of learning and memory phenomena (e.g., spatial and non-spatial learning and memory, massed and distributed training protocols, and schedules of reinforcement). Pharmacological manipulations have also been carried out using the sand maze. The NMDA antagonist, MK-801, was used to disrupt reversal learning in the sand maze. And the synthetic cannabinoid, WIN-55-212-2, was used to disrupt learning and memory and examine the state dependent properties of that drug in an abbreviated sand maze procedure. The sand maze is a versatile spatial task that produces patterns of learning and memory that are similar, if not identical, to other spatial tasks, and can be used to examine any number of learning and memory phenomena. The sand maze may serve as an alternative to aversive spatial tasks (e.g., the water maze) in some studies; in particular, those that aim to examine spatial behavior without the possible side effects of aversive tasks (e.g., potentially increased amygdala activity and stress responses).

INTRODUCTION

Spatial learning and memory is an essential survival mechanism concerned with how humans and animals navigate their environments and aids organisms in their search for food, shelter, and mates. The Morris water maze is one of the most commonly employed spatial

---

* Contact Information: Gretchen Hanson Gotthard, Ph.D. Department of Psychology, Randolph-Macon Woman's College, 2500 Rivermont Avenue, Lynchburg, VA 24503, Phone: 434-947-8647, Email: ggotthard@rmwc.edu

tasks and requires a rodent to locate a platform hidden in a pool of water (Morris, 1981). Because escape from the water is highly motivating, rats learn this task quickly and remember it well.

Although the water maze is clearly an invaluable task, it has been suggested that the aversive aspects of the task may increase stress and arousal, and ultimately produce different response strategies than appetitive spatial tasks (e.g., Whishaw and Pasztor, 2000). Therefore, performance in the water maze may provide a picture of spatial learning and memory that reflects an aversive motivational system, in addition to spatial cognition.

Increased arousal may produce altered neural input as well. While the hippocampus is essential for forming and maintaining spatial memories, the amygdala is equally critical for adding emotional salience to those memories (LeDoux, 1995; McGaugh, 2000). When a memory is especially emotional, this additional input from the amygdala helps to strengthen spatial memories being processed by the hippocampus. Therefore, increased levels of arousal produced in the water maze may result in stronger memories when compared to emotionally less salient memories created in appetitive spatial tasks. The motivational differences between these tasks may lead to variations in performance that need to be taken into account when choosing a spatial learning and memory task.

This chapter introduces an appetitive spatial task, called the sand maze (Hanson, 2003). The sand maze is essentially identical to the water maze, except it requires a rat to dig in a pool of sand to retrieve buried cereal rewards, rather than find a hidden platform in a pool of water. The sand maze may serve as an alternative to the water maze in some studies; in particular, those that aim to examine spatial behavior without the possible side effects of aversive tasks (e.g., potentially increased amygdala activity and stress responses).

The sand maze has been used to examine a number of basic learning and memory phenomena. Early studies with the sand maze aimed to determine whether the sand maze was in fact tapping spatial learning and memory, or whether it was engaging the animal in different, non-spatial forms of learning and memory. Hanson and Riccio (2001) examined the use of spatial, extramaze cues (i.e., those located outside the maze) versus non-spatial, intramaze cues (i.e., those located inside the maze). Rats were trained to find one location in the maze and then the maze was rotated 90° on the last day of training. On this last training trial, the food reward was buried in the previously correct location relative to intramaze cues; however, the maze was rotated 90° to disrupt extramaze cues. If rats used a spatial strategy to solve the task, then they would not find the buried reward, while reliance on a non-spatial strategy would allow the subjects to continue to find the buried food. The results from this study showed that rats were relying on spatial, not non-spatial, strategies to solve the task. On the rotated trial, none of the rats found the buried food reward and all rats showed an above-chance preference for the previously correct quadrant, relative to extramaze cues.

Gotthard and Hamid (2004) carried out a study that directly compared rats in the sand maze and the water maze on acquisition and retention. Both tasks produced similar patterns of responding (i.e., statistically significant decreases in latencies across trials and greater preferences for the previously correct quadrant). However, rats exhibited shorter latencies and higher quadrant preference scores in the water maze than the sand maze. These differences are likely due to differences in the motivational systems involved in these tasks (i.e., foraging in the sand maze versus escape in the water maze).

Various training procedures have been used in the sand maze. For instance, massed and distributed training protocols were used to examine the patterns of responding demonstrated during acquisition and retention in the sand maze (Hanson and Riccio, 2002). Distributed training (1 trial per day for four days) resulted in shorter latencies during acquisition than massed training (4 trials per day for one day). However, one-day and seven-day retention probe trials (with no food buried in the maze) produced no differences in responding. That is, distributed and massed training procedures both resulted in above-chance preferences for the correct quadrant.

Different schedules of reinforcement have also been examined in the sand maze (Hanson, 2003). Rats were trained with either continuous or partial reinforcement and then were tested for their retention of the correct location, followed by extinction trials. Rats found the correct location more quickly with continuous reinforcement than with partial reinforcement yet showed no differences during retention testing or extinction. During retention testing, both continuous and partial reinforcement resulted in above-chance preferences for the correct quadrant. Extinction trials produced behavior that followed a typical pattern of extinction. In particular, rats showed an initial reduction in responding, followed by spontaneous recovery, and then another reduction in responding.

Several pharmacological agents have been used to examine learning and memory in the sand maze. An NMDA antagonist, MK-801, was used in a reversal learning version of the sand maze (Gotthard and Stem, 2005). Rats were required to learn one correct location without the drug, followed by training on a new location while under the influence of the drug. Rats receiving MK-801 had more difficulty learning the new location than rats receiving a placebo injection (as indicated by increased latencies to find the new correct location).

A synthetic cannabinoid, WIN-55-212-2, also produced deficits in learning and memory in the sand maze, but in a dose-dependent fashion (Smith and Gotthard, 2005). Smaller doses of the drug (e.g., 1.5 mg/kg) produced no differences in learning and memory; conversely, larger doses (e.g., 5.6 mg/kg) produced profound impairments in learning and memory (e.g., increased latencies and chance preferences for the correct quadrant). Interestingly, there appeared to be a state dependent aspect to this drug, in that rats re-exposed to the large drug dose during testing showed improved performance and patterns of responding that did not differ from control rats receiving vehicle injections.

The experiments just described show that the sand maze is a versatile spatial task that produces patterns of learning and memory that are similar, if not identical, to other spatial tasks and can be used to examine any number of learning and memory phenomena.

METHODS

Subjects

Adult, male Long-Evans rats have been used in sand maze studies in our lab. Other types of rodents (e.g., mice) could be easily trained in this task as well, and investigators studying gender differences in spatial learning and memory may also find the sand maze a useful task.

Rats are reduced to 85% of their free-feeding weight prior to experimentation, and water is available *ad libitum*. A slow food deprivation procedure is safest for the animal and we typically allow weight reduction to occur over the course of approximately two weeks. As is true with most appetitive spatial tasks (e.g., radial arm maze), mild food deprivation is essential for motivating subjects to search for food in the sand maze. Even highly palatable rewards are not enough on their own to motivate rats to perform the task. In one study, we used highly desirable food rewards (e.g., chocolate or peanuts) without food deprivation and found that rats were not motivated enough to search for the correct location in the sand maze (Gotthard, Radke, and Hagar, 2004). From our experience, only rats that are food deprived to at least 85% of their free-feeding weights work efficiently in this task.

Apparatus

The sand maze is a round, plastic pool (see Figure 1) that measures 36 inches wide by 6 inches deep and can be purchased at most large discount stores (e.g., Target, Walmart, and Kmart). The maze is filled with a sand/crushed Froot Loops (FL) cereal mixture that measures approximately 2 inches deep. A mixture of sand and crushed FL is used to help mask the odor of the buried reward. To create the sand/crushed FL mixture, approximately 11 ounces of FL are finely crushed and mixed with 100 pounds of play sand. The maze is elevated 36 inches off the floor and multiple cues are placed external to the maze to aid subjects in their search for food.

The maze is positioned in a small, windowless room to control for lighting conditions. Overhead lighting is not used. Low lighting, through the use of a small lamp, seems to produce the best responding and the quickest acclimation to the environment and the task. Additionally, the light gradient produced by the lamp may serve as an extramaze cue. Since rats are nocturnal creatures, it seems most ethologically relevant to allow them to explore and forage for food under conditions more like those experienced under non-laboratory conditions. White noise is also played in the background to reduce any outside noises during learning and testing.

Procedure

Handling
Rats are handled every day during the food deprivation procedure for two minutes per day. This normally results in approximately two weeks of handling prior to the start of the experiment. Because the sand maze requires exploration and foraging in a novel environment, multiple handling sessions are helpful in reducing any unnecessary fear or hesitation to perform. While two weeks of handling is not essential for rats to perform well in this task, more handling usually results in faster acclimation to the task. After the final handling session, rats receive two FL in their home cage to reduce neophobia to the new food prior to experimentation.

Figure 1.

Standard Procedure

Shaping

Following handling, rats receive three days of shaping (one trial per day). All trials begin with the rat being placed in the sand maze at a North (N), South (S), East (E), or West (W) start location (positions are not magnetic N, S, E, or W). Start locations are pseudorandomly assigned so that the rat is not started from the same location on consecutive trials. Starting from a new location is critical in ensuring rats are not finding the correct location simply by making a procedural response (e.g., always turning right).

Each rat is arbitrarily assigned a single correct food location that stays consistent throughout the experiment. Correct locations are determined by dividing the maze into four quadrants (NW, NE, SW, and SE). The correct location within each quadrant is marked on the bottom of the pool as the mid-point of that quadrant as measured from all boundaries of the quadrant (see Figure 2). After determining the correct locations, a small mark is made on the bottom of the pool to indicate the correct quadrant locations.

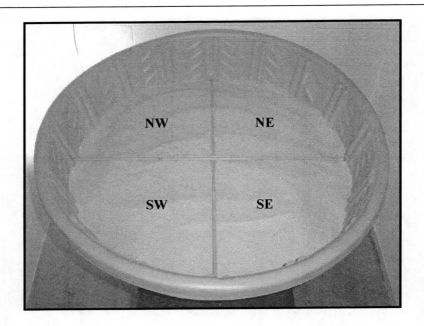

Figure 2.

Froot Loops (FL) are broken into halves and a large cache of FL are placed in the correct location on each trial (i.e., 10 ½-sized FL pieces). Rats are allowed to consume between six and eight of these ½-sized FL pieces prior to termination of all shaping and training trials. After every trial, it is important to remove any remaining FL pieces, urine, or feces left by the rat. This can be done through the use of a slotted scooper. Additionally, it is critical to wipe down the walls of the maze with a mild cleaner (e.g., unscented soap and water) and move the sand around in the maze using the slotted scooper. Rats will leave cues around the perimeter of the maze and in the sand (i.e., intramaze cues) that can be used on subsequent trials to help them locate the reward. Wiping down the walls and moving the sand around helps to remove these cues or at least spread them around so they are less useful. One caveat, using a cleaner with a strong scent will disrupt performance on subsequent trials as the rats will focus on the new scent and not the buried reward.

Day 1 of shaping consists of a single Exposed trial where the FL are completely exposed in the correct location. During this trial, rats can see and smell the reward (i.e., they are likely finding the reward based on non-spatial, intramaze cues). This trial serves mainly as an acclimation trial, in that it allows the rats to reduce neophobia to the maze and learn that searching in the maze results in a food reward.

Day 2 consists of a Partially Buried trial in which half of the FL are partially exposed while the remaining half are buried just under the surface of the sand. Again, rats can solve this trial by using non-spatial, intramaze cues, but in this case they need to dig to retrieve some of their reinforcement.

Day 3 consists of a Shallow Buried trial in which all 10 ½-sized FL pieces are completely buried, but just under the surface of the sand. It is on this trial that rats sometimes exhibit a some difficulty finding the reward (e.g., increased latencies to find the FL). This is the first trial in which they cannot rely solely on intramaze cues to find the reward.

It is important to make certain that all rats find the cache of food before being taken out of the maze on all trials, except probe trials in which no reward is buried in the sand. If a rat has not found the reward within 15 minutes of being placed in the maze, the reward should be partially exposed and the rat should be allowed to retrieve the standard reward (i.e., 6 to 8 pieces) before being removed from the maze. Removal from the maze without a reward is essentially an extinction trial and will serve to decrease exploration on subsequent trials, not increase it.

Dependent measures taken during shaping consist of latency to find the FL and the pattern of initial maze behavior. Initial maze behavior is a measure of choice and is measured on a three point scale: (1) exploring the perimeter of the maze (this behavior is mostly seen on early trials), (2) going directly to the correct location (typically seen during later training trials), and (3) going directly to an incorrect location while not exploring the perimeter of the maze (normally seen in earlier trials or during extinction trials). Several other dependent measures can be taken depending on the type of equipment employed. For example, automated tracking systems will allow for path measurements, in addition to many other useful measures.

There is no acquisition criterion for shaping. Subjects typically take the longest to eat the exposed FL (on Day 1 of shaping), but on subsequent trials will find the reward and consume several pieces within one minute. If a rat refuses to eat, dig, or explore, they do not proceed to the training phase.

Training

One day following the last shaping trial, training begins. Training trials are identical to shaping trials, except all FL are buried on all training trials. Rats receive one trial per day for four days in which the FL are buried progressively deeper from one day/trial to the next. The key to maintaining good performance in this task is not burying the FL too deep too quickly. As with shaping, if the rat does not locate the buried reward and is taken out of the maze before being reinforced, it has experienced an extinction trial that will likely decrease responding on future trials. The FL do not have to be buried at the bottom of the maze to produce good retention in this task. Rotation studies in our lab (in which the maze was rotated with FL buried in the maze) indicated that rats could not smell the buried FL when they were buried approximately 1 inch deep (Hanson and Riccio, 2001). Therefore, it is important to bury the reward only slightly deeper on each training trial to ensure that rats will be able to find them. The acquisition criterion for training is finding the buried reward in two minutes or less on two of the four training trials. If rats do not meet this criterion, additional trials may be added.

Testing

One week following training, rats receive a test trial to measure their retention for the correct location. Testing is carried out through the use of a single probe trial that is five minutes in length. Probe trials are run in the same manner shaping and training trials are run, except no FL are buried in the maze on probe trials. These trials help to test not only the subject's memory for the correct location, but also help to rule out the possibility that subjects are solving the task through the use of non-spatial, intramaze cues (like the scent of the buried reward).

The same dependent measures taken during shaping and training are measured during probe trials. Additionally, quadrant preference measures are taken. Quadrant preference is a measure of how much time the animal spends in the trained (correct) quadrant relative to the incorrect quadrants, and is computed by dividing the time spent in the correct quadrant by the total time spent in the maze on the probe trial (i.e., five minutes). Chance performance with a maze divided into four equal quadrants is .25; therefore, any preference statistically above .25 would indicate a preference for that quadrant. If not already using an automated tracking system, probe trials should be videotaped with a camera mounted over the maze so that trials can be coded for time spent in each of the four quadrants.

Abbreviated Procedure

The standard procedure requires seven shaping and training trials carried out over seven days. An abbreviated version of the sand maze has been employed in the WIN-55-212-2 studies previously mentioned (Smith and Gotthard, 2005). The abbreviated procedure presents the rat with six shaping and training trials (just one fewer than the standard procedure), but does so over the course of three days (two trials per day), rather than seven days. We have found equivalent levels of acquisition and retention using this procedure, when compared to the standard procedure.

Prior to shaping and training, rats are placed on the food deprivation procedure and are handled, as described earlier. On Day 1, rats receive two shaping trials. The first trial is an Exposed trial in which all FL are completely exposed in the correct location. The second trial on Day 1 is a Partially Buried trial, in which half of the 10 ½-sized FL pieces are exposed, while the remaining ones are buried just under the surface of the sand. A five minute inter-trial interval is used between trials. As with the standard procedure, rats are allowed to consume between 6 and 8 FL pieces before termination of all trials. The same dependent measures are taken in this procedure as in the standard procedure.

On Day 2, rats again receive two shaping trials. The first trial on Day 2 is a Partially Buried trial, and the second trial is a Shallow Buried trial, in which all FL are buried, but just under the surface of the sand.

On Day 3, rats receive two training trials, in which the FL are buried progressively deeper on each trial. As with the standard procedure, it is critical that the FL are not buried too deep too quickly or responding will be extinguished. The acquisition criterion for the abbreviated procedure requires that rats find the buried reward on training trials (i.e., Day 3 trials 1 and 2) in less than two minutes. If a rat does not meet this criterion, additional trials may be added.

Depending on the parameters of the study, either one day or one week following training, rats receive a probe trial to measure their retention of the correct location. Probe trials are run the same in the abbreviated procedure as they are run in the standard procedure.

In conclusion, the sand maze is a versatile spatial task that produces patterns of learning and memory that are similar, if not identical, to other spatial tasks, and can be used to examine any number of learning and memory phenomena. The sand maze may serve as an alternative to aversive spatial tasks in some studies (e.g., the water maze); in particular, those that aim to examine spatial behavior without the possible side effects of aversive tasks (e.g., potentially increased amygdala activity and/or stress responses).

REFERENCES

Gotthard, G. H., and Hamid, E. (2004, November). *Comparison of spatial behavior in the sand maze and the water maze.* Poster session presented at the annual meeting of the Psychonomic Society, Minneapolis, MN.

Gotthard, G. H., Radke, K., and Hagar, B. (2004). [Reward salience as a replacement for food deprivation in rats in the sand maze]. Unpublished raw data.

Gotthard, G. H., and Stem, K. (2005). *The effects of MK-801 on reversal learning in rats in the sand maze.* Manuscript in preparation.

Hanson, G. R. (2003). The sand maze: An appetitive alternative to the Morris water maze (Doctoral dissertation, Kent State University, 2003). *Dissertation Abstracts International, 63,* 4958.

Hanson, G. R., and Riccio, D. C. (2002, May). *The effects of massed and spaced training trials on acquisition, retention, and extinction in the Sand Maze.* Poster session presented at the annual meeting of the Midwestern Psychological Association, Chicago, IL.

Hanson, G. R., and Riccio, D. C. (2001, October). *The Sand Maze: An appetitive alternative to the Morris Water Maze.* Poster session presented at the annual meeting of the Pavlovian Society, New Brunswick, NJ.

LeDoux, J. E. (1995). In search of an emotional system in the brain: Leaping from fear to emotion and consciousness. In M. S. Gazzaniga (Ed.), *The Cognitive Neurosciences* (pp. 1049-1061). Cambridge, MA: The MIT Press.

McGaugh, J. L. (2000). Memory: A century of consolidation. *Science, 287*(5451), 248-251.

Morris, R. G. M. (1981). Spatial localization does not require the presence of local cues. *Learning and Motivation, 12,* 239-260.

Smith, A. R., and Gotthard, G. H. (2005, November). *Examination of the state dependent properties of WIN-55-212-2 on spatial learning and memory in rats in the sand maze.* Poster session presented at the annual meeting of the Society for Neuroscience, Washington, D.C.

Whishaw, I. Q., and Pasztor, T. J. (2000). Rats alternate on a dry-land but not swimming-pool (Morris Task) place task: Implications for spatial processing. *Behavioral Neuroscience, 114(2),* 442-446.

PART II. COMMON CONDITIONING PROCEDURES

In: Tasks and Techniques: A Sampling of the Methodologies...   ISBN 1-60021-126-7
Editor: Matthew J. Anderson, pp. 99-110   © 2006 Nova Science Publishers, Inc.

Chapter 9

PLACE CONDITIONING:
A METHODOLOGICAL ANALYSIS

Rick A. Bevins[*1] *and Christopher L. Cunningham*[2]

[1] Department of Psychology, 238 Burnett Hall,
University of Nebraska-Lincoln, Lincoln NE 68588-0308, USA
[2] Department of Behavioral Neuroscience and Portland Alcohol Research Center,
Oregon Health and Science University, 3181 SW Sam Jackson Park Road,
Portland OR 97239-3098, US

ABSTRACT

The place conditioning procedure is widely used to study choice behavior that is directed by Pavlovian conditioned motivational responses. In a typical place conditioning experiment, one set of environmental cues is paired with a biologically and motivationally relevant stimulus (e.g., food or illness); another set of distinct cues remain unpaired with this motivationally relevant stimulus. Of interest in a place conditioning experiment are the behavioral and neurobiological factors affecting the development and expression of a preference (conditioned approach) or aversion (conditioned withdrawal) for the paired environmental cues. This chapter describes many of the choices concerning apparatus construction (e.g., environmental cues, compartment number) and procedural details (e.g., intertrial duration, inclusion of a pretest, paired stimulus assignment) an investigator will face in establishing place conditioning in his or her laboratory. In discussing the methodological soundness of these choices, we conclude that it is essential to make decisions on apparatus and design that avoid interpretive difficulties (e.g., unbiased apparatus and design), use controls that allow assessment of alternative explanations (e.g., unpaired US exposure), and present data in a manner that provides a complete picture of the place conditioning effect.

---

[*] Correspondence should be addressed: Rick A. Bevins, e-mail: rbevins1@unl.edu, Tel.: 1.402.472.1189, Fax: 1.402.472.4637

INTRODUCTION

Choice behavior is clearly affected by learning history. This observation has prompted the development of several animal models to study different aspects of choice [e.g., concurrent schedules of reinforcement to measure self control (Rachlin and Green, 1972; Peters, Hunt, and Harper, 2004) and delayed matching-to-sample to study memory processes (Zentall and Hogan, 1974; Zentall and Clement, 2002) to note just two popular tasks]. The place conditioning procedure is widely used to study the importance of Pavlovian (classical) conditioning processes on choice behavior among alternative environmental stimuli (Bardo and Bevins, 2000). In a typical place conditioning experiment, the focus is on the impact of pairing one distinct environment (termed conditional stimulus or CS) with a biologically and motivationally relevant stimulus (termed unconditioned stimulus or US) on time spent in this paired environment relative to a different distinct environment. If the US has rewarding (appetitive) properties then more time is spent in the paired environmental CS. This result is sometimes referred to as a conditioned place preference and is thought to result from the environmental cues acquiring appetitive properties (conditioned reward). Stimuli that have a conditioned or unconditioned rewarding quality tend to control approach behaviors (Panksepp, Nocjar, Burgdorf, Panksepp, and Huber, 2004; Schneirla, 1959). This conditioned-approach tendency presumably increases the amount of time in the paired environment. Notably, the place conditioning procedure can also detect whether a US has an aversive quality (e.g., foot-shock, illness). If so, less time is spent in the paired environment (i.e., a conditioned-withdrawal tendency).

Although there is some research with primates (e.g., Evans, Nasser, Comer, and Foltin, 2003) and birds (e.g., Akins, Levens, Prather, Cooper, and Fritz, 2004), most place conditioning studies have been with rodents—especially mice and rats. Further, this procedure has been used to study a long list of potential USs: abused drugs (Bardo and Bevins, 2000; Tzschentke, 1998), food and sucrose solutions (Perks and Clifton, 1997), water (Ågmo, Federman, Navarro, Pudua, and Valazquez, 1993), copulatory opportunity (Meisel, Joppa, and Rowe, 1996), wheel running (Lett, Grant, Byrne, and Koh, 2000), novel objects (Bevins, Besheer, Palmatier, Jensen, Pickett, and Eurek, 2002), foot-shock (Westbrook, Harvey, and Swinbourne, 1988), lithium chloride (Cunningham and Niehus, 1993), drug withdrawal (Mucha, 1987), etc. Despite the length of this list, the place conditioning procedure has been most widely employed to study the effects of drug USs on Pavlovian conditioned choice behavior (Tzschentke, 1998). With this in mind, much of the methodological discussion in the present chapter will reference drugs (e.g., ethanol, cocaine, etc.) as the US. Finally, the primary focus of this chapter is on methodological issues. For a more detailed discussion of past research and/or a critical comparison of the place conditioning method with other reward measures, we direct the reader to key review papers that address these important issues (Bardo and Bevins, 2000; Bardo, Rowlett, and Harris, 1995; Carr, Fibiger, and Phillips, 1989; Tzschentke, 1998).

METHODS

General Procedural Considerations

Pre-Test

Before conditioning, some researchers include one or more pre-tests in which the animal is given free access to the place conditioning apparatus. Without this pre-test, the first time the animal has access to entire apparatus would be on the post-conditioning preference test. This novelty could interfere with expression of place conditioning. The pre-test also provides an initial measure of bias for the distinct environmental cues. Such a measure is used by some to derive a pre- to post-conditioning difference score as an index of conditioning (see later). Although there may be some advantages to a pre-test phase (e.g., familiarizing the test procedure), investigators should be cautious not to give too much pre-exposure to the environmental cues. Pre-exposure to potential CSs can decrease their ability to control conditioned responding thus weakening expression of place conditioning (cf. latent inhibition; Ayres, Philbin, Cassidy, Bellino, and Redlinger, 1992; Lubow, 1973). In fact, Bardo et al. (1995) in a meta-analysis of drug place conditioning concluded that effect size was greater without the pre-test phase.

Conditioning

In the conditioning phase, the animal is placed in the presence of one distinct set of environmental cues and receives the US of interest (e.g., drug, food, sucrose). In the presence of a distinctly different set of environmental cues the animal receives nothing. Although there has been some interest in one-trial place conditioning (Bardo, Valone, and Bevins, 1999; Mucha, van der Kooy, O'Shaughnessy, and Bucenicks, 1982), this alternating protocol is usually repeated for several (4 to 8) conditioning trials. Of course, counterbalancing whether the reinforced or non-reinforced trial occurs first or second within each group is necessary for avoiding any systematic influence of trial order on place conditioning. Duration of each exposure to the environmental cues depends on the nature of the US. For example, conditioning sessions with novel objects tends to be short (10 min) given the transient nature of stimulus novelty (Bevins and Bardo, 1999; Bevins et al., 2002). However, session duration is often longer with drug USs (Bardo et al., 1995; Cunningham, Dickinson, Grahame, Okorn and McMulllin, 1999; O'Dell, Khroyan, and Neisewander, 1996), though not always (Cunningham and Prather, 1992).

Whereas most investigators separate reinforced and non-reinforced trials by 24 h, there are some that include both trial types in the same day (< 12 h). Although one might gain efficiency by decreasing the conditioning phase by half the days, some methodological difficulties may arise especially if a drug US or agonist/antagonist manipulations are involved. For example, if proper counterbalancing is followed, then half the animals in a group receive drug in the first placement and vehicle in the second placement; the remaining animals receive the opposite order. Note that if a drug has a long half life, there could be overlap of the drug effect with the presumed unpaired environment in the subset of animals that received drug in the first placement making it difficult to demonstrate place conditioning. In contrast, a drug with a short half life might leave this subset of animals experiencing acute withdrawal during the second placement.[1] Because withdrawal from a drug has been shown to be an effective US for producing a place aversion (e.g., Mucha, 1987), time spent in the drug-paired environment might reflect avoidance of the unpaired environment rather than approach to the paired environment (i.e., providing an overestimation of conditioned drug reward). Problems with paired and unpaired placements in the same day may also arise when conditions of deprivation and/or satiation are employed. Satiation, for instance, might carry over if food was given in the first placement. One solution to these problems has been to always give the US on the second placement. This maneuver, unfortunately, adds an unnecessary confound of placement order into the experiment. Separating reinforced and non-reinforced trials by 24 h seems the best strategy unless special circumstances are involved (e.g., Besheer and Bevins, 2003).

Post-Conditioning Preference Test

Testing is usually conducted 24 h after the last conditioning trial. On the test day, the animal is placed in the apparatus and given free access to both sets of environmental cues (cf. pre-test). That is, testing is a choice between the paired (i.e., reinforced) or unpaired (i.e., non-reinforced) environmental cues. Most investigators conduct a single post-conditioning test in the absence of the US (i.e., extinction). Unless there is a pre-test phase, the post-conditioning preference test reflects the first day the place conditioning apparatus has been experienced without the US. The absence of the US in the presence of the paired environmental cues might make that environment more novel than the unpaired environment in which no US occurred. Because rodents tend to spend more time in novel environments, some researchers have attributed part, to all, of a place preference to this restored novelty (see Bardo and Bevins, 2000 for a more detailed discussion of this issue). Although the precise mechanism of this restored novelty can vary, there is little evidence supporting this account. In fact, explicit choice tests between an unpaired, novel, and drug-paired environmental cues reveal a preference for the drug-paired environment over the novel and unpaired environment (e.g., Parker, 1992).

General Methodological Considerations

Apparatus: Number of Compartments

There is substantial diversity in the configuration of the equipment used for place conditioning. These chambers vary in the total number of compartments, as well as in the number and modality of the stimuli that distinguish these compartments. The most commonly used configuration is an illuminated two-compartment apparatus that provides different tactile and visual cues in compartments that are spatially distinct (e.g., Cunningham, 1979). For example, one compartment might have a smooth floor with gray walls, whereas the other has a textured floor and walls with black stripes on a white background. In such configurations,

---

[1] The amount and pattern of drug administration in a place conditioning experiment is typically different from that used to demonstrate somatic withdrawal signs. However, this does not preclude the possibility of an acute withdrawal or hangover like effect once the drug has been sufficiently cleared from the system. Further, one could argue that withdrawal might also be a factor in a design that separates the paired and unpaired exposure by 24 h. Albeit less likely in a typical place conditioning protocol, this possibility deserves empirical attention.

animals are confined to one of the compartments on each conditioning trial, but given free access to both compartments on test trials.

Some investigators prefer an apparatus that contains three or more compartments. In many three-compartment configurations, the added compartment is simply a "neutral" zone that separates the two main conditioning compartments during test sessions (e.g., Bevins, 2001). By placing the animal in the neutral center compartment, one may be able to reduce unintentional bias related to the animal's initial placement in the apparatus. In other cases, additional compartments have been used to increase the number of stimulus alternatives available during choice testing (e.g., Parker, 1992). The stimuli presented in these added compartments might be novel, or they might be CSs that have been paired with other USs.

A few laboratories have also used a one-compartment apparatus for place conditioning (e.g., Cunningham and Prather, 1992; Vezina and Stewart, 1987). In these cases, the apparatus is constructed so that a different stimulus can be presented throughout the chamber on each type of trial (e.g., metal rod floor on reinforced trials versus perforated metal floor on non-reinforced trials). However, on test trials, both stimuli are available in spatially distinct locations within the single compartment (see Figure 1). A potential advantage of the one-compartment procedure is that expression of place conditioning may be enhanced because, compared to multi-compartment procedures that require confinement during conditioning, novelty of the test environment is reduced (Vezina and Stewart, 1987).

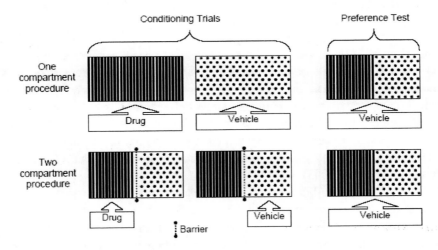

Figure 1. This figure illustrates two different ways to conduct a place conditioning experiment using a drug US. In both cases, the experiment consists of a series of drug and vehicle conditioning trials, usually presented in an alternating order across days. In the one compartment procedure (upper panel), the drug is paired with a unique stimulus that is present throughout the chamber (e.g., metal rod floor). Vehicle is paired with a different stimulus that is also present throughout the chamber (e.g., perforated metal floor). In an "unbiased" apparatus, these stimuli are selected so that the average time spent by untrained subjects in contact with each cue during a choice test is similar. In well-designed studies, the assignment of the stimulus paired with drug is counterbalanced. Drug and vehicle are also paired with different cues in the two-compartment procedure (lower panel). However, in this case, the subject is confined to a spatially distinct compartment during the conditioning phase. Both types of place conditioning procedure conclude with a preference test (usually without drug) that allows subjects to choose freely between the stimulus alternatives, which are located in spatially distinct locations within the apparatus. Some investigators have proposed that expression of place conditioning may be enhanced in the one compartment procedure because, compared to multi-compartment procedures that require confinement during conditioning, novelty of the test environment is reduced (Vezina and Stewart, 1987).

Apparatus: Stimulus Selection

Compound CSs are used in most place conditioning studies. That is, the stimuli that signal delivery of the US are composed of multiple elements, often from several modalities. The most commonly used stimuli include: visual (e.g., shapes, patterns, brightness), tactile (e.g., floor, wall textures), and olfactory (e.g., wood chips, scented cotton), in addition to spatial location within the apparatus. Although a wide variety of stimuli have been used, there is little systematic information on the relative efficacy of these stimuli or the value of using compound versus single element stimuli. Some investigators have argued that, compared to visual or olfactory cues, tactile cues (presented in a dark chamber) may be better suited for directing the spatial response required in the place conditioning task because animals must physically touch the US-paired cue in order to elicit the conditioned motivational response that presumably underlies preference for (or avoidance of) the cue (Vezina and Stewart, 1987). However, strong evidence for the superiority of any particular stimulus modality is still lacking.

[handwritten margin note: related to beh. systems theory?]

Issue of Bias

A very significant issue in the experimenter's selection of stimuli for place conditioning studies is whether there is an unlearned preference or aversion (bias) for one of the stimulus alternatives because such biases can complicate interpretation of the post-conditioning choice test (Carr et al., 1989; van der Kooy, 1987; Swerdlow, Gilbert, and Koob, 1989). It was recently suggested that distinguishing between apparatus bias and stimulus assignment bias facilitates evaluation of the role played by bias in place conditioning studies (Cunningham, Ferree and Howard, 2003). An apparatus is labeled "biased" when the average time that untrained animals spend in contact with the various stimulus alternatives differs from expectations based on chance. In contrast, an "unbiased" apparatus is one where the average time spent in contact with each stimulus is similar. Because it is reasonable to assume that conditioned preferences (or aversions) summate with unlearned preferences, apparatus bias has potential implications for the ability to detect place conditioning due to floor or ceiling effects. Thus, use of an unbiased apparatus is generally recommended (Bardo and Bevins, 2000; Cunningham et al., 2003).

The distinction between biased and unbiased place conditioning has also been applied to the experimenter's procedure for choosing the specific stimulus that is paired with the US. A stimulus assignment procedure is labeled "biased" when the experimenter's selection of the paired stimulus depends on the animal's unlearned preference or aversion for the cue (e.g., pairing a drug US with each subject's non-preferred cue). In contrast, an unbiased assignment procedure is one in which the stimulus paired with the US is randomly assigned, regardless of subject's unlearned preference or aversion for the cue. The primary argument against using the biased assignment procedure is that it raises the possibility that the effect of the US is due entirely or in part to its ability to alter motivational features of the unlearned response to the paired cue. For example, a conditioned preference produced by pairing a drug with the compartment that the animal initially avoids could be caused by a drug-induced reduction in anxiety or aversiveness rather than by a rewarding effect of the drug. To avoid such interpretive complications, use of an unbiased stimulus assignment procedure in an unbiased apparatus is generally recommended (Bardo and Bevins, 2000; Carr et al., 1989; Cunningham et al., 2003; Swerdlow et al., 1989; van der Kooy, 1987).

Design, Control Procedures and Dependent Variables

In most place conditioning studies, the experimenter's intent is to induce a learned preference (or aversion) that is linked to an association between the CS and the rewarding (or aversive) effects of the US. However, in order to support that interpretation, the study must be designed to eliminate or allow evaluation of various alternative interpretations. For example, in addition to unlearned biases, the relative novelty or familiarity of a stimulus may affect a subject's willingness to approach that stimulus during a choice test (Parker, 1992). Thus, when designing place-conditioning studies, it is important to use procedures that match overall exposure to the stimulus alternatives prior to the post-conditioning choice test. In the standard two-compartment procedure, this goal is typically achieved by exposing subjects equally often to both compartments during the conditioning phase, pairing one compartment with the US but not the other (see earlier).

A critical issue in the design of place conditioning studies is the comparison used to decide that successful conditioning has occurred. The literature reveals several different approaches, some of which are better than others. Some approaches involve within-subject comparisons based on either the difference between the time spent in each of the stimulus compartments during the test session or the difference between time spent in the US-paired stimulus compartment during the test session and time spent in that same compartment during a pre-test given before conditioning (Cunningham et al., 2003). Such comparisons may be informative, but only to the extent that there is independent evidence that these differences do not simply reflect unlearned biases or shifts in initial bias that are unrelated to CS-US pairing. In place conditioning studies involving drug USs, the experimental group is sometimes compared to a vehicle control group (i.e., a group that is matched for exposure to the CSs), but receives only vehicle on all conditioning trials. Although such controls are useful for assessing unlearned biases and the possibility that repeated CS exposure produces a shift in those biases, they are less useful for drawing conclusions about the development of conditioning because they fail to control for nonspecific aspects of repeated exposure to the US (Cunningham, 1993).

Given that place conditioning is a form of Pavlovian conditioning, selection of the control comparison for place conditioning should give consideration to the same theoretical issues that have been raised historically in the study of Pavlovian conditioning (e.g., Rescorla, 1967). Although opinions about the precise nature of the optimal control have varied over time, the control treatment favored by most contemporary experts is one in which the subject is exposed to both the CS and US, but in such as way as to avoid establishing an association between those events. One way of implementing this control in the place conditioning procedure is to present the US in the animal's home cage long before or after exposure to the CS, i.e., an "unpaired US" control procedure (Cunningham and Noble, 1992). In this case, conditioning is defined by the difference in the response (preference) of the paired experimental group compared to the unpaired control group. Another, more common approach is to use a counterbalanced, discrimination control procedure involving two CSs (Cunningham, 1993). In this procedure, one CS is paired with the US while the other is not. To eliminate interpretations of differential responding based on intrinsic properties of these CSs, the specific CS that is paired with the US is counterbalanced across groups. With this approach, conditioning is defined by the difference between the responses of these counterbalanced conditioning subgroups (Cunningham, 1993; Cunningham et al., 2003).

Locomotor Activity and Expression of Place Conditioning

An animal's ability to express a conditioned place preference or aversion clearly depends on its locomotor abilities. Consequently, an experimental treatment (e.g., brain lesion) or subject variable (e.g., genotype, age) that significantly affects locomotor activity might be expected to impact the expression of place conditioning. In fact, several studies have suggested that there may be an inverse relationship between test session activity level and strength of conditioned place preference in both rats (Vezina and Stewart, 1987) and mice (Cunningham, 1995; Cunningham et al., 1999). Thus, it is generally recommended that activity be measured during place conditioning tests in order to determine whether group differences in place preference or aversion are confounded by group differences in test activity.

Reference Place Conditioning Procedure

In the bulk of the place-conditioning studies, the experimenter sets up a situation that requires the animal to choose between US paired environmental cues and a set of non-reinforced (unpaired) cues. This situation sometime makes it difficult to see graded changes in place conditioning with changes in variables known to affect conditioned responding (e.g., US magnitude, CS-US interval). That is, maximum preference (or aversion) supported by the apparatus is often expressed once the US has crossed a threshold sufficient for place conditioning. Indeed, a consistently noted limitation of drug place conditioning is that it tends to be all-or-none (Bardo and Bevins, 2000; Wise 1989; but see Bardo et al., 1995). One suggested solution that has received very limited attention is a "reference place conditioning procedure" (Barr, Paredes, and Bridger, 1985; Bevins, 2005). This modified version of the place conditioning procedure extends the effect range by providing a known conditioning history in one environment (i.e., reference US) and then compares that to variations in conditioning history to the alternate environment. For example, Bevins (2005) found that an environment paired with 0.45 to 1.2 mg/kg intravenous (IV) cocaine was preferred over the no-drug environment in rats (i.e., standard protocol). Notably, according to this data pattern, the 0.45 and 1.2 mg/kg doses of cocaine have similar conditioned rewarding effects. However, in a reference place conditioning protocol, rats spent more time in an environment paired with 1.2 mg/kg IV cocaine over one paired with the 0.45 mg/kg reference dose of cocaine. Note that with a change in reference from no drug to a low but rewarding dose of cocaine (0.45 mg/kg) the conclusion differs from the standard protocol. That is, the higher dose of cocaine had more conditioned rewarding effects. For more detail, the reader is referred to Bevins (2005) for further discussion and to Barr et al. (1985) and Mattson, Williams, Rosenblatt, and Morrell (2001) for further examples of the utility of this procedure.

DISCUSSION

The place conditioning procedure is a powerful tool for studying choice behavior directed by Pavlovian conditioned motivational responses. Indeed, drug abuse researchers have taken advantage of this methodology to elucidate the neurobiological processes mediating the rewarding (appetitive) effects of abused drugs (Bardo and Bevins, 2000; Carr et al. 1989; Risinger, Cunningham, Bevins, and Holloway, 2002; Tzschentke, 1998). Much less research has addressed the associative learning processes involved in acquisition and expression of a place preference and aversion (Bardo and Bevins, 2000). It is unclear why this is the case given the popularity of the procedure in the drug abuse field and the interest in choice behavior by researchers in the learning field. Regardless, the narrative of this chapter clearly illustrates that establishing place conditioning in one's laboratory involves a long series of choices concerning apparatus construction (e.g., environmental cues, compartment number) and procedural details (e.g., intertrial duration, paired stimulus assignment). The methodological and hence interpretive soundness of some choices are more obvious than others: biased over non-biased apparatus versus two or three compartment chamber. There have been calls to standardize apparatus and procedures (e.g., Carr et al., 1989). A potential advantage of standardization is to increase comparability of data across laboratories. However, even with standardization there are important differences that remain (e.g., experimenter, housing, etc.) that can influence behavior (Crabbe, Wahlsten, and Dudek, 1999). Further, strong pressures to standardize a methodology in which the processes underlying the behavior are relatively poorly understood could stifle scientific advancement. An alternative strategy for increasing comparability might be to make decisions on apparatus and design that avoid interpretive difficulties, use controls and measures that allow for assessment of alternative explanations, and to present data in a manner that provides a complete picture of the place conditioning effect.

ACKNOWLEDGEMENTS

R. Bevins was partially supported by United States Public Health Service grant DA017086 and DA018114 while writing this chapter. C. Cunningham was partially supported by grants AA07702 and AA13479. Correspondence related to this article should be addressed to Rick A. Bevins, Department of Psychology, University of Nebraska-Lincoln, Lincoln NE USA 68588-0308, or e-mail rbevins1@unl.edu.

REFERENCES

Ågmo, A., Federman, I., Navarro, V., Pudua, M., and Valazquez, G. (1993). Reward and reinforcement produced by drinking water: role of opioids and dopamine receptor subtypes. *Pharmacology, Biochemistry and Behavior, 46,* 183-194.

Akins, C. K., Levens, N., Prather, R., Cooper, B., and Fritz, T. (2004). Dose-dependent cocaine place conditioning and D1 antagonist effects in male Japanese quail. *Physiology and Behavior, 82,* 309-315.

Ayres, J. J. B., Philbin, D., Cassidy, S., Bellino, L., and Redlinger, E. (1992). Some parameters of latent inhibition. *Learning and Motivation, 23,* 268-287.

Bardo, M. T., and Bevins, R. A. (2000). Conditioned place preference: what does it add to our preclinical understanding of drug reward? *Psychopharmacology, 153,* 31-43.

Bardo, M. T., Rowlett, J. K., and Harris, M. J. (1995). Conditioned place preference using opiate and stimulant drugs: a meta-analysis. *Neuroscience and Biobehavioral Reviews, 19,* 39-51.

Bardo, M. T., Valone, J. M., Bevins, R. A. (1999). Locomotion and conditioned place preference produced by acute intravenous amphetamine: role of dopamine receptors and individual differences in amphetamine self-administration. *Psychopharmacology, 143,* 39-46.

Barr, G. A., Paredes, W., and Bridger, W. H. (1985). Place conditioning with morphine and phencyclidine: Dose dependent effects. *Life Sciences, 36,* 363-368.

Besheer, J. and Bevins, R. A. (2003). The impact of nicotine withdrawal on novelty reward and related behaviors. *Behavioral Neuroscience, 117,* 327-340.

Bevins, R. A. (2001). Novelty seeking and reward: Implications for the study of high-risk behaviors. *Current Directions in Psychological Science, 10,* 189-193.

Bevins, R. A. (2005). The reference-dose place conditioning procedure yields a graded dose-effect function. *International Journal of Comparative Psychology, 18,* 101-111.

Bevins, R. A., and Bardo, M. T. (1999). Conditioned increase in place preference by access to novel objects: Antagonism by MK-801. *Behavioural Brain Research, 99,* 53-60.

Bevins, R. A., Besheer, J., Palmatier, M. I., Jensen, H. C., Pickett, K. S., and Eurek, S. (2002). Novel-object place conditioning: Behavioral and dopaminergic processes in expression of novelty reward. *Behavioural Brain Research, 129,* 41-50.

Carr, G. D., Fibiger, H. C., and Phillips, A. G. (1989). Conditioned place preference as a measure of drug reward. In J. M. Liebman and S. J. Cooper (Eds.), *Neuropharmacological basis of reward* (pp. 264-319). New York: Oxford.

Crabbe, J. C., Wahlsten, D., and Dudek, B. C. (1999). Genetics of mouse behavior: interactions with laboratory environment. *Science, 284,* 1670-1672.

Cunningham, C. L. (1979). Flavor and location aversions produced by ethanol. *Behavioral and Neural Biology, 27,* 362-367.

Cunningham, C. L. (1993). Pavlovian drug conditioning. In F. van Haaren (Ed.), *Methods in behavioral pharmacology* (pp. 349-381). Amsterdam: Elsevier.

Cunningham, C. L. (1995). Localization of genes influencing ethanol-induced conditioned place preference and locomotor activity in BXD recombinant inbred mice. *Psychopharmacology, 120,* 28-41.

Cunningham, C. L., Dickinson, S. D., Grahame, N. J., Okorn, D. M., and McMullin, C. S. (1999). Genetic differences in cocaine-induced conditioned place preference in mice depend on conditioning trial duration. *Psychopharmacology, 146,* 73-80.

Cunningham, C. L., Ferree, N. K., and Howard, M. A. (2003). Apparatus bias and place conditioning with ethanol in mice. *Psychopharmacology, 170,* 409-422.

Cunningham, C. L., and Niehus J. S. (1993). Drug-induced hypothermia and conditioned place aversion. *Behavioral Neuroscience, 107,* 468-479.

Cunningham, C. L., and Noble, D. (1992). Conditioned activation induced by ethanol: Role in sensitization and conditioned place preference. *Pharmacology, Biochemistry and Behavior, 43,* 307-313.

Cunningham, C. L., and Prather, L. K. (1992). Conditioning trial duration affects ethanol-induced conditioned place preference in mice. *Animal Learning and Behavior, 20,* 187-194.

Evans, S. M., Nasser, J., Comer, S. D., and Foltin, R. W. (2003). Smoked heroin in rhesus monkeys: Effects of heroin extinction and fluid availability on measures of heroin seeking. *Pharmacology, Biochemistry and Behavior, 74,* 723-737.

Lett, B. T., Grant, V. L., Byrne, M. J., and Koh, M. T. (2000). Pairing of a distinctive chamber with the aftereffect of wheel running produce conditioned place preference. *Appetite, 34,* 87-94.

Lubow, R. E. (1973). Latent inhibition. *Psychological Bulletin, 79,* 398-407.

Mattson, B. J., Williams, S., Rosenblatt, J. S., and Morrell, J. I. (2001). Comparison of two positive reinforcing stimuli: pups and cocaine throughout the postpartum period. *Behavioral Neuroscience, 115,* 683-694.

Meisel, R. L., Joppa, M. A., and Rowe, R. K. (1996). Dopamine receptor antagonists attenuate conditioned place preference following sexual behavior in female Syrian hamsters. *European Journal of Pharmacology, 309,* 21-24.

Mucha, R. F. (1987). Is the motivational effect of opiate withdrawal reflected by common somatic indices of precipitated withdrawal? A place conditioning study in rats. *Brain Research, 418,* 214-220.

Mucha, R. F., van der Kooy, D., O'Shaughnessy, M., and Bucenicks, P. (1982). Drug reinforcement studied by use of place conditioning in rat. *Brain Research, 243,* 91-105.

O'Dell, L. E., Khroyan, T. V., and Neisewander, J. L. (1996). Dose-dependent characterization of the rewarding and stimulant properties of cocaine following intraperitoneal and intravenous administration in rats. *Psychopharmacology, 123,* 144-153.

Panksepp, J., Nocjar, C., Burgdorf, J., Panksepp, J.B., and Huber, R. (2004). The role of emotional systems in addiction: A neuroethological perspective. In R .A. Bevins and M. T. Bardo (Eds.), *Nebraska symposium on motivation, 50, motivational factors in the etiology of drug abuse.* (pp. 85-126). Lincoln NE: University of Nebraska Press.

Parker, L. A. (1992). Place conditioning in a three- or four-choice apparatus: Role of stimulus novelty in drug-induced place conditioning. *Behavioral Neuroscience, 106,* 294-306.

Perks, S. M., and Clifton, P. G. (1997). Reinforcer revaluation and conditioned place preference. *Physiology and Behavior, 61,* 1-5.

Peters, H. L., Hunt, M., and Harper, D. N. (2004). Choice with initial and terminal link reinforcement: an alternative self-control paradigm. *Journal of Experimental Psychology: Animal Behavior Processes, 30,* 74-77.

Rachlin, H., and Green, L. (1972). Commitment, choice and self-control. *Journal of Experimental Analysis of Behavior, 17,* 15-22.

Rescorla, R. A. (1967). Pavlovian conditioning and its proper control procedures. *Psychological Review, 74,* 71-80.

Risinger, F. O., Cunningham, C. L., Bevins, R. A., and Holloway, F. A. (2002). Place conditioning: What does it add to our understanding of ethanol reward? *Alcoholism: Clinical and Experimental Research, 26,* 1444-1452.

Schneirla, T. C. (1959). An evolutionary and developmental theory of biphasic processes underlying approach and withdrawal. In M. R. Jones (Ed.), *Nebraska Symposium on Motivation, 1959* (pp. 1-42). Lincoln NE: University of Nebraska Press.

Swerdlow, N. R., Gilbert, D., and Koob, G. F. (1989). Conditioned drug effects on spatial preference: Critical evaluation. In A. A. Boulton, G. B. Baker and A. J. Greenshaw (Eds.), *Psychopharmacology (Neuromethods Vol.13)* (pp. 399-446). Clifton, NJ: Humana Press.

Tzschentke, T. M. (1998). Measuring reward with the conditioned place preference paradigm: a comprehensive review of drug effects, recent progress and new issues. *Progress in Neurobiology, 56,* 613-672.

van der Kooy, D. (1987). Place conditioning: A simple and effective method for assessing the motivational properties of drugs. In M. A. Bozarth (Ed.), *Methods of assessing the reinforcing properties of abused drugs* (pp. 229-240). New York: Springer-Verlag.

Vezina, P., and Stewart, J. (1987). Morphine conditioned place preference and locomotion: The effect of confinement during training. *Psychopharmacology, 93,* 257-260.

Wise, R. A. (1989). The brain and reward: In J. M. Leibman and S. J. Cooper (Eds.), *The neuropharmacological basis of reward* (pp. 377-424). Oxford: Clarendon Press.

Zentall, T. R., and Clement, T. S. (2002). Memory mechanisms in pigeons: evidence of base-rate neglect. *Journal of Experimental Psychology: Animal Behavior Processes, 28,* 111-115.

Zentall, T. R., and Hogan, D. E. (1974). Memory in pigeons: proactive inhibition in a delayed matching task. *Bulletin of the Psychonomic Society, 4,* 109-112.

In: Tasks and Techniques: A Sampling of the Methodologies...   ISBN 1-60021-126-7
Editor: Matthew J. Anderson, pp. 111-123   © 2006 Nova Science Publishers, Inc.

Chapter 10

BEHAVIORAL NEUROSCIENCE OF PAVLOVIAN FEAR CONDITIONING

Matthew J. Sanders and *Michael S. Fanselow*

Psychology Department, UCLA, Los Angeles, CA 90095-1563

ABSTRACT

Fear conditioning has become an increasingly important model system for the study of the neural mechanisms of learning and memory. Fear is more than a cluster of behaviors related to aversive stimuli or events; in our view, fear rather is a functional behavioral system. The fear *system* is defined by antecedent conditions (environmental stimuli and conditions that activate and modify behavior), resultant behaviors, and mediating mechanisms. The fear system functions to defend the organism against environmental threats. By combining manipulations aimed at both the antecedent conditions and putative neural substrates of the system, we can develop a powerful analysis of the role of those neural substrates in the fear system. We begin our discussion with a short account of the environmental factors that influence fear conditioning. Behavioral manipulations can be married with traditional neuroscience methods to indicate not only which neural mechanisms mediate fear but also which mechanisms may mediate specific facets of fear conditioning. Throughout this chapter, we will discuss the progress made in the search for the neural mechanisms of fear conditioning brought about by these methods. We will point out, along the way, how careful manipulation of the behavioral methodology yields powerful insight into those mechanisms. We end with a discussion of methodology and the importance of stimulus parameters in genetic and neurobiological investigations of fear conditioning.

---

[*] Address Correspondence to: Marquette University Psychology Department, PO Box 1881, Milwaukee, WI 53201-1881, matthew.sanders@marquette.edu

INTRODUCTION

The Functional Behavioral System of Fear

Fear is a psychological construct with many definitions and interpretations. The experimental study of fear requires this concept to be embedded in an empirically anchored network with clear environmental causes and measurable effects. As a result, fear becomes a tractable subject for neuroscientific inquiry. *never thought of that*

Aversively conditioned stimuli elicit behaviors that mimic those normally elicited by detection of a predator (Fanselow, 1989). In the wild, a rodent that has detected a predator will freeze. That is, it will show a complete loss of movement except that required for respiration. This response is adaptive in that it minimizes the likelihood of detection by the predator and minimizes the probability of attack should the predator detect the prey (motion is a releasing stimulus for those animals that prey on rodents). Laboratory rodents show the exact same response when presented with a (once neutral) conditional stimulus (CS) that has been paired with an aversive footshock unconditional stimulus (US). We use this freezing response as a primary measure of the threat that an animal perceives when the CS is presented. That is, the freezing response is taken as a direct measure of the amount of fear that an animal ascribes to a stimulus.

The functional behavioral system of fear is defined, in large part, by the antecedent conditions that evoke fear. The situations and stimuli that engage the fear system are integral components of our operational definition of the system. Two general classes of stimuli engage the fear system: innate threats and learned stimuli. As the fear behavioral system has evolved in a specialized fashion, it is not surprising that animals show identical responses when faced with innate and learned threat stimuli. Of the two classes of stimuli, learned stimuli have been of primary interest to psychologists and neuroscientists. The study of Pavlovian conditioning is the study of the relations among stimuli and the associations made, by the organism, between the representations of those stimuli. New responses to stimuli are used as a measure of their association but the thrust of investigation is how, and under what circumstances, stimuli are related to one another by the central nervous system. Thus, the search for the neural mechanisms of fear revolves around the study of how fear antecedent stimuli are learned, stored, and recalled later. In examining these processes, it is instructive to investigate the conditions under which the learning process takes place. These "antecedent conditions" determine the probability that fear is learned to a given stimulus. When a few seemingly minor manipulations are made in the way animals are presented with stimuli, dramatic changes can be seen in the learning of these stimuli. Manipulations in the presentation of both the US and the CS can alter significantly the fear shown by an animal on subsequent presentations of the CS.

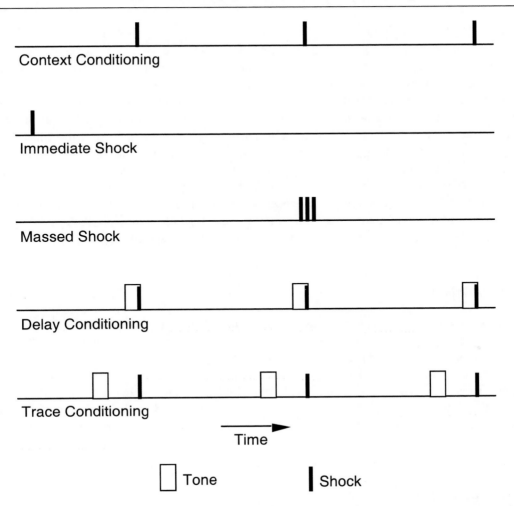

Figure 1. Some schedules used in Pavlovian fear conditioning. Each of the five diagrams represents a typical example of each type of schedule. See text for details.

When a rodent is subjected to footshock in a novel environment, it learns to fear that environment. Typically, an animal is placed in a novel chamber and, after a few minutes of exposure, is given one or a few painful shocks (Figure 1) spaced about a minute apart. Later, the animal will respond fearfully when placed back in the chamber, as indexed by the freezing response. Fear is specific to the trained context; less fear is shown in contexts that progressively differ from the original training context (Fanselow, 1981). Two temporal manipulations of the antecedent conditions have dramatic impact on the amount of context fear acquired. If the animal is shocked immediately upon placement in the chamber, it will fail to exhibit fear of the context when tested later (Figure 1). This empirical observation has been coined the "immediate shock deficit." As the deficit is caused by the temporal constraint on exposure to the previously neutral context, we take the deficit as a clue to the processes underlying context processing and context-shock association formation. If adequate time is given prior to shock but a series of shocks is presented in a more rapid fashion, at 3-second intervals for instance, then significantly less fear of the context develops than would develop if the shocks were spaced (Fanselow and Tighe, 1988; Fanselow, DeCola, and Young, 1993)

(Figure 1). This deficit may reveal how the production of unconditional and conditional responses during training can impact upon fear acquisition.

Alterations in the structure of CS and US presentations seem to affect the formation of CS-US associations dramatically. In the search for the neural underpinnings of these associations, alternative behavioral methods will lend insight into the neurobiological mechanisms of fear. In this chapter, we will argue that the techniques of neuroscience are used to their fullest advantage when combined with careful manipulations of the antecedent conditions of fear conditioning. In the following sections, we will discuss brain structures implicated in fear conditioning. We will start with the hippocampus, which may serve a crucial role in processing predictive stimuli in the fear system. We will then discuss the periaqueductal gray, a structure that organizes the resultant behaviors of the fear system. We will finish our discussion with a consideration of the amygdala, a structure thought by many to constitute a storage site for the associations made by the fear system.

The Hippocampus

The hippocampus is known to play an important role in fear conditioning. Its exact role, however, remains a bit of a mystery. In fact, the hippocampus represents an area of investigation in which improvements in the methodology of neuroscience have provided new and surprising information. The hippocampus normally is not a necessary part of the neural mechanisms underlying very simple conditioning such as that involving a contiguous tone and a footshock (delay procedure, Figure 1), but it is suspected to be involved in both the conditioning of fear to a context and the conditioning of fear to a discontiguous tone (trace procedure, Figure 1).

The Hippocampus and Context Fear

In context conditioning, the hippocampus most likely is responsible for assembling a representation of the context and conveying such a representation to other parts of the brain responsible for associating the context with an aversive event such as a footshock. Electrolytic lesions of the dorsal hippocampus, when made after conditioning, result in a loss of memory for fearful contexts (a retrograde amnesia) (Kim and Fanselow, 1992; Phillips and LeDoux, 1992; Anagnostaras, Maren and Fanselow, 1999). The effect of post-training lesions is time-limited in that lesions made within a couple of weeks of training cause impairment in context fear while lesions made after 28 days fail to cause a deficit (Kim and Fanselow, 1992). However, post-training electrolytic lesions do not affect tone fear regardless of the training-lesion interval (Kim and Fanselow, 1992). Electrolytic lesions made before training block context fear conditioning as well (Kim, Rison and Fanselow, 1993; Young, Bohenek and Fanselow, 1994; Maren, Aharonov and Fanselow, 1997).

Young et al. (1994) reported a unique combination of this electrolytic lesion method with the behavioral procedure known as context pre-exposure. Context pre-exposure acted prophylactically against the deficit seen when conditioning followed electrolytic lesions. Rats were pre-exposed to the to-be-conditioned context 28 days before receiving an electrolytic lesion of the dorsal hippocampus. One week after the lesion, they were subjected to a standard context fear conditioning protocol. Lesioned animals that had been pre-exposed to the context showed normal levels of fear (Young et al., 1994). This result indicates that the hippocampus may be necessary for forming a representation of the context for association with aversive footshock but may not be necessary at the time of footshock if given ample previous opportunity to acquire and consolidate this representation. In the case of pre-exposure, the context representation may be formed by the hippocampus and then stored in the neocortex, from where it may be associated later with the footshock. Another clue as to the nature of this extrahippocampal circuitry can be drawn from the Young et al. study. That study employed electrolytic lesions of the hippocampus, which are devastating to fibers of passage. Thus, the circuitry responsible for the spared learning with pre-exposure must not involve axons passing through the dorsal hippocampus. Retrograde amnesia for fear, caused by post-training lesions of the dorsal hippocampus, is limited to 28 days (the same amount of time for protection by pre-exposure) (Kim and Fanselow, 1992). In light of the data on retrograde amnesia, it appears that the hippocampus is necessary for learning and recall of the context for a limited time but that the representation eventually is stored in the neocortex. Again, the lesion includes fibers of passage in the dorsal hippocampus. Thus, the system that underlies this protected fear memory must not employ such fibers.

Some controversy abounds concerning the apparent difference in the effectiveness of pre- and post-training hippocampal lesions. While post-training lesions are recognized as devastating to fear memory, pre-training lesions do not have as dramatic an effect on context fear acquisition (Kim and Fanselow, 1992; Maren et al., 1997). Recent data indicate that pre-training excitotoxic lesions of the hippocampus do, indeed, result in reliable deficits in context fear conditioning. The effect of such lesions, however, depends heavily on the training conditions. In fact, the hippocampus lesion deficit emerges only when conditioning involves a single trial. When given only one shock, lesioned animals showed a significant deficit in conditioning. When given three shocks, however, lesioned animals showed normal levels of context fear (Wiltgen, Sanders, Anagnostaras, Sage and Fanselow, submitted). By carefully manipulating the antecedent conditions, this investigation clarified the discrepancy in findings from different lesion methods and, more importantly, provided further information about the mediating mechanisms that acquire fear in the absence of the hippocampus.

Our laboratory recently completed a set of investigations of sex differences in context fear in mice (Wiltgen, Sanders, Behne and Fanselow, 2001). These investigations employed the immediate shock procedure in investigating sex differences in the fear system. When shocked almost immediately upon placement in a context, neither males nor females were able to learn fear of the context. At longer intervals, both sexes showed substantial context fear (see also Paylor, Tracy, Wehner and Rudy, 1994). Males learned more fear than females, however, at intermediate placement-to-shock intervals (Wiltgen et al., 2001). These data indicate that males and females may differ in the underlying substrates of context conditioning. The sex difference seen at intermediate placement-to-shock intervals shows susceptibility to the pre-exposure effect. When given pre-exposure to the conditioning context, males and females learned equivalently over all intervals tested. Thus, just as the pre-exposure manipulation clarifies the role of the hippocampus in fear conditioning, it sheds light on the sex difference as well. In this case, males and females appear to differ in their ability to form a context representation, not in the ability to associate such a representation with footshock.

The Hippocampus and Trace Fear

When fear conditioning is implemented with contiguous footshock pairings (delay conditioning), the hippocampus is not necessary for tone fear (Kim and Fanselow, 1992; McEchron, Bouwmeester, Tseng, Weiss and Disterhoft, 1998). When fear conditioning is implemented with discontiguous tone-shock pairings (known as "trace" conditioning; Figure 1), the hippocampus plays a central role in tone fear. Trace conditioning involves the presentation of a conditional tone stimulus and an unconditional footshock stimulus with a temporal gap (known as the trace interval) between them. When trace conditioning procedures are used, tone fear relies upon the integrity of the hippocampus (McEchron et al., 1998; Quinn, Oommen, Morrison and Fanselow, 2002). More importantly, the involvement of the hippocampus depends heavily on the antecedent conditions of the experiment. Disruption of hippocampal plasticity by NMDA receptor blockade is successful in impairing trace conditioning only when the trace interval is at least 15 seconds (Misane et al., 2005). Hippocampus lesions impair trace fear following training with 30-second, but not 3-second, trace intervals (Chowdhury, Quinn and Fanselow, 2005). At short trace intervals, the mediating mechanisms for tone fear lie outside of the hippocampus (much as in delay conditioning). At longer intervals, the hippocampus plays a critical role. The hippocampus is essential for processing fear conditional stimuli (both discrete stimuli such as tones and diffuse stimuli such as contexts) but its essential nature in turn depends on the methods used in establishing fear responses.

The Periaqueductal Gray

Traditionally, the midbrain periaqueductal gray (PAG) has been seen as an essential element in the circuit producing a cluster of fear responses (Fanselow, 1991; Borszcz, Cranney and Leaton, 1989; LeDoux, Iwata, Cicchetti and Reis, 1988). The PAG is a primary target for axons from the amygdala (de Olmos, Alheid and Beltramino, 1985), a structure believed by many to be responsible for the storage of fear memories (Fanselow and LeDoux, 1999). Stimulation and lesion studies reveal that the PAG coordinates a number of defensive behaviors, including vigorous fight-or-flight behaviors as well as anticipatory freezing behavior. The dorsal and ventral portions of the PAG play different but complementary roles in responding to threat. Electrical stimulation of the dorsal PAG produces non-opioid analgesia and locomotion that mimics the circa-strike defense produced by footshock (Mayer and Liebeskind, 1974; Depaulis, Keay and Bandler, 1992; Fanselow, 1991). Lesions of the dorsal PAG eliminate the activity burst elicited by footshock (Fanselow, 1991). These lesions do not reduce freezing behavior. Stimulation of the ventral PAG produces freezing behavior (Fanselow, 1991) and lesions of the ventral PAG reduce freezing (Kim et al., 1993). Lesions of the ventral PAG have no effect on the activity burst elicited by shock (Fanselow, 1991). Thus the dorsal and ventral PAG are involved in organizing different defensive responses. In fact, some of these responses are incompatible (e.g. freezing and activity burst). The nature of the antecedent stimuli of fear determines which portion of the PAG is engaged and, hence, what defensive behavior is generated.

While much of the data cited above implicates the PAG as a simple coordinator of fear responses, more recent sophisticated manipulations of the antecedent conditions of fear have revealed the role of the PAG to be more complicated. Manipulations of both CS and US presentation indicate that the antagonistic relationship between the dorsal and ventral PAG has an influence on the acquisition of conditional fear. When shocks are administered in a massed fashion (i.e. with a small inter-shock interval), then little context conditioning develops (Fanselow et al., 1993). This massed shock effect is thought to stem from reduced processing of the conditional stimuli (in this case, the context) and an inhibition of associative processes subserving conditional fear. Lesions of the dorsal PAG eliminate this deficit in conditioning. Animals with dorsal PAG lesions show an increase in freezing overall but lesioned animals trained with a 3-second inter-shock interval show the same level of freezing as those trained with a 60-second inter-shock interval (Fanselow, DeCola, De Oca and Landeira-Fernandez, 1995). Thus the PAG is implicated in the acquisition deficit produced by massed shock presentation. Pre-exposure to either the context or the shock attenuates the massed shock deficit. Context pre-exposure allows for a pre-formed CS representation at the time of training. Shock pre-exposure reduces the unconditional response to shock. One of the unconditional responses to shock, mediated by the dorsal PAG, may be a suppression of context processing. Thus, the dorsal PAG, in producing the circa-strike response, may limit the processing of environmental stimuli.

The dorsal PAG may contribute to the conditioning deficit seen with immediate shock as well. Recall that normal rats show very little context conditioning if shocked soon after placement in a context. Rats with dorsal PAG lesions, however, show substantial context fear when trained with short placement-to-shock intervals (Fanselow, 1991). As stated previously, the immediate shock deficit may stem from inadequate processing of the context. Dorsal PAG lesions thus seem to allow for better context processing. Such lesions attenuate the circa-strike (i.e. shock elicited) reduction in CS processing that normally is initiated by the dorsal PAG.

The Amygdala

The amygdala is a small almond-shaped structure in the subcortical field of the temporal lobe. Mounting evidence suggests that the amygdala is a locus of CS-US association in fear conditioning. The amygdala represents yet another subject of investigation where refined techniques have led to surprising results.

Recent data indicate that the amygdala may be a permanent site of storage for the CS-US association. Post-training lesions of the amygdala prevent freezing to a fear-conditioned stimulus. If excitotoxic lesions are made in the amygdala after tone-shock pairings, then rats show a lack of fear to both the tone and the context in which shocks were given (Maren, Aharonov and Fanselow, 1996a). Such a loss of fear is seen even if the lesion is made 16 months after the initial training experience (Gale et al., 2004). Thus the amygdala is involved in at least the recall of an association and the expression of fear. Lesions of the amygdala made before training have a devastating effect on fear conditioning. Amygdala lesions completely prevent the acquisition of fear when typical training parameters are used (LeDoux, Cicchetti, Xagoraris and Romanski, 1990; Phillips and LeDoux, 1992). Importantly, such lesions have no effect on unconditional responses to the footshock US (LeDoux et al., 1990). This result indicates normal processing of the US, at some level, but a lack of association with the CS. One point should be kept in mind when evaluating the effects of pre-training lesions: the same lesion may affect the expression of conditional fear. Thus, the acquisition, mnemonic, and performance roles of any structure are confounded when permanent pre-training lesions are made. For a more accurate assessment of the amygdala's role, other techniques are necessary. Maren (1999) made excitotoxic lesions of the amygdala before training but used a particular manipulation aimed at the antecedent conditions of fear; He employed on "over-training" procedure with many more tone-shock pairings (up to 75) during conditioning. Under these circumstances, lesioned animals were able to learn and express conditional fear of the context to the same degree as sham controls. Thus, it appears that extra-amygdala structures are capable of fear learning under the appropriate circumstances and that the amygdala might not be necessary for fear acquisition, given particular manipulations of the antecedent conditions of fear. Clarification of its role depends on somewhat more sophisticated techniques. For example, extensive "temporary lesions" are more suited to the differentiation between learning and recall accounts of the amygdala's role in fear conditioning. Temporary inactivation of, or receptor blockade in, the amygdala can be made at either training or testing, allowing for the separate examination of the acquisition and performance roles of the amygdala in conditioned fear. Blockade of the NMDA receptor prevents fear acquisition and fear expression (Maren, Aharonov, Stote and Fanselow, 1996b Lee, Choi, Brown and Kim, 2001). Inactivation of the amygdala with muscimol prevents both the acquisition and expression of tone and context fear (Muller, Corodimas, Fridel and LeDoux, 1997). Recent efforts in our laboratory have combined these sophisticated inactivation methods with manipulations of the antecedent conditions of fear. Results indicate that the amygdala is not necessary for expression of context fear, if such context fear is acquired by structures outside of the amygdala. Animals were treated with intra-amygdala infusions of muscimol during training, testing, or both in an over-training procedure. If muscimol was infused during acquisition, a similar infusion had no effect during testing (Ponnusamy, Zelikowsky and Fanselow, 2005).

SUMMARY

The fear behavioral system is a popular model for the study of learning and memory. In recent years, standard Pavlovian fear conditioning has become a benchmark for measuring the effectiveness of pharmacological, molecular, and genetic manipulations of learning. While neuroscientists are eager to understand learning and memory at progressively reduced levels of analysis, we are still in the earliest stages of delineating the circuitry of fear learning. The hippocampus, periaqueductal gray, and amygdala surely are just a few of the important elements of the neural circuitry underlying fear conditioning. Disruption of function in any of these structures negatively affects learning and expression of fear. Under certain circumstances, the effects of these manipulations are dramatic. Under other circumstances, the effects are subtle. We argue that careful manipulation of the antecedent conditions of fear will reveal the fundamental characteristics of the mediating neural structures of the fear system. The quest for the neural underpinnings of learning and memory demands a careful, deliberate blending of somatic and behavioral manipulations.

METHODS

Fear conditioning has been used by many laboratories as an "assay" for molecular, cellular, and circuit mechanisms learning and memory. We wish to stress that there is no "correct" procedure for fear conditioning and that the proper use of fear conditioning in behavioral neuroscience depends on maximizing methods for effectively testing particular concrete hypotheses. Fear conditioning, as a laboratory phenomenon, boils down to an orderly presentation of neutral and aversive stimuli in such a fashion that the subject is able to extract the relations among those stimuli. Beyond this simple definition, the experimenter is free to arrange and present the stimuli in countless ways (Figure 1 gives some examples). Here, we do not wish to give a rigid, authoritative proclamation of the standard fear conditioning protocol. Instead, we wish to discuss briefly how particular aspects of stimuli and their presentation bear upon conditional fear. Indeed, much of the power of the Pavlovian paradigm is that it allows for quantifiable manipulation of the training variables and investigators have at their disposal explicit models that predict how such manipulation will affect behavior (e.g. Rescorla and Wagner, 1972).

Context fear conditioning can be studied in the absence of a unimodal (e.g. tone) CS. In such a case, an animal is simply placed in a distinctive context CS and exposed to an aversive US. In this case, fear levels are determined by two temporal relationships: the relationship between the context exposure and the US as well as the relationship between successive USs. The placement-to-shock interval (PSI) is defined as the time between the point at which the animal is placed in a distinct context and the point at which the aversive footshock US is presented. This interval is a critical determinant of the amount of context fear. Longer PSIs (longer than 30 s) result in substantial context fear while short PSIs (under 15 s) result in practically no context fear (Wiltgen et al., 2001; Fanselow, 1986; Fanselow, 1990). If shocks are given repeatedly, then a longer inter-shock interval results in relatively more fear than a shorter inter-shock interval (Fanselow and Tighe, 1988; Fanselow et al., 1993). Regardless of whether or not the aversive US is signaled by a single cue or only the context, the amount of conditional fear is determined directly by the intensity of the US. Stronger shocks result in more fear (Annau and Kamin, 1961; Young and Fanselow, 1992; Anagnostaras, Josselyn, Frankland and Silva, 2000; Merino, Cordero and Sandi, 2000). Of course, the amount of conditioned fear increases with the number of trials given (Fanselow and Bolles, 1979; Young and Fanselow, 1992; Inoue, Tsuchiya and Koyama, 1994).

In a typical delay, tone fear conditioning protocol, a tone (conditional stimulus; CS) is presented and ends coincident with an aversive footshock (unconditional stimulus; US). When tested later, animals typically show fear to both the tone and the context in which the training took place (the context also serves as a CS, predicting the US). The amounts of fear shown to the tone and context depend upon the particular characteristics of the tone, the context, and the shock, as well as their temporal relationship: CSs of greater intensity will engender more fear than less intense stimuli. Longer inter-trial intervals result in relatively greater tone fear than context fear (for an expanded discussion of how these parameters can affect conditioning, see Rescorla and Wagner, 1972; Mackintosh, 1974). When a tone CS predicts a shock, the tone and context compete for predictive validity. Inasmuch as longer inter-trial intervals allow for greater context-no shock experience, the tone is more predictive of shock than is the context.

In the trace conditioning procedure, a tone is presented before shock but an interval intercedes between the end of the tone stimulus and the beginning of the shock stimulus. In this case, the amount of tone and context fear is dependent upon both the interceding interval (the trace interval) and the inter-trial interval. Very long trace intervals prevent acquisition of fear to the tone. Moderately long intervals result in a hippocampus-dependent acquisition of tone fear. Short intervals result in a hippocampus-independent acquisition of tone fear, seemingly identical to that resulting from delay conditioning (Misane et al., 2005; Chowdhury et al., 2005).

The most urgent point we wish to make is that subtle changes in the antecedent conditions can produce dramatic changes in the resultant behaviors and even engage different underlying mechanisms in the process. That is to say, very certain alterations in the independent variables of behavioral experiments can have dramatic influence on the behavioral outcomes and can even change the nervous system locus for those behavioral effects. If one's goal is the investigation of central nervous system mechanisms, one must carefully craft the experimental protocol to best engage those mechanisms.

REFERENCES

Anagnostaras, S. G., Josselyn, S. A., Frankland, P. W., and Silva, A. J. (2000). Computer-assisted behavioral assessment of Pavlovian fear conditioning in mice. *Learning and Memory, 7,* 58-72.

Anagnostaras S. G., Maren S., and Fanselow M. S. (1999). Temporally graded retrograde amnesia of contextual fear after hippocampal damage in rats: within-subjects examination. *Journal of Neuroscience, 19,* 1106-1114.

Annau, Z., Kamin, L. .J. (1961). The conditioned emotional response as a function of intensity of the US. *Journal of Comparative and Physiological Psychology, 54,* 428-432.

Borszcz G. S., Cranney J., and Leaton R. N. (1989). Influence of long-term sensitization on long-term habituation of the acoustic startle response in rats: Central gray lesions, preexposure, and extinction. *Journal of Experimental Psychology: Animal Behavior Processes, 15,* 54-64.

Chowdhury, N., Quinn, J. J., and Fanselow, M. S. (2005). Dorsal hippocampus involvement in trace fear conditioning with long, but not short, trace intervals in mice. *Behavioral Neuroscience, 119,* 1396-1402.

de Olmos J., Alheid G. F., and Beltramino C. A. (1985). Amygdala, In: Paxinos G. (Ed.), *The rat nervous system I. Forebrain and midbrain.* (pp. 223-334). Academic Press.

Depaulis A., Keay K. A., and Bandler R. (1992). Longitudinal neuronal organization of defensive reactions in the midbrain periaqueductal gray region of the rat. *Experimental Brain Research, 90,* 307-318.

Fanselow M. S. (1991). The midbrain periaqueductal gray as a coordinator of action in response to fear and anxiety, In: A. Depaulis and R. Bandler, (Eds.), *The midbrain periaqueductal gray matter.* (pp. 151-173). Plenum Press.

Fanselow, M. S. (1990). Factors governing one trial contextual conditioning. *Animal Learning and Behavior, 18,* 264-270.

Fanselow, M. S. (1989). The adaptive function of conditioned defensive behavior: An ecological approach to Pavlovian stimulus substitution theory. In R. J. Blanchard, P. F. Brain, D. C. Blanchard, and S. Parmigiani (Eds.), *Ethological approaches to the study of behavior, NATO ASI Series D Vol 48.* (pp. 151-166). Boston: Kluver Academic Publishers.

Fanselow, M. S. (1981). Naloxone and Pavlovian fear conditioning. *Learning and Motivation, 12,* 398-419.

Fanselow, M. S. (1986). Associative vs. topographical accounts of the immediate shock freezing deficit in rats: Implications for the response selection rules governing species specific defensive reactions. *Learning and Motivation, 17,* 16-39.

Fanselow, M. S., Bolles, R. C. (1979). Naloxone and shock-elicited freezing in the rat. *Journal of Comparative and Physiological Psychology, 93,* 736-744.

Fanselow M. S., DeCola J. P., De Oca B. M., and Landeira-Fernandez J. (1995). Ventral and dorsolateral regions of the midbrain periaqueductal gray (PAG) control different stages of defensive behavior. *Aggressive Behavior, 21,* 63-77.

Fanselow M. S., DeCola J. P., and Young S. L. (1993). Mechanisms responsible for reduced contextual conditioning with massed unsignaled unconditional stimuli. *Journal of Experimental Psychology: Animal Behavior Processes, 19,* 121-137.

Fanselow M. S., LeDoux J. E. (1999). Why we think plasticity underlying Pavlovian fear conditioning occurs in the basolateral amygdala. *Neuron, 23,* 229-232.

Fanselow, M. S., Tighe, T. J. (1988). Contextual conditioning with massed versus distributed unconditional stimuli in the absence of explicit conditional stimuli *Journal of Experimental Psychology: Animal Behavior Processes, 14,* 187-199.

Gale, G. G., Anagnostaras, S. G., Godsil, B. P., Mitchell, S., Nozawa, T., Sage, J. R., Wiltgen, B., and Fanselow, M. S. (2004). Role of the basolateral amygdala in the storage of fear memories across the adult lifetime of rats. *Journal of Neuroscience, 24,* 3810-3815.

Inoue, T., Tsuchiya K., and Koyama, T. (1994). Regional changes in dopamine and serotonin activation with various intensity of physical and psychological stress in the rat brain. *Pharmacology, Biochemistry, and Behavior, 49,* 911-920.

Kim J. J., Fanselow M. S. (1992). Modality-specific retrograde amnesia of fear. *Science, 256,* 675-677.

Kim J. J., Rison R. A., and Fanselow M. S. (1993). Effects of amygdala, hippocampus, and periaqueductal gray lesions on short- and long-term contextual fear. *Behavioral Neuroscience, 107,* 1093-1098.

LeDoux J. E., Cicchetti P., Xagoraris A., and Romanski L. M. (1990). The lateral amygdaloid nucleus: Sensory interface of the amygdala in fear conditioning. *Journal of Neuroscience, 10,* 1062-1069.

LeDoux J. E., Iwata J., Cicchetti P., and Reis D. J. (1988). Different projections of the central amygdaloid nucleus mediate autonomic and behavioral correlates of conditioned fear. *Journal of Neuroscience, 8,* 2517-29.

Lee, H. J., Choi, J. S., Brown, T. H., and Kim, J. J. (2001). Amygdalar NMDA receptors are critical for the expression of multiple conditional fear responses. *Journal of Neuroscience, 21,* 4116-4124.

Mackintosh, N.J. (1974). *The psychology of animal learning.* New York: Academic Press.

Maren S. (1999). Neurotoxic basolateral amygdala lesions impair learning and memory but not the performance of conditional fear in rats. *Journal of Neuroscience, 19,* 8696-8703.

Maren S., Aharonov G., and Fanselow M. S. (1996a). Retrograde abolition of conditional fear after excitotoxic lesions in the basolateral amygdala of rats: absence of a temporal gradient. *Behavioral Neuroscience, 110,* 718-726.

Maren, S., Aharonov, G., Stote, D. L., and Fanselow, M. S. (1996b). N-methyl-D-aspartate receptors in the basolateral amygdala are required for both acquisition and expression of conditional fear in rats. *Behavioral Neuroscience, 110,* 1365-1374.

Maren S., Aharonov G., and Fanselow M. S. (1997). Neurotoxic lesions of the dorsal hippocampus and Pavlovian fear conditioning in rats. *Behavioral Brain Research, 88,* 261-274.

Mayer D. J., Liebeskind J. C. (1974). Pain reduction by focal electrical stimulation of the brain: an anatomical and behavioral analysis. *Brain Research, 68,* 73-93.

McEchron, M. D., Bouwmeester, H., Tseng, W., Weiss, C., and Disterhoft, J. F. (1998). Hippocampectomy disrupts auditory trace fear conditioning and contextual fear conditioning in the rat. *Hippocampus, 8,* 638-646.

Merino, J.J., Cordero, M.I., and Sandi, C. (2000). Regulation of hippocampal cell adhesion molecules NCAM and L1 by contextual fear conditioning is dependent upon time and stressor intensity. *European Journal of Neuroscience, 12,* 3283-3290.

Misane, I., Tovote, P., Meyer, M., Spiess, J., Ogren, S.O., and Stiedl, O. (2005). Time-dependent involvement of the dorsal hippocampus in trace fear conditioning in mice. *Hippocampus, 15,* 418-426.

Muller J., Corodimas K. P., Fridel Z., and LeDoux J. E. (1997). Functional inactivation of the lateral and basal nuclei of the amygdala by muscimol infusion prevents fear conditioning to an explicit conditioned stimulus and to contextual stimuli. *Behavioral Neuroscience, 111,* 683-691.

Paylor R., Tracy R., Wehner J., and Rudy J.W. (1994). DBA/2 and C57BL/6 mice differ in contextual fear but not auditory fear conditioning. *Behavioral Neuroscience, 108,* 810-817.

Phillips R. G., LeDoux J. E. (1992.) Differential contribution of amygdala and hippocampus to cued and contextual fear conditioning. *Behavioral Neuroscience, 106,* 274-285.

Ponnusamy, R., Zelikowsky, M., and Fanselow, M.S. (2005). Assessment of BLA-independent learning, memory and expression of context fear using muscimol inactivation. Program No. 414.22. *2005 Abstract Viewer/Itinerary Planner.* Washington, DC: Society for Neuroscience, 2005. Online.

Quinn, J. J., Oommen, S. S., Morrison, G. E., and Fanselow, M. S. (2002). Post-training excitotoxic lesions of the dorsal hippocampus attenuate forward trace, backward trace, and delay fear conditioning in a temporally specific manner. *Hippocampus, 12,* 495-504.

Rescorla, R.A., Wagner, A.R. (1972). A theory of Pavlovian conditioning: Variations in the effectiveness of reinforcement and non-reinforcement. In: A. Black and W. Prokasy (Eds.) *Classical conditioning II: Current research and theory.* (pp. 64-99). New York: Appleton-Century-Crofts.

Wiltgen, B. J., Sanders, M. J., Behne, N. S., and Fanselow, M. S. (2001). Sex differences, context preexposure, and the immediate shock deficit in Pavlovian context conditioning with mice. *Behavioral Neuroscience, 115,* 26-32.

Wiltgen, B. W., Sanders, M. J., Anagnostaras, S. G., Sage, J. R., and Fanselow M. S. (submitted). Factors controlling anterograde amnesia for context fear following damage to the hippocampus.

Young, S. L., Fanselow, M. S. (1992). Associative regulation of Pavlovian fear conditioning: Unconditional stimulus intensity, incentive shifts, and latent inhibition *Journal of Experimental Psychology: Animal Behavior Processes, 18,* 400-413.

Young S. L., Bohenek D. L., and Fanselow M. S. (1994). NMDA processes mediate anterograde amnesia of contextual fear conditioning induced by hippocampal damage: immunization against amnesia by context preexposure. *Behavioral Neuroscience, 108,* 19-29.

In: Tasks and Techniques: A Sampling of the Methodologies...   ISBN 1-60021-126-7
Editor: Matthew J. Anderson, pp. 125-138   © 2006 Nova Science Publishers, Inc.

Chapter 11

THE CONDITIONED TASTE AVERSION PREPARATION: PRACTICAL APPLICATIONS AND TECHNICAL CONSIDERATIONS

Kevin B. Freeman [*] *and Anthony L. Riley*

Psychopharmacology Laboratory, Department of Psychology
American University, Washington, DC 20016

ABSTRACT

When an animal consumes a flavored substance that is novel and subsequently experiences nausea, future presentations of the flavor will result in the animal's reduced consumption or complete rejection of the flavored substance. This phenomenon is referred to as conditioned taste aversion (CTA) learning and is thought to occur when the animal associates the novel flavor with subsequent malaise. Since the time of its first empirical demonstration (Garcia et al., 1955), CTA learning has proven to be a highly sensitive, replicable tool for the assessment of drug toxicity and side effects. In this chapter, we present some practical applications of the CTA preparation in addition to an overview of some technical issues that should be considered for researchers planning on using the CTA preparation. Finally, we give a detailed description of a CTA experiment run in our own laboratory as a demonstration of its application.

INTRODUCTION

When an animal consumes a novel flavor (food or solution) and subsequently experiences nausea, the animal will likely avoid consuming that substance on future encounters (Garcia et al., 1968; Rozin and Kalat, 1971). This phenomenon is referred to as a conditioned taste

---

[*] Please address all correspondence to: Kevin B. Freeman, Psychopharmacology Laboratory, Department of Psychology, American University, Washington, DC 20016, Phone: (202) 302-4514, Fax: (202) 885-1081, email: kf6802a@american.edu

aversion (CTA) and is thought to occur when an animal forms an association between an ingested flavor and contiguous malaise. Conditioned taste aversions were first demonstrated in the laboratory in the mid-1950s by John Garcia and colleagues during a series of experiments assessing the effects of ionizing radiation on a number of behavioral endpoints (Garcia et al., 1955). After noticing that rats decreased their food consumption during periods of radiation administration, Garcia sought to determine if radiation could condition an avoidance response to a discriminative taste. To assess this, Garcia administered gamma radiation (unconditioned stimulus [US]) to rats during their consumption of saccharin-flavored water (conditioned stimulus [CS]) and measured the amount of fluid consumed on a subsequent radiation-free presentation of the flavored solution. On this later presentation, rats previously treated with radiation dramatically decreased their preference for the saccharin solution relative to sham-irradiated controls, demonstrating that aversions could be conditioned to tastes when paired with experimentally-induced nausea. Since that demonstration, the effective list of USs in aversion learning has grown to include not only a variety of emetic agents, but numerous other compounds not traditionally considered emetics that appear to induce their effects through a diverse array of processes (Hunt and Amit, 1987; Riley and Tuck, 1985).

The conditioning that occurs in taste aversion learning is highly robust in that learning can occur in a single trial (CS-US pairing), with relatively long intervals separating the presentations of the CS and the US and at drug doses that appear ineffective in other preparations (Garcia and Ervin, 1968; Riley and Tuck, 1985; Rozin and Kalat, 1978). In addition, the strength of conditioning has been shown to vary as a function of the animal's sex, strain, age and drug history (for reviews, see Klosterhalfen and Klosterhalfen, 1985; Riley and Freeman, 2004a). These factors make the CTA preparation a highly sensitive, replicable tool and have led to its widespread usage in the assessment of drug side effects (Riley and Tuck, 1985). However, the applications of the CTA preparation, although rooted in behavioral toxicology, have expanded to include a number of other research issues. Some of these include the characterization of its physiological underpinnings (Bures et al., 1998), the management of wildlife predation (Gustavson and Nicolaus, 1987), the etiology of cancer anorexia (Bernstein, 1999), the pharmacological characterization of the motivational effects of abused drugs (Fenu et al., 2005, Freeman et al., 2005ab; Hunt et al., 1985), the occurrence of drug interactions (Busse et al, 2005b; Grakalic and Riley, 2002), the treatment of autoimmune diseases (Ader and Cohen, 1985) and the determination of taste psychophysics (Scott and Giza, 1987).

One particularly useful application of the CTA assay is in the experimental assessment of implicit learning and memory function. Being a form of Pavlovian conditioning (Rozin and Kalat, 1971), the CTA design inherently contains a learning component (development of a CS-US association) and a memory component (retention). Having the added advantages of fast acquisition (i.e., single-trial learning) and long-term retention (Klosterhalfen and Klosterhalfen, 1985), the CTA preparation allows for rapid assessments of factors either underlying or modifying the acquisition of learning and the retention of memory (Welzl et al., 2001). A recent study by Janus et al. (2004) used the CTA preparation to assess memory functioning in a mouse model of Alzheimer's disease. Given that memory deficits are a hallmark of Alzheimer's disease, it was hypothesized that transgenic mice with a double mutated allele of the human amyloid precursor protein (APP; a neural marker of Alzheimer's disease) would show impaired taste aversion acquisition and/or retention of conditioning to a

LiCl-paired saccharin solution if implicit memory functions were affected by Alzheimer's symptomatology. The results are shown in Figure 1. Panel B shows that there were no differences between the transgenic mice and controls in baseline saccharin preference. However, the results in Panel A reveal deficits in aversion acquisition in the transgenic mice (relative to controls). Furthermore, the rate of extinction for the transgenic mice was faster than that seen in controls (although one could argue this interpretation is confounded by the initial differences in the strength of acquisition). Thus, implicit memory function, as indexed by the retarded acquisition of the aversion in the transgenic mice, seems to be affected by a neural marker of Alzheimer's disease (i.e., the mutated APP), in much the same way that explicit (hippocampal) memory function is affected.

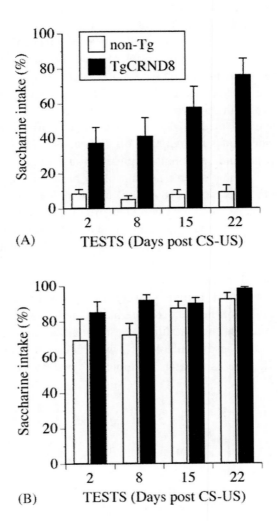

Figure 1. Conditioned transgenic mice consumed more saccharin solution (acquiring a significantly weaker taste aversion) than non-transgenic mice and displayed a significantly faster extinction of a taste aversion during the whole testing period (A). In control (saline injected) conditions, both transgenic mice and the non-transgenic littermates showed strong preferences for saccharin throughout the test (B). *Reprinted from Neurobiology of Aging, 25, Janus et al., Impaired conditioned taste aversion learning in APP transgenic mice, 1213-1219, Copyright (2004), with permission from Elsevier.*

Another interesting application of the CTA preparation is in the characterization of the pharmacological bases for the motivational properties of abused drugs (Freeman et al., 2005ab, Hunt et al., 1985). Similar to emetic USs, self-administered (SA) compounds are capable of conditioning aversions to flavored solutions with which they have been paired, although the mechanisms underlying the suppressive effects of these compounds appear to be qualitatively distinct from those of emetics (for reviews, see Hunt and Amit, 1987; Parker, 2003; also see Grigson, 1997). There have been numerous reports demonstrating that SA compounds have motivational properties that are both rewarding (Nomikos and Spyraki, 1988; Wise et al., 1992) and aversive (Ettenberg, 2004; Koob et al, 1997). Interest in the aversive properties of SA compounds stems from the notion that drug acceptability may be a function of the balance between its rewarding and aversive effects (Riley and Simpson, 2001). Although the mechanisms underlying the rewarding effects of most SA compounds have been well characterized (Kalivas and Volkow, 2005; Ritz et al., 1987), there is relatively little known about the physiological bases for the aversive side effects of these drugs. To address this issue, researchers have used the CTA design to characterize the pharmacological processes mediating the aversive motivational properties of SA compounds (Freeman et al., 2005ab, Hunt et al., 1985). In our own laboratory, we have recently used this preparation to elucidate the neurochemical mediation of cocaine-induced taste aversions (Freeman et al., 2005b). Because cocaine blocks the reuptake of all three monoamine neurotransmitters (i.e., dopamine, norepinephrine and serotonin; Woolverton and Johnson, 1992), it is difficult to determine which aspects of this diverse pharmacology are mediating its aversive effects. By comparing cocaine to matched doses (18 mg/kg) of the three monoamine reuptake inhibitors GBR 12909 (dopamine), desipramine (norepinephrine) and clomipramine (serotonin), we were able to determine that cocaine's noradrenergic actions play a major role in its aversive effects as evidenced by the similar suppression patterns of cocaine and desipramine (see Figure 2).

Although a thorough discussion of the numerous applications of the CTA preparation is beyond the scope of this chapter, there are several reviews within which the interested reader could find the application of interest (Klosterhalfen and Klosterhalfen, 1985; Riley and Freeman, 2004a; Scalera, 2002). In addition, we maintain an annotated bibliography in the form of an electronic database available at www.ctalearning.com (Riley and Freeman, 2004b). Within this site, one can search for topics of interest by author, date, keyword or journal title.

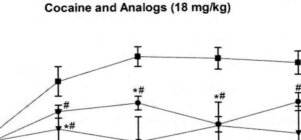

Figure 2. Mean saccharin consumption (ml) for subjects in Groups Veh (saline-injected), Cocaine, GBR 12909, Desipramine and Clomipramine (n = 8 per group; all doses 18 mg/kg) on each of four conditioning Trials and the Aversion Test (Test). Bars above and below each point represent S.E.M. *Significantly different from Group Veh. #Treatment groups significantly different from Group Cocaine. *Reprinted from Pharmacology, Biochemistry and Behavior, 82, Freeman et al., Assessment of monoamine transporter inhibition in the mediation of cocaine-induced conditioned taste aversion, 583-589, Copyright (2005), with permission from Elsevier.*

TECHNICAL CONSIDERATIONS

There are numerous procedural factors that modulate CTA learning, and consideration should be given to these critical parameters during the experimental design process. In addition to aiding in the avoidance of pitfalls, understanding the impact that the following factors have on CTA learning will enable the researcher to better refine the procedure so that the questions of interest are addressed in the most direct manner possible.

One-Bottle vs. Two-Bottle Test

Although CS-US pairings in CTA typically consist of the presentation of a single bottle containing the flavored solution, the researcher has the option of using a one-bottle or two-bottle method for the final aversion test. In a one-bottle test, the animal is presented with the CS only (see Figure 3a), and the total amount of solution consumed serves as the index of the CTA. However, another option is to give a two-bottle test wherein the animal is presented with a bottle containing the CS in addition to an adjacent, identical bottle containing water (see Figure 3b). In this case, the CTA is indexed by the amount of CS consumed relative to total fluid intake, usually expressed in percentage form. Because the animal is not driven by thirst to drink the CS, the two-bottle method is thought to be a more sensitive test, best suited for preparations using relatively weak USs (Dragoin et al., 1971). However, the one-bottle test is more appropriate for preparations looking at graded functions of the US (e.g., dose comparisons), because USs of varying magnitudes may appear equivalent in two-bottle tests if animals generally consume water rather than the CS solution (e.g., see Van Haaren and Hughes, 1990). As a final note, researchers choosing to use the two-bottle test should counter-balance the right/left order of the bottle positions for the CS and water to avoid any possible effects of bottle position on consumption choice.

Figure 3. Rats drinking during a one-bottle test (A) and a two-bottle test (B).

Single Trial vs. Repeated Trials

Although taste aversions are often acquired after a single CS-US pairing, the magnitude of the aversion usually increases over repeated trials. This repeated trial design can often reveal aversive side effects of drugs that may be too weak to produce significant suppression after only one CS-US pairing. Interestingly, the repeated trial design may also reveal the development of tolerance to a drug's aversive effects, as rats receiving a morphine US show a typical aversion acquisition function after a few CS-US pairings, but then start to increase consumption of the paired flavor over continuing trials (Siegel et al., 1995).

Extension of the CS-US Interval

One of the hallmarks of CTA learning is that animals can be conditioned with relatively long delays between the presentations of the CS and the US at intervals that are otherwise ineffective in other traditional learning preparations (Revusky and Garcia, 1970). This type of long-delay learning has been demonstrated with numerous emetics (Revusky and Garcia, 1970), with self-administered compounds (D'Mello et al., 1977; Freeman and Riley, 2005; Goudie et al., 1978) and forced swimming (Masaki and Nakajima, 2004). Furthermore, the effect of the CS-US interval extension on conditioning strength has been shown to vary as a function of the animal's age and/or metabolic rate (Hinderliter et al., 2002; Misanin et al., 2002). Although conditioning is possible with long delays in the CS-US interval in CTA learning, the strength of conditioning generally decreases with the extension of the CS-US interval (Nachman and Jones, 1974).

CS Pre-Exposure

When an animal is pre-exposed to the CS before conditioning, the magnitude of the conditioned response tends to be weaker than for animals that receive a novel CS at the time of conditioning. In traditional learning theory, this phenomenon is known as latent inhibition (Lubow, 1973). In CTA learning, the effects of latent inhibition are evident when preexposed animals drink more of the US-paired CS relative to those that experience the CS as novel upon conditioning (Kalat and Rozin, 1973).

US Pre-Exposure

Similar to the effects of CS preexposure, US preexposure results in the expression of weaker CTAs (for review, see Riley and Simpson, 2001). This effect is robust and has been demonstrated with numerous compounds. In addition, cross-drug preexposure has been shown to have similar effects when using two compounds with established efficacy as USs (Ford and Riley, 1984). As such, appropriate considerations should be made when using animals with drug histories in a CTA preparation.

Strain of the Animal

In CTA learning, strain-dependent differences in conditioning have been reported to occur with a variety of US compounds (Glowa et al., 1994; Risinger and Brown, 1996; Risinger and Cunningham, 2000). Because differential sensitivities among strains appear to exist for a variety of drugs, researchers interested in expanding on previous CTA research should consider conserving the strain in their follow-up studies. In addition, strains that have established differential baselines in other preparations (behavioral or physiological) can be compared in CTA learning to assess the roles of these known parameters on aversion learning (Grabus et al., 2004; Kosten and Ambrosio, 2002).

Sex of the Animal

Although most CTA experiments use only one sex in a single assessment, numerous studies have reported sex-dependent differences in taste aversion learning (Busse et al., 2005a; Chambers et al, 1981; Randall-Thompson et al., 2003). Typically, males show faster acquisition and/or slower extinction rates than do females (Chambers et al., 1997). Furthermore, these differences appear to be hormone-dependent as gonadectomized males exhibit an extinction rate comparable to females. In addition, both females and gonadectomized males treated with testosterone show extinction rates comparable to intact males (Chambers, 1976). As such, the sex of the animal should be held constant when conducting an investigation over serial assessments unless the research aim is to examine the impact of sex on aversion learning.

Drug Dose and Route of Administration

As a general rule, the magnitude of the US intensity is directly correlated with the strength of conditioning (Mackintosh, 1974). In CTA learning, US intensity varies with the dose of the drug. Specifically, the expression of taste aversions increases in magnitude as the dose of an aversive drug is increased (Dacanay et al., 1984). Furthermore, the expression of aversions can vary with the drug's route of administration. For example, cocaine produces much stronger aversions when administered subcutaneously than when given intraperitoneally (Ferrari et al., 1991). Such differences in the expression of aversions may be a function of differential absorption, distribution and net metabolism of the drug across varying administration routes. As such, researchers should note the route of administration used in previous experiments demonstrating CTAs with the compound of interest.

EXAMPLE DESIGN

In the following, we describe a CTA experiment conducted in our laboratory using saccharin-flavored water as the CS and cocaine as the US. Embedded in this design is a dose response function (5, 10, 20 and 32 mg/kg) and an aversion acquisition function (repeated CS-US pairings). Saccharin solution is typically used as the CS in the CTA preparation because it is both palatable to the rat and non-caloric, thus allowing for the marginalization of nutritive factors in the interpretation of the conditioning data.

Subjects

We used 40 male Sprague-Dawley rats weighing between 325-450 g at the start of the experiment. The animals were housed in separate hanging wire-mesh cages in a room maintained on a 12:12 h light-dark cycle and at an ambient temperature of 23° C. Animals were handled daily beginning 2 weeks prior to the start of the experiment in order to limit any effects of handling stress during conditioning and testing.

Phase I: Habituation

During this phase, animals were taken off of *ad-libitum* water and put on a fluid deprivation schedule. Specifically, the animals were given 20-min access to water (presented in graduated 50-ml Nalgene tubes [see Figure 4]) each day until all animals reached a stable baseline that persisted for 3 days. The total amount of water consumed was determined by calculating the difference between the pre-consumption and post-consumption volumes (ml). To ensure that each animal got exactly 20-min of water access, we spaced the bottle presentation and removal between each animal by 15-sec (i.e., the bottle presentation and subsequent removal for Animal #1 preceded that for Animal #40 by 10 min [600 sec]).

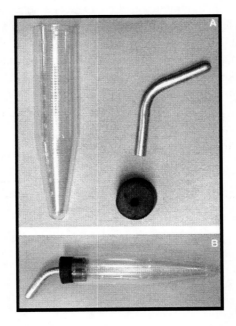

Figure 4. The drinking apparatus consists of a 50-ml Nalgene tube, rubber stopper (Size No. 5 ½, Fisherbrand) and a bent 3½" sipper tube (A). The fully assembled drinking bottle (B).

Phase II: Conditioning

On the morning of this phase, cocaine was prepared as a 10 mg/ml solution in 0.9 % saline and a 0.1% (1 g/L) saccharin solution was prepared with tap water. A separate set of 50-ml Nalgene tubes was used for the saccharin presentation. We strongly recommend permanently designating a set of drinking tubes for saccharin use only, as any mixing of the water and saccharin bottles could result in taste contamination on water-only days. At the time of day designated for water presentation in the habituation phase, the animals were given 20-min access to the novel saccharin solution. Immediately following saccharin access, all subjects were ranked according to the volume of their saccharin consumption and assigned to five groups (n=8 per group) such that each group was comparable in the volume of saccharin consumption on this initial presentation. Approximately 20-min after saccharin access, each subject was removed from its home cage, taken to a separate room and injected subcutaneously with cocaine at one of four doses (5, 10, 20 or 32 mg/kg) or the drug vehicle (saline) equivolume to the highest cocaine dose. Following the injection, each animal was returned to its respective home cage. On the following 3 days, all animals were given 20-min of water access to recover their drinking baselines. No injections were given following water access on these days. This alternating procedure of conditioning/water-recovery was repeated until all subjects received four complete cycles. On the day following the final water-recovery session, all subjects were given 20-min access to saccharin in a one-bottle test of the aversion to saccharin (Aversion Test). No injections were given following the test. Fluid consumption was recorded on all conditioning and water-recovery sessions.

Figure 5 illustrates the mean consumption of saccharin for all subjects on Trials 1-4 and the Aversion Test. Cocaine treatment resulted in a dose-dependent decrease in saccharin consumption after a single CS-US pairing with the magnitude of this suppression increasing over repeated pairings at 20 and 32 mg/kg. The acquisition of the aversion for a treatment group can be defined as a statistical difference in saccharin consumption from control animals on a given trial (between-group comparison) or as a statistical difference between a particular group's baseline consumption (Trial 1) and the consumption on the Aversion Test (within-group comparison).

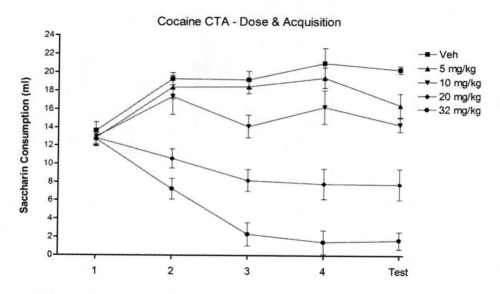

Figure 5. Mean saccharin consumption (ml) for subjects in Groups Veh (saline-injected), 5 mg/kg, 10 mg/kg, 20 mg/kg and 32 mg/kg ($\underline{n}$ = 8 per group) on each of four conditioning Trials and the Aversion Test (Test). Bars above and below each point represent S.E.M.

REFERENCES

Ader, R., and Cohen, N. (1985). CNS-immune system interactions: Conditioning phenomena. *Behav. Brain Sci.* 8, 379-394.

Bernstein, I.L. (1999). Taste aversion learning: A contemporary perspective. *Nutrition,* 15, 229-334.

Bures, J., Bermudez-Rattoni, F., and Yamamoto, T. (1998). *Conditioned Taste Aversion: Memory of a Special Kind.* New York: Oxford University Press.

Busse, G.D., Freeman, K.B., and Riley, A.L. (2005a). The interaction of sex and route of drug administration in cocaine-induced conditioned taste aversions. *Pharmacology, Biochemistry and Behavior,* 81, 814-820.

Busse, G.D., Verndeev, A., Jones, J., and Riley, A.L. (2005b). The effects of cocaine, alcohol and cocaine/alcohol combinations in conditioned taste aversion learning. *Pharmacology, Biochemistry and Behavior*, 82, 207-214.

Chambers, K.C. (1976). Hormonal influences of sexual dimorphism in rate of extinction of a conditioned taste aversion. *Journal of Comparative and Physiological Psychology*, 90, 851-856.

Chambers, K.C., Sengstake, C.B., Yoder, R.L., and Thornton, J.E. (1981). Sexually dimorphic acquisition of a conditioned taste aversion in rats: Effects of gonadectomy, testosterone replacement and water deprivation. *Physiology and Behavior*, 27,83-88.

Chambers, K.C., Yuan, D., Brownson, E.A., and Wang, Y. (1997). Sexual dimorphisms in conditioned taste aversions: Mechanism and function. In: Bouton M.E., and Fanselow M.S., (Eds.), *Learning, motivation, and cognition: The functional behaviorism of Robert C. Bolles* (pp. 195-224). Washington, DC: American Psychological Association.

Dacanay, R.J., Mastropaolo, J.P., Olin, D.A., and Riley, A.L. (1984). Sex differences in taste aversion learning: An analysis of minimal effective dose. *Neurobehavioral Toxicology and Teratology*, 6, 9-11.

D'Mello, G.D., Stolerman, I.P., Booth, D.A., and Pilcher, C.W.T. (1977). Factors influencing flavour aversions conditioned with amphetamine in rats. *Pharmacology, Biochemistry and Behavior*, 7, 185-190.

Dragoin, W., McCleary, G.E., and McCleary, P. (1971). A comparison of two methods of measuring conditioned taste aversions. *Behavior Research Methods Instruments and Computers*, 3, 309-310.

Ettenberg, A. (2004). Opponent process properties of self-administered cocaine. *Neuroscience and Biobehavioral Reviews*, 27, 721-728.

Fenu, S, Rivas, E., and Di Chiara, G. (2005). Differential role of dopamine in drug- and lithium-conditioned saccharin avoidance. *Physiology and Behavior*, 85, 37-43.

Ferrari, C.M., O'Connor, D.A,, and Riley, A.L. (1991). Cocaine-induced taste aversion: Effect of route of administration. *Pharmacology, Biochemistry and Behavior*, 38, 267-271.

Ford, K.A., and Riley, A.L. (1984). The effects of LiCl preexposure on amphetamine-induced taste aversions: An assessment of blocking. *Pharmacology, Biochemistry and Behavior*, 20, 643-645.

Freeman, K.B., Konaklieva, M.I., and Riley, A.L. (2005a). Assessment of the contributions of Na^+ channel inhibition and general peripheral action in cocaine-induced conditioned taste aversion. *Pharmacology, Biochemistry and Behavior*, 80, 281-288.

Freeman, K.B., Rice, K.C., and Riley, A.L. (2005b). Assessment of monoamine transporter inhibition in the mediation of cocaine-induced conditioned taste aversion. *Pharmacology, Biochemistry and Behavior*, 82, 583-589.

Freeman, K.B., and Riley, A.L. (2005). Cocaine-induced conditioned taste avoidance over extended conditioned stimulus-unconditioned stimulus intervals. *Behavioural Pharmacology*, 16, 591-595.

Garcia, J., and Ervin, F.R. (1968). Gustatory-visceral and telereceptor-cutaneous conditioning-adaptation in internal and external milieus. *Communications in Behavioral Biology*, 1 (Pt. A), 389-415.

Garcia, J., Kimeldorf, D.J., and Koelling, R.A. (1955). Conditioned aversion to saccharin resulting from exposure to gamma radiation. *Science*, 122, 157-158.

Glowa, J.R., Shaw, A.E., and Riley, A.L. (1994). Cocaine-induced conditioned taste aversions: Comparisons between effects in LEW/N and F344/N rat strains. *Psychopharmacology*, 113, 229-232.

Goudie, A.J., Dickins, D.W., and Thornton, E.W. (1978). Cocaine-induced conditioned taste aversions in rats. *Pharmacology, Biochemistry and Behavior*, 8, 757-761.

Grabus, S.D., Glowa, J.R., and Riley A.L. (2004). Morphine- and cocaine-induced c-Fos levels in Lewis and Fischer rat strains. *Brain Research*, 13, 20-28.

Grakalic, I., and Riley, A.L. (2002). Asymmetric serial interactions between ethanol and cocaine in taste aversion learning. *Pharmacology, Biochemistry and Behavior*, 73, 787-795.

Grigson, P.S. (1997). Conditioned taste aversions and drugs of abuse: A reinterpretation. *Behavioral Neuroscience*, 111, 129-136.

Gustavson, C.R., and Nicolaus, L.K. (1987). Taste aversion conditioning in wolves, coyotes, and other canids: Retrospect and prospect. In: Frank, H., (Ed.), *Man and Wolf* (pp. 169-200). Dordrecht, The Netherlands: Dr. W. Junk Publishers.

Hinderliter, C.F., Goodhart, M., Anderson, M.J., and Misanin, J.R. (2002). Extended lowered body temperature increases the effective CS-US interval in conditioned taste aversion for adult rats. *Psychological Reports*, 90, 800-802.

Hunt, T., and Amit, Z. (1987). Conditioned taste aversion induced by self-administered drugs: Paradox revisited. *Neuroscience and Biobehavioral Reviews*, 11, 107-130.

Hunt, T., Switzman, L., and Amit, Z. (1985). Involvement of dopamine in the aversive stimulus properties of cocaine in rats. *Pharmacology, Biochemistry and Behavior*, 22, 945-948.

Janus, C., Welzl, H., Hanna, A., Lovasic, L., Lane, N., St. George-Hyslop, P., and Westaway, D. (2004). Impaired conditioned taste aversion learning in *APP* transgenic mice. *Neurobiology of Aging*, 25, 1213-1219.

Kalat, J.W., and Rozin, P. (1973). "Learned safety" as a mechanism in long-delay learning in rats. *Journal of Comparative and Physiological Psychology*, 83, 198-207.

Kalivas, P.W., Volkow, N.D. (2005). The neural basis of addiction: A pathology of motivation and choice. *American Journal of Psychiatry*, 162, 1403-1413.

Klosterhalfen, S., and Klosterhalfen, W. (1985). Conditioned taste aversion and traditional learning. *Psychological Research*, 47, 71-94.

Koob, G.F., Caine, S.B., Parsons, L., Markou, A., and Weiss, F. (1997). Opponent process model of psychostimulant addiction. *Pharmacology, Biochemistry and Behavior*, 57, 513-521.

Kosten, T.A., Ambrosio, E. (2002). HPA axis function and drug addictive behaviors: Insights from studies with Lewis and Fischer inbred strains. *Psychoneuroendocrinology*, 27, 35-69.

Lubow, RE. (1973). Latent inhibition. *Psychological Bulletin*, 79, 389-407.

Mackintosh, N.J. (1974). *The Psychology of Animal Learning*. London: Academic Press.

Masaki, T., and Nakajima, S. (2004). Taste aversion learning induced by delayed swimming activity. *Behavioural Processes*, 67, 367-362.

Misanin, J.R., Collins, M., Rushanan, S., Anderson, M.J., Goodhart, M., and Hinderliter, C.F. (2002). Aging facilitates long-trace taste-aversion conditioning in rats. *Physiology and Behavior*, 75, 759-764.

Nachman, M., and Jones, D.R. (1974). Learned taste aversions over long delays in rats: The role of learned safety. *Journal of Comparative and Physiological Psychology*, 86, 949-956.

Nomikos, G.G., and Spyraki, C. (1988). Cocaine-induced place conditioning: importance of route of administration and other procedural variables. *Psychopharmacology*, 94, 167-173.

Parker, L.A. (2003). Taste avoidance and taste aversions: Evidence for two different processes. *Learning and Behavior*, 31, 165-172.

Randall-Thompson, J.F., and Riley, A.L. (2003). Morphine-induced conditioned taste aversions: Assessment of sexual dimorphism. *Pharmacology, Biochemistry and Behavior*, 76, 373-381.

Revusky, S., and Garcia, J. (1970). Learned associations over long delays. In: Bower, G., and Spence, J., (Eds.), *Psychology of Learning and Motivation: Advances in Research and Theory* (Vol. 4; pp. 1-84) New York, NY: Academic Press.

Riley, A.L., and Freeman, K.B. (2004a). Conditioned flavor aversions: Assessment of drug-induced suppression of food intake. In: Crawley, J.N., Gerfen, C., McKay, R., Rogawski, M., Sibley, D.R., and Skolnick, P., (Eds.) *Current Protocols in Neuroscience* (8.6E.1-.12) New York, NY: Wiley.

Riley, A.L., and Freeman, K.B. (2004b). Conditioned taste aversion: A database. *Pharmacology, Biochemistry and Behavior*, 77, 655-656.

Riley, A.L., and Simpson, G.R. (2001). The attenuating effects of drug preexposure on taste aversion conditioning: Generality, experimental parameters, underlying mechanisms and implications for drug use and abuse. In: Mowrer, R.R., and Klein, S.B., (Eds.), *Contemporary learning theory*, 2nd Edition (pp. 505-559), Hillsdale, NJ: Lawrence Erlbaum Associates.

Riley, A.L., and Tuck, D.L. (1985). Conditioned taste aversions: A behavioral index of toxicity. *Annals of the New York Academy of Sciences*, 443, 381-437.

Risinger, F.O., and Brown, M.M. (1996). Genetic differences in nicotine-induced conditioned taste aversion. *Life Sciences*, 58, 223-229.

Risinger, F.O., and Cunningham, C.L. (2000). DBA/2J mice develop stronger lithium chloride-induced conditioned taste and place aversion than C57BL/6J mice. *Pharmacology, Biochemistry and Behavior*, 67, 17-24.

Ritz, M.C., Lamb, R.J., Goldberg, S.R., and Kuhar, M.J. (1987). Cocaine receptors on dopamine transporters are related to self-administration of cocaine. *Science*, 237, 1219-1223.

Rozin, P., and Kalat, J.W. (1971). Specific hungers and poison avoidance as adaptive specializations of learning. *Psychological Review*, 78, 459-486.

Scalera, G. (2002). Effects of conditioned food aversions on nutritional behavior in humans. *Nutritional Neuroscience*, 5, 159-188.

Scott, T.R., and Giza, B.K. (1987). A measure of taste intensity discrimination in the rat through conditioned taste aversions. *Physiology and Behavior*, 41, 315-320.

Siegel, S., Parker, L.A., and Moroz, I. (1995). Morphine-induced taste avoidance is attenuated with multiple conditioning trials. *Pharmacology, Biochemistry and Behavior*, 50, 299-303.

van Haaren, F., and Hughes, C.E. (1990). Cocaine-induced conditioned taste aversions in male and female Wistar rats. *Pharmacology, Biochemistry and Behavior*, 37, 693-696.

Welzl, H., D'Adamo, P., and Lipp, H.P. (2001). Conditioned taste aversion as a learning and memory paradigm. *Behavioural Brain Research*, 125, 205-213.

Wise, R.A., Bauco, P., and Carlezon, W.A. (1992). Self-stimulation and drug reward mechanisms. *Annals of the New York Academy of Sciences*, 654, 192-198.

Woolverton, W.L., and Johnson, K.M. (1992). Neurobiology of cocaine abuse. *Trends in Pharmacological Sciences*, 13, 193-200.

In: Tasks and Techniques: A Sampling of the Methodologies...   ISBN 1-60021-126-7
Editor: Matthew J. Anderson, pp. 139-144   © 2006 Nova Science Publishers, Inc.

Chapter 12

PASSIVE AVOIDANCE

*Paula M. Millin**

Kenyon College, Gambier, OH 43022

ABSTRACT

Passive avoidance is an efficient and convenient learning task, in which animals are trained in a single trial to avoid a portion of the training apparatus that has been paired with mild footshock. This chapter will discuss the advantages and appropriate uses of passive avoidance, as well as present a small sampling of empirical findings from the psychology and neuroscience literature that has been obtained using this procedure. Additionally, a detailed description of the methodology for using this valuable task will be provided.

INTRODUCTION

Passive avoidance (PA) is a fast, reliable method for producing robust learning in laboratory animals. This task involves a unique combination of operant and classical fear conditioning (for a discussion, see Randall and Riccio, 1969) in which rats are punished with a mild footshock for shuttling from the white to the black side of a two-compartment chamber (see figure below). Since rats naturally prefer dark spaces to light, there is no "training" required to elicit the punished response, and the test, which measures the latency of a trained rat to cross from white to black, challenges the animal's innate behavior, providing an especially compelling demonstration of learning and memory.

---
* Address correspondence to: Paula M. Millin, Department of Psychology, Kenyon College, Gambier, OH 43022, Office: 740-427-5891, Fax: 740-427- 5237, millinp@kenyon.edu

Figure 1. A typical passive avoidance chamber

Upon their first exposure to the apparatus, most rats will perform the cross response within about 60 seconds of being placed in the apparatus, making PA an extremely efficient paradigm. It is also quite well retained, as in the case of pilot work from my laboratory demonstrating near perfect performance at 90 days post training. These qualities have made PA an extremely popular paradigm among psychologists and neuroscientists for decades.

While the cross through procedure is the most conventional PA method, a step-down version, in which the rat is punished for stepping off of a suspended platform onto an electrified grid, is also relatively common (for example, see Medina, Nadja, and Izquierdo, 1999). A newer variation of the cross through procedure punishes the rat for crossing to the black compartment by administering a strong puff of air to its face. Although rodents are used most commonly, modifications of the procedure (and apparatus) have been used with other species. For example, in a study investigating the state-dependent properties of the protein synthesis inhibitor, anisomycin, chicks pecked a metallic bead soaked in either water or an aversive bitter tasting solution. Six hours later, chicks were presented with a non-flavored metallic bead and the amount of pecking during a 30-second test measured memory for the initial exposure. Chicks that remembered the initial aversive exposure passively avoided the aversive stimulus at test by refusing to peck (Bradley and Galal, 1988).

In addition to the obvious advantage of enabling the training of a large number of animals in a short time, PA offers a number of other methodological benefits. First, it is simple to administer and requires very little technical expertise on the part of the experimenter. Moreover, although this procedure is aversively motivated, exposure to the noxious stimulus is brief, making this paradigm less stressful than other tasks involving footshock, such as active avoidance, which requires the animal to escape from a constantly electrified grid to a "safe" compartment (a procedure that often requires multiple trials).

From a theoretical standpoint, the single trial nature of PA training makes it ideal for the study of memory deficits such as anterograde and retrograde amnesias, since the precise moment of learning is more clearly identifiable than in procedures requiring multiple training trials (possibly continuing across days). For example, Quevedo, Vianna, Roesler, de-Paris, Izquierdo, and Rose (1999) investigated the effect of inrahippocampal infusions of the protein synthesis inhibitor, anisomycin, either 15 minutes before, or 0, 3, or 6 hours after training on a step-down passive avoidance response. Rats injected either 15 minutes before or 3 hours after training demonstrated impaired memory (amnesia) when tested at a 24-hour delay. This interesting outcome may suggest a bi-phasic critical period for hippocampal protein synthesis.

It is important to note that like many learning tasks, PA is context dependent. In other words, memory for the PA task is sensitive to contextual changes that occur between training and testing. In a recent study, Millin and Riccio (2004) found a reliable decrement in PA performance when training and testing (24 hours later) occurred in different physical locations. Changes in the internal physiological context of the animal have also been shown to have a detrimental effect on PA performance (for example, see Khavandgar, Homayoun, Torkaman-Boutorabi, and Zarrindast, 2002). Thus, unless a study is explicitly designed to study the effects of a context shift, care should be taken to keep all experimental stimuli consistent between training and testing, including the room, apparatus, experimenters, and time of day.

It is also important to note that when PA is used to investigate the effects of a drug on learning or memory, one must control for any possible motor or motivational effects the drug may have on performance. This issue is irrelevant when the drug is administered following training. For example, in a recent study investigating the effects of glucose on infantile amnesia (accelerated forgetting in immature animals), Flint and Riccio (1999) reported that glucose injected immediately after passive avoidance training enhanced memory for the task 24 hours later in 18-day-old rat pups as compared to animals that had received saline injections following training. If, on the other hand, the experiment requires the drug to be present in the animal's system during either training or testing (or both), an appropriate control group (or groups) would be crucial to a clear interpretation of the results. Consider, for example, a study that investigated the effects of pre-test amphetamine on PA performance in a shifted context (Millin and Riccio, 2004). In this study, rats demonstrated the typical context shift effect (poorer performance in a test context that differed from the training context) unless they had received an injection of amphetamine twenty minutes prior to testing. Although amphetamine generally increases locomotion, which would tend to decrease cross latencies, it could be argued that the good performance (i.e. long cross latencies) in the amphetamine treated group was the result of some non-specific drug effect (e.g. the drug causes generalized fear resulting in a freezing response). To rule out this alternative explanation, a "psuedotrained" control group was included. This group was treated exactly as the experimental group except that they received no shock upon crossing to the black compartment during training. One hour after "pseudotraining", the animals received a non-contingent footshock (identical to the standard shock) in a separate apparatus. In this way, the control group had the same experience with all elements of training, but in a non-contingent manner. This control group also received amphetamine prior to testing, but performed poorly (i.e. they had very short cross latencies). Poor performance in this group ruled out the possibility that some non-specific effect of amphetamine accounted for the long latencies in the trained animals that received amphetamine prior to test.

METHODS

As with all procedures involving laboratory animals, it is advisable to handle each rat for several minutes a day for several days prior to training. Handling simply involves picking the animal up, petting, rubbing, and manipulating its body. Although this added step is time consuming when a study involves many animals, it reduces the stress the animal experiences during training and makes for a more calm and compliant subject, thus reducing the experimenter's stress! Handling is especially important when the procedure includes an injection, since more relaxed animals are easier to restrain.

The passive avoidance apparatus should be housed in an isolated area, preferably in a private, sound-attenuated room. Even minor disturbances, such as a door opening or closing, can disrupt the animal's behavior, causing a freezing response that could interfere with normal cross-through behavior. It is also important that the chosen area, including the equipment and other furniture in the room, be left undisturbed between sessions. It is best not to share the apparatus and room, since it might introduce new odors, functionally changing the experimental context and causing unwanted changes in performance (see the above discussion of context dependency of PA).

Although PA apparatuses are available in a number of designs with different features, a standard PA unit consists of a two-chamber Plexiglas or acrylic box (approximately 43cm x 18cm x 18cm) that is divided in half by a guillotine or sliding door (the door may be set to open automatically on newer units, while older models may require manual operation). As noted in the introduction, the walls and lid of one compartment are opaque black, allowing no light to enter the chamber except from underneath the floor. The other compartment has opaque white walls with a clear ceiling, which typically contains a small light (see figure above). This dual chamber box sits on top of a stainless steel grid floor (grids approximately 2-mm wide, spaced 1-mm apart center to center) and has a hinged lid for moving the animal in and out of the apparatus. The floor of the apparatus is connected to a shock generator and a console that allows the experimenter to determine the length, intensity, and delay of onset (following the cross response) of the footshock.

Prior to the training session, each animal should be transported individually in its home cage to the experimental room housing the PA apparatus. Allowing the animal to sit undisturbed for a minute or two in the new room before being placed in the PA box will permit it to acclimate to the novel environment and decrease its excitation from being transported. Following the acclimation period, the rat should be placed into the white compartment of the PA box with the door between chambers closed. Once the lid of the chamber is quietly closed, allow 15 seconds to elapse before the door between compartments is opened (or, if you have an automated system, set the console to delay the opening of the door for 15 seconds once the timer is started). Once the door opens, begin timing in seconds (or tenths of a second) the latency of the animal to cross from the white to the black compartment. How a "cross" (the dependent variable) is determined will largely depend on the level of sophistication of your PA equipment. Newer models may be equipped with a tilting floor, such that when the weight of the rat shifts to the black compartment, the floor tilts slightly, completing a circuit and stopping the timer (as well as closing the door behind the animal). Other models use infrared beams to detect the location of the rat within the chamber. When the rat breaks a beam in the black side of the box, the timer stops. If the PA unit is older and not automated, the experimenter must operationally define his or her criterion for a cross response. A common criterion has been to record a cross when the animal has placed all four feet within the black compartment (for example, see Millin and Riccio, 2004).

As an aside, automated systems have the advantage of offering a high level of consistency in recording the dependent measure, however, an animal may trip the circuit by stretching across the threshold without ever actually crossing into the black compartment (some tilting floor models have a damper that can be used to decrease the sensitivity of the mechanism). On the other hand, systems that require the experimenter to determine when a cross has occurred (usually by observing the placement of the animal's feet using a mirror placed underneath the grid floor) allow for more variability and potential human bias.

Once the animal has made the cross-through response, the guillotine door should be closed, confining it to the black compartment. After a delay of around ten seconds, the rat should receive a single, brief (usually 1 second) footshock. The delay between entry into the black compartment and shock delivery is meant to allow the rat time to process the features of the conditional stimulus (CS; the black compartment) prior to onset of the unconditional stimulus (UCS; the shock). Determining the appropriate level of shock intensity will depend on the specific goals of your study (such as how long you wish the memory to last, the level of avoidance you wish to achieve, etc.), however, between 0.5-1.0mA is generally sufficient to produce robust learning and memory. It is always recommended that the lowest level of shock sufficient to achieve your empirical goals be used. The rat should remain in the black compartment for 15 seconds following shock (to allow for further exposure to the CS), after which the animal should be removed from the apparatus and returned to the colony room in its home cage. Be sure to record the training cross latency before training another subject. It is advisable to wipe down the walls and floor of the PA box with clean water (do not use cleaning solutions that introduce a new odor into the apparatus) to remove any urine or feces before placing another subject in the apparatus.

The delay at which you test for memory of the PA task will depend on the specific questions under investigation. Many investigators use a 24-hour training-to-test interval since rats generally show very good retention at that delay. Test trials should be conducted identically to the training trial with the exception that the rat is not punished for crossing from the white to the black compartment. Some investigators take only a cross latency measure and terminate the test as soon as the rat makes the response (or after 5 to 10 minutes if no cross is made). Others take an additional measure known as total time on white (TTW). This measure involves calculating the total amount of time the rat spends in the white side of the box during a 10-minute (or less) test, and is considered by some to be a more sensitive test of memory, since an animal may cross quickly, but then immediately return to the white compartment for the remainder of the test. If you wish to include this measure, simply leave the door open between chambers after the rat makes its initial cross such that it may move freely between compartments until the test period is over. TTW may even be preferable to cross latency if the apparatus used is highly sensitive and frequently records false crosses (such as when the animal stretches across the threshold, but spends no actual time in the black compartment). A good approach may be to take both measures until it is determined whether TTW offers redundant or novel information about the animals' memory for training.

As can be seen, PA is a reliable and efficient learning paradigm. It allows many animals to be trained quickly and is well retained. In addition, it offers the advantage that the precise moment of learning is clearly identifiable. This feature is a great benefit when one wishes to impose a manipulation just prior to or following the learning episode. Although PA equipment can be expensive (costing thousands of dollars), its efficiency and usefulness have made it one of the most heavily utilized tasks for the study of learning and memory in animal subjects.

REFERENCES

Bradley, P.M. and Galal, K.M. (1988). State-dependent recall can be induced by protein synthesis inhibition: behavioral and morphological observations. *Brain Research,* 468, 243-251.

Flint, R. W. and Riccio, D.C. (1999). Post-training glucose administration attenuates forgetting of passive-avoidance conditioning in 18-day-old rats. *Neurobiology of Learning and Memory*, 72(1), 62-67.

Khavandgar, S., Homayoun, H., Torkaman-Boutorabi, A., and Zarrindast, M. R. The effects of adenosine receptor agonists and antagonists on morphine state-dependent memory of passive avoidance. *Neurobiology of Learning and Memory,* 78(2), 390-405.

Medina, J.H., Nadja, S., and Izquierdo, I. (1999). Two different properties of short- and long-term memory. *Behavioural Brain Research*, 103(1), 119-121.

Millin, P.M. and Riccio, D.C. (2004). Is the context shift effect a case of retrieval failure? The effects of retrieval enhancing treatments on forgetting under altered stimulus conditions in rats. *Journal of Experimental Psychology,* 30(4), 325-334.

Quevedo, J., Vianna, M.R.M., Roesler, R., de-Paris, F., Izquierdo, I., and Rose, S.P.R. (1999). Two Time Windows of Anisomycin-Induced Amnesia for Inhibitory Avoidance Training in Rats: Protection from Amnesia by Pretraining but not Pre-exposure to the Task Apparatus. *Learning and Memory,* 6(6), 600-607.

Randall, P.K. and Riccio, D.C. (1969). Fear and punishment as determinants of passive-avoidance responding. *Journal of Comparative and Physiological Psychology*, 69(3), 550-553.

In: Tasks and Techniques: A Sampling of the Methodologies...   ISBN 1-60021-126-7
Editor: Matthew J. Anderson, pp. 145-162   © 2006 Nova Science Publishers, Inc.

Chapter 13

SEXUAL CONDITIONING METHODS: THEORETICAL AND PRACTICAL CONSIDERATIONS

Michael Domjan[*] and Adem Can
University of Texas at Austin, Texas, USA

ABSTRACT

The sexual behavior system has been found to be no less susceptible to conditioning than other aspects of behavior and shows many standard conditioning effects. However, because sexual conditioning is not as familiar as conditioning with food or shock, procedural details that are usually taken for granted require explicit consideration and proper tuning. In particular investigators have to consider the motivational state of the organism, what to use as the sexual reinforcer, how to pace conditioning trials, what conditioned stimulus to use, and what aspects of behavior to measure to characterize the resultant learning. Examination of these variables has helped to identify effective sexual conditioning procedures and has also provided valuable insights that can help us understand learning more generally.

INTRODUCTION

Conditioning procedures can be used to modify responding in the sexual behavior system, just as they are frequently employed in studies of conditioning and learning in the feeding and defensive behavior systems. However, the procedures have to be adapted to accommodate special features of the sexual behavior system. These accommodations involve the reinforcer and how the reinforcer is delivered, the subject's motivation or readiness to engage in relevant behavior, and how conditioned responses are identified and measured. Studies of sexual conditioning have been conducted with a wide range of model species including ring doves (*Streptopelia risoria*), (Burns- Cusato, Cusato and Daniel, 2005), fruit

[*] Corresponding Address: Michael Domjan, Department of Psychology, University of Texas A8000, Austin, Texas 78712, Tel: 512-471-7702, Email: Domjan@psy.utexas.edu, ademcan@mail.utexas.edu.

fly (*Drosophila melanogaster*) (Siwicki and Ladewski, 2003; McBride et al., 1999, Dukas, 2005), Mongolian gerbil (*Meriones unguiculatus*) (Villarreal and Domjan, 1998), male threespine stickleback (*Gasterosteus aculeatus*) (Jenkins, 1997), blue gourami (*Trichogaster-Trichopterus*) (Hollis, Cadieux, and Colbert, 1989), and humans (Hoffmann, Janssen, and Turner, 2004). However, the most frequently used species in studies of sexual conditioning are rats and domesticated quail. Therefore, we will mainly focus on those two species.

TYPES OF SEXUAL CONDITIONING

From a basic conceptual point of view, the only thing that distinguishes sexual conditioning from more conventional methodologies for the study of learning is the reinforcer or unconditioned stimulus (US) that is used. Rather than the familiar food, water, or foot-shock that are employed in conventional conditioning experiments, in a sexual conditioning study the reinforcer is access to a sexually receptive member of the opposite sex. Once an effective sexual reinforcer has been identified, it can be used in both instrumental and Pavlovian conditioning procedures. In an instrumental conditioning procedure, a response specified by the experimenter is required before access to the sexual reinforcer. In contrast, in a Pavlovian conditioning procedure a signal or conditioned stimulus (CS) is presented shortly before the US (or reinforcer), but, unlike with instrumental conditioning, no response is required to get access to the US, and the point of interest is the conditioned responding that develops as the CS comes to be associated with the US. Although both instrumental and Pavlovian conditioning paradigms have been employed in studies of sexual learning, Pavlovian procedures have been used more often and will be the focus of this chapter (for some examples of studies of instrumental sexual conditioning, see Sheffield, Wulff and Barker, 1951; Everitt et al., 1987.)

Many research methods that are used in traditional Pavlovian and instrumental conditioning paradigms have also been utilized in sexual behavior research, though with differing levels of success. Even though conditioning in the sexual behavior system appears to be relatively straightforward, an experimenter should keep in mind that simply replacing a common reinforcer or unconditioned stimulus, like the food or water, with mating in a typical conditioning experimental design may not necessarily be the best experimental strategy in sexual conditioning. Unlike food or water, sexual interaction with an opposite sex conspecific is a rather complex experience for the subject. Sexual conditioning experiments usually involve mating or some other kind of interaction with a partner animal. These partner subjects have important effects on the sexual behavior of the experimental subjects. Therefore, when selecting and treating these partner subjects, great care should be taken to ensure that they play no role in creating confounding variables. Because of this, experimental conditions must control both types of subjects even though partner animals often are not used directly in data collection. This is often a source of mistakes and cannot be overemphasized. Experiments aimed at investigating sexual learning should be designed with these concerns in mind. We will address these issues in this chapter.

MOTIVATIONAL PREREQUISITES FOR SEXUAL CONDITIONING

Sexual reinforcement is a form of positive reinforcement, like food and water. Food and water are effective reinforcers only if the subject is food or water deprived. Likewise, sexual deprivation is necessary for access to a sexual partner to be an effective reinforcer. In addition, both the subject being conditioned and its sexual partner who provides the sexual reinforcement have to be sexually receptive. For seasonal breeders, this restricts studies of sexual conditioning to the breeding season. For species that are sexually active throughout the year, sexual receptivity is governed generally by the cycles of receptivity of the female.

Of the two species commonly used in studies of sexual conditioning, domesticated quail are seasonal breeders, whereas laboratory rats typically breed all year round. However, both species can be induced to engage in sexual behavior under laboratory conditions throughout the year.

As is common in avian species, the reproductive readiness of quail depends on the daily photoperiod that controls the hormonal state of the animal (Dawson et al., 2001). An increase in the daily photoperiod in the laboratory from 8 to 16 hours of light per day serves to mimic the transition from winter to spring and summer and results in recruitment of the reproductive physiology of the birds. Sexually mature females start to lay eggs and become sexually receptive, and males begin to crow and become sexually active as the daily photoperiod is increased. The birds remain in reproductive condition provided that the photoperiod remains at 16 hours of light per day (Mills et al., 1997). This makes it highly convenient to study sexual behavior and sexual conditioning in domesticated quail.

In laboratory rats, sexual behavior and receptivity of the females typically depends on the estrous cycle (Beach, 1976; Madlafousek and Hlinak 1977). Although endogenous hormonal fluctuations can lead to reliable periods of sexual activity, for convenience and increased experimental control, investigators typically employ females who have been ovariectomized and induce sexual receptivity with injections or implants of estradiol benzoate and progesterone (Albert et al. 1991). This hormonal treatment regimen has been shown to induce higher preference in ovariectomized female rats for male rats compared to ovariectomized but oil-treated counterparts (Clark et al. 2004). Similarly, Delville and Balthazart (1987) showed that sexual receptivity can be induced in ovariectomized female quail with injections of estradiol benzoate.

[handwritten margin note: — how is this natural? or does it more closely resemble humans]

THE NATURE OF THE SEXUAL REINFORCER

As we noted above, what distinguishes sexual conditioning from other conditioning procedures is the access to a receptive sexual partner as the reinforcer. Access can be in the form of an opportunity to copulate with the sexual partner or exposure to the stimuli provided by a potential sexual partner behind a barrier. Visual exposure to a female conspecific has been successfully used as the reinforcer in sexual conditioning of both the male gourami (a species of fish) (Hollis, Cadieux, and Colbert, 1989), and male domesticated quail (Crawford and Domjan, 1993). Copulatory access to a female has been also frequently used as the reinforcer in the sexual conditioning of male domesticated quail (e.g., Domjan, Cusato and Krause. 2004) and male rats (Pfaus, Kippin and Centeno, 2001). A few studies have also examined the relative effectiveness of copulation vs. noncopulatory or limited copulatory access to a female as the reinforcer. It has been shown that in male quail copulatory access to a female conspecific produces significantly higher levels of conditioned responding than just visual access to a female behind a barrier (Holloway and Domjan, 1993). The superiority of full copulatory access to limited interaction with a sexual partner as a reinforcer has also been found in studies with rats (Kagan, 1955; Whalen, 1961; Zamble et al. 1985). For example, while sexually naïve male rats can learn to run down a straight alley to get non-contact exposure to a sexually receptive female, those subjects that were permitted to have physical contact with a receptive female and ejaculate increased their running speed (López, Olster, and Ettenberg, 1999).

Both males and female have been the focus of attention in studies of sexual conditioning. In domesticated quail, conditioning effects have been more subtle and more difficult to detect in females than in males (Gutierrez and Domjan, 1997), perhaps because procedures that insure that sexual interaction is reinforcing for the female have yet to be identified. In rats, various studies showed that sexual reinforcement for the female appears to depend on the opportunity for her to pace her sexual interactions with the male. In other words, being able to control copulation and sexual stimulation is more rewarding for female rats than just passively accepting males' advances (Paredes, and Vazquez, 1999). While in their natural environment, which consists of interconnected burrows, female rats can actively solicit, initiate, and terminate copulation. In an experimental setting in which there is no impediment to stop the male rat from chasing the female during mating, however, the sexual behaviors of the female that are indicative of her sexual motivation are limited to lordosis and, in some cases, defensive behaviors against the male (Pfaus, Smith and Coopersmith, 1999). In addition, in such settings, it is difficult for the experimenter to isolate the male's contribution to an interaction from the female's contribution.

The paced mating method is devised to solve these problems by mimicking the natural habitat of the rats. The paced mating chamber consists of at least two compartments that are connected via a hole that is just big enough for the female, but not the male, rat to pass through. The female rat, as it is smaller than her male counterpart, can then travel back and forth between the compartments through holes that the male cannot pass, confining it to its compartment. This freedom to choose between compartments allows the female to control, or "pace", the sexual interaction. Modified versions of the paced mating chamber can also be used to study mate selection phenomena. As shown in the cleverly designed paced mating chamber in Figure 1, the number of compartments may be increased to fulfill experimental needs, and simple materials are adequate for building these kinds of experimental chambers. (Ferreira-Nun~o et al. 2005).

Experimental evidence supports the idea that paced mating is more effective as a sexual reinforcer. Paredes and Alonso (1997) found that if female rats are placed in a distinctive context right after paced mating sessions, they conditionally prefer this context over an alternative, whereas this preference is not induced if non-paced mating precedes the context exposure. In a similar study by Coria-Avila et al. (2005), females were given paced-mating trials in which the male copulation partner was scented with a neutral odor (almond), and non-paced mating trials in which the male was unscented. In the preference test that followed training, the females showed more solicitation behaviors towards the scented than the unscented male and generally selected the scented male for the first ejaculation.

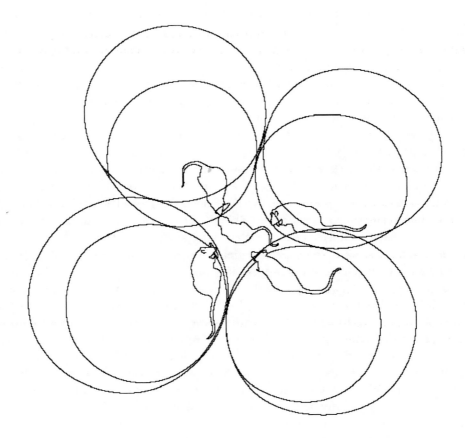

Figure 1. Apparatus that permits paced mating and female choice in rats. A male rat is confined to the central area, with females in the four side chambers. (Adapted from Ferreira-Nun̄o et al. 2005, by Susanna Douglas.)

TRIAL SPACING IN STUDIES OF SEXUAL CONDITIONING

In traditional studies of learning the target subject is placed in a conditioning chamber for daily training sessions and receives numerous conditioning trials in each session. For example, rabbit eye-blink conditioning experiments typically involve sessions in which as many as 60 trials are conducted, with intertrial intervals of 60-90 sec. Appetitive conditioning with food is often conducted in a similar fashion. Multiple, closely-spaced trials are possible because the reinforcer remains effective despite its repeated presentation during the course of a conditioning session.

Multiple daily conditioning trials can also be employed in a sexual conditioning experiment if the reinforcer is exposure to a sexual partner behind a visual or wire-mesh barrier. However, as we noted above, noncopulatory exposure to a conspecific is less effective in sexual conditioning than is the opportunity to copulate with a sexual partner. This has encouraged investigators to use copulation as the reinforcer in studies of sexual conditioning. However, an important consequence of using copulation is that successive conditioning trials have to be widely spaced. Since, for most vertebrate species, copulation is an exhaustive event and repeated copulations decrease the level of sexual motivation, the number of training trials that can be conducted is fairly constrained in sexual conditioning compared to other conditioning experiments.

Once a male has copulated with a female several times, he is not likely to copulate again for some time. Copulatory behavior is typically followed by a refractory period that is substantially longer than for other appetitive reinforcers. To avoid presenting a conditioning trial during the refractory period from the last trial, trials are typically separated by at least one or more days. In one of the early studies, Beach and Jordan (1956) showed that some male rats require up to two weeks to fully recover from the effects of total sexual exhaustion, and that males that ejaculated only once a day may show some signs of sluggishness in response to sexual stimuli. More recently, Fernández-Guasti and Rodríguez-Manzo (2003) reported that only after seven days of rest did all of the male rats recover enough from the effects of sexual satiation to be able to complete one ejaculatory series.

Sexual satiation has also been shown to greatly suppress conditioned responses to a CS as well as to the US in male domesticated quail. This has been seen even after a single 5-minute copulation opportunity, and nearly complete lack of responding to a female occurs after 8 such successive trials (Hilliard and Domjan, 1995; Hilliard et al. 1998).

Given these empirical findings, it would be a safe strategy for a researcher to space trials with long rest periods between trials when designing a sexual conditioning experiment that involves copulation. If such long intertrial intervals produce other confounding variables (e.g. aging), or there are other time constraints in the experimental design, the researcher should consider constraining copulatory access by limiting the number of intromissions or ejaculations or by using shorter periods of copulatory interaction to prevent sexual satiation. It is also important to regard the condition and welfare of partner animals throughout an experiment. Sexual interaction, while positive for the male, may cause distress and aversive stimulation for females, especially with extensive trials. Although using the same animals as partners in successive trials with different experimental subjects reduces the number of animals required in a study, the partner's resistance toward sexual interactions after multiple matings may be more detrimental to the experiment than the benefits obtained from using fewer partner animals.

CONDITIONED STIMULI

A large variety of conditioned stimuli have been used in studies of sexual conditioning. A red light was used as the CS in experiments with blue gourami (Hollis, Cadieux and Colbert, 1989), and in an early study of sexual conditioning in male quail (Domjan et al., 1986). Since then, a variety of other stimuli have been used as CSs in studies with quail, including orange feathers attached to a female (Domjan, O'Vary, and Greene, 1988), orange feathers mounted on a foam block (Holloway and Domjan, 1993), a wood block lowered from the ceiling (Köksal et al., 1994), and a terrycloth object presented with or without species typical cues (see Figure 2). Contextual cues provided by a distinctive environment can also be successfully used as a CS in sexual conditioning of quail (Hilliard et al., 1997).

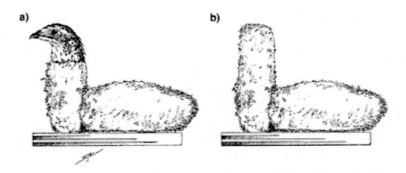

Figure 2. CS objects used in sexual conditioning of quail, with (a) and without (b) limited female cues.

Unlike with quail, studies of sexual conditioning with rats have generally focused on olfactory and contextual cues rather than localized visual stimuli. As they are nocturnal, with relatively few cones in the retina, rats have relatively poor vision (Jacobs, Fenwick and Williams, 2001), and selective breeding for albinism in laboratory rats often results in even lower visual acuity (Prusky et al. 2002). Olfaction is an important source of information in the rat's sexual behavior system. For example, airborne odors from estrus females are alone effective in inducing penile erections in male rats (Sachs, 1997). By the same token, olfactory CSs can be used in sexual conditioning experiments with rats. Kippin et al. (1998) showed that not just natural estrous odors but neutral odors too (e.g. almond) can be associated with a sexual US. In this experiment, male rats that were previously allowed to copulate with an artificially scented receptive female showed a preference for ejaculating with females with the same scent over unscented receptive females. In another experiment, similar training produced more contacts and mounts toward nonreceptive but scented females (Kippin and Pfaus, 2001a).

Subsequent studies demonstrated that this preference results from exposure to the scented female just after ejaculation (Kippin and Pfaus, 2001b). In other words, the post-ejaculatory state appears to be a potent sexual US in male rats. Studies of conditioned place preference also support this idea. If a male rat is placed in a distinctive context right after a copulation that has ended with ejaculation, the subject develops a conditioned place preference for that context (e.g Agmo and Berenfeld, 1990).

The variety of stimuli that have been successfully used as CSs in studies of sexual conditioning might imply that the type of CS is of little consequence. However, that is far from the case. The CS employed often determines the topography of the conditioned response that emerges, as we will discuss in the next section. In addition, studies with male quail have indicated that the type of CS also determines the rate of learning and how learning phenomena are manifested.

In most definitions of Pavlovian conditioning, the CS is characterized as unrelated to, or arbitrary, with respect to the US at the outset of training. This is typically the case in the laboratory, and, because of that, pairings of the CS with the US have to be arranged by the experimenter. The experimenter is unavailable to arrange CS-US pairings in an animal's natural environment. Therefore, in the natural environment, conditioned stimuli are generally cues that have an inherent relationship to the US. They are typically cues that are natural precursors to the US or occur early in the causal chain of events that naturally leads to the US.

To identify such CSs, one has to consider the natural history of the species under investigation.

Quail live in areas with tall grass. Therefore, a male looking for a female may only see her head at a distance at first. Thus, limited visual cues of a female may be natural precursors of sexual reinforcement and may serve as CSs in the wild. Such a naturalistic CS may be modeled in the laboratory using the type of CS object that is illustrated in the left panel of Figure 2. The second CS object shown in Figure 2 was designed to be of similar shape and size but lacks limited female cues. An extensive series of experiments has been conducted to compare the relative effectiveness of these two types of CSs in studies of sexual conditioning. In general, the more naturalistic CS supports more rapid learning and a wider range of conditioned responses (see following section). In addition, conditioned responding with the naturalistic CS is more robust in the sense that it is not as easily disrupted by an increase in the CS-US interval, it is not as susceptible to the blocking effect, it leads to more second-order conditioning, and the responding is much more resistant to extinction (see Domjan, Cusato, and Krause, 2004).

IDENTIFYING AND MEASURING SEXUALLY CONDITIONED RESPONSES

How to measure learning is rarely an issue in conventional learning preparations because these practices have been tuned over the years to produce good data. On the other hand, one cannot easily rely on convention when one ventures to use a novel behavior system or species. Therefore, the choices of responses to be measured as indices of learning have to be carefully considered.

Learning does not invariably lead to an obvious, easy to identify behavioral change. To observe behavioral evidence of learning, one has to know where to look. In the case of sexual conditioning, probably the first and foremost consideration is the selection of a specific behavior related to the scientific question under investigation. Obviously, the nature of the response would be determined by the species of subjects. For example, while the number of intromissions performed prior to ejaculation is a good index of sexual motivation in male rats, a researcher using an avian species which has no penis should be looking at other responses such as cloacal contacts to measure an analogous phenomenon.

After characteristics of the subject's species are carefully examined, the experimenter should concentrate on sex differences in the subjects' behavior. Sex differences in responses to conditioned and unconditioned stimuli are particularly important in sexual behavior studies. Since the sexual behaviors of males and females differ, the same behavior may indicate a totally different motivation for males and females. For example, while male quail actively search for a copulation partner and perform sexual responses quite intensely, in female quail, increased immobility and related responses, such as squatting behavior, (Delville, Sulon and Balthazart, 1986) indicate sexual receptivity. Therefore, while heightened locomotion in males indicates increased sexual motivation, the same in females indicates a lack of sexual receptivity.

Conventional notions of stimulus substitution or conditioned compensatory behavior are often not helpful. Stimulus substitution, for example, predicts that if the unconditioned response is copulatory contact with a sexual partner, the conditioned response will involve attempts to copulate with the CS. Although conditioned copulation with the CS has been reported, it is observed only under special circumstances (Koksal et al. 2004). Noncopulatory conditioned responses are more commonly observed.

In considering potential sexually conditioned responses, we have found the behavior systems theory formulated by Timberlake (2001) to be particularly useful. This theory views behavior as organized into functional systems designed to accomplish various biological tasks such as feeding, defense, and reproduction. Each functional system of behavior consists of a sequence of response modes. Each response mode is, in turn, assumed to have its own specific activating stimulus and response output. Timberlake has examined the behavior system for feeding in considerable detail. Since sexual behavior is a form of appetitive behavior, the basic structure of the feeding system can be used as a guide in examining the sexual behavior system.

From a behavior systems perspective, the sexual behavior system may be conceptualized as consisting of a general search mode, in which the subject seeks a potential sexual partner in the absence of specific cues that identify the partner's location. In the general search mode, increased nondirected locomotor behavior is expected to ensue. Once the partner's possible location has been identified, a focal search mode is activated that involves responses with greater spatial specificity. Finally, upon direct encounter with the sexual partner, species typical courtship and copulatory responses are expected to occur. Thus, sexual behavior involves a transition from appetitive response modes to a consummatory response mode.

Conditioning procedures typically involve creating the required motivational state (such as food deprivation) and periodically presenting the reinforcer in the experimental context. These manipulations serve to activate the relevant behavior system. The specific Pavlovian or instrumental conditioning procedure is then conducted in the context of this behavior system. The sexual behavior system will be activated if subjects are in the breeding season, if they are sexually deprived, and if they are in a place where they are likely to encounter a sexual partner.

A Pavlovian conditioning procedure consists of presenting a CS prior to access to the sexual partner or reinforcer. According to behavior systems theory, the CS becomes incorporated into the sexual behavior system as a result of the CS–US pairings and comes to elicit responses appropriate to its temporal relation to the US. Thus, a sexually conditioned CS that is sequentially paired with a US should come to elicit behaviors that ordinarily precede rather than mimic copulatory behavior.

In the case of male quail, the use of a short CS–US interval results in focal search, or approach to the CS. This behavior is similar to the sign tracking that is typically observed when a light is paired with food in pigeons. As with pigeon sign tracking, sexually conditioned approach behavior is resistant to omission training (Crawford and Domjan, 1993) and occurs even if the CS is located far from the US (Burns and Domjan, 1996). If a relatively long CS–US interval is used (e.g., 20 min), the conditioned response that develops is more akin to general search behavior and consists of increased nondirected locomotion (Akins, Domjan, and Gutiérrez, 1994).

The appetitive responses that best reflect sexual learning depend on the species. In rats, a particularly sensitive index of sexual conditioning was identified using a bilevel chamber, which is illustrated in Figure 3. Conditioned sexual anticipation can be measured as an increase in locomotion between the two levels (Pfaus, Mendelson and Phillips, 1990).

A bilevel chamber (see Figure 3) basically is a small, transparent box with two long and narrow platforms, one placed above another and connected with ramps. These two platforms, or levels, allow subjects to stand or copulate. Since the platforms are connected by ramps, the male rat is not able to restrict the female to a particular location. Rather, the female can move freely and pace the mating episodes to a degree. The number of level changes prior to the introduction of the female and the latency to change levels have been reported as indices of male rats' sexual motivation (VanFurth and VanRee 1996a; VanFurth and VanRee 1996b).

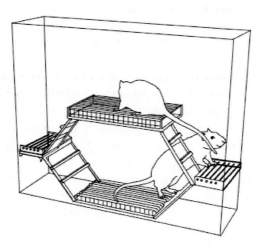

Figure 3. Bilevel chamber used in tests of sexual motivation in rats. (Adapted from Mendelson and Gorzalka, 1987, by Susanna Douglas).

Another advantage of the bilevel chamber is that the narrow platforms force the subjects to mate in a consistent orientation, thus allowing the researcher to observe the subjects' flanks, which facilitates the identification of stereotypical sexual behaviors like lordosis and intromissions (Mendelson and Gorzalka 1987; Mendelson and Pfaus 1989).

Appetitive sexual responses are most commonly observed when a CS becomes associated with sexual reinforcement. However, conditioned consummatory responses have also been obtained in male quail under other circumstances. One important requirement is that the CS be a three-dimensional object that can support copulatory behavior. Two examples of such CSs are presented in Figure 2. Each is made of terrycloth and consists of a horizontal section that a male quail can mount, and a vertical section that it can grab with its beak. Conditioned copulatory responding is more likely to develop with a CS object that includes taxidermically prepared portions of a female quail (Cusato and Domjan, 1998). However, some males also come to copulate with a terrycloth object that lacks female cues after extensive training (Köksal et al., 2004). The most effective way to develop conditioned copulation with a terrycloth object is to use a fading procedure. In this procedure a taxidermically prepared female quail is initially paired with access to a live female to initiate copulation with the inanimate object. The female cues are then gradually covered up across successive trials. With the proper fading steps, copulation that started with the taxidermic model of a female persists when the CS object consists entirely of terrycloth (Domjan, Huber-McDonald, and Holloway, 1992).

As was noted earlier, each response mode is tuned to a range of eliciting stimuli. Easily localized stimuli (such as a light or a wood block) can come to elicit focal search responses. Such responses are not likely to be observed with contextual cues that are more spatially distributed. One might predict that if contextual cues are used as the CS, the conditioned response would be some form of increased locomotion or pacing. That outcome has not been observed with male quail. Rather, conditioned contextual cues have been found to potentiate responses to limited female cues. Thus, in the presence of conditioned contextual cues, male quail are more likely to approach and copulate with a taxidermic model that contains limited female species typical cues (Domjan, Greene, and North, 1989; Hilliard, Nguyen, and Domjan, 1997). It is important to note that in this situation the taxidermic model is used probe stimulus and is only presented during post-conditioning test trials. It is not presented as a CS during training.

The increased responsiveness to female cues that occurs with exposure to conditioned contextual cues has been also found to facilitate copulatory behavior. Male rats, for example, achieve ejaculation more quickly if they encounter a female after exposure to sexually conditioned contextual cues (e.g., Zamble et al., 1985).

CONDITIONED CHANGES IN RESPONDING TO A SEXUAL UNCONDITIONED STIMULUS

Pavlovian conditioning is typically defined and measured in terms of conditioned changes in responding to the conditioned stimulus. However, of equal importance is the way in which subjects change their behavior in response to the sexual unconditioned stimulus or the sexual partner, as a consequence of Pavlovian conditioning. In fact, in some situations the effects of sexual conditioning are evidenced only by facilitation of copulatory interactions with a sexual partner or US. In an early study of sexual conditioning in rats, Zamble et al. (1985) found that males ejaculated with shorter latencies if their encounter with the female occurred after exposure to a sexually conditioned stimulus. Furthermore, this decrease in ejaculatory latency was the only evidence that the CS had acquired conditioned properties. In a related study, Kippin et al. (1998) found that a CS can modify ejaculatory preferences of male rats, without creating any changes in appetitive responding (e.g. level changing behavior) between experimental and control groups.

In female quail, sexual conditioning is also only evident in the way in which the female interacts with its sexual partner. Gutiérrez and Domjan (1997) found that females do not approach a signal that has been paired with access to a male. However, conditioned female quail are more likely to squat and permit the male to mount if the male is encountered following exposure to a sexually conditioned stimulus.

Although sexual conditioning in male quail and male gourami typically results in appetitive conditioned responses that occur during the CS, important conditioned changes in responding are also observed to the sexual partner or US in these species as well. Hollis et al. (1997), for example, found that male blue gourami that are allowed to interact with a female after exposure to a sexually conditioned stimulus show less aggression and more clasping behavior with the female, spend more time nest building, and have shorter latencies to spawn. Most significantly, these responses result in the production of more offspring.

Male quail have shorter latencies to copulate after exposure to a conditioned stimulus, which provides an advantage in sexual competition (Gutiérrrez and Domjan, 1996). Male quail also copulate with a female more efficiently if the female is presented following a Pavlovian signal. This copulatory efficiency is evident in the fact that each mounting attempt by the male is more likely to be successful (Mahometa and Domjan, 2005). Copulations that follow exposure to a conditioned stimulus are more likely to result in fertilization of the female's eggs (Adkins-Regan and MacKillop, 2003; Mahometa and Domjan, 2005). These findings indicate that copulatory efficiency and fertilization rate or numbers of offspring produced can be good measures of conditioned sexual behavior.

TYPICAL SEXUAL CONDITIONING PROCEDURE FOR QUAIL

In the remaining section of the chapter, we provide methodological details for conducting sexual conditioning in domesticated quail. In a typical quail sexual conditioning experiment, the first step is to select subjects and partner animals. Quail become sexually mature around 45 days of age. To be sure subjects are sexually mature, we prefer to use animals that are at least 2 months old (Mills et al., 1997). In order to prevent unwanted nonexperimental copulations, male and female birds are separated at 30 days of age, when secondary sexual characteristics are clearly visible. At this point, we house males individually to avoid having them fight with each other. Females are less likely to engage in aggression and can be housed in groups.

Before being selected to participate in an experiment, male quail undergo a pretest trial to assess their sexual competence. In the pretest, a sexually receptive female is introduced into the male's home cage and the two birds are allowed to interact for 5 min. To be considered a viable experimental subject, the male should show at least one full sequence of copulatory behavior: a grab, mount, and cloacal contact. When female quail are used as experimental subjects, the selection criterion is that the female should lay one egg per day on average to ensure sexual maturity.

Once subjects are selected, they go through a phase of habituation, since fear-related behaviors, such as jumping and freezing, are common in novel environments. During the habituation phase, the birds are handled and placed in the experimental chambers repeatedly. If the subjects are going to spend long periods of time in the experimental chambers, food and water should be available.

Experimental chambers are often made of wire mesh and sealed wood, but chambers made of Plexiglas and hardened plastics are good alternatives because of their ease of cleaning and durability. A typical experimental chamber is rectangular, with a wide viewing angle for video recording. If ambient illumination is insufficient for video recording, additional house lights can be put in the chambers. However, if houselights are used, they should always be on when subjects are present to avoid creating confounding variables.

In order to increase experimental control, the partner animal should be placed in the side cage even when no US is going to be introduced on a particular trial, so that the experimental animal does not associate cues (e.g. sounds) coming from the partner animal in the side cage with the US. Similarly, the presence of the experimenter may become a cue for the introduction of US. To prevent this, the researcher or other laboratory personnel should visit the experiment room at random times when the US or sexual partner is not released into the chamber.

In our sexual conditioning experiments, when localized cues, such as a key light or a three dimensional object, are used as conditioned stimuli, they are often presented on one side of the longer length of the rectangular chamber, and the area around the CS is marked as a CS approach zone for data collection (see Figure 4). Whenever the subject enters this area with both feet, it is considered to be in the CS zone. The size or shape of the CS approach area is something the researcher needs to design. However the general principle is that the area around the CS should be big enough to reflect conditioned approach responses, but small enough to minimize accidental, non-CR entries by subjects into the CS zone.

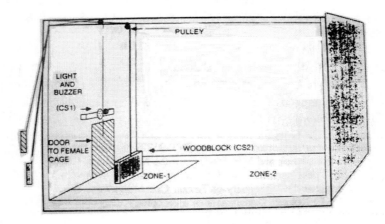

Figure 4. Typical experimental chamber for the study of sexual conditioning in quail. A wood block or a light are provided as potential conditioned stimuli (From Koksal, et al., 1994). Zone 1 identifies approach to the CS. Reprinted with permission from the Psychonomic Society.

The length of CS presentations are often short, 30 seconds to 1 minute, and are followed by the presentation of the US, which is usually a 5 minute opportunity to copulate with an opposite sex conspecific. Partner animals are often placed in smaller side cages during the experiment and are released to the main experimental chamber through a sliding door controlled by the experimenter (see Figure 4). Depending on the experimental procedure, the sliding door can be placed either on the same side of the chamber as the CS or on the opposite side (Burns and Domjan, 1996).

The intertrial interval in sexual conditioning experiments with quail is usually at least one day to ensure high levels of sexual motivation for each trial. When there is enough space, subjects may be left in the experimental chambers throughout the experiment. This is preferable, since it minimizes handling and intervention by the experimenter. But if there are not enough experimental chambers to run all of the subjects at the same time, subjects may be assigned to two different squads that spend alternate days in the experimental chamber. This alternative also provides ample context exposure and minimizes handling of the subjects just before each conditioning trial.

ACKNOWLEDGEMENTS

The preparation of the manuscript was supported by grant MH39940 from the National Institute of Mental Health. We wish to thank Emily Gean for her help with the manuscript.

REFERENCES

Adkins-Regan, E., and MacKillop, E.A. (2003). Japanese quail (*Coturnix japonica*) inseminations are more likely to fertilize eggs in a context predicting mating opportunities. *Proceedings of the Royal Society of London Series B-Biological Sciences, 270,* 1685-1689.

Agmo, A., and Berenfeld, R. (1990). Reinforcing properties of ejaculation in the male rat: The role of opioids and dopamine. *Behavioral Neuroscience. 104,* 177–182.

Akins, C.K., Domjan, M., and Gutiérrez, G. (1994). Topography of sexually conditioned behavior in male Japanese quail (*Coturnix japonica*) depends on the CS-US interval. *Journal of Experimental Psychology: Animal Behavior Processes, 20,* 199-209.

Albert, D. J., Jonik R. H., Gorzalka B.B., and Newlove, T., Webb B, and Walsh M.L. (1991). Serum estradiol concentration required to maintain body-weight, attractivity, proceptivity, and receptivity in the ovariectomized female rat. *Physiology and Behavior, 49,* 225-231

Beach, F., and Jordan, L. (1956). Sexual exhaustion and recovery in the male rat. *Quarterly Journal of Experimental Psychology, 8,* 121-133.

Beach, F. (1976). Sexual attractivity, proceptivity, and receptivity in female mammals. *Hormones and Behavior, 7,* 105-138.

Burns, M., and Domjan, M. (1996). Sign tracking versus goal tracking in the sexual conditioning of male Japanese quail (*Coturnix japonica*). *Journal of Experimental Psychology: Animal Behavior Processes, 22,* 297-306.

Burns-Cusato, M., Cusato, B.M., and Daniel, A. (2005). A new model for sexual conditioning: The ring dove (Streptopelia risoria). *Journal of Comparative Psychology, 119,* 111-116.

Clark, A.S., Kelton, M.C., Guarraci, F.A., and Clyons, E.Q. (2004). Hormonal status and test condition, but not sexual experience, modulate partner preference in female rats. *Hormones and Behavior, 45,* 314-323.

Coria-Avila, G. A., Ouimet, A. J., Pacheco, P., Manzo, J., and Pfaus, J. G. (2005). Olfactory conditioned partner preference in the female rat. *Behavioral Neuroscience, 89,* 716–725.

Crawford, L.L., and Domjan M. (1993). Sexual approach conditioning - omission contingency tests. *Animal Learning and Behavior, 21,* 42-50.

Cusato, B., and Domjan, M. (1998). Special efficacy of sexual conditioned stimuli that include species typical cues: Tests with a CS preexposure design. *Learning and Motivation, 29,* 152-167.

Dawson, A, King, V.M., Bentley, G. E., and Ball, G.F. (2001). Photoperiodic control of seasonality in birds. *Journal of Biological Rhythms, 16,* 365-380.

Delville, Y. and Balthazart, J. (1987). Hormonal control of female sexual behavior in the Japanese quail. *Hormones and Behavior, 21,* 288-309.

Delville, Y., Sulon, J. and Balthazart, J. (1986). Diurnal variations of sexual receptivity in the female Japanese quail Coturnix coturnix japonica. *Hormones and Behavior, 20,* 13-33.

Domjan, M., Lyons, R., North, N. C., and Bruell, J. (1986). Sexual Pavlovian conditioned approach behavior in male Japanese quail (*Coturnix coturnix japonica*). *Journal of Comparative Psychology, 100,* 413-421.

Domjan, M., O'Vary, D., and Greene, P. (1988). Conditioning of appetitive and consummatory sexual behavior in male Japanese quail. *Journal of the Experimental Analysis of Behavior, 50,* 505-519.

Domjan, M., Greene, P., and North, N. C. (1989). Contextual conditioning and the control of copulatory behavior by species-specific sign stimuli in male Japanese quail. *Journal of Experimental Psychology: Animal Behavior Processes, 15,* 147-153.

Domjan, M., Huber-McDonald, M., and Holloway, K. S. (1992). Conditioning copulatory behavior to an artificial object: Efficacy of stimulus fading. *Animal Learning and Behavior, 20,* 350-362.

Domjan, M., Cusato, B., and Krause, M. (2004). Learning with arbitrary versus ecological conditioned stimuli: Evidence from sexual conditioning. *Psychonomic Bulletin and Review, 11,* 232-246.

Dukas, R. (2005). Learning affects mate choice in female fruit flies. *Behavioral Ecology,* 16, 800-804.

Everitt B. J., Fray P, Kostarczyk E., Taylor S., and Stacey P. (1987). Studies of instrumental behavior with sexual reinforcement in male-rats (*rattus-norvegicus*) .1. Control by brief visual-stimuli paired with a receptive female. *Journal of Comparative Psychology, 101,* 395-406.

Fernandez-Guasti A., and Rodriguez-Manzo G. (2003). Pharmacological and physiological aspects of sexual exhaustion in male rats. *Scandinavian Journal of Psychology, 44,* 257-263.

Ferreira-Nuño, A., Morales-Otal, A., Paredes, R.G., and Velázquez-Moctezuma, J. (2005). Sexual behavior of female rats in a multiple-partner preference test. *Hormones and Behavior, 47,* 290-296

Gutierrez, G., and Domjan, M. (1997). Differences in the sexual conditioned behavior of male and female Japanese quail (coturnix japonica). *Journal of Comparative Psychology, 111,* 135-142

Hilliard, S., and Domjan, M. (1995). Effects of sexual conditioning of devaluing the US through satiation. *Quarterly Journal of Experimental Psychology, 48B,* 84-92.

Hilliard, S., Nguyen, M., and Domjan, M. (1997). One-trial appetitive conditioning in the sexual behavior system. *Psychonomic Bulletin and Review, 4,* 237-241.

Hilliard, S., Domjan, M., Nguyen, M., and Cusato, B. (1998). Dissociation of conditioned appetitive and consummatory sexual behavior: Satiation and extinction tests. *Animal Learning and Behavior,* 26, 20-33.

Hollis, K.L., Cadieux, E.L., and Colbert, M.M. (1989). The biological function of Pavlovian conditioning - a mechanism for mating success in the blue gourami (*trichogaster-trichopterus*). *Journal of Comparative Psychology, 103,* 115-121.

Hollis, K.L., Pharr, V.L., Dumas M.J., Britton G.B., and Field, J. (1997). Classical conditioning provides paternity advantage for territorial male blue gouramis (*Trichogaster trichopterus*). *Journal of Comparative Psychology, 111,* 219-225.

Holloway, K. S., and Domjan, M. (1993). Sexual approach conditioning: Unconditioned stimulus factors. *Journal of Experimental Psychology: Animal Behavior Processes, 19*, 38-46.

Hoffmann H., Janssen E., and Turner S.L. (2004). Classical conditioning of sexual arousal in women and men: Effects of varying awareness and biological relevance of the conditioned stimulus. *Archives of Sexual Behavior, 33*, 43-53.

Jacobs, G.H., Fenwick J.A., and Williams, G.A. (2001). Cone-based vision of rats for ultraviolet and visible lights. *The Journal of Experimental Biology, 204*, 2439-2446.

Jenkins, J. (1997). Pavlovian conditioning of sexual behavior in male threespine stickleback (*Gasterosteus aculeatus*). *Behavioural Processes, 41*, 133-137.

Kagan, J. (1955). Differential reward value of incomplete and complete sexual behavior. *Journal of Comparative and Physiological Psychology, 48*, 59-64.

Kippin, T. E., Talinakis, E., Schattmann, L., Bartholomew, S., and Pfaus, J. G. (1998). Olfactory conditioning of sexual behavior in the male rat (*Rattus norvegicus*). *Journal of Comparative Psychology, 112*, 389–399.

Kippin, T. E., and Pfaus, J. G. (2001a). The development of olfactory conditioned ejaculatory preferences in the male rat: I. Nature of the unconditioned stimulus. *Physiology and Behavior, 73*, 457–469.

Kippin, T. E. and Pfaus, J. G. (2001b). The nature of the conditioned response mediating olfactory conditioned ejaculatory preference in the male rat. *Behavioural Brain Research, 122*, 11-24.

Koksal, F., Domjan, M., Kurt, A., Sertel, O., Orung, S., Bowers, R., Kumru, G. (2004). An animal model of fetishism. *Behaviour Research and Therapy, 42*, 1421-1434.

Köksal, F., Domjan, M., and Weisman, G. (1994). Blocking of the sexual conditioning of differentially effective conditioned stimulus objects. *Animal Learning and Behavior, 22*, 103-111.

Lopez H.H., Olster D.H., and Ettenberg, A. (1999). Sexual motivation in the male rat: the role of primary incentives and copulatory experience. *Hormones and Behavior, 36*, 176– 85.

Madlafousek, J., and Hlinak, Z. 1977. Sexual-behavior of female laboratory rat - inventory, patterning, and measurement. *Behaviour, 63*, 129-174.

Mahometa, M. J., and Domjan, M. (2005). Classical conditioning increases reproductive success in Japanese quail, *Coturnix japonica. Animal Behaviour, 69*, 983-989.

Mendelson, S.D., and Gorzalka, B.B. (1987). An improved chamber for the observation and analysis of the sexual-behavior of the female rat. *Physiology and Behavior, 39*, 67-71.

Mendelson, S.D.,and Pfaus, J.G. (1989). Level searching - A new assay of sexual motivation in the male-rat. *Physiology and Behavior, 45*, 337-341.

McBride, S.M.J., Giuliani, G., Choi, C., Krause, P., Correale, D., Watson, K., Baker, G., and Siwicki, K.K. 1999. Mushroom body ablation impairs short-term memory and long-term memory of courtship conditioning in Drosophila melanogaster. *Neuron, 24*, 967-977.

Mills A.D., Crawford L.L., Domjan M., and Faure J.M. 1997. The behavior of the Japanese or domestic quail, Coturnix japonica. *Neuroscience and Biobehavioral Reviews, 21*, 261-281.

Paredes, R. G., and Alonso, A. (1997). Sexual behavior regulated (paced) bythe female induces conditioned place preference. *Behavioral Neuroscience, 111*, 123–128.

Paredes R.G., and Vazquez B. (1999). What do female rats like about sex? Paced mating. *Behavioural Brain Research, 105*, 117-127.

Pfaus, J. G., Mendelson, S. D., and Phillips, A. G. (1990). A correlational and factor analysis of anticipatory and consummatory measures of sexual behavior in the male rat. *Psychoneuroendocrinology, 15,* 329–340.

Pfaus, J.G., Smith, W.J., and Coopersmith, C.B. (1999). Appetitive and consummatory sexual behaviors of female rats in bilevel chambers - I. A correlational and factor analysis and the effects of ovarian hormones. *Hormones and Behavior, 35,* 224-240.

Pfaus, J.G., Kippin, T.E., and Centeno, S. (2001). Conditioning and sexual behavior: A review. *Hormones and Behavior, 40,* 291-321.

Prusky G.T., Harker, K.T., Douglas R.M., and Whishaw I.Q. (2002). Variation in visual acuity within pigmented, and between pigmented and albino rat strains. *Behavioural Brain Research, 136,* 339-348.

Sachs, B.D. (1997). Erection evoked in male rats by airborne scent from estrous females. *Physiology and Behavior, 62,* 921-924.

Sheffield, F.D., Wulff, J.J., and Barker, R. (1951). Reward value of copulation without sex drive reduction. *Journal of Comparative and Physiological Psychology,* 44, 3-8.

Siwicki, K.K., and Ladewski, L. (2003). Associative learning and memory in Drosophila: beyond olfactory conditioning. *Behavioural Processes, 64,* 225-238.

Timberlake W. (2001). Motivational modes in behavior systems. *Handbook of contemporary learning theories,* eds. Mowrer, R.R, Klein, S.B.: 155-209. Mahwah, NJ: Erlbaum.

Van Furth, W. R., and Van Ree, J. M. (1996a). Appetitive sexual behavior in male rats: 1. The role of olfaction in level-changing behavior. *Physiology and Behavior. 60,* 999–1005.

Van Furth, W. R., and Van Ree, J. M. (1996b). Appetitive sexual behavior in male rats: 2. Sexual reward and level-changing behavior. *Physiology and Behavior. 60,* 1007–1012.

Villarreal, R., and Domjan, M. (1998). Pavlovian conditioning of social-affiliative behavior in the Mongolian gerbil (*Meriones unguiculatus*). *Journal of Comparative Psychology, 112,* 26-35.

Whalen, R. E. (1961). Effects of mounting without intromission and intromission without ejaculation on sexual behavior and maze learning. *Journal of Comparative and Physiological Psychology,* 54, 409-415.

Zamble, E., Hadad, G. M., and Mitchell, J. B. (1985). Pavlovian conditioning of sexual arousal: First- and second-order effects. *Journal of Experimental Psychology*: Animal Behavior Processes, 11, 598-610.

In: Tasks and Techniques: A Sampling of the Methodologies...   ISBN 1-60021-126-7
Editor: Matthew J. Anderson, pp. 163-175   © 2006 Nova Science Publishers, Inc.

Chapter 14

METHODS USED IN EYEBLINK CLASSICAL CONDITIONING

Jo Anne Tracy and Joseph E. Steinmetz*
Indiana University, Bloomington, IN 47405

ABSTRACT

Eyeblink classical conditioning has proven very useful for studying behavioral features of simple associative learning as well as the neural correlates of simple learning and memory processes. In this chapter, an overview of the basic behavioral procedures used during eyeblink classical conditioning is presented. In addition, a brief presentation of how variations of the basic paradigms have been used to study the neural correlates of conditioning is provided.

INTRODUCTION

For several decades now eyeblink classical conditioning has attracted attention as a means of studying motor learning and the neural correlates associated with simple associative learning. All mammalian species tested to date show similar patterns of learning this simple behavioral task, as well as similar neural substrates that form the bases for the learning. That is, the learning and memory of eyeblink classical conditioning seems to be dependent on the same brain structures when one looks across mammalian species. (Steinmetz and Woodruff-Pak, 2000).

One structure that is known to be essential for eyeblink conditioning is the cerebellum. Because of this fact, eyeblink conditioning has been well established as a useful tool for assessing the integrity of cerebellar function (Steinmetz, 2000). Other brain regions, such as discrete regions of the brain stem, the hippocampus, the neostriatum, and the amygdala appear to modulate activity generated in the cerebellum to provide the variations in responding that occur when parameters are manipulated or when variations of the basic excitatory conditioning process are undertaken (Lavond and Steinmetz, 2003).

In recent years, there has been increased interest in using eyeblink classical conditioning to study human as well as animal behaviors. It has chiefly been used to assess learning phenomena associated with clinical pathologies (Sears, Finn, and Steinmetz, 1994; Tracy, Ghose, Stecher, McFall, and Steinmetz, 1999), to explore hypothesized differences between declarative and non-declarative memories (Clark, Manns, and Squire, 2001), to answer questions regarding the role of awareness during associative, procedural learning (Clark and Squire, 1999), and, importantly, to bring a clearer understanding of the role of the cerebellum with regard to both motor and cognitive functioning (Woodruff-Pak and Steinmetz, 2000).

Thanks in large part to the efforts of a number of researchers, much is known about behavioral aspects of this type of Pavlovian conditioning (Brandon, Betts, and Wagner, 1994; Gormezano and Kehoe, 1981; Gormezano, Kehoe, and Marshall, 1983; Gormezano, Schneiderman, Deaux, and Fuentes, 1962). For example, optimal training conditions have been determined and the effects of varying key parameters such as inter-stimulus interval length, inter-trial interval timing, conditioned stimulus and unconditioned stimulus intensity, and response timing have been widely researched and delineated (Gormezano et al., 1983; Grevert and Moore, 1970; Kehoe and Napier, 1991). In this chapter, we describe how classical conditioning is accomplished from a methodological standpoint, including a brief discussion of how manipulations of the basic procedure have been used to explore brain function.

THE BASIC DELAY AND TRACE PARADIGMS

There are a number of variations of the basic eyeblink conditioning procedure that have proven useful for studying basic behavioral and neural correlates of associative learning. Regardless of the specific paradigm, though, all eyeblink conditioning involves, at minimum, the paired presentation of a neutral conditioned stimulus (CS), such as a tone or a light, and an unconditioned stimulus (US), such as a mild air puff or sub-dermal shock presented to the region of the eye. The US consistently evokes a reflexive eyeblink, the unconditioned response (UR). Repeated paired presentation of the CS and US pair results in the development of an anticipatory eyeblink response: a blink that precedes and predicts the occurrence of the US. This response is the conditioned response (CR). Unpaired presentations of the CS and the US do not produce CRs and conditioning does not occur if the US is presented before the CS. Also, if after training the CS is presented without the US or if unpaired presentations of the CS and US are given, the anticipatory CR disappears (i.e., behavioral extinction occurs).

The two most popular eyeblink classical conditioning procedures in use today are delay conditioning and trace conditioning. In the delay procedure, perhaps the most commonly employed procedure, the CS and US overlap to some degree at the end of the CS presentation. In trace conditioning, the CS terminates and time elapses before the presentation of the US, thus forcing the subject to form a memory "trace" of the CS because the CS does not overlap

* Address Correspondence to: Joseph E. Steinmetz, Ph.D., University of Kansas, College of Liberal Arts and Sciences, 1450 Jayhawk Blvd, Strong Hall 200, Lawrence, KS, 66045-7535, jsteinmetz@ku.edu.

with the US. These two paradigms have been used extensively to study the function of the cerebellum and hippocampus. It is well established that the cerebellum is necessary for both delay and trace conditioning (Krupa, Thompson, and Thompson, 1993). However, trace conditioning requires not only an intact cerebellum, but a hippocampus as well (Moyer, Deyo, and Disterhoft, 1990). Indeed, because trace conditioning is a bit more difficult to learn and, insofar as it does require the hippocampus, has been used as a model of declarative learning (Kim, Clark, and Thompson, 1995).

One of the very interesting features of eyeblink classical conditioning is that the CR that forms as a result of paired CS and US presentations is incredibly well timed: That is, in a well-trained subject, the peak of the CR occurs at the time when the US is anticipated. This is easily demonstrated by manipulations of the interstimulus interval (ISI), which is defined as the time between CS onset and US onset. The relationship of the conditioning stimuli that define different eyeblink conditioning paradigms, features of timing and stimulus intensity, as well as brief considerations of apparatus and application will be considered here.

COMMON EXPERIMENTAL PARAMETERS FOR EYEBLINK CONDITIONING

The learning curves for acquisition of the conditioned eyeblink response vary a bit with species and with specific features and parameters of the stimuli. Most non-human animals, however, require two or three training sessions to reliably acquire the conditioned response while humans learn the response much quicker. Sessions typically consist of a series of 50 – 120 paired CS-US trials. Figure 1 provides a comparative look at acquisition rates in humans, rabbits and rats.

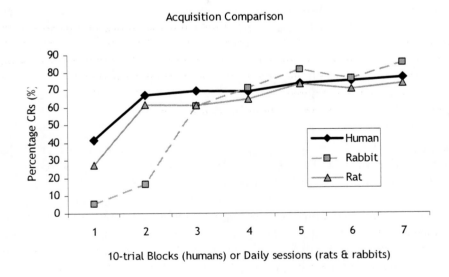

Figure 1. Comparison of learning curves for humans, rabbits and rats. The percentage of CRs increases daily for the animals, reaching an asymptotic level by day 3 of paired training. The human subjects reach an asymptotic level of responding in the first (and often only) day of training by the third block of trials.

DEFINING THE STIMULI USED IN CONDITIONING

The CS

The CS used in eyeblink conditioning is normally a neutral stimulus, which means that when it is presented alone to a naïve animal, no observable behavioral response is seen. In some species, however, such as humans and rats, the presentation of a tone or light CS will produce an orienting response (sometimes referred to as an "alpha" response) that typically disappear over conditioning trials. The CR should be discrete, mainly because eyeblink conditioning studies often measure some aspect of the timing of the CR, either as a reflection of motor learning, or as a correlate to some physiological measure. Accurate determination of the timed response requires the delivery of precisely timed stimuli, which can only be accomplished with a discrete stimulus such as a tone, light, or tactile stimulus. Stimuli with variable onsets and uncontrollable, or those which are difficult to control and deliver (such as olfactory stimuli), make measurement of the timed responses much less reliable and hence are used less often.

A pure tone, delivered at 70 – 90 dB (depending on species) is perhaps the most commonly used CS. Auditory CSs are very effective and work in a range of frequencies, from 700 – 10,000 Hz, depending upon the species being tested. Bursts of white noise are equally effective as CSs. CSs that engage the visual and tactile systems have also proven to be very effective when conditioning. Light CSs may be constructed from light emitting diodes (LEDs) or from incandescent lamps (Tracy, Britton, and Steinmetz, 2001). Tactile CSs have also been used with good results (Lewis, LoTurco, and Solomon, 1987). Vibration applied to the back of the subject via a mechanical stimulating device is effective as a CS for eyeblink conditioning. The rate of conditioning is directly related to strength of the CS. Simply put, the louder tone or the brighter the light, the faster the rate of conditioning. There is an upper limit to the intensity of the CS, however, as very loud tones and very bright lights can produce strong alpha responses that compromise the assumed neutral nature of the CS (Clark and Prokasy, 1976; Moore and Mis, 1973; Scavio and Gormezano, 1974; Smith, 1968; Suboski, 1967).

The US

Two types of USs are typically used during eyeblink conditioning—a gentle puff of air delivered to the cornea of the eye or a mild electric shock that is delivered to the skin surrounding the eye. The air puff US or periorbital shock US are typically strong enough to elicit a reflexive response, though not so strong as to elicit large amounts of fear and anxiety which may introduce competing behaviors that interfere with acquisition of the CR. An air puff US, which is typically used for human or rabbit studies, can range from 3 – 8 psi and are 50-100 ms duration. Periorbital shock USs are most often used in rat and mouse studies. It is important that the type and duration of shock that is used is taken into consideration. For example, a train of short pulses, each about 5 ms wide delivered at approximately 60 pps, makes for a very effective US. As is the case with the CS, the intensity of the US influences the rate of conditioning and the intensity is inversely related to the duration. For example, at

100 ms, a 1.5 mA shock will usually result in robust learning while at shorter durations, such as 25 ms, a 3 mA may be necessary for learning to occur.

Stimulus Timing

In a typical eyeblink conditioning experiment, the CS and US are temporally arranged so that the CS occurs for a short period of time, typically 200 – 1000 ms, and the US occurs for an even shorter period, 25 – 100 ms. One critical feature in determining the rate of conditioning is the ISI; the time between the onsets of the CS and US. The range of effective ISIs for conditioning is 100 ms to 2000 ms. That is, eyeblink conditioning does not occur with ISI less than 100 ms or so or greater than approximately 2000 ms. A well-described inverted-U shaped function describes the ISI training function for all mammals that have been studied (Schneiderman, 1964; Smith, 1968). Thus, it is clear that the length of the ISI plays an important role in a subject's ability to acquire the eyeblink CR. It appears that most species learn best with an ISI of approximately 200-350 ms and demonstrate relatively poor learning when ISI are greater than 1000 ms. Non-human animals tend to learn well with relatively short ISIs while humans can acquire eyeblink CRs quite well upwards of 1200 ms (Clark and Squire, 1998). However, long ISIs can pose problems in human conditioning experiments in that cognitive factors come into play in the conditioning process.

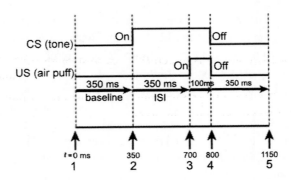

Figure 2. Trial stimuli timing parameters for a typical delay conditioning experiment: 1) Trial onset, which is the beginning of the recording period for the response, 2) CS onset, which occrs 350 ms after trial onset; 3) US onset, which occurs 350 ms after and 700 ms after trial onet; 4) CS and US offset when the two stimuli co-terminated (450 ms after CS onset and 800 msec after trial onset and; 5) Trial offset, which occurs 1150 ms after trial onset.

Trial Timing

Conditioning sessions typically consist of a series of discrete trials, the length of which are determined in part by the stimulus parameters. In general, a single trial will consist of three parts: 1) an initial blank baseline period before CS onset when baseline eyeblinking rate can be established as well as the relative position of the eyeblink; 2) the CS period, which is the time between CS onset and US onset. During this time anticipatory CRs are found and scored; and 3) the US period, defined as the time from US onset to the end of the trial-scoring period, when measurements concerning the topography of the US can be taken. Using a 350 ms CS, and a 100 ms US, a typical eyeblink conditioning trial may consist of the parameters illustrated in Figure 2.

Session Length

Setting the number of trials that are delivered in a daily training session is very important because this number combined with the intertrial interval (ITI) defines the session length. In a typical daily session, 60-120 trials are delivered. In general, rabbits take upwards of 200 trials to reach criterion while rats often condition in 70 – 100 trials and humans require only 60 or fewer trials to reach criterion (see Figure 1). Individual trials are relatively short, one or 2 seconds long, but the time between trials, the inter-trial interval (ITI), requires careful consideration. Eyeblink studies that have systematically varied the ITI show that at least 10 s is required between trials for eyeblink conditioning to succeed (Nordholm, Lavond, and Thompson, 1991). If the inter-trial interval (ITI) is too short conditioning will be delayed or may not occur at all. Indeed, there are suggestions in the literature that suggest that the ITI should be at least 1.5 times the ISI to support learning (Rescorla, 1988). In general, the ratio of ITI to ISI may be inversely proportional with the number of trials required for learning to occur (Gallistel and Gibbon, 2000). For example, with an ISI of 500 ms, the subject being trained at 30 s ITI will reach a learning criterion faster than one being trained at 10 s ITI. We have observed that an even greater ratio is required for discrimination learning, a type of learning that requires responding to one CS but not another (see below). The minimum ITI : ISI ratio required for learning to occur in a simple delay paradigm often is not sufficient to support learning in a discrimination-type paradigm.

While the ITI should be as long as possible, it is often desirable to keep the entire session under 60 – 90 minutes. Increasing the number of trials/session necessarily decreases the ITI. Hence, a session that consists of 80 trials of two seconds each could employ an ITI up to 40 s each while a session that consists of 120 trials of two seconds each would have to keep the ITI under 30 s. Furthermore, in order to minimize the possibility of temporal conditioning, the exact ITI should be somewhat randomized to within +/- 10 s so that the CS onset is not predictable based on timing alone. In the first example of 80 trials, the ISI would vary between 30 and 50 s, with a mean ITI of 40 s.

MEASURING THE EYEBLINK RESPONSE

As important as stimulus and temporal control are in eyeblink conditioning, precise measurements of the eyeblink CR and UR are critical. A number of approaches for quantifying eyeblink responses are readily available, including electromyographic (EMG) recording, mechanical methods (e.g., using variable-resistance minitorque potentiometers), and light-spectral detection devices (e.g., infrared emitter-detector systems). Each of these systems measures a slightly different aspect of the eyeblink response, but all seem to be highly correlated.

EMG recordings are typically taken from the obicularis oculi muscles around the eye by imbedding small, large-impedance wires into the musculature and measuring the electrical activity of the muscles. This method is most desirable for kinematic studies in which precise measurement of the eye-blinking musculature response is desired. Variable-resistance potentiometers were traditionally used to measure the movement of the rabbit nictitating membrane (NM), which retracts across the eyeball passively as the eye retracts into the socket in preparation of a blink. The optical measurement systems, such as infrared emitter/detector and photodiode systems, are non-invasive measures that respond to changes in the light reflectance or absorption as the eyelid crosses the subjects' eye, a technique that works equally well in both human and rabbit subjects (Lavond and Steinmetz, 2003).

All the measurement techniques described above quantify the eyeblink response in terms of voltages and voltage changes over time. Features that result from these changes can be used to describe conditioning and can be analyzed to determine the rate and efficacy of conditioning under varying experimenter manipulations. Typically, the descriptors used for eyeblink conditioning include the overall percentage of trials in which a CR occurred (percent CRs), the amplitude of the blinks, and timing features such as onset latency (defined as the time from CS onset to the beginning of the CR) and peak latency (defined as the time from CS onset to the CR's maximum amplitude) of the blinks.

How much eyelid movement is required for a blink to be recognized and defined? Most species blink spontaneously at relatively high rates. The exception to this is the rabbit, a species with an exceptionally low rate of spontaneous blinking, making it an ideal subject for measuring conditioned eyeblink responses. There is little or no ambiguity in determining a when a blink occurs in rabbits, as they do not show alpha responses, or any kind of response for that matter, to the CS before it becomes conditioned. Hence, any variation from baseline, the level of blink activity occurring in the period preceding the CS, can be considered significant.

Other species are not so cooperative when it comes to defining what constitutes a blink. Both rats and humans blink frequently, and those blinks are likely to show up at any time during a conditioning session complicating the reliable determination of a conditioned response. There are studies examining the kinematics of spontaneous vs. non-spontaneous blinks, and descriptors for differentiating voluntary from involuntary blinks as well (Gruart, Blazquez, and Delgado-Garcia, 1994; Ojakangas and Ebner, 1994; Welsh, 1992). However, one need not go to such lengths to determine the presence of conditioned eyeblink responses. A few rules-of-thumb seem to suffice.

First, a conditioned response can be determined statistically. Within-animal rates of spontaneous blink activity tend to be fairly constant, so that a conditioned response can be considered on the basis of variation from baseline: A number of standard deviations beyond that baseline mean or median can be used to define a CR. Second, conditioned responses are constrained by experimenter-controlled variables. A conditioned response, by definition, must occur within some interval around the ISI. Hence, a CR cannot occur prior to the CS. Nor, for physiological reasons, can one occur within the first 30 ms or so following the onset of the CS. Blinks that occur just prior to or just after the onset of the CS are typically classified as "Bad Trials" – trials in which a spontaneous blink was already in progress at the time of stimulus presentation. These trials are not scored for CRs or URs and are excluded from analyses.

Third, the topography of a conditioned response changes over time. In particular, CR amplitude increases as training progresses and this increase is in general inversely proportional to the unconditioned reflexive responses. Some species produce alpha responses, startle, or orienting responses to the CS. The alpha response is unconditioned and, like the UR, tends to diminish over time. As the CR increases in frequency and amplitude, the UR and the alpha response (if present) decrease in amplitude. Figure 3 serves to illustrate the course of conditioning for a single human subject. These particular data were collected optically using an infrared eyeblink detection system. The top trace shows the average blink response for the first 10 training trials. The trace indicates voltages measured over time, in this case, 1.5 seconds. The upward deflection of the line indicates increased voltages as a result of eyelid closure. Following the CS onset, indicated by the first vertical line, an alpha response is clearly present. There is no other blink activity on this first block of trials until the US is presented, indicated by the second vertical line, followed closely by the UR. Note as conditioning progresses, the amplitude of the alpha and unconditioned responses decrease, although the timing of those responses remains constant, occurring reliably at 20 - 30 ms after stimulus onset. In contrast, the conditioned response becomes apparent in the second block of trials and gradually increases in amplitude over the remaining trials. By the final block of training (bottom trace), the CR is well developed and almost indistinguishable from the UR. The alpha response is almost entirely absent.

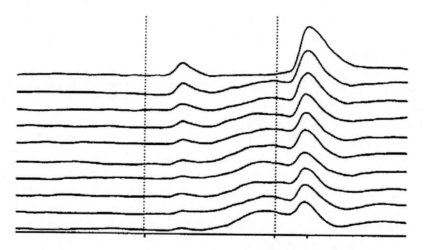

Figure 3. Plot of average blink activity for each block of ten trials. The top trace represents the average blink for the first 10 trials; the second trace the second 10 trials, etc. The vertical lines indicate CS onset and US onset respectively.

SOME PARADIGM VARIATIONS AND FUTURE DIRECTIONS

Over the years, variations of the basic delay and trace procedures have been used to study behavioral and neural function. Discrimination/reversal learning has been used to study inhibitory learning and the role of the hippocampus in conditioning (Churchill, Voss, Miller, Steinmetz, and Garraghty, 1998; Miller and Steinmetz, 1997). During discrimination learning, two CSs are used (such as tones of two different intensities). One CS is followed by the US while the second CS is presented in isolation. Subjects learn to respond to the reinforced CS and not to respond to the other CS. Reversal learning is simply the switching of the roles of the two CSs and the subsequent response acquisition to the new reinforced CS and inhibition of responding to the previously reinforced CS. Discrimination training using two different ISIs (signaled by two different CSs) has been recently employed to study the behavioral and neural correlates of CR timing (Green and Steinmetz, 2005)

Latent inhibition and blocking are procedures that have been used frequently to study the behavioral and neural correlates of inhibitory learning (Garcia and Mauk, 1998; Giftakis and Tait, 1998; Katz, Rogers, and Steinmetz, 2002; Schmajuk, Lam, and Christiansen, 1994; Solomon and Moore, 1975). In latent inhibition, several presentations of the CS alone are given prior to paired CS and US trials. The net effect of the CS alone presentations is to retard the rate of learning compared to subjects who are exposed to the training context but not pre-exposed to the CS.

The blocking procedure is a bit more complicated. Subjects are first given extensive paired training with a CS and US (e.g., a tone and air puff) so that the CS reliably elicits the CR. In the next stage, subjects are given training with a compound CS consisting of the original CS and a novel one (e.g., a tone CS and a light CS together) with the US. In the third stage, the second CS (i.e., the light) is presented by itself and CR generation noted. What is typically found is that responding to the second CS is low or not existent during the test phase. In other words, CRs to the second CS are blocked when in compound with the first CS, even though the second CS was paired with the US.

Varying the basic eyeblink conditioning procedure such as in trace, discrimination and blocking experiments has proven useful for exploring brain function. While this topic is beyond the scope of this chapter, an example will suffice to make this point. We recognize that the cerebellum is critical for the acquisition and performance of all motor CRs that are expressed. Other brain areas appear to become involved in eyeblink conditioning as the paradigm becomes more complex. As already noted, there is much evidence that trace conditioning requires an intact hippocampus, perhaps to account for the trace memory period that exists between CS offset and US onset (Beylin et al., 2001; James, Hardiman, and Yeo, 1987). There is also evidence that the hippocampus is involved in discrimination/reversal learning, perhaps contributing to overall contextual processing (Miller and Steinmetz, 1997). While blocking does not seem to be hippocampal-dependent, pre-cerebellar areas of the brain appear to play a fundamental role in the inhibitory process (Allen, Padilla, Myers, and Gluck, 2002; Nicholson and Freeman, 2002). Recent data suggests that the amygdala plays a major role in encoding fear and aversive aspects of the conditioning process (Rorick-Kehn and Steinmetz, 2005). Our major point here is that the variations of the basic eyeblink conditioning procedures have generated a rich data set concerning how the brain encodes the conditioning process. We predict many more discoveries in the future as this paradigm is used in additional experiments.

CONCLUSION

We have presented a relatively brief overview of the behavioral methods used in eyeblink classical conditioning experiments and a very brief mention of how the procedure has been used to study neural correlates of associative learning. For a more in-depth treatment of this subject, interested readers are directed to Lavond and Steinmetz's 2003 book, "Handbook of Classical Conditioning," which provides more details on eyeblink conditioning and its use to study behavioral and neural correlates of associative learning.

REFERENCES

Allen, M. T., Padilla, Y., Myers, C. E., and Gluck, M. A. (2002). Selective hippocampal lesions disrupt a novel cue effect but fail to eliminate blocking in rabbit eyeblink conditioning. *Cognitive, Affective and Behavioral Neuroscience, 2*(4), 318-328.

Beylin, A. V., Gandhi, C. C., Wood, G. E., Talk, A. C., Matzel, L. D., and Shors, T. J. (2001). The role of the hippocampus in trace conditioning: Temporal discontinuity or task difficulty? *Neurobiology of Learning and Memor, 76*(3), 447-461.

Brandon, S. E., Betts, S. L., and Wagner, A. R. (1994). Discriminated lateralized eyeblink conditioning in the rabbit: An experimental context for separating specific and general associative influences. *Journal of Experimental Psychology: Animal Behavior Processes, 20*(3), 292-307.

Churchill, J. D., Voss, S. E., Miller, D. P., Steinmetz, J. E., and Garraghty, P. E. (1998). Phenytoin blocks the reversal of a classically conditioned discriminative eyeblink response in rabbits. *Epilepsia, 39*(6), 584-589.

Clark, C. G., and Prokasy, W. F. (1976). Manipulation of response-contingent unconditioned-stimulus intensity in human eyelid conditioning: A two-phase model analysis. *Memory and Cognition, 4*(3), 277-282.

Clark, R. E., and Squire, L. R. (1998). Classical conditioning and brain systems: The role of awareness. *Science, 280*, 77-81.

Clark, R. E., and Squire, L. R. (1999). Human eyeblink classical conditioning: Effects of manipulating awareness of the stimulus contingencies. *Psychological Science, 10*(1), 14-18.

Clark, R. E., Manns, J. R., and Squire, L. R. (2001). Trace and delay eyeblink conditioning: Contrasting phenomena of declarative and nondeclarative memory. *Psychological Science, 12*(4), 304-308.

Gallistel, C. R., and Gibbon, J. (2000). Time, rate, and conditioning. *Psychological Review, 107*(2), 2890344.

Garcia, K. S., and Mauk, M. D. (1998). Pharmacological analysis of cerebellar contributions to the timing and expression of conditioned eyelid responses. *Neuropharmacology, 37*(4-5), 471-480.

Giftakis, J. E., and Tait, R. W. (1998). Blocking of the rabbit's classically conditioned nictitating membrane response: Effects of modifications of contextual associative strength. *Learning and Motivation, 29*(1), 23-48.

Gormezano, I., and Kehoe, E. J. (1981). Classical conditioning and the law of contiguity. In P. Harzem and M. D. Zeiler (Eds.), *Predictability, Correlation, and Contiguity* (pp. 1-45). New York: John Wiley and Sons.

Gormezano, I., Kehoe, E. J., and Marshall, B. S. (1983). Twenty years of clasical conditioning with the rabbit. *Progress in Psychobiology and Physiological Psychology, 10*, 197-275.

Gormezano, I., Schneiderman, N., Deaux, E., and Fuentes, I. (1962). Nictitating membrane: classical conditioning and extinction in the albino rabbit. *Science, 138*, 33-34.

Green, J. T., and Steinmetz, J. E. (2005). Purkinje cell activity in the cerebellar anterior lobe after rabbit eyeblink conditioning. *Learning & Memory, 12*(3), 260-269.

Grevert, P., and Moore, J. W. (1970). The effect of unpaired US presentations on conditioning of the rabbit's nictitating membrane response: consolidation or contingency. *Psychonomic Science, 20*, 177-179.

Gruart, A., Blazquez, P., and Delgado-Garcia, J. M. (1994). Kinematic analyses of classically-conditioned eyelid movements in the cat suggest a brain stem site for motor learning. *Neuroscience Letters, 175*, 81-84.

James, G. O., Hardiman, M. J., and Yeo, C. H. (1987). Hippocampal lesions and trace conditioning in the rabbit. *Behavioural Brain Research, 23*(2), 109-116.

Katz, D. B., Rogers, R. F., and Steinmetz, J. E. (2002). Novel factors contributing to the expression of latent inhibition. *Behavioral Neuroscience, 116*(5), 824-836.

Kehoe, E. J., and Napier, R. M. (1991). Temporal specificity in cross-modal transfer of the rabbit nictitating membrane responses. *Journal of Experimental Psychology*, 26-35.

Kim, J. J., Clark, R. E., and Thompson, R. F. (1995). Hippocampectomy impairs the memory of recently, but not remotely, acquired trace eyeblink conditioned responses. *Behavioral Neuroscience, 109*(2), 195-203.

Krupa, D. J., Thompson, J. K., and Thompson, R. F. (1993). Localization of a memory trace in the mammalian brain. *Science, 260*, 989-991.

Lavond, D. G., and Steinmetz, J. E. (2003). *Handbook of Classical Conditioning*. Boston: Kluwer Academic Publishing.

Lewis, J. L., LoTurco, J. J., and Solomon, P. R. (1987). Lesions of the middle cerebellar peduncle disrupt acquisition and retention of the rabbit's classically conditioned nictitating membrane response. *Behavioral Neuroscience, 101*(2), 151-157.

Miller, D. P., and Steinmetz, J. E. (1997). Hippocampal activity during classical discrimination-reversal eyeblink conditioning in rabbits. *Behavioral Neuroscience, 111*(1), 70-79.

Moore, J. W., and Mis, F. W. (1973). Differential conditioning along two dimensions and stimulus generalization of the rabbit's nictitating membrane response. *Bulletin of the Psychonomic Society, 1*(2), 123-125.

Moyer, J. R., Deyo, R. A., and Disterhoft, J. F. (1990). Hippocampectomy disrupts trace eye-blink conditioning in rabbits. *Behavioral Neuroscience, 104*, 243-252.

Nicholson, D. A., and Freeman, J. H., Jr. (2002). Medial dorsal thalamic lesions impair blocking and latent inhibition of the conditioned eyeblink response in rats. *Behavioral Neuroscience, 116*(2), 276-285.

Nordholm, A. F., Lavond, D. G., and Thompson, R. F. (1991). Are eyeblink respones to tone in the decerebrate, decerebellate rabbit conditioned responses? *Behavioral Brain Research, 44*, 27-34.

Ojakangas, C. L., and Ebner, T. (1994). Purkinje cell complex spike activity during voluntary motor learning: Relationship to kinematics. *Journal of Neurophysiology, 72*(6), 2617-2630.

Rescorla, R. A. (1988). Behavioral studies of Pavlovian conditioning. *Annual Review of Neuroscience, 11*, 329-352.

Rorick-Kehn, L. M., and Steinmetz, J. E. (2005). Amygdalar unit activity during three learning tasks: Eyeblink classical conditioning, Pavlovian fear conditioning, and signaled avoidance conditioning. *Behavioral Neuroscience, 119*(5), 1254-1276.

Scavio, M. J., and Gormezano, I. (1974). CS intensity effects on rabbit nictitating membrane conditioning, extinction and generalization. *Pavlovian Journal of Biological Science, 9*(1), 25-34.

Schmajuk, N. A., Lam, Y.-W., and Christiansen, B. A. (1994). Latent inhibition of the rat eyeblink response: Effect of hippocampal aspiration lesions. *Physiology and Behavior, 55*(3), 597-601.

Schneiderman, N. (1964). Interstimulus interval function of the nictitating membrane response of the rabbit under delay versus trace conditioning. *Journal of Comparative and Physiological Psychology, 57*(2), 188-195.

Sears, L. L., Finn, P. R., and Steinmetz, J. E. (1994). Abnormal classical eye-blink conditioning in autism. *Journal of Autism and Developmental Disorders, 24*(6), 737-751.

Smith, M. C. (1968). CS-US interval and US intensity in classical conditioning of the rabbit's nictitating membrane response. *Journal of Comparative and Physiological Psychology, 66*(3), 679-687.

Solomon, P. R., and Moore, J. W. (1975). Latent inhibition and stimulus generalization of the classically conditioned nictitating membrane response in rabbits (Oryctolagus cuniculus) following dorsal hippocampal ablation. *Journal of Comparative and Physiological Psychology, 89*(10), 1192-1203.

Steinmetz, J. E. (2000). Brain substrates of classical eyeblink conditioning: A highly localized but also distributed system. *Behavioural Brain Research, 110*(1-2), 13-24.

Steinmetz, J. E., and Woodruff-Pak, D. S. (2000). Animal Models in Eyeblink Classical Conditioning. In D. S. Woodruff-Pak and J. E. Steinmetz (Eds.), *Eyeblink Classical Conditioning: Volume II Animal Models*. Norwell, Massachusetts: Kluwer Academic Publishers.

Suboski, M. D. (1967). UCS intensity and the latency of the classically conditioned eyelid response. *Journal of Experimental Psychology, 74*(1), 31-35.

Tracy, J. A., Britton, G. B., and Steinmetz, J. E. (2001). Comparison of single unit responses to tone, light, and compound conditioned stimuli during rabbit classical eyeblink conditioning. *Neurobiology of Learning and Memory, 76*(3), 253-267.

Tracy, J. A., Ghose, S. S., Stecher, T., McFall, R. M., and Steinmetz, J. E. (1999). Classical conditioning in a nonclinical obsessive-compulsive population. *Psychological Science, 10*(1), 9-13.

Welsh, J. P. (1992). Changes in the motor pattern of learned and unlearned responses following cerebellar lesions: a kinematic analysis of the nictitating membrane reflex. *Neuroscience, 47*, 1-19.

Woodruff-Pak, D. S., and Steinmetz, J. E. (2000). *Eyeblink Classical Conditioning: Volume I Applications in Humans*. Boston: Kluwer Academic Publishers.

PART III. SOCIAL AND COGNITIVE ISSUES

In: Tasks and Techniques: A Sampling of the Methodologies...   ISBN 1-60021-126-7
Editor: Matthew J. Anderson, pp. 177-187   © 2006 Nova Science Publishers, Inc.

Chapter 15

THE RESIDENT-INTRUDER PARADIGM: AN ANIMAL MODEL OF AGGRESSIVE BEHAVIOR AND SOCIAL STRESS

Elizabeth E. Caldwell[*]
Tufts University, Medford, MA 02155

ABSTRACT

Behavioral scientists have employed a variety of methodologies to examine aggressive behavior in animals over the past several decades. Many laboratory protocols offer sound techniques for examining at least some forms of aggression, but are limited either in their scope of aggressive behaviors measured, lack experimental flexibility, or have proved inadequate in their ability to generalize findings to other subject populations. For these reasons, the most widely used naturalistic paradigm for studying aggressive behavior in animals is the resident-intruder paradigm. The resident-intruder paradigm is a laboratory protocol that has developed over time to become an excellent tool for behavioral scientists interested in a variety of intraspecific agonistic and social behavior. Both male and female aggressive behavior can be studied using the resident-intruder design, and the protocol may be used to study multiple species of rodents, fish, spiders, and pigs, among others. The present chapter will introduce the basic aims and applications of the resident-intruder paradigm, and will outline the specific procedures routinely used for aggression research. Although the resident-intruder protocol is useful for studying multiple species and also female aggressive behavior, the main focus of this chapter is on intermale rodent (i.e. rat and mouse) aggression, which represents, to date, the most frequently studied subject population using this design.

[*] Contact Info: Elizabeth E. Caldwell, Address: 530 Boston Ave, Medford MA 02155, Phone: 617.627.5465, Fax: 617.627.3939, Email: Beth.Caldwell@tufts.edu

INTRODUCTION

One major issue invariably arises when designing an animal model of motivated behavior with the goal of understanding human mental health. The primary concern is whether a laboratory can elicit a naturally-occurring behavior in animals that is also representative of maladaptive behavior in humans. Aggression is a motivated behavior which is often viewed as socially maladroit in human beings. However, in animals normative levels of aggressive behavior can be evolutionarily stable, termed as such because aggression can serve to protect highly-valued resources and increase potential for reproductive success. The study of aggressive behavior and defeat is important for identifying therapeutic interventions for human populations adversely affected by violence and other social stressors. Animal models of aggression and social stress offer contributions to the study of human populations because social stress is an unavoidable component of the human experience. Indeed, applications of community social services often target individuals subjected to chronic social stressors like poverty, racism, drug abuse, domestic violence, and child abuse. Although a broad variety of techniques have been employed over the last few decades to study aggressive behavior in animals, it has been difficult to elicit aggressive behavior in animal populations that adequately models pathological violence in humans.

The study of aggressive behavior in nonhuman animals has been conducted using several different animal models, each methodology designed to provide a detailed analysis of a particular ethological behavior. For many years, aggression protocols were chosen based on the particular behavior of interest. In 1968, K. E. Moyer published a paper called "Kinds of aggression and their physiological basis," in which he outlined seven distinct types of agonistic behavior: irritable, territorial, maternal, instrumental, predatory, inter-male, and fear-induced, and later Moyer (1976) added sexual aggression. Moyer's taxonomy generated considerable controversy for many reasons. Many of the motivated behaviors had a good deal of overlap with other categories, some researchers argued that all aggressive behaviors have an instrumental basis, and some aggressive behaviors were necessarily excluded (e.g., paternal). Classifications such as "irritable" and "fear-induced" essentially implied an emotional etiology of aggressive behavior, which is difficult to assess in animal experimentation. At the center of the debate is the fact that the term "aggression" refers to several various complex behaviors, and identifying an exact construct for a sound experiment is an important obstacle for any behavioral scientist (see Brain, 1994, for a detailed discussion).

Animal models of aggression developed over time that took advantage of certain naturally-occurring behaviors which could be readily elicited in laboratories. Maternal aggression protocols (e.g. Al-Maliki, Brain, Childs, and Benton, 1979) were developed to study female aggression, shock-induced aggression was designed to study reflexive pain-induced aggression (Ulrich, 1966; Viken and Knutson, 1992), isolation-induced aggression attempted to model the effect of stress from social deprivation (see Brain, 1975, for a critique of isolation-induced stress), and irritable aggression was examined using frustration- or schedule-induced aggression paradigms (de Almeida and Miczek, 2002).

 Over time, several problems arose with many of the existing animal aggression designs. For example, shock-induced aggression was used extensively for many years, but major criticisms existed over confounds inherent in this method. Some researchers argued that aggression elicited by shock was actually an artifact of the laboratory technique. Upon the initiation of shock, animals predictably reared upright on their hindpaws and directed bites and forepaw blows toward the head of the other animal. Once the shock terminated, the animals ceased their fighting behavior (see Ulrich, 1966; also Viken and Knutson, 1992, for reviews). This topography of fighting ("boxing" with the opponent) did not resemble normative intermale fighting. Although the factors associated with aggression measured using this method were well correlated with other more naturalistic approaches, other problems remained difficult to resolve. For example, onset and termination of shock resulted in positive and negative reinforcement of fighting behavior, and the possibility existed that both cooperative escape and fighting behavior occurred simultaneously (Ulrich 1967; 1969; see Viken and Knutson, 1992). The resident-intruder paradigm (Miczek, 1979) emerged as a new protocol which avoided specific problems that arose with this and other methodologies.

The resident-intruder paradigm entails the introduction of an animal (the "intruder) into the home cage of a conspecific animal (the "resident") for the purpose of measuring social and agonistic behaviors. This protocol is used by researchers studying a broad range of species including pigs (D'Eath and Pickup, 2002), hamsters (Potegal, Ferris, Hebert, Meyerhoff, and Skaredoff, 1996), fish (Hollis, Dumas, Singh and Fackelman, 1995), spiders (Moya-Larano, Orta-Ocana, Barrientos, Bach, and Wise, 2002), mice and rats (Miczek, 1979). The overall objectives of the protocol are to identify and examine social and agonistic behaviors typical for the species of interest in the most naturalistic setting possible. The range of uses for the protocol include the study of normative aggression in males or females, social and affiliative behavior (Bielsky and Young, 2004), territorial behavior (Bartolomucci, et al., 2005; Bielsky and Young, 2004), and defeat or social stress (Bartolomucci et al., 2005; Nikulina, Covington, Ganschow, Hammer, and Miczek, 2004). Importantly, the use of the resident-intruder paradigm has allowed researchers to identify differences between dominant and submissive animals with respect to behavioral, physiological, or neurological outcomes of agonistic encounters (Ebner, Wotjak, Landgraf, and Engelmann, 2005; Oyegbile and Marler, 2005; Tornatzky, Cole, and Miczek, 1998; van Erp and Miczek, 2000) or repeated episodes of social defeat stress (Bartolomucci et al., 2005; Nikulina et al., 2004; Rygula et al., 2005; Tidey and Miczek, 1996).

Animal models of escalated, pathological aggressive behavior, such as frustration- induced and social instigation of aggressive behavior (de Almeida and Miczek, 2002) and the identification of aggressive behavioral phenotypes in mice (see Miczek, Maxson, Fish, and Faccidomo, 2001), have emerged in recent years which incorporate the resident-intruder paradigm into their methodologies. Fish, DeBold and Miczek (2002) developed an elegant protocol that measures animals' motivation to perform operant responses rewarded by the opportunity to fight an intruder. Such uses of the resident-intruder methodology have given the study of aggressive behavior a broader range of clinical applications, most notably in the field of psychopharmacology. Research using animal models of aggression and social defeat are currently being used to identify neurobiological and pharmacological targets aimed at reducing escalated aggressive behavior. Such research may be useful for identifying behavioral interventions and pharmacological treatments that will alleviate suffering associated with violence and related behavioral disorders in human clinical populations.

METHODS

Animals

Miczek (1979) originally used small colonies of rats, each consisting of two males and two females. A colony model may be useful if the experiment specifically compares behavior between dominant and subordinate males. However, confounds of group housing with more than one male can arise due to differences that emerge in dominant-subordinate dyads. Most experiments today use one resident male living in a single male-female breeding pair, and an intruder housed in isolation, same-sex pairs, or same-sex groups of 3 or more animals.

Both resident and intruder animals used in the resident-intruder paradigm must be sexually mature adults, and it is essential that all animals serving as subjects (resident or intruder) be reared under identical housing conditions, as prior social experience will affect later aggressiveness (see Brain and Kamal, 1989; Oyegbile and Marler, 2005). The ideal age for a resident rat at the onset of the experiment is five months old (see de Boer, van der Vegt, and Koolhaas, 2003, for discussion). Resident rats should be at least one month older than intruders, and should outweigh intruders by approximately 25%. If intruders are too large/small, or too old/young relative to residents, normative aggressive behavior tends to decline. Although mouse aggression is less likely than that of rats to be affected by intruder size, larger, older intruder mice may be more likely to attack a resident. Thus, younger intruders are also ideal when using mouse models.

Home Cage Residency

Breeding Pairs

Resident males should cohabitate in breeding pairs for at least 21 days, the minimum duration necessary for a pair to produce a litter. This minimum time-frame is ideal because aggressive behavior is most likely to emerge and quickly reach stable levels if animals cohabitate for a full breeding cycle. Because animals are kept in breeding pairs, litter control is an important ethical issue when using the resident-intruder paradigm. Litters may be culled at weaning age if the breeding pairs are housed with adequate space and husbandry practices. However, if space is limited or animals are on food or water restriction, the experimenter may consider performing a fallopian tube ligation or partial hysterectomy (removal of uterus only while ovaries remain intact) to prevent pregnancy in females cohabitating with resident males. Some experimenters have conducted research only on males in the breeding colonies of their laboratory to avoid the problem of unwanted litters. Research employing male or female mice as residents may benefit from leaving litters intact until weaning, since reproductive success has been shown to be a factor influencing aggressive behavior of mice (Palanza, Della Seta, Ferrari, and Parmigiani, 2005). Importantly, each experimenter should consult with the animal facilities' veterinarian and Institutional Animal Care and Use Committee to determine the most appropriate method for litter control prior to initiation of the experiment.

Cage Characteristics

The resident-intruder paradigm necessarily requires all aggression testing to be performed in the home cage of the resident male. Most laboratories house mice in polypropylene cages (11½" x 7½" x 5"), which provide adequate space, both for housing breeding pairs and for aggression testing. However, if the experimenter has chosen one of several rat strains for experimentation, it is highly recommended that the male-female dyad be housed in a larger cage than current husbandry guidelines requires. Increasing the size of the resident's living quarters will ensure that each agonistic encounter represents behaviors typically demonstrated under naturalistic conditions, and allows experimenters to view the full spectrum of social and aggressive behaviors exhibited during confrontations. Feral rats (Rattus rattus) observed in their natural habitat have been found to live in extensive burrow systems with long tunnel-like runs, and burrows are occupied by multiple colony members (Pye, Swain, and Seppelt, 1999). Thus, a typical resident-intruder confrontation is likely to result in an attack and chase, while the intruder or subordinate male has the ability to flee or, alternatively, display submissive appeasement signals. If the laboratory cages used have insufficient space, crowding becomes a serious consideration because normative social behaviors are compromised.

In addition to size requirements, resident cage substrate at the time of aggression testing must be sufficiently soiled. Urine and other scent marking is essential for the establishment of home cage residency (Brown, 1992). Rats and mice each have specific ways of scent-marking, wherein animals deposit various odors (e.g., urine, preputial gland secretions) which help convey territoriality (Gawienowski et al., 1976; Gray and Hurst, 1995). Clean cages or new sawdust/bedding can add ambiguity to established residency, and subsequently reduce a resident's ability to quickly signal dominance (Brown, 1992; Mink and Adams, 1981). This is also important when studying social defeat stress because each exposure to the resident male should have consistent levels of stimulus odors across testing sessions.

Generally, 48 hours between cage cleaning and aggression testing is sufficient, but experimenters may choose to wait longer or control home-cage odors by partial cleanings on a semi-daily basis. David Riccio and I examined aggressive behavior after cage cleanings in our laboratory (unpublished observations, 2001), and found that attack latencies were increased when soiled substrate was replaced. Attack latencies increased further when animals were tested one hour after being replaced in newly cleaned cages (i.e., clean, polycarbonate cages, cage tops, water bottles, and fresh substrate). Furthermore, number of biting attacks made by the residents were significantly lower when animals were tested in clean cages compared to those tested in soiled cages (See Figure). Mice are highly sensitive to changes in housing substrate, often exhibiting home-cage aggression following even partial cleanings (Gray and Hurst, 1995). Therefore, mice need to be given ample time to adjust to any substrate changes before aggression testing commences.

Resident Aggressive
Behavior by Substrate Condition

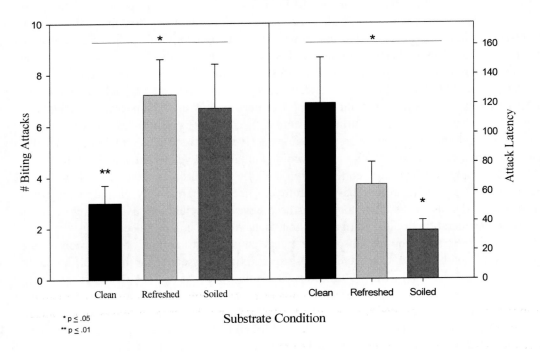

Figure: Caldwell and Riccio (unpublished data, 2001). Kent State University. Resident male rats demonstrated more aggressive behavior when tested in soiled home cages than when tested in refreshed (new sawdust, soiled polypropylene shell) or clean cages, as evidenced by greater attack frequencies ($F_{(2,27)}$ = 3.269, p = .05) and shorter latencies ($F_{(2,27)}$ = 4.331, p = .02). Post-hoc tests showed animals tested in clean cages had lower attack frequencies compared to animals tested in either soiled or refreshed cages, and animals tested in soiled cages had lower attack latencies compared to those tested in clean cages (all p's < .05).

Circadian Cycle

The light/dark cycle should be modified so that residents are maintained under a 12/12-hour light/dark cycle with the light cycle reversed (i.e. lights off during the day). Because rats and mice are nocturnal animals, the reversed light cycle allows for aggression-testing during the animals' most active waking hours. If the experiment is designed to study the effects of social stress in intruder animals, intruders should also be maintained under a reversed light cycle. During the lights off period, the room can be illuminated with red light bulbs so experimenter may better view the colony, and laboratory cameras may have infrared lights to help illuminate videotaped interactions.

Aggression Testing

Aggression Screening

Resident animals need to be screened for aggression multiple times prior to inclusion in the experiment. All resident males should reach explicitly-defined criteria for agonistic behavior before the application of experimental treatments. Certainly, all resident males should demonstrate a reliable propensity to attack an intruder. Yet, the degree and stability of attack behavior required for inclusion will be determined based on the specific constructs identified in the experiment. First, an experimenter needs to ascertain when animals' aggressive behavior is stable from one encounter to another (i.e. rate of threats and attacks occur within 15% of mean for each individual). Once animals demonstrate stable aggressive behavior, each resident animal's baseline can be calculated, after which the researcher will randomly assign animals to experimental manipulations. With multiple screenings, most rodents will become sufficiently experienced in intermale conflict. Therefore, once animals are properly screened, any observed changes in aggressive and social behavior will represent assignment to the assigned experimental condition rather than general changes in behavior over time.

Some important differences exist between rats and mice with regard to aggressive behavior. Rats naturally live in colonies with multiple males and well-established dominance hierarchies, while mice are typically male intolerant. Mice demonstrate a propensity to attack an intruder more reliably that that observed with rats, and also show a higher biting attack frequency. Rats spend a significant amount of time in aggressive threats and postures, while mice attack in "bursts" of several successive bites (Miczek, Weerts, Tornatzky, DeBold, and Vatne, 1992). Also, rats direct the majority of their bites toward the back and shoulders, while mice primarily bite the intruder's rump. Mice tend to need more screenings to reach stable attack rates compared to rats, but mice can encounter the same intruder male for multiple screenings and still reach a stable baseline. Rats become successively less aggressive each time a familiar intruder is introduced into the home cage. After one or two encounters with the same intruder, rats will often exhibit longer attack latencies and fewer biting attacks, along with less exploration of the intruder. Therefore, rats should meet novel intruders as often as possible during aggression testing.

Although mice will exhibit stable aggressive behavior with a familiar intruder over several screenings, initial screenings are characterized by low levels of aggression and high rates of exploration. Once residents have been introduced to conspecific male intruders, mouse aggression escalates rapidly during subsequent tests. If mice are tested repeatedly with the same *familiar* intruder, frequency and severity of aggressive behaviors will decline over time and reach stable levels, while introduction of unfamiliar intruders will elicit higher attack rates (see Brain and Kamal, 1989, for review). Occasionally, an intruder will attack a resident mouse, even after having experienced several defeats. This may cause the resident's baseline aggressive behavior to cease or else decline substantially. Thus, intruders should be excluded from further aggression testing if threats and biting attacks are directed toward a resident male.

Basic Aggression-Testing Procedure

Once stable baseline aggressive behavior has been established, aggression testing may begin. The experimenter will remove the female and any pups from the resident's home cage, place an intruder into the cage, and record the latency of the first attack. Depending on the aims and objectives of the experiment, an agonistic encounter may last upwards of 30 minutes. However, most laboratories observe a dyad for 5 or10 minutes after the first biting attack. All resident-intruder encounters should be videotaped for later observational scoring.

Social Instigation

Experimenters sometimes employ various social instigation techniques when studying aggression. The social instigation protocol, previously referred to as "priming" has been employed in a variety of species, including rats, mice, hamsters, and fish (de Almeida and Miczek, 2002; Hollis, 1999; Hollis, et al., 1995; Potegal, et al., 1996). Usually, this procedure entails first allowing the resident to explore the intruder through a protective barrier, such as a stainless steel mesh cage. The intruder is placed in the resident's cage for a specified time period, after which the resident gains full access to the intruder. The instigation procedure serves to substantially increase attack behavior following removal of the partition (de Almeida and Miczek, 2002). When studying social defeat stress, use of a protective barrier for all or part of the encounter may be quite useful. Researchers may use this protective barrier to address potential confounds, such as pain and injury. An intruder is protected from tissue damage while underneath the enclosure, while fully able to view and smell the resident, while residents are still able to exhibit threats toward the enclosure.

Social Instigation: The Resident-Intruder paradigm may be conducted with the intruder animal protected beneath a protective mesh cage. Both resident and intruder are exposed to stimuli associated with an agonistic encounter without physical contact. This procedure is useful for protecting subjects from injury in experiments employing social defeat stress, and may also be used in protocols that call for increased aggressive attacks by resident males.

Aggressive and Social Behaviors

Resident male rodents engage in a number of fairly predictable species-typical behaviors during an agonistic encounter. Upon entry into the resident's cage, an intruder will explore the environment while the resident explores the intruder. Rats will spend a fair amount of time engaged in anogenital contact early on, and such contact will continue intermittently throughout the encounter. Most experienced rats will attack an intruder within the first 90 seconds of an encounter. Experienced mice typically show extremely short (< 5 seconds) latencies to initiate an attack. Both rats and mice exhibit piloerection, and may also show an aggressive form of contact with the intruder, termed "allogrooming," which has the appearance of forceful grooming with the mouth and nose (mice) or paws (rats). Allogrooming often immediately precedes an attack. Mice display "tail-rattling," and demonstrate threats by posturing themselves around the front of the intruder's upright body, aiming the nose at the rump. Rats use a lateral sideways threat, pressing their body against the intruder's, and will spend a considerable amount of time in aggressive posturing, "pinning" the intruder into a supine position. Rats can also be observed exhibiting a "tooth-rattle," which is identified by evidence of a hissing or chattering sound while the resident is maintaining a close face-to-face position with the intruder. Tooth rattling in rats, however, can be difficult to score reliably, because it is very subtly applied.

Observational Analyses

Trained observers will score aggressive, social, and non-social behaviors. This is best accomplished by videotaping interactions and scoring behaviors afterward. Frequency of attack bites, along with frequency and duration of threats and aggressive posturing are the primary aggressive behaviors the experimenter quantifies. Frequency and duration of tail-rattling (in mice) is often scored by experimenters, but may be difficult to interpret, since this behavior has a great deal of individual variability. Duration of exploratory contact (the "anogenital sniff" and "allogroom") with the intruder, and time spent in pursuit of (chasing) intruders, should all be measured. Non-social behaviors such as walking, rearing, grooming, and digging are all useful behaviors to examine, since any change in aggressive behavior could be attributed to general inactivity or hyperactivity in the experiment's final analyses. Because observational analysis is not perfectly objective, it is essential that observers be properly trained by experienced researchers to observe and score behaviors, and are able to demonstrate good inter-rater and test-retest reliability.

In conclusion, the resident-intruder paradigm has become a widely recognized, naturalistic animal model for aggressive behavior within the fields of psychology, behavioral neuroscience, and psychopharmacology. If properly designed and thoroughly applied, this protocol is an excellent resource for behavioral scientists. The resident-intruder paradigm has given scientists a broad understanding of ethological differences between multiple species of animals, and has allowed scientists to advance pharmacotherapies and behavioral interventions for human populations affected by aggressive behavior or social stress. This paradigm has proved to be remarkably flexible and has the ability to examine escalated, or maladaptive, aggressive behavior. In short, the resident-intruder has become the protocol of choice for studying aggression, social interaction, and defeat stress in animals, and will likely continue to be used extensively in research employing animal models of human mental health.

REFERENCES

Al-Maliki, S., Brain, P. F., Childs, G., and Benton, D. (1979). Factors influencing maternal attack on conspecific intruders by lactating female "TO" strain mice. *Aggressive Behavior, 6,* 103-117.

Bartolomucci, A., Palanza, P., Sacerdote, P., Panerai, A. E., Sgoifo, A., Dantzer, R., and Parmigiani, S. (2005). Social factors and individual vulnerability to chronic stress exposure. *Neuroscience and Biobehavioral Reviews, 29,* 67-81.

Brain, P. F. (1975). What does individual house mean to a mouse? *Life Sciences, 16,* 187-200.

Brain, P. F., and Kamal, K. B. H. (1989). Effects of prior social experiences on individual aggressiveness in laboratory rodents. *Rassegna di Psicologia, 6,* 37-43.

Brown, R. E. (1992). Responses of dominant and subordinate male rats to the odors of male and female conspecifics. *Aggressive Behavior, 18,* 129-138.

D'Eath, R. B., and Pickup, H. E. (2002). Behaviour of young growing pigs in a resident-intruder test designed to measure aggressiveness. *Aggressive Behavior, 28,* 401-415.

de Almeida, R. M. M., and Miczek, K. A. (2002). Aggression escalated by social instigation or by discontinuation of reinforcement ("frustration") in mice: inhibition by anpirtoline: a 5-HT1B receptor agonist. *Neuropsychopharmacology, 27,* 171-181.

de Boer, S. F., van der Vegt, B. J., and Koolhaas, J. M. (2003). Individual variation in aggression of feral rodent strains: a standard for the genetics of aggression and violence? *Behavior Genetics, 33,* 485-501.

Ebner, K., Wotjak, C. T., Landgraf, R., and Engelmann, M. (2005). Neuroendocrine and behavioral response to social confrontation: residents versus intruders, active versus passive coping styles. *Hormones and Behavior, 47,* 14-21.

Fish, E. W., DeBold, J. F., and Miczek, K. A. (2002). Aggressive behavior as a reinforcer in mice: activation by allopregnanolone. *Psychopharmacology, 163,* 459-466.

Gawienowski, A. M., Denicola, D. B., and Stacewiczsapuntzakis, M. (1976). Androgen dependence of a marking pheromone in rat urine in mice. *Brain Research, 898,* 232-241.

Gray, S., and Hurst J. L. (1995). The effects of cage cleaning on aggression within groups of male laboratory mice. *Animal Behavior, 49,* 821-826.

Hollis, K. L. (1999). The role of learning in the aggressive and reproductive behavior of blue gouramis, Trichogaster trichopterus. *Environmental Biology Of Fishes 54,* 355-369.

Hollis, K. L., Dumas, M. J., Singh, P., and Fackelman, P. (1995). Pavlovian conditioning of aggressive-behavior in blue gourami fish (Trichogaster-Trichopterus) - winners become winners and losers stay losers. *Journal Of Comparative Psychology, 109,* 123-133.

Miczek, K. A. (1979) A new test for aggression in rats without aversive stimulation: Differential effects of d-amphetamine and cocaine. *Psychopharmacology, 60,* 253-259.

Miczek, K. A., Maxson, S. C., Fish, E. W., and Faccidomo, S. (2001). Aggressive behavioral phenotypes in mice. *Behavioural Brain Research, 125,* 167-181.

Miczek, K. A., Weerts, E. M., Tornatzky, W., DeBold, J. F., and Vatne, T. M. (1992). Alcohol and "bursts" of aggressive behavior: Ethological analysis of individual differences in rats. *Psychopharmacology, 107,* 551-563.

Mink, J. W., and Adams, D. B. (1981). Why offense is reduced when rats are tested in a strange cage. *Physiology and Behavior, 26,* 567-573.

Moya-Larano J., Orta-Ocana J.M., Barrientos J.A., Bach C., and Wise, D.H. (2002). Territoriality in a cannibalistic burrowing wolf spider. Ecology, 83, 356-361.

Moyer, K. E. (1968). Kinds of aggression and their physicological basis. *Communications in Behavioural Biology*, 2, 65-87.

Moyer, K. E. (1976). *The psychobiology of aggression.* New York: Harper and Row Publishers.

Nikulina, E., M., Covington, H. E., Ganschow, L., Hammer, R. P., and Miczek, K. A. (2004). Long-term behavioral and neuronal cross-sensitization to amphetamine induced by repeated brief social defeat stress: fos in the ventral tegmental area and amygdala. *Neuroscience, 123*, 857-865.

Oyegbile, T. O., and Marler, C. A. (2005). Winning fights elevates testosterone levels in California mice and enhances future ability to win fights. *Hormones and Behavior, 48*, 259-267.

Palanza, P., Della Seta, D., Ferrari, P. F., and Parmigiani, S. (2005). Female competition in wild house mice depends upon timing of female/male settlement and kinship between females. Animal Behaviour, 69, 1259–1271.

Potegal, M., Ferris, C. F., Hebert, M., Meyerhoff, J., and Skaredoff, L. (1996). Attack priming in female Syrian golden hamsters is associated with a c-fos-coupled process within the corticomedial amygdala. *Neuroscience, 75*, 869-880.

Pye, T., Swain, R., and Seppelt, R. D. (1999). Distribution and habitat use of the feral black rat (Rattus rattus) on subantarctic Macquarie Island. *Journal of Zoology (London), 247*, 429-438.

Rygula, R., Abumaria, N., Flugge, G., Fuchs, E., Ruther, E., and Havemann-Reinecke, U. (2005). Anhedonia and motivational deficits in rats: Impact of chronic social stress. *Behavioural Brain Research, 162*, 127-134.

Tidey, J. W., and Miczek, K. A.(1996). Social defeat stress selectively alters mesocortico-limbic dopamine release: an in vivo microdialysis study. *Brain Research, 721*, 140-149.

Tornatzky, W., Cole, J. C., and Miczek, K. A. (1998). Recurrent aggressive episodes entrain ultradian heart rate and core temperature rhythms. *Physiology and Behavior, 63*, 845-853.

Ulrich, R. (1966). Pain as a cause of aggression. *American Zoologist, 6*, 643-661.

Ulrich, R. (1967). Interaction between reflexive fighting and cooperative escape. *Journal of the Experimental Analysis of Behavior, 10*, 311-317.

Ulrich, R. (1969). Punishment of shock-induced aggression. *Journal of the Experimental Analysis of Behavior, 12*, 1009-1015.

van Erp, A. M. M., and Miczek, K. A. (2000). Aggressive behavior, increased accumbal dopamine, and decreased cortical serotonin in rats. *The Journal of Neuroscience, 20*, 9320-9325.

Viken, R. J., and Knutson, J. F. (1992). Relationship between shock-induced aggression and other laboratory tests of agonistic behavior in rats. *Aggressive Behavior, 18*, 53-63.

In: Tasks and Techniques: A Sampling of the Methodologies...   ISBN 1-60021-126-7
Editor: Matthew J. Anderson, pp. 189-208   © 2006 Nova Science Publishers, Inc.

Chapter 16

AN ANIMAL MODEL FOR STUDYING THE BEHAVIOR OF COOPERATING

Richard Schuster and Barry D. Berger**

Department of Psychology, University of Haifa, Haifa 31905, Israel

ABSTRACT

An animal model of cooperation is described that was designed for use with laboratory rats *Rattus norvegicus* to study the behavior of cooperating and to address explanatory issues concerning both why and how cooperation occurs. Most laboratory models derive from an economic perspective that reduces cooperation to individual behaviors. Using pairs or groups of subjects that are anonymous and physically isolated, inter-dependent contingencies specify that the reinforcements for each individual are linked both to its own behavior and also to that of others. In the natural world of cooperation, however, such contingencies are inseparable from social dimensions of cooperating including coordination, communication, spontaneous interactions and jointly-obtained outcomes that are absent when an individual opts for non-cooperation. These differences between cooperation (C) and non-cooperation (NC) were incorporated into a model in which C is represented by a pair of rats that are positively reinforced for coordinating their shuttling from one end to the other end of a shared rectangular chamber; NC, in contrast, is represented by individual shuttling, even if another animal is present. The only cues available during C are the behaviors and locations of the animals themselves. The model is validated as one of social cooperation by data showing: a) partners using each other's behaviors and locations to coordinate; b) a bias to cooperate when outcomes for C and NC are matched; c) sensitivity of the model to the cooperating partners, including sex differences and pairs composed of two live animals vs one inanimate "partner"; and d) differential sensitivity of C and NC to housing, hormones and psychoactive drugs. Overall, the model demonstrates the importance – both for method and theory - of incorporating more of nature into laboratory models of social behaviors such as cooperation.

* Address Corresspondence to: Telephones Richard Schuster: 972 4 8240924 (office); 972 4 8253069 (home); 972 4 8240966 (fax); Telephone Barry D. Berger: 972 4 8249374 (office); E-mails: Schuster@psy.haifa.ac.il; bberger@psy.haifa.ac.il

INTRODUCITON

This chapter describes an animal model of cooperation that was designed for use with laboratory rats Rattus norvegicus to study the behavior of cooperating. Also discussed is how this kind of model can address some of the explanatory issues concerning both why and how cooperation occurs. Behaviors like cooperation and altruism have long posed difficult theoretical problems because of the implication that individuals, when they choose to cooperate, are working together with others on common tasks for shared outcomes. There is also the implication that cooperation can be to some extent altruistic: individuals might be doing so in part for the benefit of others. In other words, cooperation usually implies some kind of intrinsically social behavior. When explaining cooperation, however, most current theories tend to treat cooperation not as a social behavior but as a behavior performed by individuals when the outcomes happen to depend also on the behaviors of others (Skinner, 1953). This difference in explanatory perspectives has, however, not been only about theory. It has also been the main influence on the design of laboratory models regarding the degree to which they represent cooperation as a social or an individual behavior.

The study of cooperation as an individual-level behavior is closely linked to an economic perspective: individuals are expected to be rational and opportunistic, in other words selfish when behaving cooperatively and also when choosing whether or not to cooperate. Individuals are assumed to cooperate only if they themselves can gain greater benefits for themselves or for their kin. Beneficial outcomes have been the currency of evolutionary theories of cooperation (Trivers, 1985; Mesterton-Gibbons and Dugatkin, 1992; Clement and Stephens, 1995; Dugatkin, 1997; Stephens and Anderson, 1997; Stevens and Stephens, 2004). The same underlying assumption has dominated Psychology: evolutionary selfishness is assumed to be matched by adaptive behavioral selfishness. Individuals are expected to cooperate only when they can maximize a quantity called "expected utility" which is roughly an index of the value of the outcomes obtained (Edwards, 1954; Ostrom, 1998). And underlying both evolution and psychology is the unifying assumption that utility and fitness are linked by the ability to adopt adaptive strategies.

This emphasis on individual behaviors and economics has led to a long history of laboratory models of cooperation based on behaviors and outcomes that are reduced to individual events by using subjects that are anonymous and physically isolated when behaving. The only cooperative feature of such models is a contingency of reinforcement that is inter-dependent: the reinforcements obtained by each participant are linked to its own behavior and also to that of others (Skinner, 1953; Lindsley, 1966; Hake and Vukelich, 1972). From an economic perspective, cooperation can still be claimed even in the complete absence of social interaction (Hake and Vukelich, 1972; Stephens and Anderson, 1997). Colman (2003) characterized this approach to modelling as "the bedrock of methodological individualism." Simple cooperation models reinforce the coordination of brief acts such as bar presses or key pecks (e.g., Skinner, 1953; Lindsley, 1966; Hake and Vukelich, 1972). More complex models offer cooperation as an option in "social dilemmas" derived from Game Theory such as the prisoner's dilemma. This game offers "players" a choice between whether or not to cooperate (e.g., in humans, Rapoport and Chammah, 1965; Axelrod and Hamilton, 1981; in animals, Flood, Lendenmann, and Rapoport, 1983; Clements and Stephens, 1995; Green, Price and Hamburger, 1995; Baker and Rachlin, 2002a).

The use of isolated and anonymous subjects is inseparable from the core assumption of economics: all behavior is ultimately individual action determined by individual outcomes. To show that this assumption also applies to cooperation, differences between the behavioral expressions of cooperation and non-cooperation were erased by reducing both to brief individual acts linked to reinforcing outcomes that are also experienced alone. Although human subjects are sometimes influenced by the minimal social properties of such models to cooperate more than expected by pure self-interest (e.g., Palameta and Brown, 1999; Colman, 2003), the behavior of animals is dominated by the larger immediate reinforcements that lead them to prefer non-cooperation or "defection" (e.g., Stephens, Nishimura, and Toyer, 1986; Clements and Stephens, 1995).

A Bias to Cooperate

The influence of individual-level economics on cooperation is challenged by examples of animal species in the natural world in which individuals continue to cooperate *in sensu* behavior, i.e., work together, but are not adequately compensated or are not compensated at all at the time of performance (e.g., Boesch and Boesch, 1989; Brosnan and de Waal, 2002; Schuster, 2002; Schuster and Perelberg, 2004). In other words, cooperation in the natural world occurs more than expected from immediate material gains alone. Examples of this apparent insensitivity to immediate economic outcomes include the following:

a) cooperation may be preferred even when non-cooperation is immediately more beneficial (e.g., in lions, Packer, Scheel and Pusey, 1990);

b) individuals may behave together but then divide the outcomes unfairly (Schuster and Perelberg, 2004; Boesch and Boesch, 1989; Brosnan and de Waal, 2002; Packer, Scheel and Pusey, 1990);

c) individuals may be more likely to share outcomes if they have been achieved by cooperating (e.g., in capuchin monkeys, de Waal and Berger, 2000);

d) the behavior is learned, despite extended periods with few or no material rewards (in lions, Scheel and Packer, 1991; in chimpanzees, Boesch, 2002);

In humans, this bias to cooperate exists in both the natural world (e.g., Frank, 1988) and, as noted above, also in game- theory models despite the isolation and anonymity (Palameta and Brown, 1999; Colman, 2003). Apparently, human subjects are aware to some degree that other players are involved. Providing this knowledge can affect both behavior (Baker and Rachlin, 2002b) and brain imaging (Rilling et al., 2002).

A major focus of our research has been to ask why cooperation would occur at levels not predicted by immediate reinforcements. Evolution offers one kind of explanation. It is likely that cooperation exists because it is ultimately beneficial in an adaptive sense, that is, engaging in cooperation leads eventually to beneficial economic outcomes for individuals that would elevate individual fitness and thereby influence natural selection. Lions, for example, seem to eat less following a group hunt because the single prey is shared among many individuals, some of whom (typically the larger males) do not even participate (Packer, Scheel and Pusey, 1990; Scheel and Packer, 1991). Chimpanzees that hunt monkeys together also divide small prey unequally and then share the meat with others that did not hunt

(Boesch and Boesch, 1989). But it is possible that both lions and chimpanzees ultimately benefit from cooperative hunting by forging social ties that influence success in inter-group aggression during a later stage of their lives, and it is this success that provides the main influence on increased fitness and evolution (Packer, Scheel and Pusey, 1990; Mitani and Watts, 2001; Schuster, 2002; Schuster and Perelberg, 2004). In this respect, cooperation would be analogous to play behaviors that often occur without any obvious immediate benefit but can lead in the long run to adaptive skills (Bekoff and Byers, 1998).

COOPERATION AS A SOCIAL BEHAVIOR

This ability to hunt cooperatively, and the evidence for a cooperation bias, invite interest in the behavoral/ psychological processes that motivate and reinforce such behaviors at the time of performance, i.e., the proximate short-acting processes that underlie the performance of a behavior when it is not adequately reinforced by immediate material success. Our hypothesis has been that the answer probably is linked to differences between the behavioral expressions of cooperation and non-cooperation in the natural world. A hungry lioness, for example, can choose between cooperative hunting with her pride-mates for shared outcomes or non-cooperative hunting performed alone (Packer, Scheel and Pusey, 1990). The existence of a cooperation bias suggests to us that the psychological reasons why individuals might choose to cooperate are not only economic - about immediate beneficial outcomes - but also about differences between how individuals are affected by engaging in cooperation and non-cooperation (Schuster, 2002; Schuster and Perelberg, 2004). These differences could arise from a number of dimensions of cooperation, any one of which could be responsible for the bias (Schuster, 2002; Schuster and Perelberg, 2004):

- individuals during cooperation engage in con-joint, cohesive actions for shared outcomes;
- coordination of actions is based on using each other's behaviors and locations;
- coordination includes the possibility of different and complementary roles that are consistently adopted by the same individuals, and would be ineffectual if used individually, e.g., in the coordinated hunts of both lions (Stander, 1992) and chimpanzees (Boesch and Boesch, 1989);
- cooperating individuals enjoy unrestricted social interaction before during and after acts of cooperation, such as physical contact, grooming and even fighting;
- shared outcomes following cooperation can also evoke social interactions and dominance that determine allocations.

It is likely that the kinds of cooperation relevant to the above scenarios are especially relevant to more "cognitively complex species" in which cooperation involves mutual recognition, expectations regarding the future actions of others, and concomitant social interactions. Species such as lions, chimpanzees and hyenas hunt together in ways consistent with some level of shared intentionality by launching their trap even before the target has been identified (Schuster, in press). From the perspective of behavioral/ psychological processes in such animals, the choice between whether or not to cooperate becomes a choice between two different ways of gaining access to material outcomes: by joint action with shared success, or by individual action and individual success (Schuster, 2002; Schuster and Perelberg, 2004).

By suggesting that the behaviors of cooperating might be central to explanations of cooperation, we are questioning the validity of the economic perspective and the isolation models that it has spawned. According to an economic point of view, the actual behaviors used when cooperating are not relevant to the reasons why individuals might actually cooperate but only to the secondary question of what individuals actually do when they cooperate (e.g., Stephens and Anderson, 1997; Dugatkin, 1997). The only dimension of behaviour that seems to matter is the reinforcement following an individual's behavior that is also dependent on the behavior of others (Skinner, 1953; Weingarten and Mechner, 1966; Lindsley, 1966; Hake and Vukelich, 1972; Mesterton-Gibbons and Dugatkin, 1992; Dugatkin, 1997). Hence, isolation models can be offered as a legitimate technique for understanding cooperation even though the influence of social interactions is minimized if not entirely eliminated.

The limitation of economic theories and models is that they attach no importance to the fact that, in the natural world, the social dimensions of cooperative behaviors are usually inseparable from inter-dependent reinforcement contingencies. The existence of a bias to cooperate, however, suggests that cooperating individuals are influenced by working together for shared outcomes because the behavior is linked to underlying processes of intrinsic motivation and reinforcement (Schuster 2002; Schuster and Perelberg 2004). Thus, the likelihood of engaging in an act of cooperating would be governed by two kinds of immediate reinforcements: (1) tangible economic gains, i.e., the usual material reinforcers with immediate benefits such as food and mating opportunities, that can be directly observed and measured; and (2) positive affective states evoked by the social dimensions of behaving cooperatively.

Intrinsic reinforcement is consistent with many examples of coordinated behaviors that seem to exert a powerful influence on both animals and humans. In humans, excitement and unity are evoked by orchestrated group ceremonies based on coordinated marching, praying, singing and dancing (McNeill,1995) and there is evidence also for increased rapport between people that unconsciously adopt similar postures and gestures via a process of mimicry or "behavior matching" (Lakin and Chartrand 2003). Many species of animals employ behavioral matching of coordinated and ritualized acts in contexts as varied as courtship (Maynard Smith, 1978) and aggression (Leuthold, 1977) that are mutually beneficial (Schuster, 2002). If emotions are associated with cooperating together for shared outcomes, this would add intrinsic positive valence beyond immediate economic outcomes. From a functional/evolutionary perspective, intrinsic reinforcement would also circumvent the problem of sharp discounting in the value of reinforcement that is long-delayed (Kagel, Green and Caraco, 1986; Stephens, Nishimura and Toyer, 1995). Immediate affective outcomes can thereby provide a way for cooperation to be learned and performed even when immediate material reinforcements are inadequate or entirely absent. If such cooperation can thereby lead eventually to beneficial outcomes, this would be consistent with the idea that the processes underlying intrinsic reinforcement are adaptive.

A MODEL OF COOPERATIVE COORDINATION

Our research on animal cooperation is designed to address the kinds of issues outlined above: how do cooperation and non-cooperation differ in their behavioral expressions; whether these differences impact on the individuals performing them; and whether the performance of cooperation provides additional incentive and reinforcement above and beyond primary material reinforcements such as food. The cooperation model described below was therefore developed to incorporate the kinds of differences between cooperation (hereafter C) and non-cooperation (hereafter NC) in the natural world. C is modeled by individuals acting together for shared outcomes; NC is modeled by individuals acting alone for their own outcomes. .

We call the model of C the Zugia, from the Hebrew word "zug" for pair. This model shares many features with a pioneering experiment on cooperation in which pairs of rats had to coordinate an exchange of locations within a shared chamber to obtain reinforcements while also avoiding electric shocks (Daniel, 1942). The core of the model is a pair of rats that are both reinforced (usually with 3 mM saccharine solution presented in two adjacent cups) for coordinating their shuttling from one end to the other end of a shared rectangular chamber. There are no artificial cues such as lights or tones that could facilitate the coordination. Normally, there is also no separation barrier between the two partners so that social interactions – whether affiliative or agonistic – are unrestricted. (Barriers of all kinds can be added to manipulate the extent of social interaction during cooperation, including bars or solid partitions that are transparent or opaque.) Under these conditions, the only cues available during coordination are the behaviors and locations of the animals themselves. Without barriers, some pairs also develop behaviors such as contact, anal investigation and social grooming that appear to serve as cues facilitating coordination (Daniel, 1942; Schuster, Berger and Swanson, 1993). There are also intra-pair asymmetries in the use of such behaviors whereby they are initiated more by one partner who thereby seems to adopt the role of controller over the frequency and level of coordination (Schuster, 2001; Schuster and Berger, in prep). Overall, the cooperation model incorporates many of the social dimensions that characterize the performance of behaviors such as cooperative hunting and aggression in the real world in which two (or more) animals are also forced to use each other's behaviors and locations when coordinating movements in space (Boesch and Boesch, 1989; Schuster, 2002; Schuster and Perelberg, 2004).

Another advantage of the model is that non-cooperation (NC) can be modeled within the same chamber by reinforcing individual animals for their own back-and-forth shuttling, even if a second animal is also present. C and NC are thereby represented by animals reinforced for performing two different behaviors that are nevertheless topographically and energetically comparable at the level of individual action: back-and-forth shuttling. In this way, the essential differences between C – a coordinated social act - and NC – an individual act - can be isolated: C becomes a behavior associated with intrinsic social dimensions associated with cooperating that are absent when engaging in NC. Moreover, the differences between C and NC become analogous to the differences between an animal such as a lioness that hunts cooperatively or individually.

Reinforcement Contingencies

The behavioral differences between C and NC can be appreciated from their respective reinforcement contingencies. Both are run in identical experimental chambers diagrammed in Figure 1. These are rectangular, 94 cm long, with three contiguous floors identified as N, M and D, respectively located near, in the middle and distant from the place where the two reinforcement cups are presented adjacent to Floor N. In all of the experiments reported below, the locations of subjects were detected by four micro-switches located under the four corners of each floor. We are currently testing a prototype of a new chamber in which the locations of animals are monitored by three video cameras located on the ceiling above the three floors.

Operationally, reinforcement is contingent upon animals positioned only on Floor D for a minimum of 0.5 sec followed by animals positioned only on Floor N for a minimum of 0.5 sec. The difference between C and NC, diagrammed in Figure 2, resides in whether the Floor D →Floor N contingency is satisfied by behaving individually (NC) or by a pair coordinating their behaviors (C):

a) Cooperation: Pairs are reinforced for C when both partners are first positioned together on Floor D for at least 0.5 sec and then together again on Floor N for at least 0.5 sec. There is no restriction placed on how a pair actually satisfies this contingency, whether by shuttling together or sequentially, by one animal calling to the other, or in some other way such as one animal forcing the other to move. All that matters is that the pair is at some point standing together on Floor D for at least 0.5 sec and then again on Floor N. If pairs do not arrive together onto a floor, the contingency can only be satisfied if the first partner to reach a floor awaits the arrival of its partner. Coordination errors are also possible when the first animal to reach a floor – either D or N - does not wait for the arrival of its partner. In this case, the error on the D-floor must first be corrected before the N-floor requirement can be satisfied. Only then is the reinforcement delivered. A decline in errors provides direct evidence that partners are paying attention to each other's behaviors and locations.

b) Non-cooperation. Individuals are reinforced for NC by satisfying the same Floor D→Floor N contingency by means of individual shuttling to Floor D and back to Floor N. NC can be represented by animals run alone (individual non-cooperation) or in pairs (social non-cooperation) in which each animal is reinforced independently for its own shuttles regardless of the behaviors and outcomes of the other. Social non-cooperation provides a way to isolate the influence of the presence of another animal from the influence of cooperating by means of coordination.

Rats run in pairs were sensitive to this difference in C and NC contingencies when reinforcement probabilities were matched for individual subjects (Schuster, 2002; Schuster and Perelberg, 2004; Schuster and Berger, in prep). The result, shown in Figure 3, was that cumulative running times were comparable for the two groups, but increased coordination was displayed only by the C group. This result is important because it demonstrates that coordination does not emerge spontaneously when rats are independently reinforced in each other's presence. The emergence of cooperative coordination depends instead upon the inter-dependent contingency of reinforcement to which the rats were sensitive.

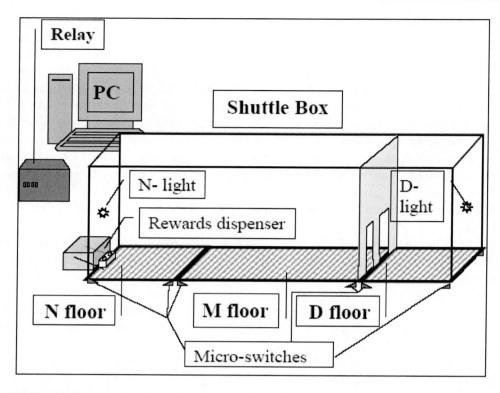

Figure 1. Schematic diagram of the learning chamber for both cooperation (C) and non-cooperation. (NC). See text for explanation.

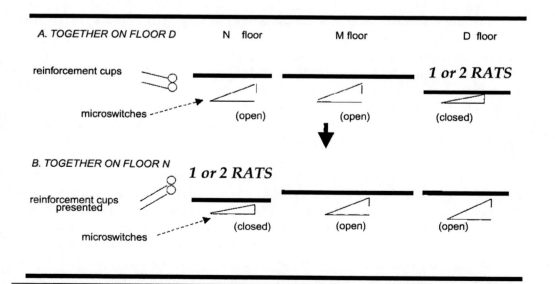

Figure 2. Schematic diagram of the operational reinforcement contingencies for both cooperation (C) and non-cooperation. (NC). See text for explanation. Reprinted from *Behavioural Processes, 66*, Schuster and Perelberg, Why cooperate? An economic perspective, 261-277, (2004), with permission from Elsevier.

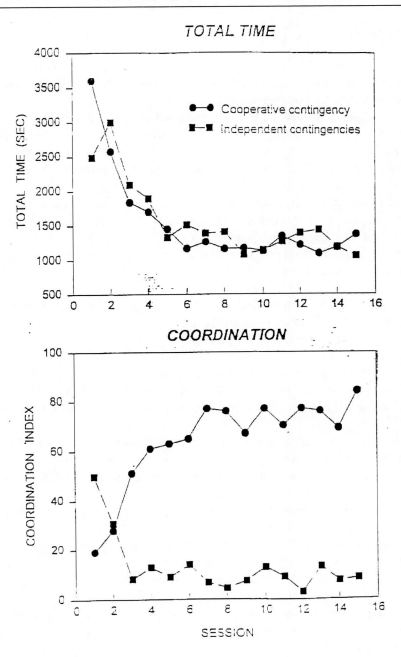

Figure 3. Comparison of total time (upper) and percent of errorless coordinations (lower) between pairs reinforced for cooperating (n = 3 pairs) and pairs in which each animal was reinforced independently for individual shuttling within a single shared chamber (n = 3 pairs). This figure shows that paired rats are sensitive to the difference between the C and NC contingencies of reinforcement. Copyright c (2002) by Aldine Publishers. Reprinted by permission of AldineTransaction, a division of Transaction Publishers.

Measures

The following measures of C and NC are collected automatically on line by PCs programmed for on-line running and data collection of those measures based only on floor locations of subjects without the need to identify individual partners:

-**Rate of performance**: Performance rate and learning during a session are measured by: a) total session duration to complete a pre-determined number of reinforced coordinations (C) or individual shuttles (NC), up to a maximum session duration if that number is not achieved; b) rate of completed coordinations (C) or individual shuttles (NC) measured as the number of completed behaviors/ unit time.

-**Intra-pair proximity:** Measures of proximity between partners during performance provide one index of coordination level since well-coordinated pairs are usually characterized by mean levels of intra-pair separation during a session that are lower than in pairs whose coordination is poor. Proximity measures are measured indirectly by measures of intra-pair separation that include the following:

a) Total numbers of $N \cap D$ closures that can only occur when partners are maximally separated within the experimental chambers;
b) Cumulative duration of $N \cap D$ closures.

The combination of both of the above measures provides an accurate picture of intra-pair separation since the numbers of $N \cap D$ closures can be small not only if partners shuttle together but also if partners shuttle slowly or remain stationary while widely separated on the N and D floors.

-**Anticipatory running speed**: Anticipatory emotional states prior to engaging in C vs NC are measured by running speed of subjects in alleys leading to chambers associated respectively with C and NC. Timing is initiated from photocells near the entrance to the alleys and terminated when subjects enter a chamber.

Trained observers record behaviors that depend upon identification of individual partners during C and social NC. These behaviors include the following:

-**Social interactions**: Species-typical affiliative and agonistic behaviors are scored by observers based in part on behavioral descriptions in Grant and Mackintosh (1963). These data provide a picture of the relationships between partners during C and can also be correlated with rate measures of C. Higher aggression, for example, is correlated with the poor learning and performance of male rats housed in isolation (Berger and Schuster, 1980; Schuster, Rachlin, Rom and Berger, 1982; Swanson and Schuster, 1987; Schuster, Berger and Swanson, 1988, 1993).

-**Coordination**: Errors in coordination (see definition above in the section on C contingency of reinforcement) are scored in order to calculate the proportion of completed coordinations that are performed with or without errors. Lower error scores are indicative of pairs that are better at using each other's behaviors and locations during coordination.

-**Precedence**: Precedence is calculated as the proportion of shuttles in which each partner leads the other. Higher intra-pair precedence is indicative of both the social cues used when shuttling and intra-pair asymmetries in roles (Schuster, Berger and Swanson, 1993). When cooperating partners compete over single outcomes, dominants also tend to precede subordinates in running from Floor D to Floor N (Schuster and Tsoory, in prep).

VALIDATING COORDINATED SHUTTLING
AS A MODEL OF SOCIAL COOPERATION

The validity of C as a social model of cooperation invites verification of the claim that this kind of model can better represent cooperation in the natural world in comparison with models based on isolation and anonymity. The issue of validity was already addressed above with reference to sensitivity of pairs to the difference between the C and NC contingencies (Figure 3) and the emergence or intra-pair role differences as measured by precedence (Schuster, 2001). Additional support comes from the following:

-**Social cues**. Figure 4 shows that pairs were markedly impaired when reinforced for coordinating shuttles in separate chambers (the "yoked" group) without the access to social cues or the provision of non-social cues to aid coordination (Schuster and Perelberg, 2004; Schuster and Berger, in prep). This result confirms that partners have learned to use each other while cooperating when in each other's presence within a shared space.

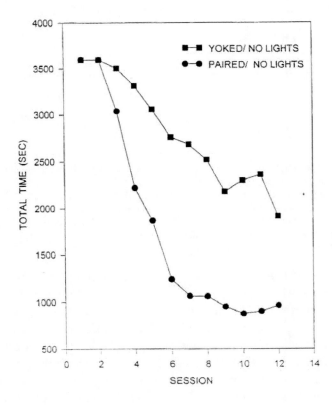

Figure 4. Comparison of paired (shared chamber) and yoked (separate chambers) groups on the measure of mean total time per session. The figure shows that learning in the yoked group of isolated partners without social cues was impaired. The decrease in session duration in the yoked group was linked to a gradual increase in the speed of uncoordinated back-and-forth running that increased the likelihood of satisfying the cooperation contingency by chance.

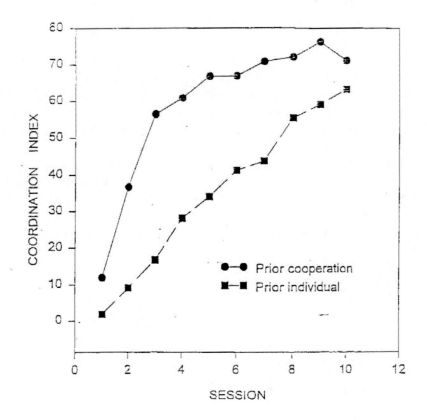

Figure 5. Comparison of learning to coordinate by pairs in which one partner was naive and the other was experienced either in coordinating (n = 10 pairs) or in individual shuttling (n = 10 pairs). The measure is the coordination index: mean percent of errorless coordinations per session. The figure demonstrates that learning by new pairs was facilitated by prior cooperation experience that can be transferred to new pairs. This result is consistent with cooperating pairs that have learned to coordinate, presumably by using cues from each other's behaviors and locations. Copyright c (2002) by Aldine Publishers. Reprinted by permission of AldineTransaction, a division of Transaction Publishers.

-Pairs learn to work together. The same message can be gained from an experiment that was designed to ask whether cooperating pairs have actually learned to work together. This was tested by comparing C learning by pairs composed of one experienced and one naïve partner when the prior experience of the experienced partner was either in C or individual NC. Figure 5 shows that prior learning of C facilitated subsequent cooperation learning (Schuster, 2002; Schuster and Perelberg, 2004; Schuster and Berger, in prep).

-Competition and dominance over outcomes. The unrestricted social conditions of the model also allow for modeling competition during the outcome phase of a cooperative act by intermittently presenting only single reinforcement cups and determining how these are allocated between partners (Schuster and Tsoory, in prep). It then becomes possible to examine the extent to which competition and dominance are tolerated within cooperative relationships. In the majority of male pairs, dominance emerged whereby one partner "invaded" and appropriated most of the single cups – both his own and those of the partner.

Despite the within-pair asymmetry in obtained reinforcements, allocation had no influence on the performance of cooperation (Schuster and Tsoory, in prep). This result is reminiscent of cooperative hunting in chimpanzees in which outcomes were unfairly allocated without obvious influence on future collaboration (Boesch and Boesch, 1989).

-Readiness to learn. Both male and female rats readily learn to cooperate (Berger, Mesch and Schuster, 1980; Schuster et al., 1982; Swanson and Schuster, 1987; Schuster, Berger and Swanson, 1988, 1993; Schuster, 2001, 2002; Schuster and Perelberg, 2004). Asymptotic rates of shuttling are generally reached within 4 or 5 sessions after individual partners first learn to shuttle individually. Recent experiments have confirmed that completely naïve pairs can also learn to cooperate during a single extended session without prior individual learning or shaping of approach to the reinforcement cups.

It may seem surprising that rat pairs so readily acquire the behavior of cooperating in this model since Norway rats do not normally cooperate in the wild. Rats however are a highly social and adaptable species that normally live in large colonies characterized by dominance and a repertoire of social signals (Grant and Mackintosh, 1963; Barnett, 1975). Rats also exhibit social learning whereby feeding habits can transfer between individuals in a variety of ways (Galef, 1990). In the wild, there are also examples of species that learned to coordinate hunting even though they typically hunt alone, such as the Harris' hawk *Parabuteo unicinctus* (Bednarz, 1988) and the cheetah *Acimonyx jubatus* (Caro, 1994). Coordinated hunting is also known between unrelated species, badgers *Taxidea taxus* and coyotes *Canis latrans* (Minta, Minta and Lott, 1992). We suggest that a necessary condition for the ability of a species to cooperate with its own kind or with members of another species may be sensitivity to the presence and behaviors of others. And rats in this respect are a highly social species.

Differential Sensitivity of C and NC

The model's validity also emerges from experiments in which the two behaviors C and NC were compared under conditions that would be expected to differentially impact on social and individual behaviors. These have included housing (Berger and Schuster, 1980; Schuster, Rachlin, Rom and Berger, 1982; Schuster, Berger and Swanson, 1988, 1993), and psychoactive drugs (Berger and Schuster 1982, 1987). A difference between C and NC was also shown by offering a choice between them after both were experienced separately (Schuster, 2001, 2002; Schuster and Perelberg, 2004). Finally, important evidence for the difference between C and NC comes from evidence that the identity of the partners is important. Studies have shown differential sensitivity of C and NC to sex and strain differences (Schuster, Berger and Swanson, 1988, 1993) and to the difference between cooperating with a live partner vs. inanimate stimuli (Schuster, 2001; Schuster and Berger, in prep.)

In the following section, a sample of these data will be presented with the aim of demonstrating the validity of the cooperation model, and of the differences between C and NC:

-Sensitivity to housing. Figure 6 shows one example of the marked differential effect of individual housing on C and NC. Learning of C was severely impaired, whereas NC was unaffected (Berger Mesch and Schuster, 1980; Schuster, Rachlin, Rom and Berger, 1982; Berger and Schuster, 1982, 1987). The deficit in C was associated with violent aggression by dominants and freezing by subordinates that was sustained across sessions. We have obtained this difference when males were housed individually for as little as 7 days (Berger, unpublished).

-**Sensitivity to partner. 1. Sex and strain differences.** The influence of partner was shown by the detrimental effect of isolated housing on C that was mainly limited to males, and only in 2 of 3 strains that were compared: S3 (maze-dull) and Sprague-Dawley. (Schuster, Berger and Swanson, 1988; 1993). In Wistar rats, both males and females readily learned after both social and isolated housing. The deficit in male Sprague Dawley rats was linked to the male sex hormone testosterone. Intact males and castrated males with hormone replacement were impaired after isolated but not social housing, whereas castrated males without hormone replacement were unimpaired (Swanson and Schuster, 1987).

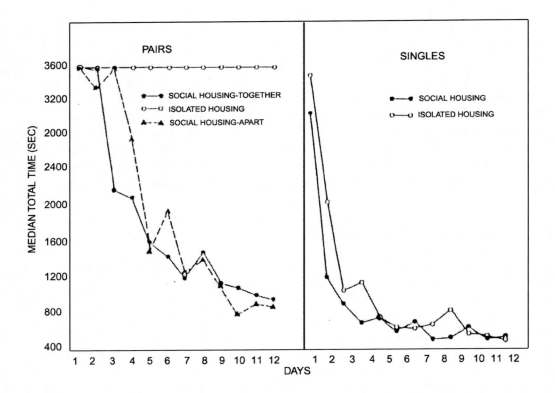

Figure 6. Comparison between the effects of social vs. isolated housing on cooperation (C) individual non-cooperation (NC) in male rats. The figure shows that housing had no differential effect on NC whereas C was impaired in animals housed in isolation. There was no difference between cooperating by socially-housed pairs when housed together or separately with other cage mates. Reprinted from *Aggressive Behavior, 8*, Schuster, Rachlin, Rom, and Berger, An animal model of dyadic social interaction: Influence of isolation, competition and shock-induced aggression, 116-121, (1982), with permission from John Wiley and Sons, Inc.

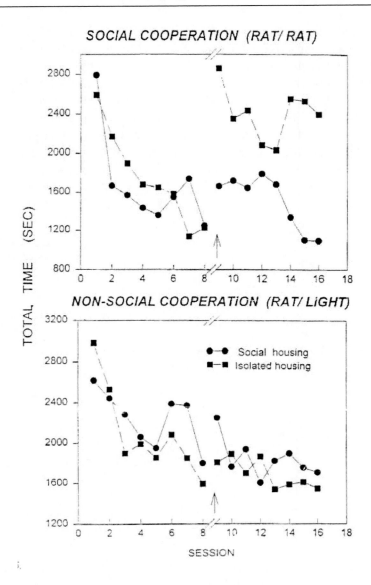

Figure 7. Comparison between the cooperation of rat / rat pairs and the "cooperation" of rat / light pairs (n = 8 per group) when socially housed (sessions 1-8) and when half the pairs were switched from social to individual housing (sessions 9-16). The switch from social to isolated housing is shown by the ⇑. The figure shows that rat / rat pairs were selectively impaired by the switch to isolated housing whereas rat / light pairs were unimpaired. The results can be interpreted as showing that the coordinated behavior of individual animals cooperating with a non-living "partner" is not comparable to the coordinating of two animals acting together. From Schuster (2001). Reprinted with permission from the Mexican Society for Behavior zAnalysis.

-**Sensitivity to partner. 2. Live vs inanimate "partner." Figure 7** shows the results of an experiment that perhaps provides the most direct validation of C as a social model of cooperation. The detrimental effects of social vs. isolated housing on C were used to compare two kinds of cooperating pairs: two live rats vs. pairs composed of one live rat coordinating with a sequence of light presentations that mimicked the shuttling of a live rat (Schuster,

2001; Schuster and Berger, in prep). In the latter "pair," the model is effectively reduced to a single-animal model comparable to the isolation models of Skinner (1953) and others outlined above in which individual animals are behaving and reinforced for "cooperating." We expected that rats would readily learn to coordinate with an inanimate sequence of stimuli. The question was whether the learned behavior is comparable to coordination between two animals. The differential effects of social vs. isolated housing offered a way to do this. Both kinds of pairs first learned to cooperate when housed socially. Then half of the subjects were switched to isolated housing. Figure 7 shows that isolated housing once again impaired the behavior of the live pairs housed in isolation, whereas the behavior of rat + lights was unaffected.

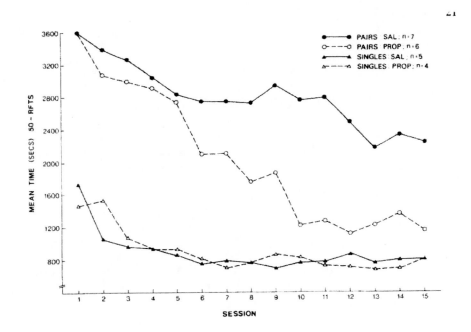

Figure 8. Comparison between the effects of the beta receptor blocker propranolol on cooperation (C) individual non-cooperation (NC) in male rats when animals were housed individually (isolated housing). The figure shows that propranolol selectively led to the improvement of C relative to animals injected with saline, whereas NC was unaffected by the drug. From *Ethopharmacology of Agonistic Behaviour in Animals and Humans*, 1987, page 21, Pharmacological Aspects of Social Cooperation, Schuster and Perelberg, Figure 4, copyright notice Brill Academic Publishers. With kind permission of Springer Science and Business Media.

-**Sensitivity to psychoactive drugs**. **Figure 8** shows an example of another kind of differential sensitivity of C and NC: the influence of psychoactive drugs, in this case the adrenergic beta-blocker propranolol (Berger and Schuster, 1982, 1987). When male rats were housed in isolation, administration of this drug had no effect on the behavior of NC but the usual deficit in C was substantially blocked. Males were now able to cooperate, associated with marked reduction in both violent fighting and freezing. Propranolol also allowed for the recovery of C in pairs whose behavior was previously impaired by isolated housing. The above references summarize data from other drugs on this differential sensitivity.

-**Preference.** Two experiments confirmed the cooperation bias in the laboratory when a choice was offered between two chambers in which the same outcome - saccharine-flavored water – was equally available by either C or NC (Schuster and Perelberg, 2004). The cooperation option was preferred by c. 3-to-1 even though reinforcing outcomes for the two behaviors were matched. This experiment is the first step towards isolating the dimensions of cooperation responsible for the preference.

-Physiological substrates. Qualitative differences between cooperation and non-cooperation are also supported by evidence for differential activation of brain structures associated with performance. This would run counter to the claim that, at the level of performance, all behavior – whether social or individual - is ultimately an individual event controlled by the same processes (e.g., Skinner, 1953). In a preliminary study, C and NC were associated with a different profile of neurotransmitter activity as measured by high pressure liquid chromatography -HPLC (Tsoory, Youdim and Schuster, in prep). An analogous result was shown in humans playing prisoner's dilemma games using fMRI (Rilling et al., 2002).

Final Comments

Perhaps the main point that underlies this article is the importance of incorporating more of nature into our laboratory models of social behaviors such as cooperation. This is sometimes described as the problem of external validity (Bolles, 1975). Isolation models of cooperation, rooted in economics and evolution, were designed to emphasize individual actions and decisions when outcomes are inter-dependent. But if the models are stripped of the social dimensions that differentiate between cooperation and non-cooperation in the natural world, there is no direct way to examine how the behavior of cooperating influences individuals and their actions. Instead, isolation models reduce cooperation to another example of how reinforcement determines individual behavior in a model such as a Skinner Box for individual subjects. It is hardly surprising that animals, when isolated in separate chambers, were unable to cooperate in prisoner's dilemma games (Flood, Lendenmann, and Rapoport, 1983; Clements and Stephens, 1995; Green, Price and Hamburger, 1995; Baker and Rachlin, 2002).

The Zugia model of cooperation described here, by bringing elements of natural cooperation into the laboratory, allows the study of why and how cooperation occurs in the real world between individuals that are not isolated and anonymous. The existence of a behavioral process such as intrinsic reinforcement offers the advantage of freeing explanations of cooperation from the limitation that all participants must immediately profit materially. Instead, cooperation can still be claimed in all those examples of joint actions that persist and improve despite individuals that gain little or nothing at the time of cooperating (Brosnan and de Waal, 2002; Schuster, 2002; Schuster and Perelberg, 2004). The key is to understand the social dimensions of behaving cooperatively, and this was the aim of the model.

ACKNOWLEDGEMENTS

The writing of this paper and some of the research reported herein were supported in part by grants to RS from the US-Israel Binational Science Foundation (1979-1982; 1997-2000) and the Israel Academy of Sciences (2005-2008).

REFERENCES

Axelrod, R. and Hamilton, W.D., (1981). The evolution of cooperation. *Science, 211*:1390-1396.

Baker, F. and Rachlin, H., (2002a). Self-control by pigeons in the prisoner's dilemma. *Psychonomic Bulletin and Review, 9:* 482-488.

Baker, F. and Rachlin, H., (2002b). Teaching and learning in a probabilistic prisoner's dilemma. *Behavioral Processes, 57:* 211-226.

Barnett, S.A., (1975). *The Rat: A Study in Behavior* (2nd Ed.). Chicago, University of Chicago Press.

Bednarz, J.C., (1988). Cooperative hunting in Harris' hawks (*Parabuteo unicinctus*). *Science, 239*: 1525-1527.

Bekoff, M. and Byers, J. A., (1998). *Animal Play: Evolutionary, Comparative, and Ecological Perspectives.* New York: Cambridge University Press.

Berger, B.D., Mesch, D., and Schuster, R., (1980). An animal model of "cooperation" learning. In: R.F. Thompson, L.H. Hicks, and V.B. Shvyrkov (Editors), *Neural Mechanisms of Goal-directed Behavior,* New York, Academic Press, pp. 481-492.

Berger, B.D. and Schuster, R. (1982). An animal model of social interaction: implications for the analysis of drug action. In: M.Y. Spiegelstein and A. Levy (Eds.), *Behavioral Models and the Analysis of Drug Action.*Amsterdam: Elsevier, pp. 415-428.

Berger, B.D. and Schuster, R. (1987). Pharmacological aspects of social cooperation. In B. Olivier, J. Mos, and P.F. Brain (Eds.), *Ethopharmacology of Agonistic Behavior in Animals and Humans.* Dordrecht: Martinus Nijhoff.

Boesch, C. (2002). Cooperative hunting roles among Taï chimpanzees. *Human Nature, 13*: 27-46.

Boesch, C. and Boesch, H., (1989). Hunting behavior of wild chimpanzees in the Tai National Park. *American Journal of Physical Anthropology, 78*: 547-573.

Bolles, Robert C. (1975). *Theory of Motivation. 2nd edition* Harper and Row

Brosnan, S.F. and de Waal, F.B.M., (2002). A proximate perspective on reciprocal altruism. *Human Nature, 13:* 129-152.

Caro, T.M., (1994). *Cheetahs of the Serengeti Plains: Group Living in an Asocial Species.* Chicago, University of Chicago Press.

Clements, K.C. and Stephens, D.W., (1995). Testing models of non-kin cooperation: mutualism and the Prisoner's Dilemma. *Animal Behaviour, 50*: 527-535.

Colman, A.M., (2003). Cooperation, psychological game theory, and limitations of rationality in social interaction. *Behavioral and Brain Sciences, 26*: 139-198.

Daniel, W.J., (1942). Cooperative problem solving in rats. *Journal of Comparative Psychology, 34:* 361-368.

de Waal, F.B.M. and Berger, M.L., (2000). Payment for labour in monkeys. *Nature, 404:* 563.

Dugatkin, L.A., (1997). *Cooperation Among Animals: An Evolutionary Perspective.* Oxford, Oxford University Press.

Edwards, W., (1954). The theory of decision making. *Psychological Bulletin, 51:* 380-417.

Flood, M, Lendenmann, K., and Rapoport, A., (1983). A 2 x 2 game played by rats: different delays of reinforcement as payoffs. *Behavioral Science, 28:* 65-78.

Frank R.H., (1988). *Passions Within Reason: The Strategic Role of the Emotions.* New York, W.W. Norton.

Galef, B.G. Jr., (1990). An adaptationist perspective on social learning, social feeding, and social foraging in Norway rats. In: D.A. Dewsbury (Editor), *Contemporary Issues in Comparative Psychology,* Sunderland, Mass., Sinauer, pp. 55-79.

Grant, E.C., and Mackintosh, J.H., (1963). A comparison of the social postures of some common laboratory rodents. *Behaviour, 21:* 246-259.

Green, L., Price P. C. and Hamburger, M. E., (1995). Prisoners dilemma and the pigeon: control by immediate consequences. *Journal of the Experimental Analysis of Behavior, 64:* 1-17.

Hake, D.F., and Vukelich, R., (1972). A classification and review of cooperation procedures. *Journal of the Experimental Analysis of Behavior, 18:* 333-343.

Kagel, J.H., Green, L. and Caraco, T. (1986). When foragers discount the future: constraint or adaptation? *Animal Behaviour, 34:* 271-283.

Lakin, J.L.and Chartrand, T.L. (2003). Using unconscious behavioral mimicry to create affiliation and rapport. *Psychological Science, 14:* 334-339.

Leuthold, W., (1977). *African Ungulates: A Comparative Review of Their Ethology and Behavioral Ecology.* Berlin, Springer-Verlag.

Lindsley, O.R., (1966). Experimental analysis of cooperation and competition. In *The Experimental Analysis of Behavior,* (Ed. By T. Verhave), pp. 470-501. New York: Appleton-Century-Crofts.

Maynard Smith, J. (1978). *The Evolution of Sex.* Cambridge, England, Cambridge University Press.

McNeill, W.H., (1995). *Keeping Together in Time: Dance and Drill in Human History.* Cambridge, Mass., Harvard University Press.

Mesterton-Gibbons, M. and Dugatkin, L.A., (1992). Cooperation among unrelated individuals: evolutionary factors. *The Quarterly Review of Biology, 67:* 267-281.

Minta, S.C., Minta, K.A. and Lott, D.F., (1992). Hunting associations between badgers (*Taxidea taxus*) and coyotes (*Canis latrans*). *Journal of Mammalogy, 73:* 814-820.

Mitani, J and Watts, D., 2001. Why do chimpanzees hunt and share meat? Animal Behaviour, 61: 915-924.

Ostrom, E.A. (1998). Behavioral approach to the rational choice theory of collective action. *American Political Science Review, 92:* 1-22.

Packer, C., Scheel, D and Pusey, A.E., (1990). Why lions form groups: food is not enough. *American Naturalist, 136:* 1-19.

Palameta, B. and Brown, W.M., (1999). Human cooperation is more than by-product mutualism. *Animal Behaviour, 57:* F1-F3.

Rapoport, A. and Chammah, A. M., (1965). *Prisoner's Dilemma: A study in conflict and cooperation.* Ann Arbor, Michigan, University of Michigan Press.

Rilling, J.K., Gutman, D.A., Zeh, T.R., Pagnoni, G., Berns, G.S. and Kilts, C.D., (2002). A neural basis for social cooperation. *Neuron, 35*: 395-405.

Scheel, D. and Packer, C., (1991). Group hunting behavior of lions: a search for cooperation. *Animal Behaviour, 41:* 697-709.

Schuster, R., (2001). An animal model of cooperating dyads: methodological and theoretical issues. *Mexican Journal of Behavior Analysis, 27*: 165-200.

Schuster, R., (2002). Cooperative coordination as a social behavior: experiments with an animal model. *Human Nature, 13*: 47-83.

Schuster, R. (In press). Why not chimpanzees, lions and hyenas too. Commentary on Tomasello et al., Understanding and sharing intentions: The origins of cultural cognition. *Behavioral and Brain Sciences.*

Schuster, R., Berger, B.D. and Swanson, H.H., (1988). Cooperative social coordination and aggression: sex and strain differences in the effects of housing on gonadectomized rats with hormone replacement. *Aggressive Behavior, 14:* 275-290.

Schuster, R., Berger, B.D. and Swanson, H.H., (1993). Cooperative social coordination and aggression. II. Effects of sex and housing among three strains of intact laboratory rats differing in aggressiveness. *Quarterly Journal of Experimental Psychology, 46B*: 367-390.

Schuster, R and Perelberg, A. (2004). Why cooperate? An economic perspective is not enough. *Behavioral Preocesses, 66:* 261-277.

Schuster, R., Rachlin, H., Rom, M., and Berger, B.D., (1982). An animal model of dyadic social interaction: Influence of isolation, competition and shock-induced aggression. *Aggressive Behavior, 8*: 116-121.

Skinner, B.F., (1953). *Science and Human Behavior.* New York, Macmillan.

Stander, P.E., (1992). Cooperative hunting in lions: the role of the individual. *Behavioral Ecology and Sociobiology, 29*: 445-454.

Stephens, D.W. and Anderson, J.P., (1997). Reply to Roberts: cooperation is an outcome, not a mechanism. *Animal Behaviour, 53:* 1363-1364

Stephens, D.W., Nishimura, K. and Toyer, K.B. (1986). Error and discounting in the iterated Prisoner's Dilemma. *Journal of Theoretical Biology, 176*: 457-469.

Stevens, J. R. and Stephens, D. W. (2004). The economic basis of cooperation: tradeoffs between selfishness and generosity. *Behavioral Ecology, 15,* 255–261.

Swanson, H.H. and Schuster, R., (1987). Cooperative social coordination and aggression in male laboratory rats: effects of housing and testosterone. *Hormones and Behavior, 21*: 310-330.

Trivers, R., (1985). *Social Evolution.* Menlo Park, CA, Benjamin/Cummings.

Weingarten, K., and Mechner, F., (1966). The contingency as an independent variable of social interaction. In: T. Verhave (Editor), *The Experimental Analysis of Behavior.* New York, Appleton-Century-Crofts, pp. 447-459.

In: Tasks and Techniques: A Sampling of the Methodologies...   ISBN 1-60021-126-7
Editor: Matthew J. Anderson, pp. 209-222   © 2006 Nova Science Publishers, Inc.

Chapter 17

METHODOLOGICAL ISSUES IN THE STUDY OF IMITATIVE LEARNING BY ANIMALS

Thomas R. Zentall[*]
University of Kentucky, Lexington, KY 40506

ABSTRACT

Imitation is a phenomenon that is most easily defined by excluding several alternative mechanisms that could produce a correspondence between the behaviors of two organisms. By a process of analysis involving the design of critical experiments one can rule out or control for these alternative accounts including: matching behavior that is predisposed (eating), that merely involves manipulation the motivation of the observer (social facilitation), that functions merely by attracting the attention of the observer to a particular object or location (stimulus or local enhancement), or that might not require the presence of a demonstrator (affordance learning or object movement reenactment). The cognitive implications of imitation can be further demonstrated by examining the role of specific variables such as demonstrator reinforcement, observer motivation, the ability to defer imitation for some time after observation, and the ability to imitate a behavioral sequence. Both pigeons and Japanese quail show such response matching, in spite of the fact that from their perspective, their own behavior appears quite different from that demonstrated (opaque imitation). Although imitation has been demonstrated in birds and several primates, we are still not certain how they do it.

INTRODUCTION

The field of comparative cognition (animal intelligence) often requires that inferences be made about processes that cannot readily be seen. For this reason, the strategy used by many researchers is to identify various alternative accounts and develop experimental designs that

[*] Send Correspondence to: Thomas R. Zentall, Department of Psychology, University of Kentucky, Lexington, KY 40506, Phone: 859-257-4076, Fax: 859-323-1979, E-mail: Zentall@uky.edu

allow one to isolate the process in question. If one can rule out all of the alternative hypotheses, one may be left with evidence for the cognitive process under study.

Imitative learning, a form of social learning, is one of those areas of research that must include in its definition not only the matching of behavior but also that it does not result from any of a number of alternative nonimitative processes. The special interest in imitation in animals comes from the cognitive implications thought to be present when it occurs in children. According to Piaget (1962), the ability to imitate the actions of another (a model) requires that one appreciate the relation between one's own behavior and the behavior of the model. Often this may involve behavior that can be seen when demonstrated by another but cannot be seen when one performs it oneself. Examples of such so called *opaque* behavior are placing one's hand on one's head or clasping one's hand's behind one's back. The question raised by Piaget was how does a child coordinate these two very different sources of stimulus input – what it sees and what it does. In other words, how does the observer know what to do. Piaget reasoned that under such conditions one must be able to take the perspective of a third person and ask, 'what must I do such that this third person would say that my behavior and that of the model are similar?' Whether perspective taking is required for imitation involving opaque behavior is not clear but it would be of some theoretical interest to know if animals are capable of such imitative behavior.

To isolate this form of imitation, I will first identify other sources of facilitated responding attributable to other, perhaps simpler, mechanisms. Then I will suggest designs to isolate imitation from these other processes. Finally, I will present converging suggestive evidence that imitation is the process underlying the facilitated performance found.

SOCIALLY FACILITATED RESPONDING
AND NONIMITATIVE SOCIAL LEARNING

Bird Song

Acquisition of species typical song by birds is often genetically predisposed and may occur even in isolation but some birds acquire a regional dialect from others at an early age (Petrinovitch, 1988). Most researchers place learned song in the category of vocal mimicry, however, rather than imitation because the listener can match the sound that it hears to the sound that it makes (i.e., the behavior is transparent, see e.g., Fritz and Kotrschall, 2002). Thus, bird song can be viewed as a special case of identity matching of stimuli (Zentall Edwards and Hogan, 1983).

Contagious Behavior

Birds sometimes act in concert when they flock or attack a predator as a group (mobbing). These are species-typical defensive reactions shown by all members of the species. These behaviors are considered contagious because naturally occurring behavior is released by the sight of others engaged in that activity. Similarly, social eating behavior may be considered contagious when it occurs in an animal presumed to be stated (as evidenced by refraining from eating) but eating resumes when a hungry animal is introduced. The term contagion is appropriate when the target behavior is clearly species typical and when the effect on the observer persists only while the performing demonstrator is present.

Motivational Factors

Social Facilitation

It has been shown that the mere presence of another animal may affect the motivation or arousal of the observer (Zajonc, 1965). An increase in motivation may cause the animal to be more active and thus, because it is more likely to interact with its environment, it may be more likely to acquire a new response through individual learning. Similarly, in a novel fear-inducing environment, the mere presence of another animal may have a fear reducing effect and fear reduction can also lead to increased activity (Morrison and Hill, 1967).

Incentive Motivation

Being in the presence of a demonstrator that is eating may increase arousal and activity beyond the level induced by a demonstrator's mere presence (see Zentall and Levine, 1972) and once again, individual learning may be facilitated. A change in incentive motivation may also occur when the behavior to be acquired through observation is motivated by avoidance of an aversive effect. In this case, the motivation of the demonstrator may transfer to the observer either directly as a consequence of the demonstrators contact with the aversive event (e.g., shock) or indirectly through behavioral evidence of the demonstrator's fear (John, Chesler, Bartlett, and Victor, 1968). Such transfer of fear may sensitize the observer to the aversive event, thus increasing its effect which, in turn, could facilitate the acquisition of the avoidance response.

Perceptual Factors

When the observation of a demonstrator draws attention to the consequences of a response (e.g., a lever press), it may alter the salience of the lever (stimulus enhancement) or the place where the lever is located (local enhancement).

Local Enhancement

Local enhancement refers to the facilitation of learning that results from drawing attention to a locale or place associated with reinforcement (Roberts, 1941). For example, Lorenz (1935) noted that ducks enclosed in a pen may not react to a hole large enough for them to escape unless they happen to be near another duck as it is escaping from the pen. The sight of a duck passing through the hole in the pen may serve to draw attention to the hole that might not otherwise have been seen.

Local enhancement has also been implicated in the finding that puncturing the top of milk bottles by great tits spread in a systematic way from one neighborhood to another (Fisher and Hinde, 1949). The technique of pecking through the top of the bottle may be learned through observation, however, the mere presence of birds feeding from the bottles appears to be sufficient for observer birds to acquire the milk-bottle-opening behavior (Sherry and Galef, 1990).

Similarly, Zentall and Hogan (1976) found that pigeons that observed another pigeon pecking at a response key for food were more likely to peck that key, when given the opportunity, than pigeons that had observed another pigeon not pecking at the key but eating from the feeder. However, attention to the demonstrator's pecking may have drawn sufficient attention to the response key to account for facilitation of response acquisition by the observers.

Stimulus Enhancement

When the activity of the demonstrator draws the attention of the observer to a particular *object* (e.g., something that can be manipulated) such facilitation of responding is referred to as stimulus enhancement. Often, the stimulus object is at a particular location, so local and stimulus enhancement effects are confounded. For this reason, the term stimulus enhancement is used primarily when there are two similar objects to be manipulated, one for the demonstrator the other for the observer, and they appear in different locations (e.g., the duplicate-chamber, Zentall and Levine, 1972). Under these conditions, although attention to the location of the demonstrators object should remove the observer's attention from its own object, the similarity between the two may result in attention to the observer's object as well.

Nonimitative Social Learning

Observational Conditioning

The observation of a performing demonstrator can do more than merely draw attention to the object being manipulated (e.g., a colored food patch). Because the observer's orientation to the object is often followed immediately by access to food by the demonstrator, a Pavlovian association may be established. This form of conditioning, in which the observer learns the relation between some part of the environment and the reinforcer (e.g., an initially neutral stimulus and an aversive event, Mineka and Cook, 1988, or depression of a lever and the food that follows, Heyes, 1994) has been called observational conditioning or valence transformation. Although such conditioning would have to take the form of higher-order conditioning (because the observer would not actually experience the unconditional stimulus), there is evidence that such higher-order conditioning can occur even in the absence of a demonstrator (Zentall and Hogan, 1975). The presence of a demonstrator drawing additional attention to the object (by pecking at it) and to the reinforcer (by eating it) may further enhance associative processes in the absence of imitative learning. What characterizes observational conditioning is that the associative process makes it more likely that the observer will approach the CS (the lever or pecking key) and press it by chance.

Affordance Learning or Emulation

A form of learning that is similar to observational conditioning is affordance learning or emulation. Affordance learning involves reproducing the *results* of a demonstrators actions. For example, it is possible for an observer to learn about the consequences of the actions of the demonstrator without actually learning about the actions themselves (Tomasello, 1996).

For example, if a pigeon sees another pigeon pulling the stopper from a tube to obtain grain from the tube (Beauchamp, Giraldeau, and Dugatkin, 1994) the observer may learn that stoppers can be removed from tubes to get the grain inside without learning how to remove the stopper from the tube. Tomasello (1990) has argued that reproducing results does not necessarily imply an understanding of the behavior that led to those results. A clear example, attributable to emulation, is provided by Meltzoff (1988). In his experiment, young children who were shown a toy that could be pulled apart by the experimenter, pulled the toy apart themselves more often than control children who were also shown the toy but did not see it pulled apart. The problem is, seeing that the toy comes apart may be sufficient to produce the pulling-apart response (Meltzoff, 1996; Huang, Heyes, and Charman, 2002).

It should be noted, however, that learning about the affordances of the environment, although different from imitation, may not be a less complex process. In fact, the translation of an observed environmental relationship into behavior that produces the same consequence is a quite remarkable ability (see Klein and Zentall, 2003).

Affordance learning is also likely to have been involved in an experiment reported by Huber, Rechberger, and Taborsky (2001) in which keas (a New Zealand parrot) observed a demonstrator removing several locking devises to open a box. The observers explored the devices more and succeeded in unlocking more devices than birds that had not observed demonstrators.

IMITATION

The traditional means of isolating a variable is by use of a control group that includes all of the factors present in the experimental group (e.g., in the case of imitation, social facilitation) except the one under study. However, it may not be possible to control adequately, by a process of elimination, for all of the nonimitational factors that have been described here (e.g., by including a group that is not exposed to a performing demonstrator but controls for stimulus enhancement, observational conditioning, and learning affordances that may result from observation of a moving manipulandum followed by the appearance of a reinforcer). An alternative approach is to demonstrate different specific body movements to different observers. For example, Moore (1992) would wave his hand at his Grey parrot while saying "caio" and found that the parrot waved back while saying "caio". Similarly, Moore would say "look at my tongue" while sticking out his tongue and the parrot would do the same.

The Bidirectional Control Procedure

Moore's (1992) approach can be incorporated into a better controlled design by defining different responses to be imitated that have individual topographies but have the same consequence. Half of the observers are exposed to one of the topographies and the other half exposed to another. Following observation, the observers are able to perform either topography to obtain reinforcement. The question is, what is the correlation between the topography of the response performed by the demonstrator and that performed by the observer?

The strength of this design is in the fact that it controls for many of the alternative mechanisms described earlier. Because both groups have similar experiences with a demonstrator and with vicarious reward, their motivational level should be comparable. Because the consequences of both topographies are similar, local and stimulus enhancement should be comparable for the two groups. And finally, because the results of the demonstrator's responses, and their relationship to reward, should be the same for the two groups, affordance learning should be comparable as well.

The first study to use a design of this type was reported by Dawson and Foss (1965). But rather than define two response topographies, they allowed demonstrators to discover on their own how to obtain reward from a loosely covered container. By chance, the five demonstrators learned to remove the lid in three quite different ways, two by pushing the lid back with the beak, two by twisting the lid off with the beak, and one by pulling the lid off with the foot. Each of the demonstrators was observed by an observer and when the observers were then presented with the covered containers, all of them removed the lid in the same way that they had seen it removed. Although a later attempt to replicate this effect (Galef, Manzig, and Field, 1986) produced weaker evidence of imitation, the potential strength of the design was recognized.

A similar approach was used by Campbell, Heyes, and Goldsmith (1999). Starlings, in the presence of conspecific observers, selected one of two distinctly colored stoppers and either pushed it into a container or pulled it out of the container, to obtain food reward. When the observers were given the opportunity, they selected the same color and they acted on it in the same way as their demonstrator (see also Fritz and Kotrschal, 1999; Heyes and Saggerson, 2002). However, in this particular experiment, selecting the same color can be explained in terms of stimulus enhancement. Furthermore, repeating the push or pull action may be influenced by the two different outcomes, the stopper moving into the container, in one case, or out of the container, in the other (i.e., differential affordance learning; see Fawcett, Skinner, and Goldsmith, 2002).

Heyes and Dawson (1990) developed a variation of this procedure which they called the bidirectional control. In this procedure, rats observed demonstrators that were expressly trained to push a vertical overhead pole either to the left or to the right (see Figure 1). When the observers were then given access to the pole, Heyes and Dawson found that the rats tended to push the pole in the same direction as their demonstrator pushed it. Later research suggested, however, that olfactory cues, specific to the side of the pole against which the demonstrators pushed, were probably responsible for this response-matching effect (Mitchell, Heyes, Gardener, and Dawson, 1999; Heyes and Ray, 2000).

Bi-Directional Control

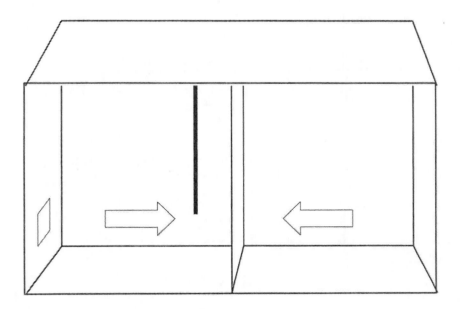

Figure 1. The apparatus used in the bidirectional control procedure with rats (after Heyes and Dawson, 1990).

Recently, evidence for response matching was found using the bidirectional control procedure in an experiment using Japanese quail (Akins, Klein, and Zentall, 2002). In this experiment, a screen that could be pushed either to the left or to the right was placed in front of the feeder and demonstrators were trained to push the screen in one direction or the other (see Figure 2). After each demonstrator performed the screen pushing response, the observer was given access to the screen. As with the rats, the Japanese quail showed a significant tendency to push the screen in the same direction that they has seen it pushed. Akins et al. also included control groups that saw the screen move either to the left or to the right by the experimenter, by means of a wire attached to the screen. To control for the possible effects of the presence of another animals, an inactive demonstrator was also present. These *ghost controls* allow one to assess the effect on screen-movement matching of merely seeing the screen move in one direction or the other (i.e., affordance learning). When given access to the screen, these groups showed no evidence of matching the direction they saw the screen move.

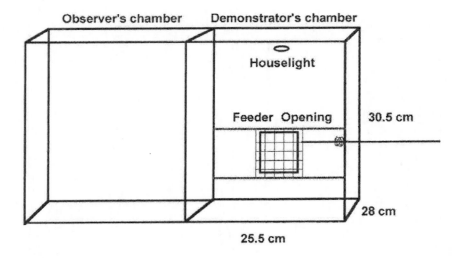

Figure 2. The apparatus used in the bidirectional control procedure with quail and pigeons (after Akins, Klein, and Zentall, 2002).

In a more recent experiment (Klein and Zentall, 2003) the results of the screen pushing task were replicated with pigeons. Furthermore, Klein and Zentall included a group of observers that were exposed to screen pushing demonstrators (either left or right) but their view of the demonstrator was blocked. These groups served as a control for the contribution of possible olfactory and auditory cues to response matching. When these pigeons were then given access to the screen, they showed no evidence of response matching. Thus, olfactory and auditory cues are insufficient to account for the response matching that was found.

The Two-Action Procedure

It should be noted that the bidirectional control procedure suffers from an inherent interpretational problem. Because the manipulated object (i.e., the overhead pole, the stopper, or the feeder screen) moves in a different direction for the two observation groups, it is possible that response matching is facilitated by affordance learning of the movement of the object rather than imitation of the demonstrator's screen-pushing response. To rule out differential affordance learning, ideally, the object should move in the same way independently of the differential response made to it. A refined version of the bidirectional control procedure, developed by Zentall, Sutton, and Sherburne (1996), accomplished this requirement. To preclude differential learning about the environmental consequences of the two responses, the manipulated object, a treadle located just above the floor of the operant chamber, was constrained in how it could move (see Figure 3). The treadle moved down only; similar to a rat lever, it was spring loaded to come back up. One group of demonstrators was trained to depress the treadle with the beak while another group was trained to depress the treadle with the foot. Thus, in this experiment the environmental consequences of both responses were the same and the only variable manipulated was of the topography of the demonstrator's response.

Following observation, when observers were given access to the treadle, Zentall et al. (1996) found a significant correlation between the topography used by the observers and that used by their respective demonstrator. Furthermore, when control pigeons were exposed either to demonstrators that were not depressing the treadle at all or to an empty demonstrator compartment, there was no tendency for the observers to either peck at or step on the treadle (Kaiser, Galef, and Zentall, 1997; see also Akins and Zentall, 1996).

An important point about this procedure is that the two responses were likely to have been quite opaque. That is, there is likely to have been very little similarity between the visual stimulus seen by the observer during observation and that seen by the observer during its own performance of that response. Specifically, to the observer, the demonstrator's beak on the treadle must have appeared quite different from the observer's own beak on the treadle. Similarly, though perhaps not so obviously, when a bird stepped on the treadle (located at the front of the chamber near the common wall between the demonstrator and the observer) it pulled back its head and thrust its body forward. Thus, it could not see its foot making contact with the treadle. Therefore, to the observer, the demonstrator's response to the treadle must have appeared quite different from the observer's own response to the treadle.

Treadle Push – Peck versus Step

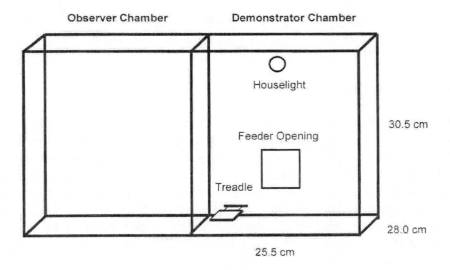

Figure 3. The apparatus used in the two-action procedure with pigeons and quail (after Zentall, Sutton, and Sherburne, 1996).

OTHER FACTORS IMPLICATING COGNITION IN IMITATION

As imitation is defined indirectly by the matching of behavior that cannot be accounted for by other processes, converging evidence would provide additional support for the hypothesis that an imitation-like process was involved.

Demonstrator's Incentive

If imitation is a process that reflects the observer's understanding of the behavior of the demonstrator and its consequences (Tomasello, 1990), whether the demonstrator's behavior is rewarded could be important to the observer. That is, one might expect that observers would be more likely to imitate if the demonstrator's behavior results in reward. Alternatively, it may be that imitation is a reflexive behavior that will occur independently of demonstrator reward.

This hypothesis was tested in an experiment with Japanese quail (Akin and Zentall, 1998). Observers were exposed to demonstrators that were either responding (pecking or stepping) for food or were responding at a comparable rate without receiving food. The results indicated clear response matching for the groups that observed demonstrators that received food for responding, but no response matching for those that observed demonstrators that did not receive food for responding.

Although observational conditioning may also be involved, this mechanism does not provide an alternative to imitation because it cannot account for the differential responses produced by the two observation groups (pecking vs. stepping). Observational conditioning may explain why the observer approaches the treadle (because it is associated with the sight of food) but it can not explain why the response elicited would be different for the two groups.

Observer's Motivation

A manipulation that is perhaps related to observation of rewarded responding is the degree to which the correlation between the demonstrator's reward and the motivational state of the observer at the time of observation affects the likelihood of response matching. In an experiment that attempted to answer this question, demonstrator Japanese quail either pecked at or stepped on a treadle in the presence of observers that were or were not food deprived. When the observers were later tested, those that were not food deprived while observing showed little evidence of imitation (Dorrance and Zentall, 2001). However, those quail that observed while food deprived showed good evidence of imitation when tested at levels of motivation comparable to the other group. These results are consistent with the hypothesis that the observer must be motivated at the time of observation if it is to benefit from that opportunity.

Deferred Imitation

Bandura (1969) made an important distinction between imitation that occurred at the same time as demonstration (or immediately thereafter) and observational learning that occurred some time after demonstration of the target behavior. Those who make this distinction consider immediate response matching to be of a simpler kind (e.g., a form of contagious behavior). According to this view, deferred imitation, on the other hand, cannot be reflexive but must represent the internalization of the demonstrator's behavior. Thus, it exemplifies a higher level of cognitive behavior.

As part of a larger study investigating the effects of observer motivation at the time of observation, Dorrance and Zentall (2001) included a group of quail that observed the demonstration of treadle pecking or treadle stepping and were given the opportunity to perform 30 min later. These quail showed response matching that was comparable to a standard imitation group that was tested immediately after observation. Thus, Japanese quail show deferred imitation for up to a half hour. Whether deferred imitation reflects a higher level of cognitive behavior than immediate imitation or not, deferred imitation does serve to rule out contagion or the elicitation of a reflexive response in the presence of the demonstrator's behavior as an explanation of the response matching found in earlier studies.

Sequence Imitation

Recently, Byrne (2002) has suggested that the imitation of actions such as those described here may be produced by a form of predisposed reflex response that he calls response facilitation. Of course, such reflexes would have to (1) be predisposed for each response individually, (2) be directed toward a particular object, (3) occur only when the demonstrator is rewarded, and (4) be capable of being deferred following observation for as long as 30 min.

Alternatively, Byrne (2002) suggested that if an animal could imitate a sequence of responses it would indicate a more cognitive integrative process. Recently we have investigated sequence imitation in pigeons (Nguyen, Klein, and Zentall, 2005). In a 2 x 2 design, demonstrator pigeons were trained to either peck at a treadle or step on the treadle and then push a screen, either to the left or to the right, away from a feeder opening. To obtain food, observer pigeons could step or peck and then push the screen to the left or to the right with any of the four possible sequences. In support of sequence imitation by pigeons, we found that the sequence produced by the observers was significantly correlated with the sequence demonstrated.

CONCLUSIONS

The approach described in this chapter exemplifies a means of studying psychological processes that cannot be directly observed. I started by identifying numerous genetically predisposed, motivational, perceptual, and learning alternatives to imitation and designing experiments to isolate them from imitation – an analytic approach. Then, I described several characteristics of an imitative process that has cognitive properties such as the consequences of the behavior for the demonstrator, the motivation of the observer, the ability to defer performance of the observed behavior, and the ability to imitate a sequence of two observed actions, and showed that Japanese quail or pigeons showed learning that was consistent with those cognitive properties – a synthetic approach. This combination of analysis and synthesis can provide a developing picture of imitation by nonprimate species that is also appropriate for studying other cognitive processes in animals.

AUTHOR NOTES

Much of the research described in this chapter was supported by Grants MH 55118, MH 59194, and MH 63726 from the National Institute of Mental Health and Grant IBN 9414589 from the National Science Foundation. Correspondence concerning this chapter can be addressed to Thomas R. Zentall, Department of Psychology, University of Kentucky, Lexington, KY 40506-0044. Email zentall@uky.edu

REFERENCES

Akins, C. K., Klein, E. D., and Zentall, T. R. (2002). Imitative learning in Japanese quail (*Coturnix japonica*) using the bidirectional control procedure. *Animal Learning and Behavior, 30,* 275-281.

Akins, C. K., and Zentall, T. R. (1996). Imitative learning in male Japanese quail (*Coturnix japonica*) using the two-action method. *Journal of Comparative Psychology, 110,* 316-320.

Akins, C. K., and Zentall, T. R. (1998). Imitation in Japanese quail: The role of reinforcement of the demonstrator's response. *Psychonomic Bulletin and Review, 5,* 694-697.

Bandura, A. (1969). Social learning theory of identificatory processes. In D. A. Goslin (Ed.). *Handbook of socialization theory and research* (pp. 213-262). Chicago: Rand-McNally.

Beauchamp, G., Giraldeau, L.-A., and Dugatkin, L. A. (1994). The relationship between individual and social learning in pigeons. Human Frontiers in Science Program, Workshop on Social Learning. Mattingly, UK.

Byrne, R. W. (2002). Imitation of novel complex actions: What does the evidence from animals mean? *Advances in the Study of Behavior, 31,* 77-105.

Campbell, F. M., Heyes, C. M., and Goldsmith, A. R. (1999). Stimulus learning and response learning by observation in the European starling in a two-object/two-action test. *Animal Behaviour, 58,* 151-158.

Dawson, B. V. and Foss, B. M. (1965). Observational learning in budgerigars. *Animal Behaviour, 13,* 470-474.

Dorrance, B. R., and Zentall, T. R. (2001). Imitative learning in Japanese quail depends on the motivational state of the observer at the time of observation. *Journal of Comparative Psychology, 115,* 62-67.

Fawcett, T. W., Skinner, A. M., and Goldsmith, A. R. (2002). A test of imitative learning in starlings using a two-action method with an enhanced ghost control. *Animal Behaviour, 64*, 546-556.

Fisher, J., and Hinde, R. A. (1949). The opening of milk bottles by birds. *British Birds, 42*, 347-357.

Fritz, J., and Kotrschal, K. (2002). On avian imitation: Cognitive and ethological perspectives. In K. Dautenhahn and C. L. Nehaniv (Eds.), *Imitation in animals and artifacts* (pp. 133-155). Cambridge, MA: MIT Press.

Galef, B. G., Jr., Manzig, L. A., and Field, R. M. (1986). Imitation learning in budgerigars: Dawson and Foss (1965) revisited. *Behavioral Processes, 13*, 191-202.

Heyes, C. M., and Dawson, G. R. (1990). A demonstration of observational learning in rats using a bidirectional control. *Quarterly Journal of Experimental Psychology, 42B*, 59-71.

Heyes, C. M., and Ray, E. D. (2000). What is the significance of imitation in animals. *Advances in the study of behavior, 29*, 215-245.

Heyes, C., and Saggerson, A. (2002). Testing for imitative and nonimitative learning in the budgerigar using a two-object/two-action test. *Animal Behaviour, 64*, 851-859.

Huang, C. T., Heyes, C. and Charman, T. (2002). Infants' Behavioral Reenactment of "Failed Attempts": Exploring the Roles of Emulation Learning, Stimulus Enhancement, and Understanding of Intentions. *Developmental Psychology 38*, 840-855

Huber, L., Rechberger, S., and Taborsky, M. (2001). Social learning affects object exploration and manipulation in keas, *Nestor notabilis*. *Animal Behaviour, 62*, 945-954.

John, E. R., Chesler, P., Bartlett, F., and Victor, I. (1968). Observational learning in cats. *Science, 159*, 1489-1491.

Kaiser, D. H., Zentall, T. R., and Galef, B. G., Jr. (1997). Can imitation in pigeons be explained by local enhancement together with trial-and-error learning? *Psychological Science, 8*, 459-465.

Klein, E. D., and Zentall, T. R. (2003). Imitation and affordance learning by pigeons (*Columba livia*). Journal of Comparative Psychology.

Lorenz, K. (1935). Der kumpanin der umvelt des vogels: die artgenosse als ausloesendesmoment socialer verhaltensweisen. *Journal fur Ornithologie, 83*, 137-213, 289-413.

Meltzoff, A. N. (1988). The human infant as *homo imitans*. In T. R. Zentall and B. G. Galef, Jr. (Eds.), *Social learning: Psychological and biological perspectives* (pp. 319-341). Hillsdale, NJ: Erlbaum.

Meltzoff, A. N. (1996). The human infant as imitative generalist: A 20-yesr progress report on infant imitation with implications for comparative psychology. In C. M. Heyes and B. G. Galef (Eds.), *Social learning in animals: The roots of culture* (pp. 347-370). San Diego, CA: Academic Press.

Mineka, S. and Cook, M. (1988). Social learning and the acquisition of snake fear in monkeys. In T. R. Zentall and B. G. Galef, Jr. (Eds.), *Social learning: Psychological and biological perspectives* (pp. 51-75). Hillsdale, NJ: Erlbaum.

Mitchell, C. J., Heyes, C. M., Gardner, M. R., and Dawson, G. R. (1999). Limitations of a bidirectional control procedure for the investigation of imitation in rats: Odour cues on the manipulandum. *Quarterly Journal of Experimental Psychology, 52*, 193-202.

Moore, B. R. (1992). Avian movement imitation and a new form of mimicry: Tracing the evolution of a complex form of learning. *Behaviour, 122*, 231-263.

Morrison, B. J., and Hill, W. F. (1967). Socially facilitated reduction of the fear response in rats raised in groups or in isolation. *Journal of Comparative and_Physiological Psychology, 63*, 71-76.

Nguyen, N. H., Klein, E. D., and Zentall, T. R. (2005). Imitation of two-action sequences by pigeons. *Psychonomic Bulletin and Review, 12*, 514-518.

Petrinovitch, L. (1988). The role of social factors in white-crowned sparrow song development. In T. R. Zentall and B. G. Galef, Jr. (Eds.), *Social learning: Psychological and biological perspectives* (pp. 119- 139). Hillsdale, NJ: Erlbaum.

Piaget, J. (1962). Play, dreams, and imitation in childhood. New York: Horton.

Roberts, D. (1941). Imitation and suggestion in animals. *Bulletin of Animal_Behaviour, 1*, 11-19.

Sherry, D. F., and Galef, B. G., Jr. (1990). Social learning without imitation: More about milk bottle opening by birds. *Animal Behaviour, 40*, 987-989.

Tomasello, M. (1990). Cultural transmission in the tool use and communicatory signaling of chimpanzees? In S. Parker and K. Gibson (Eds.), *"Language" and intelligence in monkeys and apes: Comparative developmental_perspectives*, pp. 271-311. Cambridge, UK: Cambridge University Press.

Tomasello, M. (1996). Do apes ape? In C. M. Heyes and B. G. Galef (Eds.), *Social learning in animals: The roots of culture* (pp. 319-346). San Diego, CA: Academic Press.

Zajonc, R. B. (1965). Social facilitation. *Science, 149*, 269-274.

Zentall, T. R., Edwards, C. A., and Hogan, D. E. (1983). Pigeons' use of identity. In M. L. Commons, R. J. Herrnstein, and A. Wagner (Eds.), *The quantitative analyses of behavior: Vol. 4. Discrimination processes* (pp. 273-293). Cambridge, MA: Ballinger.

Zentall, T. R. and Hogan, D. E. (1975). Key pecking in pigeons produced by pairing key light with inaccessible grain. *Journal of the Experimental Analysis of Behavior, 23*, 199-206.

Zentall, T. R. and Hogan, D. E. (1976). Imitation and social facilitation in the pigeon. *Animal Learning and Behavior, 4*, 427-430.

Zentall, T. R. and Levine, J. M. (1972). Observational learning and social facilitation in the rat. *Science, 178*, 1220-1221.

Zentall, T. R., Sutton, J. and Sherburne, L. M. (1996). True imitative learning in pigeons. *Psychological Science, 7*, 343-346.

In: Tasks and Techniques: A Sampling of the Methodologies...   ISBN 1-60021-126-7
Editor: Matthew J. Anderson, pp. 223-233   © 2006 Nova Science Publishers, Inc.

Chapter 18

METHODOLOGICAL ISSUES IN THE STUDY OF COGNITIVE MAPPING IN ANIMALS

Rebecca A. Singer and Thomas R. Zentall[*]
University of Kentucky, Lexington, KY 40506-0044

ABSTRACT

Cognitive mapping is a method of navigation that implies that there is a cognitive representation of the environment. Cognitive mapping must be distinguished from other means of navigation such as landmark use (memory for objects in the environment) and path integration (the ability to know the distance and direction to a central location) neither of which relies on an unseen representation of the environment. One means of testing for cognitive mapping in rats involves the ability to use a novel path when familiar paths are blocked under conditions that rule out the use of familiar landmarks. As predicted by cognitive mapping, we have found that rats show a significant tendency to use novel paths appropriately but only when landmarks are provided during training. Thus, path integration is not likely to be involved.

INTRODUCTION

Having a cognitive map implies the development of an internal representation of the spatial relationship among objects or landmarks in the environment. The problem with this definition is it proposes the presence of an unseen representational mechanism which may be too vague and general to capture the variety of tools an animal uses to navigate in its environment. As Macintosh (2002) has noted, if the term cognitive map is used uncritically to denote generally what an animal learns about the location of objects in its environment, it loses its explanatory value. On the other hand, if the term is meant to imply something quite

[*] Send Correspondence to: Thomas R. Zentall, Department of Psychology, University of Kentucky, Lexington, KY 40506-0044, Phone: 859-257-4076, Fax: 859-323-1979, Email: zentall@uky.edu

specific and different from other simpler mechanisms it may not be sufficiently distinguishable from them to allow for an adequate test.

However, the concept of a cognitive map can be useful if it is used to indicate a specific ability that can be clearly distinguished from other simpler mechanisms. Two such simpler mechanisms that have been proposed are landmark use and path integration. Landmark use refers to an animal's ability to use objects in the environment as cues by which to orient and find goal locations (Cartwright and Collett, 1983). Path integration is the ability to keep track of one's position in the environment (vector and distance from home) in the absence of external cues (Andel and Wehner, 2004). Although both landmark use and path integration allow animals to effectively forage and return home, neither implies a cognitive representation of the environment.

LANDMARK USE

A landmark may be an object located at or near a goal location that indicates where the goal can be found (e.g., a single landmark may mark the location of a food source). The use of landmarks can be thought of as using snapshot memory. Animals learn to use the view of the landmark from the goal. On succeeding trips they move to a location where the present view of the landmark matches their snapshot memory of the view of the landmark. The test of landmark use is whether the animal can find the goal with the landmark removed. For example, Cartwright and Collett (1983) studied the use of landmarks in bees. Bees were trained to fly to a sucrose solution placed near a fixed landmark (a black cylinder) in an experimental room. When the landmark was removed from the room, the bees no longer searched near the goal location, but searched in a random pattern. This finding suggests that the bees used the presence of the landmark to locate the sucrose solution. Animals may also use a combination of multiple landmarks to locate a food source. Collett, Cartwright, and Smith (1986) trained gerbils to dig for sunflower seeds that had been buried in a test arena a fixed distance south of an imaginary line joining two identical landmarks (white cylinders) and equidistant from both. In test, when one of the two landmarks was removed from the arena, the gerbils searched in two locations for the buried seed at an appropriate distance to the left and to the right of the remaining landmark. Thus, the gerbils appear to have used the relationship between landmarks to locate a food source and, when faced with a single landmark, the gerbils were unable to determine whether the remaining landmark was the left or right one.

PATH INTEGRATION

Path integration is a process by which animals use information about distance and direction traveled to update their current location relative to a start location. In the absence of landmarks, both ants (Müller and Wehner, 1988; Wehner and Srinivasan, 1981) and golden hamsters (Etienne, Maurer, and Saucy, 1988) appear to be able to use path integration to return to their nest after foraging excursions.

Desert ants forage along a long and circuitous route to find food, often traveling several hundred meters. However, their return journey does not retrace their outward path. Rather, these ants travel along a relatively straight trajectory from the goal location back to their nest. Evidence that the ants are not using landmarks comes from studies where ants are displaced once they find food. After displacement, ants travel along a straight trajectory back to where the nest would have been had they not been displaced and begin a focal search of the area where home would have been (Müller and Wehner, 1994; Kohler and Wehner, 2005). This suggests that the ants had used the direction and distance from the nest to determine the return route to their nest.

Similarly, animals that travel in darkness may also rely on path integration to navigate. Etienne (1992) studied the ability of golden hamsters to locate a food source and return to their nest box in the dark. The hamsters were initially trained, with the lights on, to go directly to hazelnuts buried at the center of a circular arena. The behavior of interest was how efficient the hamsters were at returning to the nest box once they had collected the hazelnuts. Test trials were conducted in total darkness. Hamsters went directly from the nest box to the center of the arena and then returned to a point very close to the nest box. Thus, in the absence of external cues, the hamsters were able to use distance and direction information to locate the nest box.

Path integration would appear to be sufficient to allow animals to navigate successfully; however, path integration has its limits. Errors in calculating distance and direction often accumulate as the distance traveled is extended. Therefore, although path integration is reasonably reliable on relatively short journeys, long-distance orientation often includes the use of landmarks.

Path integration and landmarks should provide an animal with sufficient information to find its way around in most environments. Circumstances may arise however, in which direct or familiar paths are blocked and novel pathways must be taken. In such cases it might be useful if an animal had a general sense of where in the environment it was relative to its goal.

COGNITIVE MAPS

Tolman (1948) was the first to use the term 'cognitive map' when describing navigation in rats. He proposed that "something like a field map of the environment gets established in the rat's brain" (p.192). O'Keefe and Nadel (1978) followed with a formal theory of cognitive mapping. They proposed that animals use a combination of sensory and motor information to establish their location in space. In addition, the animals use the relationship of landmarks within the environment to locate their position within the map, as well as to locate a goal.

Poucet (1993) proposed a theory of cognitive mapping that states there are two pieces of information needed to form a cognitive map, topological information and metric information. Topological information refers to the relationship between objects, such as whether one object is above, below, or next to a second object. Metric information provides quantitative information about the objects, such as the distance between the two and the angle formed by the objects relative to a fixed location, such as a starting point. The integration of both topological and metric information could allow for the formation of internal representations of objects within an environment. Therefore, cognitive maps are built by the organization of information about the spatial relationship among the landmarks.

One difficulty with these definitions is how to disambiguate these definitions from the alternative navigational strategies of path integration and landmark use. The focus of a cognitive mapping definition should be on 'representation'. Objects in the environment may be necessary for the formation of cognitive maps, but their presence or absence should not be necessary to guide navigation. Landmarks may serve as the organizing features of a cognitive map, but once the animal is oriented, they should not be needed for an animal to locate the goal (Golledge, 1999).

Intuitively, having a representation of one's environment should allow one to travel to familiar places using novel paths when either familiar paths are unavailable (i.e., detours are required) or when shortcuts provide more efficient paths to the goal. Although one might be comfortable with an intuitive notion of a cognitive map, a useful definition must allow one to distinguish a cognitive map from other mechanisms such as path integration and landmark use. Unfortunately, much that purports to show the use of cognitive maps has failed to rule out alternative explanations for subjects' successful navigation.

Use of Detours

Using a detour implies that one can use an appropriate, often longer, alternative path when a familiar shorter path is blocked. In one study of detour use, Tolman and Honzik (1930) trained rats to run to a single goal box by way of three separate paths that differed in their distance to the goal (see Figure 1). After the rats had experience with all three paths and the shortest path was blocked, they chose the second shortest path. However, when the shortest path was blocked beyond the point in the maze where the second shortest path rejoined the first path, the rats went directly to the third path, the only path that still allowed access to the goal (see also Tolman, Richie, and Kalish, 1946).

The idea is, when seen from the perspective of the shortest path, the rats must have been able to recognize that in the first case, the exit from the next shortest path would have allowed the rats to proceed beyond the blockage. However, the rats also must have been able to recognize that in the second case, the exit from the next shortest path would not allow them to proceed beyond the blockage. Instead, to gain access to the goal, the rats would have to take the third path, the only path that exited beyond the blockage.

Novel Shortcut Design

Alternatively, tests for a cognitive map may involve the use of a novel path. Tolman (1948) used the novel shortcut design in his original cognitive mapping experiment. In this experiment, rats were trained to run from a start box to a goal box along an alley that made a series of turns, both towards and away from the goal box. In test, rats were given a choice among several new alleys leading away from the start box (see Figure 2). On test trials, the rats chose the most direct path to the goal box. Thus, Tolman concluded that they had learned about the spatial relationship of the start box to the goal box.

Unfortunately, there was a single light hung directly above the goal box during both training and testing. Therefore, the rats could have learned to use that light as a landmark, rather than learning about the spatial relationship of the start and goal boxes.

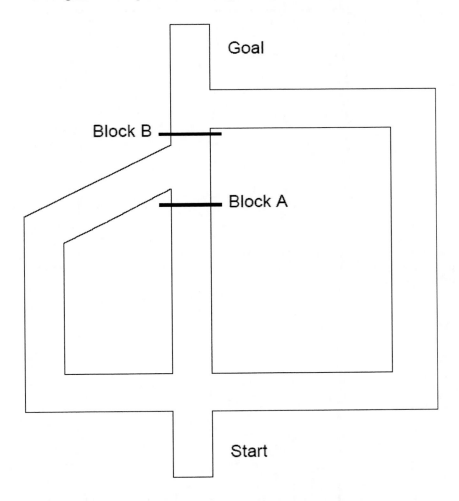

Figure 1. Novel path apparatus used by Tolman and Honzik (1930). After experience with all three paths, rats took the left path when tested with Block A but they took the right path when tasted with Block B.

Walker and Olton (cited in Olton, 1979) also examined the use of novel routes by rats. Their apparatus involved a series of thirteen interconnected boxes, with the center box serving as the goal box (see Figure 3). The four boxes adjacent to the goal box were start boxes. Rats were trained to travel from three of the four start boxes to the center goal box. Test trials examined the rats' behavior when placed in the fourth start box. Although the rats had never been in the fourth start box and had never traveled the path from the fourth start box to the center start box, they took the novel path almost 80% of the time, even on the first test trial. Walker and Olton demonstrated that rats were able to learn where the goal was and use that information when placed at an unfamiliar start location. However, the apparatus did not have a cover, so it is possible that cues above the apparatus may have served as landmarks that could have been used to find the goal.

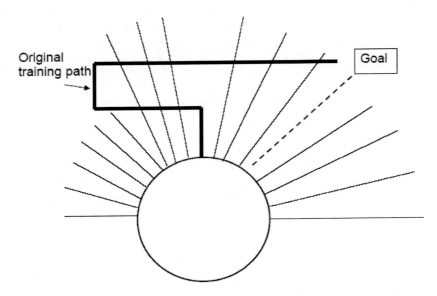

Figure 2. Novel path apparatus used by Tolman (1948). Rats learned to approach goal by taking the original training path. When this path was blocked, they took the most direct path to the goal (dotted line) rather than a path closest to the training path.

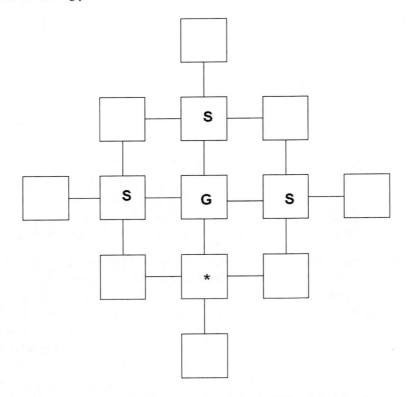

Figure 3. Novel path apparatus used by Walker and Olton (cited by Olton, 1979). Rats learned to run to goal box (G) from start boxes (S). When placed in a novel start box (*) they went directly to the goal box along a novel path in a novel direction.

A more recent experiment with dogs provides an alternative procedure for studying cognitive mapping in animals (Chapuis and Varlet, 1987). In an open field, dogs were led from a starting point to a location where a food item was hidden. The dogs were shown the food item, and wre led back to the starting point. Then the dogs were led to a second hidden food location, somewhat farther away and at an angle of about 30 degrees from the original starting point. They were shown the food there and were then led back to the starting point. In test, the dogs were let off their lead and allowed to find the hidden food in both locations. The dogs first ran to the food location closest to the starting point and then ran directly to the second hidden food location, without going back to the starting point. This ability to take a novel shortcut suggested that the dogs had some representation of the environment and where the second food location was relative to the first. The fact that the dogs were trained in an open field without distinctive local cues suggests that they were not using landmarks. However, in such a natural setting, it may be impossible to eliminate distal landmarks (e.g., trees, bushes, and houses) that might be used as cues to indicate the direction of the second goal.

Better evidence for cognitive mapping ability in animals should use a test involving a novel path as well as eliminate landmarks at the point where the animal must choose between novel paths. Singer, Abroms, and Zentall (in press) developed a method of testing for cognitive mapping in rats that meets this criterion.

The apparatus was a three-arm maze with a goal box at the end of each arm (see Figure 4). Rats were trained to find food rewards in two of the three goal boxes. For each rat, the same two arms were consistently baited (either the center and left or center and right arms). Rats had access to all three arms during the training phase. The entire maze was covered with a translucent cover and the maze was rotated 90° each day to prevent the possible use of external landmarks (possible shadows) to guide navigation. On test trials, the rats were released into the central platform but both side arms were blocked. They only had access to the center arm. Once they entered the center goal box, they could choose between two novel pathways (shown in black in Figure 4), one that led to the arm that had been consistently baited in training (designated correct), while the other led to the arm that had been unbaited during training. Both side goal boxes were baited during test trials to control for the possible use of odor cues.

Singer, et al. (in press) were also interested in the role played by landmarks in the formation of cognitive maps. The apparatus just described may be modified to incorporate landmarks to help identify the arms. Textured arm inserts, in the side arms of the three-arm maze (hardware cloth in one arm and sheet metal in the other) served this role (see Figure 4). Importantly, these arm inserts ended prior to the goal box area. Thus, on test trials, these inserts could not be seen from the center goal box and on test trials, could not be used to guide choice behavior. For a separate group of rats, all three arms were made similar in size, texture, and color (see Figure 5). If landmarks are necessary for the development of a cognitive map then the rats for which these landmarks were not available should have had difficulty forming a cognitive map.

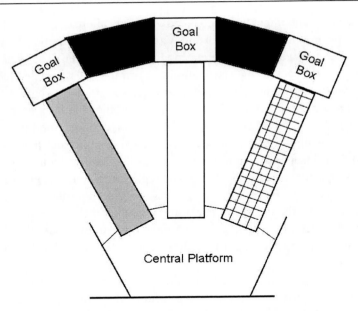

Figure 4. Novel path apparatus with distinctive arms used by Singer et al. (in press). Rats were trained to find food in center and one side arm (paths between goal boxes were blocked). When the two side arms were blocked and the novel paths between goal boxes were opened, rats took the novel path that in training led to the baited side goal box.

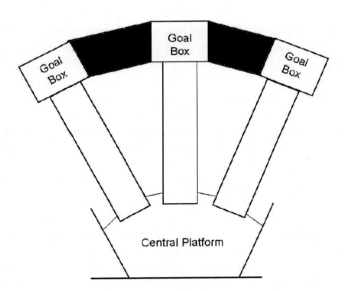

Figure 5. Novel path apparatus with nondistinctive arms used by Singer et al. (in press). Rats were trained to find food in center and one side arm (paths between goal boxes were blocked). When the two side arms were blocked and the novel paths between goal boxes were opened rats took the two novel paths about equally.

Singer, et al. (in press) found that when the textured arm inserts were present during training rats demonstrated a significant tendency to choose the novel shortcut that led to the baited goal box in training, but not when the arms were not distinctive. Thus, it appears that rats are able to form a simple cognitive map with the use of landmarks and they can then use that map in the absence of distinctive landmarks.

The typical view of path integration is that it provides a vector and distance from home, allowing an animal to return directly after foraging (e.g. Wehner and Wehner, 1986; Kohler and Wehner, 2005). Thus, according to this definition, path integration cannot account for performance on test trials found by Singer, et al. (in press). However, an alternative view of path integration is that it can also be used to navigate from home to a familiar goal by way of a novel path (Etienne, Maurer, and Séguinot, 1996). Animals may be able to update direction and distance as they move around the maze in training and that information should be able to get them to a goal by a novel path. However, an account based on path integration should not distinguish between the two conditions used by Singer, et al. That is, selection of the correct novel path should not depend on the presence in training of distinct arm cues. Yet Singer, et al. found that only the rats that had distinctive arm cues present during training showed reliable choice of the correct novel path. It may be that the role of those distinctive arm cues is to 'stitch together' the pieces of the cognitive map. That is, for example, the texture of the hardware cloth may mediate the association between the rat's original choice at the central platform and the consequences of that choice in the goal box.

CONCLUSION

When cognitive mechanisms are poorly defined, they can suffer from being overly general and vague. When the term cognitive map is used to describe an animal's general ability to navigate in its environment, it is not a useful concept. However, if the use of a cognitive map can be empirically distinguished from other presumably simpler mechanisms such as path integration and landmark use, it may provide a useful means of characterizing how an animal represents its environment. We believe that we have provided such a definition and have provided preliminary supportive evidence that under certain conditions rats can develop a simple cognitive map.

AUTHOR NOTES

Some of the research described in this chapter was supported by Grant MH 63726 from the National Institute of Mental Health. Correspondence concerning this chapter can be addressed to either Rebecca A. Singer, Department of Psychology, University of Kentucky, Lexington, KY 40506-0044 (email rasing2@uky.edu) or Thomas R. Zentall, Department of Psychology, University of Kentucky, Lexington, KY 40506-0044 (email zentall@uky.edu).

REFERENCES

Andel, D., and Wehner, R. (2004). Path integration in desert ants, *Cataglyphis*: how to make a homing ant run away from home. *Proceeding of the Royal Society of London, 271,* 1485-1489.

Cartwright, B. A., and Collett, T. S. (1983). Landmark learning in bees. *Journal of Comparative Physiology A, 151,* 521-543.

Chapius, N., and Varlet, C. (1987). Short cuts by dogs in natural surroundings. *The Quarterly Journal of Experimental Psychology, 39,* 49-64.

Collett, T. S., Cartwright, B. A., and Smith, B. A. (1986). Landmark learning and visuo-spatial memories in gerbils. *Journal of Comparative Physiology A, 158,* 835-85.

Etienne, A. S. (1992). Navigation of a small mammal by dead reckoning and local cues. *Current Directions in Psychological Science I,* 48-52.

Etienne, A. S., Maurer, R., and Saucy, F. (1988). Limitations in the assessment of path dependent information. *Behavior, 106,* 81-111.

Etienne, A. S., Maurer, R., and Séguinot, V. (1996). Path integration in mammals and its interaction with visual landmarks. *The Journal of Experimental Biology, 199,* 201-209.

Golledge, R. G. (1999). Human wayfinding and cognitive maps. In Golledge, R.G. (Ed.), *Wayfinding Behavior* (pp. 5-45). Baltimore, Maryland: The Johns Hopkins University Press.

Kohler, M., and Wehner, R. (2005). Idiosyncratic route-based memories in desert ants, *Melophorus bagoti*: How do they interact with path integration vectors? *Neurobiology of Learning and Memory, 83,* 1-12.

Mackintosh, N. J. (2002). Do not ask whether they have a cognitive map, but how they find their way about. *Psicológica, 23,* 165-185.

Müller, M., and Wehner, R. (1994). The hidden spiral: Systemataic search and path integration in desert ants, *Cataglyphis fortis. Journal of Comparative Physiology,* A175, 525-530.

Müller, M., and Wehner, R. (1988). Path integration in desert ants, *Cataglyphis fortis. Proceedings of the National Academy of Science, 85,* 5287-5290.

O'Keefe, J., and Nadel, L. (1978). The hippocampus as a cognitive map. Oxford, U.K.: Oxford University Press.

Olton, D.S. (1979). Mazes, map, and memory. *American Psychologist, 34,* 583-596.

Poucet, B. (1993). Spatial cognitive maps in animals: New hypotheses on their structure and neural mechanisms. *Psychological Review, 100(2),* 163-182.

Singer, R. A., Abroms, B. D., and Zentall, T. R. (in press). Formation of simple cognitive maps in rats. *International Journal of Comparative Psychology.*

Tolman, E. C. (1948). Cognitive maps in rats and man. *Psychological Review, 55,* 189-208.

Tolman, E. C., and Honzik, C. H. (1930a). Insight in rats. *University of California Publications in Psychology, 4,* 215-232.

Wehner, R., and Srinivasan, M. V. (1981). Searching behavior of desert ants, genus *Cataglyphis* (Formicidae, Hymenoptera). *Journal of Comparative Psychology A, 142,* 315-338.

Wehner, R., and Wehner, S. (1986). Path integration in desert ants. Approaching a long-standing puzzle in insect navigation. *Monitore Zoologico Italiano, 20,* 309-331.

In: Tasks and Techniques: A Sampling of the Methodologies...   ISBN 1-60021-126-7
Editor: Matthew J. Anderson, pp. 233-244   © 2006 Nova Science Publishers, Inc.

Chapter 19

BASIC TEMPORAL DISCRIMINATION PROCEDURES

Mika L.M. MacInnis[*] and Paulo Guilhardi

Brown University, Providence, RI 02912

ABSTRACT

Many psychophysical temporal discrimination procedures have been designed and used to measure the ability of animals and humans to time interval durations. This chapter introduces three basic psychophysical temporal discrimination procedures that have been used across a wide range of species: the fixed-interval procedure, the peak procedure, and the bisection procedure. This chapter provides an in-depth description of the three procedures as they are executed in standard operant chambers for rats, and methods for data analysis. Standard results, as well as some of the traditional interpretations of the results, are presented. A brief examination of the application of the procedures to different questions and how they have been used to answer these questions is included.

INTRODUCTION

Psychophysical procedures have been developed that use behavior as a measure of time discrimination. This chapter describes three basic psychophysical procedures that have produced similar and robust results in many laboratories and across a variety of species, such as humans (e.g. Allan and Gibbon, 1991; Green Ivry, and Woodruff-Pak, 1999), rats (e.g. Crystal, 2002; Kirkpatrick and Church, 2003), and pigeons (Machado and Keen, 2003; Santi, Hornyak, and Miki, 2003). These procedures are the fixed-interval procedure (Schneider, 1969; Ferster and Skinner, 1957), the peak procedure (Catania, 1970; Catania and Reynolds, 1968; Roberts, 1981), and the bisection procedure (Stubbs, 1976; Church and Deluty, 1977).

---

[*] Address Correspondence to: Mika L.M. MacInnis, Department of Psychology, Box 1853, Brown University, Providence, RI 02912, Telephone: 401 863 3979, Fax: 401 863 1300, email: Mika_Macinins@Brown.edu

The Fixed-Interval Procedure

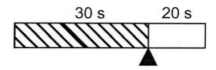

Figure 1. Fixed-interval 30 s procedure.

The fixed-interval procedure is an appetitive procedure that consists of a stimulus that is turned on (e.g. a light), and after a target duration (e.g. 30 s) the next response (e.g. head entry to the food cup) delivers food and terminates the stimulus. After a period with no stimulus the stimulus is turned on again and the cycle is repeated. An example of a cycle from a FI 30-s procedure is shown in Figure 1. The striped bar indicates the stimulus. The black triangle indicates food. The results from three FI procedures, 30, 60, and 120 s, are shown in Figure 2 (data from Guilhardi and Church, 2004). The top left panel shows response rate as a function of time averaged over five sessions (the second half of a total of 10 training sessions consisting of 60 cycles each), for the three groups (four rats in a group). The slope of the response gradients decreased as a function of interval duration. Response rate was inversely related to interval duration. When the relative response rate was plotted as a function of relative time since stimulus onset, the three curves superpose. This superposition is shown in the bottom left panel of Figure 2.

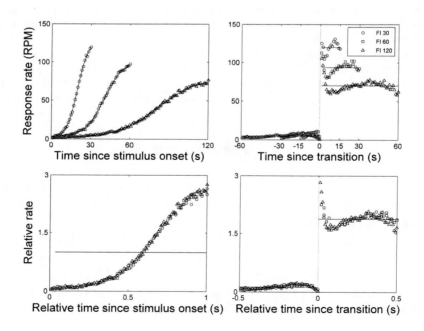

Figure 2. Results from the FI 30-, 60-, and 120-s procedure. (Adapted from Guilhardi and Church, 2004, by the authors).

On a single cycle, responding can be described as a step function, with responses at a low rate in the beginning of the cycle, and at a fast relatively stable rate at the end of the cycle (Schneider, 1969). The ogival response rate gradients shown in the left panels of Figure 2 are the average of step functions with variability in the time of transition from a low to a high state of responding. The top right panel of Figure 2 shows response rate plotted as a function of the transition point (see methods for a description of the mathematical definition of the transition). The difference in response rate across the three fixed intervals is evident following the transition point. When the relative response rate is plotted as a function of relative time, the functions also superposed (bottom right panel of Figure 2).

The results from fixed-interval procedures provide evidence for the four principles of timing (Gibbon, 1977): timescale invariance (when plotted on a relative scale, estimations of different interval durations will superpose), proportionality (time is perceived proportionately rather than absolutely), the scalar property (variability in timing increases linearly with interval duration), and Weber's law in timing (a constant ratio of the standard deviation to the mean of the interval timed). These principles have also been shown in results from FI procedures designed to measure the dynamics of temporal discrimination (e.g. Guilhardi and Church, 2005), to examine the ability to time multiple intervals simultaneously (Meck and Church, 1984; Church, Guilhardi, Keen, MacInnis, and Kirkpatrick, 2003; Guilhardi, Keen, MacInnis, and Church, 2005), to investigate the effects of neurological disorders such as Parkinson's disease on timing (e.g. Malapani, Rakitin, Levy, Meck, Dweer, Dubois, and Gibbon, 1998), as well as to compare time discrimination across species (e.g. Lejeune and Wearden, 1991).

The Peak Procedure

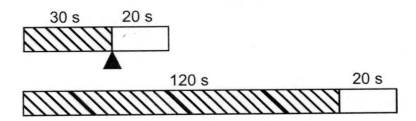

Figure 3. Peak procedure.

The peak procedure is a timing procedure in which animals are exposed to two types of cycles. Standard cycles are identical to cycles in a fixed-interval procedure. On peak cycles the stimulus is turned on but responses do not produce food nor terminate the stimulus that remains on for several times the length of the target duration. Figure 3 shows the standard (top) and peak (bottom) cycles in the peak procedure.

The results from a peak procedure 120 s are shown in Figure 4 (data from Church, Meck, and Gibbon, 1994). The response rate gradients averaged across peak cycles increased until around the time of reinforcement and then decreased relatively symmetrically (top panel). On individual cycles (bottom panels), the pattern of responding was characterized by a low-high-low states of responding with two transition points, t_1 (low-high, left panel) and t_2 (high-low, right panel).

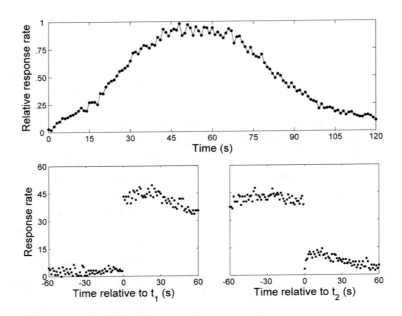

Figure 4. Results from the peak procedure. (Adapted from Church, Meck, and Gibbon, 1994, by the authors).

The peak procedure has been used extensively to study the effects of drugs, as well as neurological disorders (e.g. Parkinson's disease) on time discrimination. The location and spread of the peak in the response gradient is used as a measure of timing accuracy and precision. A shift in the gradient to the left has been produced with the administration of dopamine agonists such as methamphetamine (e.g. Maricq, Roberts, and Church, 1981). A shift to the right has been produced with the administration of haloperidol and other dopamine antagonists (e.g. Drew, Fairhurst, Malapani, Horvitz, and Balsam, 2003). The shifts have been interpreted as an increase and decrease (respectively) in the speed of an internal clock.

The Bisection Procedure

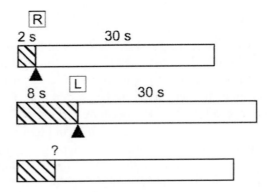

Figure 5. Bisection procedure.

On a bisection procedure, animals are trained to respond differentially (e.g. right or left lever presses) after the presentation of a short (e.g. 2 s) or a long (e.g. 8 s) stimulus duration. Once differential responding to the short and long intervals has been trained, the stimuli are presented for intermediate durations intermixed with the short and long durations. The animal's responses on the intermediate duration cycles and some of the short and long duration cycles are not reinforced. Church and Deluty (1977) trained eight rats on four pairs of intervals: 1-4 s, 2-8 s, 3-12 s, and 4-16 s (a different pair for each phase of the experiment, the order of which was counterbalanced between rats). After the stimulus was presented, two levers were inserted into the box, and the rat received food if it made a right response for the short interval and a left response for the long interval (counterbalanced across subjects). After a response had been made a 30-s intercycle interval began.

The results from the Church and Deluty (1997) bisection procedure are shown in Figure 6. The proportion of "long" responses increased as a function of the target interval. The slopes of the curves were inversely related to the target interval. The time at which the rat was equally likely to respond "long" as "short" is the point of subjective equality (the bisection point). This point was approximately the geometric mean of the long and short intervals. The proportion "long" functions superposed when plotted as a function of time relative to the geometric mean between the short and long durations (bottom panel). These and similar results (e.g. Meck, Church, and Gibbon, 1985) provided evidence for the principle of timescale invariance.

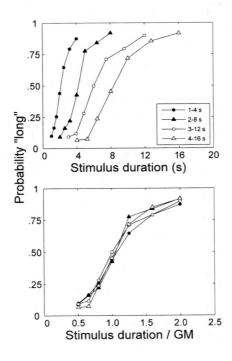

Figure 6. Results from the bisection procedure. (Adapted from Church and Deluty, 1977, by the authors).

The bisection procedure has been used extensively in humans (Allan and Gibbon, 1991), rats (Crystal, Maxwell, and Hohmann, 2003), and pigeons (Machado and Keen, 1999), as well as to study drug effects in rats (Crystal et al., 2003) on temporal discrimination. A leftward shift in the bisection point has been interpreted as an increase, and a rightward shift as a decrease, in the speed of an internal clock. A change in the slope of the function is an indication in the variability of time perception.

METHODS

This section of this chapter provides a general description of the equipment and basic protocol followed by the Timing Lab at Brown University when conducting temporal discrimination experiments with rats. Moreover, this section provides specific instructions for the use of the three procedures described above and a description of the methods of data analysis.

Animals

Naive male Sprague Dawley rats (Taconic Laboratories, Germantown, NY) are used. Although female rats can be used, there is evidence that changes in hormones levels may affect timing performance (Ross and Santi, 2000). Traditionally, only male rats have been used to control for potential effects of the estrous cycle on timing behavior. The rats are 30 to 37 days old upon arrival and housed individually in a colony room on a 12:12 hour light/dark cycle (lights off at 9:30 am). Dim red light illuminates the colony room and the testing room during the lights off portion of the day. Because rats are nocturnal animals, this reverse light/dark cycle ensures that the animals are tested during the "waking" part of their day.

During the first week following arrival, the rats are maintained on ad libitum food (FormuLab 5008). After the first week, the rats are restricted to 15 grams of food daily. Testing begins following one week of food restriction. After testing begins, the daily ration of food is given in the home cage after the testing session. The rats receive 15 grams of food in addition to the food they receive during the testing sessions provided the total amount of daily food does not exceed 20 g. Weekly weights are taken to ensure a minimum of weight gain of approximately five grams per week. If the minimum weight gain is not reached, an additional three grams of food is given daily until minimum weight gain occurs. Water is available *ad libitum* in both the home cages and the experimental cages throughout the experiments.

The rats are handled daily from arrival to the onset of the experiment. Handling consists of the handler removing the rat from the home cage by lifting it under the forelegs with the ungloved hand, holding it in the gloved hand, and stroking it with the other (ungloved) hand for approximately two minutes. The glove used is a leather gardening glove that protects the handler against getting scratched by the rat's nails. The more relaxed the handler is when handling the rat, the calmer the rats are, and the more regular the data are.

Testing begins approximately two weeks following arrival. After testing begins, daily handling ceases, although the animals are hand-carried to the experimental chambers in a manner similar to handling, rat sitting in the gloved hand, and held loosely in place with the ungloved hand.

Apparatus

Twelve extra tall modular operant test chambers (30.5 x 24.1 x 21.0 cm, Model ENV-007, Med Associates, St. Albans, VT) with stainless steel grid floors (Model ENV-005, Med Associates, St. Albans, VT), each located inside a ventilated, noise-attenuating box (66.0 cm x 55.9 cm x 35.6 cm, Model ENV-016M, Med Associates, St. Albans, VT), are used in testing. Each chamber is equipped with a food cup (5 × 5 × 2 cm, Model ENV-200R2M, Med Associates, St. Albans, VT) located in the middle of the right wall. Each head entry into the food cup is transduced by a LED-photocell (Model, ENV-254, Med Associates, St. Albans, VT). Both the times of head entry and withdrawal to the food cup are recorded. A magazine pellet dispenser (Model ENV-203M, Med Associates, St. Albans, VT) delivers 45-mg Dustless Precision Pellets (Bio-Serv, Rodent Grain-Base Formula, Frenchtown, NJ) into the food cup. To the left and right of the food cup are retractable levers (7 cm above the grid, 4.5 cm wide, extending 2 cm into the chamber and requiring approximately 18 g to operate, Model ENV-112, Med Associates, St. Albans, VT) that can be automatically inserted or removed from the chamber depending upon the procedure. A water bottle is mounted on the outside of the left wall of the experimental chamber. Water is available through a tube that passes through a hole in the middle of the wall (opposite the food cup). Licks on the water tube are recorded via a contact lickometer (Model ENV-250RM). A houselight with a diffuser (Model ENV-227M) is mounted above the water bottle. Two Gateway Pentium computers, running the Med-PC Medstate Notation Version 2.0 (Tatham and Zurn, 1989), control experimental events and record the times at which events occur with 2-ms resolution.

The overall number of responses emitted by each animal during each session is recorded in a notebook at the end of the session in order to have a prompt daily indication of its performance as well as identify unusual, but possible, equipment problems (e.g., light bulbs burned, feeder malfunction). Prior to each test session, a boxtest program is run to ensure that all stimulus generators and response recorders are functioning properly. If some component of the box is malfunctioning, it is either repaired or replaced before the start of the session. If a part malfunctions during a session, it is recorded in the notebook, with a detailed description of the problem and when it occurred (e.g. at cycle 15), and repaired after all other animals have finished the test session and the animals have been taken back to their home cages. Additionally, any changes in environment that could affect behavior (e.g. animal was dropped on the way to the experimental chamber; there was construction in the building causing excessive noise) are recorded.

Procedures

Fixed-Interval Procedure

A cycle of a FI procedure is shown in Figure 1. A stimulus (e.g. white noise, houselight, clicker) is turned on for the target duration (e.g. 30 s). The reinforcer is made available (primed) at the target duration, but delivered only after the first response (e.g. head entry into food cup, lever press) following reinforcer prime. This response also terminates the stimulus and begins a 20-s interval with no stimulus. At the end of 20 s, the stimulus is turned on and the cycle is repeated. The cycle is repeated 60 times a session. Rats learn the target duration very quickly within the first five sessions, but performance will continue to change with training (e.g. Guilhardi and Church, 2004). In the timing laboratory at Brown University, rats are generally tested for at least 20 sessions on a fixed interval procedure, and the last 10 sessions used for steady state performance. In some cases, three intervals signaled by different stimuli are presented intermixed in a session for within subjects comparison (Guilhardi and Church, 2005).

Peak Procedure

The peak procedure consists of two types of cycles shown in Figure 3. The reinforced cycle is identical to a cycle from a FI procedure. The stimulus is turned on for a fixed duration (e.g. 30 s) and the first response following reinforcer prime terminates the stimulus and delivers the food. On the peak cycles the stimulus is turned on for an interval duration that is at least four times longer than the target duration (e.g. 120 s), responses have no effect, and no food is delivered. After stimulus termination, the stimulus remains off for 20 s for both cycle types. The cycles are presented randomly, with a determined probability (e.g. .5). At the beginning of each cycle, the computer, using a random number generator, determines what type of cycle is presented (e.g. if the number generated from a uniform distribution between zero and one is under .5, a standard cycle is presented, if the number is above .5, a peak cycle is presented). Generally, 60 cycles are presented in a session.

Bisection Procedure

In a bisection procedure, there is a long and a short cycle type, shown in the top two panels of Figure 5. The durations for the long and short cycles are generally of a 1:4 ratio (e.g. 1 and 4 s, 2 and 8 s, 3 and 12 s, etc.). On each cycle, the stimulus comes on for its target duration and then terminates (independent of any response from the animal). At stimulus termination the levers are extended into the box. The first lever press response of the animal is recorded, the levers are retracted, and the intercycle interval (e.g. 30 s) begins. The animals are first trained to make the lever press response. The animals are then trained to respond differentially to the short and long stimuli (e.g. right lever press on short cycles, and left lever press on long cycles). Only correct responses are reinforced. During training, a correction procedure can be implemented, such that if the animal makes the incorrect response, that cycle type is repeated on the next cycle, until the correct response is made. In training, short and long cycles are presented with a probability of .5. Following training, cycles of intermediate duration are added to the procedure. There are usually approximately five logarithmically spaced intermediate intervals between the two extremes. The extreme cycles are presented with a probability of .25, and the cycles of intermediate duration are presented with equal probability on the other cycles.

Data Analysis

The data are recorded with 2-ms resolution. For each session, one file is saved for each animal. File names are recorded using the identification number of the animal. The file extension indicates session number (in three-digit format, e.g. '001'). Each input event to the procedure (e.g. stimulus onset, food delivery) and each output event from the animal (e.g. head entry into the food cup, licks to the water tube) are recorded. The resulting data file consists of a single column of numbers, shown to three decimal places. The numbers before the decimal point indicate the time since session start in 2-ms units. The numbers following the decimal point indicate the event that took place at the recorded time. Detailed documentation of the numbers that correspond to the events is maintained to facilitate future analysis of the data. Additionally, this makes secondary data analysis possible, should other aspects of behavior that may have not been the focus of the study at the time it was first conducted come under investigation (e.g. drinking behavior on a fixed-interval schedule of reinforcement).

The data are analyzed in Matlab using existing Matlab functions, as well as specialized functions written to compute dependent measures of interest. All figures are created in Matlab. Inferential statistics are computed in SPSS.

The data are first translated from a single column of numbers into two columns of numbers: time since session start (the numbers before the decimal point) and event (the numbers after the decimal point). Each session's data are then parsed into cycles, and the relative time since cycle start for each event determined. Working with the data in this format makes determining multiple dependent measures straightforward. (For a review of the dependent measures that can be derived from data collected on fixed-interval procedures, see Guilhardi and Church, 2004.)

For any dependent measure, the value is computed for each cycle, of each session, and each subject independently. The calculated values can then be stored in a three-dimensional table, with time or cycle as the first dimension, session as the second dimension, and animal as the third dimension. Storing the data in this way enables computation of statistics at several levels of complexity. It allows the experimenter not only to examine overall mean performance of the group, but also the mean performance of any individual across sessions, for any specific session, or even for cycles.

The dependent measures shown in this chapter include responses per minute, the time of transition from a low response state to a high response state (or vice versa), and proportion "long" responses. A precise definition of the dependent measure used in an experiment is a critical component of the description of the results.

Responses Per Minute

Responses per minute in a cycle are computed by dividing the frequency of the response by the opportunity to make that response in each time bin of the cycle, and the units are changed from responses per bin length to responses per minute. The data shown in this paper are in 1-s bins. Responses per minute as a function of time is used to describe performance on FI and peak procedures.

Times of Transition

The times of transition from a low response rate state to a high response rate state (t_1) and from a high response rate state to a low response rate state (t_2) are defined on individual peak cycles based on the maximization of the index A (Church, Meck, and Gibbon, 1994): $A = t_1(r-r_1)+ (t_2- t_1)*(r_2-r)+ (t_3- t_2)* (r-r_3)$, where t_3 is the time of the end of the peak cycle, r is the overall mean response rate, and $r_1, r_2,$ and r_3 are the rates from cycle start to t_1, from t_1 to t_2, and from t_2 to t_3, respectively. All possible values of A are calculated with t_1 set as the time of each response in a cycle until the second to the last response, and t_2 set as the time of each response in a cycle from the second response until the last response, with the restriction that t_2 is always greater than t_1, and t_3 is greater than t_2 ($t_3>t_2>t_1$). In fixed-interval procedures, only t_1 is determined with $A = t_1(r-r_1)+ (t_4- t_1)*(r_4-r)$, where t_4 is the time of the end of the cycle, and r_4 is the rate from t_1 to t_4 (Guilhardi and Church, 2004).

Proportion "Long" Responses

The proportion of "long" responses is perhaps the simplest dependent measure shown here. It is used in procedures where the subject makes differential responses depending on what stimulus is presented. It is calculated by dividing the number of "long" responses for a certain cycle type (e.g. 2 s), by the total number of cycles of that type that were presented. In a bisection procedure, this is done for each of the intervals that are presented.

Secondary Data Analysis

Secondary data analysis is becoming more feasible with the development of the world wide web. Data can be uploaded to the web after an experiment is conducted, and made available to other researchers who may have research questions of their own that could be answered by analyzing data that has already been collected, rather than taking the time and the resources to set up a similar, if not identical, study. Some organizations maintain online archives of material that supplements published articles (e.g. the Psychonomic Society's archive of norms, stimuli, and data at www.psychonomic.org/archive). In addition, the Timing Lab at Brown University archives its data, within the lab and online, to facilitate secondary data analysis both by lab members as well as anyone else who might have interest in the data. After testing is complete the data are archived within the lab on CDs. The CDs include a description of the experiment, the data collected, the programs written to run the experiment, and the Matlab programs written for data analysis. When a paper is in press, the data for that paper are uploaded to the Timing Lab archive, with the abstract, as well as any documentation that is needed to analyze the data (e.g. the event codes specific to that experiment). The archive can be accessed at the following address: http://www.brown.edu/Research/Timelab.

ACKNOWLEDGMENT

Preparation of this chapter is supported by National Institute of Mental Health Grant MH44234 to Brown University.

REFERENCES

Allan, L.G. and Gibbon, J. (1991). Human bisection at the geometric mean. *Learning and Motivation, 22*, 39-58.

Catania, C.A. (1970). Reinforcement schedules and psychophysical judgments: A study of some temporal properties of behavior. In W. N. Schoenfeld (Ed.). *The Theory of Reinforcement Schedules.* New York: Appleton-Century-Crofts.

Catania, C.A. and Reynolds, G.S. (1968). A quantitative analysis of the responding maintained by interval schedules of reinforcement. *Journal of the Experimental Analysis of Behavior, 11*, 327-383.

Church, R.M. and Deluty, M.Z. (1977). Bisection of temporal intervals. *Journal of Experimental Psychology: Animal Behavior Processes, 3*, 216-228.

Church, R. M., Meck, W. H., and Gibbon, J. (1994). Application of scalar timing to individual trials. *Journal of Experimental Psychology: Animal Behavior Processes, 20*, 135-155.

Church, R. M., Guilhardi, P., Keen, R., MacInnis, M., and Kirkpatrick, K. (2003). Simultaneous Temporal Processing. In H. Helfrich (Ed.), *Time and Mind II: Information Processing Perspectives.* Gottingen, Germany: Hogrefe and Huber Publishers, pp 3-19.

Crystal, J.D. (2002). Timing inter-reward intervals. *Learning and Motivation, 33*, 311-326.

Crystal, J.D., Maxwell, K.W., and Hohmann, A.G. (2003). Cannabinoid modulation of sensitivity to time. *Behavioural Brain Research, 144*, 57-66.

Drew, M.R., Fairhurst, S., Malapani, C., Horvitz, J.C., and Balsam, P.D. (2003). Effects of dopamine antagonists on the timing of two intervals. *Pharmacology, Biochemistry, and Behavior, 75,* 9-15.

Ferster, C.B. and Skinner, B.F. (1957). *Schedules of Reinforcement.* East Norwalk, CT: Appleton-Century-Crofts.

Gibbon, J. (1977). Scalar expectancy theory and Weber's law in animal timing. *Psychological Review, 84*, 279-325.

Green, J.T., Ivry, R.B., and Woodruff-Pak, D.S. (1999). Timing in eyeblink classical conditioning and timed-interval tapping. *Psychological Science, 10*, 19-23.

Guilhardi, P., and Church, R. M. (2004). Measures of temporal discrimination: A case study in archiving data. *Behavior Research Methods, Instruments, and Computers, 36*, 661-669.

Guilhardi, P., and Church, R. M. (2005). Dynamics of temporal discrimination. *Learning and Behavior, 33*, 399-416.

Guilhardi, P., Keen, R., MacInnis, M. L. M., and Church, R. M. (2005). How rats combine temporal cues. *Behavioural Processes, 69*, 189-205.

Kirkpatrick, K. and Church, R.M. (2003). Tracking of the expected time to reinforcement in temporal conditioning procedures. *Learning and Behavior, 31*, 3-21.

Lejeune, H. and Wearden, J.H. (1991). The comparative psychology of fixed-interval responding: Some quantitative analyses. *Learning and Motivation, 22*, 84-111.

Machado, A. and Keen, R.G. (1999). Learning to time (LET) or scalar expectancy theory (SET)? A critical test of two models of timing. *Psychological Science, 10*, 285-290.

Machado, A. and Keen, R. (2003). Temporal discrimination in a long operant chamber. *Behavioural Processes, 62*, 157-182.

Malapani, C., Rakitin, B., Levy, R., Meck, W.H., Deweer, B., Dubois, B., and Gibbon, J. (1998). Coupled temporal memories in Parkinson's disease: A dopamine-related dysfunction. *Journal of Cognitive Neuroscience, 10,* 316-331.

Maricq, A.V., Roberts, S., and Church, R.M. (1981). Methamphetamine and time estimation. *Journal of Experimental Psychology: Animal Behavior Processes, 7,* 18-30.

Meck, W.H. and Church, R.M. (1984). Simultaneous temporal processing. *Journal of Experimental Psychology: Animal Behavior Processes, 10,* 1-29.

Meck, W.H., Church, R.M., and Gibbon, J. (1985). Temporal integration in duration and number discrimination. *Journal of Experimental Psychology: Animal Behavior Processes, 11,* 591-597.

Roberts, S. (1981). Isolation of an internal clock. *Journal of Experimental Psychology: Animal Behavior Processes, 7, 242-268.*

Ross, L., and Santi, A. (2000). The effects of estrogen on temporal and numerical processing in ovariectomized female rats. *Psychobiology, 28,* 394-405.

Santi, A., Hornyak, S. and Miki, A. (2003). Pigeons' memory for empty and filled time intervals signaled by light. *Learning and Motivation, 34,* 282-302.

Schneider, B.A. (1969). A two-state analysis of fixed-interval responding in the pigeon. *Journal of the Experimental Analysis of Behavior, 12,* 677-687.

Stubbs, D.A. (1976). Scaling of stimulus duration by pigeons. *Journal of the Experimental Analysis of Behavior, 26,* 15-25.

Tatham, T.A. and Zurn, K.R. (1989). The Med-PC experimental apparatus programming system. *Behavioral Research Methods, Instruments, and Computers, 21,* 294 – 302.

In: Tasks and Techniques: A Sampling of the Methodologies…   ISBN 1-60021-126-7
Editor: Matthew J. Anderson, pp. 245-259   © 2006 Nova Science Publishers, Inc.

Chapter 20

SEQUENCE PRODUCTION PARADIGMS FOR EXPLORING THE ORGANIZATION OF SEQUENTIAL BEHAVIOR

Stephen B. Fountain[*1], *James D. Rowan*[2],
Melissa D. Muller[1], *Denise P.A. Smith*[1],
Amber M. Chenoweth[1], *and Douglas G. Wallace*[3]

[1]Department of Psychology, Kent State University, Kent, OH 44242
[2]Department of Psychology, Wesleyan College, Macon, GA 31210
[3]Department of Psychology, Northern Illinois University, DeKalb, IL 60115

ABSTRACT

Some of the most interesting features of behavior and cognition are found in animals' responses to sequential problems that require them to organize their behavior through time. If we are to characterize and understand behavior of this complexity, especially how multiple psychological processes act concurrently to produce sequential behavior, then we will have to study forms of sequential behavior that are sufficiently complex that they would likely recruit multiple processes concurrently. Our sequence production paradigm for rats seems to be well-suited for this purpose. In our paradigm, rats rather quickly learn to produce long and elaborate sequences of responses. The sequence production paradigm we use is a functional analogue of nonverbal human pattern learning tasks that require participants to choose buttons or other manipulanda in a spatial array in the proper sequential order that produces a repeating pattern of responses. In our paradigm, rats learn to press levers in a circular array in the proper sequential order that produces a repeating pattern of responses. Our method is an improvement over earlier methods used with rats and even primates because it allows us to study how rats learn long, elaborate serial patterns and because it provides measures of correct-response rates, error rates, and "intrusion" rates (i.e., the number of specific kinds of errors produced at

---

[*] Address Correspondence to: Stephen B. Fountain, Department of Psychology, Kent State University, Kent, Ohio 44242-0001, Phone: (330) 672-3826, FAX:(330) 672-3786, E-mail: sfountai@kent.edu

particular locations in the pattern) on a trial-by-trial basis throughout the serial pattern. We have applied the sequence production paradigm to examine the psychological and neural systems that subserve sequential behavior and the effects of drugs, toxic chemicals, and brain lesions on these neurobehavioral systems. The sequence production paradigm is a rich and flexible methodology for studying the complex interactions of the multiple psychological and neural processes that mediate the organization of sequential behavior.

INTRODUCTION

Some of the most interesting features of behavior and cognition are found in animals' responses to sequential problems that require them to organize their behavior through time. Models of sequential learning attempt to describe how humans and other animals learn to predict elements of event sequences or produce response sequences that occur in the same serial order, that is, in serial patterns. Recently, there has been an upsurge in interest in the psychological and neural bases of sequential learning. This type of learning has been shown to be a fundamental human and nonhuman animal capacity involved in "human activities ranging from reasoning to language, and from everyday skills to complex problem solving" (Sun, 2000, p. 1), yet the psychological and neural processes that subserve it have not been identified and properly characterized.

In recent years it has become clear that humans and other animals have much in common in terms of sequential behavior and the processes that seem to be responsible for sequential behavior (Fountain, 2006; Fountain and Rowan, 1995a; Kesner, 2002; McGonigle and Chalmers, 2002; Sands and Wright, 1980; Sands and Wright, 1982; Terrace and McGonigle, 1994). However, rather than a consensus emerging regarding the nature of the mechanisms responsible for sequential behavior, competing hypotheses and theories to describe sequential behavior abound. Sequential learning theories have ranged from those positing simple associative learning mechanisms to those proposing that sequential learning depends on abstract cognitive capacities. The picture of sequential learning that is emerging for rats, for example, like that emerging for primates and humans (Botvinick and Plaut, 2004; Chen, Swartz, and Terrace, 1997; Harris and Washburn, 2005; Keele, Ivry, Mayr, Hazeltine, and Heuer, 2003; Palmer and Pfordresher, 2003; Terrace, 2005; Treichler, Raghanti, and Van Tilburg, 2003), is perhaps more complex than is generally imagined. Evidence suggests that rats learn to perform complex behavioral sequences by concurrently monitoring several sources of information and encoding the most valid information selected from the stimulus characteristics of pattern elements, the structural relations among elements, the characteristics of extra-sequence cues, and the relative timing of sequential events (Fountain, Wallace, and Rowan, 2002; Fountain, 2006). This idea also fits with recent behavioral and neurobehavioral studies implicating multiple concurrent psychological and neural processes in rat serial pattern learning (Fountain, 2006; Fountain and Rowan, 2000; Fountain and Benson, Jr., 2006).

If we are to characterize and understand behavior of this complexity, especially how multiple psychological processes act concurrently to produce sequential behavior, then we will have to study forms of sequential behavior that are sufficiently complex that they would likely recruit multiple processes concurrently. Our sequence production paradigm for rats seems to be well-suited for this purpose. In our paradigm, rats rather quickly learn to produce long and elaborate sequences of responses. With this method, we can train rats to perform serial response patterns with many sequential items that can be associated, with spatial and temporal cues that are relevant, with particular pacing or rhythmic structures, and with patterns of movements that can potentially be coded internally as motor patterns or as rule-based structures. Typically, many of these cues and features are concurrently available to the rat as the sequence training takes place, and it appears that rats concurrently make use of multiple sources of cues and multiple psychological and neural processes to learn to navigate these serial patterns.

A SEQUENCE PRODUCTION PARADIGM FOR RATS

The sequence production paradigm we use is a functional analogue of nonverbal human pattern learning tasks that require participants to choose buttons or other manipulanda in a spatial array in the proper sequential order that produces a repeating pattern of responses (Hartman, Knopman, and Nissen, 1989; Knopman and Nissen, 1991; Reber, 1989; Restle, 1970; 1973; Restle and Brown, 1970a; 1970b; Willingham, 1998; Willingham, Nissen, and Bullemer, 1989). In our paradigm (Fountain and Rowan, 1995a; Rowan, Fountain, Kundey, and Miner, 2001), rats learn to press levers in an array in the proper sequential order that produces a repeating pattern of responses. Response patterns of this sort are remarkably easy for rats to learn even when patterns are composed of 24, 30, or even more successive elements (Fountain and Rowan, 1995a). In many studies, we have overcome constraints on daily training typically associated with food and water reinforcement procedures by using hypothalamic brain-stimulation reward (BSR) to reinforce correct responses. Because rats do not satiate to the rewarding quality of electrical brain stimulation of the hypothalamus, this form of reward allows us to train rats on patterns composed of many pattern elements with over 100 pattern presentations per day in some experiments. Our method also has the advantage that it allows us to collect accuracy and latency measures on a trial-by-trial basis while the rat performs the task at its own pace. This method is an improvement over earlier methods used with rats and even primates because it allows us to study how rats learn long, elaborate serial patterns and because it provides measures of correct-response rates, error rates, and "intrusion" rates (i.e., the number of specific kinds of errors produced at particular locations in the pattern) on a trial-by-trial basis throughout the serial pattern (Fountain and Rowan, 1995a; Rowan et al., 2001).

Subjects, BSR Electrode Implantation, and Shaping

We have typically used as subjects naïve male hooded rats (*Rattus norvegicus*) at least 90 days of age. Rats are housed in individual cages with food and water freely available. They are maintained on a 15:9-hr light-dark cycle. Testing occurs during the light portion of the cycle. Both food and water are freely available in the home cage.

For behavioral studies of sequential learning and memory, all rats are implanted with bipolar electrodes (MS301, Plastic Products, Roanoke, VA) for hypothalamic BSR (coordinates, skull level: 4.5 mm posterior, 1.5 mm lateral, 8.5 mm below the surface of the skull). Prior to stereotaxic surgery, each rat is deeply anesthetized by i.p. pre-injection of xylazine and atropine followed by isoflurane anesthesia. Rats also receive antibiotics (60,000 units penicillin i.m.) following surgery to reduce the chance of infection. They are carefully monitored for infection following surgery and are allowed at least 1 week for recovery from surgery. One important advantage of BSR is that a rat can be reinforced immediately for every correct response without requiring the rat to pause to consume food or water. The result is that rats often produce sequential response rates of 1 response every second or two, similar to sequential response rates observed in analogous human sequence production studies (Fountain and Rowan, 1995a; Restle and Brown, 1970a; 1970b). This can be compared to pattern presentation rates of 1 element every minute or two, or slower, that are common in other sequential learning procedures involving rats and food reinforcement (e.g., Fountain, Henne, and Hulse, 1984; Capaldi, Verry, Nawrocki, and Miller, 1984). An additional advantage of using BSR is that rats do not have to be food- or water-deprived throughout experiments that may last weeks or even months.

Rats are shaped to leverpress for BSR in two shaping chambers (30 X 30 X 30 cm), each equipped with a single retractable response lever mounted 5.0 cm above the floor and a commutating device centrally located in the ceiling. Each box is constructed from clear Plexiglas with a floor of stainless steel rods. Each is enclosed in a sound-attenuating shell made of particleboard (20 X 60 X 65 cm). These shaping chambers are housed in a room separate from those of the test chambers. Both shaping chambers and the sequence production apparatus are controlled from an adjoining room by a microcomputer and interface (interface and Med-State Software, Med Associates, Inc., Fairfield, VT).

Throughout all phases of the experiment, rats receive reinforcement consisting of one or more 200-ms BSR "pulses" of a 60-Hz sinusoidal pulse train from a constant current source of 20-100 μA. Stimulators were fabricated in-house (based on a step-down transformer and a variable potentiometer) and are controlled by the computer and interface. In initial stage of shaping, at the beginning of the session, the lever is inserted into the chamber and remains inserted throughout the 30-min session. Rats are required to make at least 1000 leverpress responses within a 30-min session to be admitted to a study. Rats that fail to meet the criterion within several daily shaping sessions are excluded from the study. The day before starting the sequence production procedure, rats receive one 30-min session of discrete-trial shaping, wherein the lever is retracted briefly then reinserted into the chamber during the intertrial interval (ITI), to familiarize them with the discrete trial procedure they will experience in the pattern production procedure.

The Sequence Production Apparatus: The Circular Lever Array

As shown in Figure 1, the training chamber for the sequence production paradigm (Fountain and Rowan, 1995a, 1995b) is octagonal in shape with clear Plexiglas walls 15 cm wide by 30 cm tall and measures approximately 40 cm between parallel walls. In our apparatus, a retractable response lever (fabricated in-house based on a solenoid to insert the lever arm and springs to affect retraction) is centered on each wall 5.0 cm above the floor producing a circular array of levers around the perimeter of the chamber. We refer to the levers as Levers 1 through 8 in clockwise order with Lever 8 adjacent to Lever 1. Each lever requires approximately 0.15-N force for activation. Rats in the testing chamber are connected to a stimulator by way of a flexible cord (Plastic Products MS304) and a commutating device centrally located in the ceiling of the chamber.

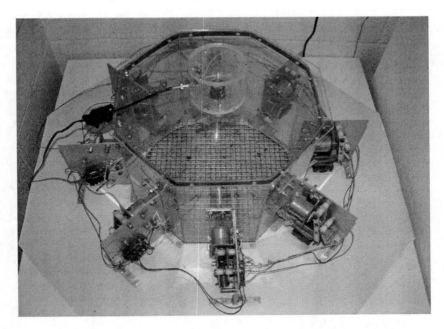

Figure 1. An octagonal operant chamber equipped with a retractable lever on each wall to form a circular array of levers. Rats are connected by a flexible cord to a commutating device in the ceiling of the chamber so that they can be reinforced with pulses of brain-stimulation reward for correct responses.

Such a chamber is easily constructed from relatively inexpensive but durable materials. To begin, cut an octagonal hole in ¾" melamine particle board large enough to accommodate the 8 Plexiglas walls. In each piece of Plexiglas that will serve as a wall, pre-drill a hole for the lever aperture and any supporting hardware, 2 holes for wood screws at the bottom of the wall, and 2 holes for small nuts and bolts at the top of the wall. Use wood screws to attach the bottom of each wall to the inside of the octagonal hole so that the bottom of each wall is flush with the bottom of the melamine board. Use small nuts and bolts to attach a lightweight metal strap around the outside top of the walls to hold the walls rigidly in place. Your Plexiglas can be lightweight (1/8" thickness) if the levers you use rest on the melamine board, or you may need to use heavier Plexiglas (e.g., 1/4" thickness) if the walls must support the levers. Use a hinge to attach an octagonal Plexiglas ceiling to the top of one wall of the chamber using the nuts and bolts that also hold the strap in place.

The chamber rests upon a floor of stainless steel hardware cloth. We have found it convenient to cut a second melamine board with a corresponding round hole slightly larger than the octagonal hole of the chamber, then add approximately 2-cm blocks on each side of the bottom of the support structure to serve as spacers. The hardware cloth sits on this support structure with the chamber atop it. As shown in Figure 2, the spacers allow us to slide standard bedding trays in and out below the hardware cloth floor for cleaning. The weight of the chamber immobilizes the hardware cloth, yet it is easy to remove the hardware cloth for cleaning simply by lifting one edge of the chamber.

Two such operant chambers are side-by-side in each of two testing rooms (approximately 2.0 X 2.6 m); the two chambers in each room are separated by a vertical partition and illuminated throughout testing by fluorescent lighting. The only major distal cues in the rooms are wall-mounted electrical outlet panels on two walls, the partition separating chambers, and white curtains on the remaining side. Mounted above each chamber is a closed-circuit television camera so that rats' activity can be monitored and shaped as necessary throughout testing from the computer and interface located in an adjoining room.

Figure 2. The octagonal operant chamber raised on one side to reveal the arrangement of the stainless steel hardware cloth floor, support structure, and bedding tray.

The Sequence Production Procedure

The sequence production procedure is a discrete-trial 8-choice procedure with correction. At the beginning of each trial, all 8 levers are inserted into the chamber. If the rat makes a correct choice, BSR is immediately administered and all levers are retracted for the next ITI. For incorrect choices, all levers but the correct lever are withdrawn and the rat must locate the correct lever and respond correctly; after the correct response, BSR is immediately administered and the lever is retracted for the next ITI. On each trial, the lever chosen and the latency to the first response are recorded. Rats learn to perform sequences of responses that involve pressing the eight levers in serial patterns. Two of the patterns we have found to be most useful are:

Perfect "Runs"   123-234-345-456-567-678-781-81<u>2</u>

Violation "Runs"   123-234-345-456-567-678-781-81<u>8</u>

Integers in the patterns refer to the clockwise position of the levers in the octagonal chamber and the correct order they are to be pressed. Dashes indicate temporal pauses that differ from other ITIs and serve as "phrasing cues" that can dramatically affect pattern learning (Fountain et al., 1984; Fountain and Rowan, 1995a; Stempowski, Carman, and Fountain, 1999; Fountain, Benson, and Wallace, 2000). Phrasing cues can be either longer or shorter temporal intervals than other ITIs (Stempowski et al., 1999). In our studies, we typically use 1-sec ITIs and 3-sec phrasing cues or, more recently, 2-sec ITIs and 0.5-sec phrasing cues. Intervals can be set to the same length as ITIs, phrasing cues, or can be discriminably longer to mark the beginning of each new pattern, for example, by using a 9-sec interval. Phrasing cues typically facilitate pattern learning (Stempowski et al., 1999) when they correspond to the inherent structure of patterns, that is, when they are positioned at formally defined chunk boundaries and thus cue chunk boundary elements (Fountain et al., 1984). In this pattern, elements within chunks obey a simple rule, namely, move one to the right until the phrasing cue is encountered. Underlined integers at the end of the patterns indicate where the patterns differ. The underlined element, "2," in the Perfect "Runs" pattern fits with the general rules governing elements in all other 3-element chunks. This pattern is formally simple—described by few such rules—with no exceptions and is easily learned by rats to a high criterion within a week of training. The underlined element in the Violation "Runs" pattern does not obey the same rule; it is a "violation" or "exception-to-the-rule" and is difficult for rats to learn. Rats can learn to anticipate this particular violation element and produce the correct response in this particular pattern in 2-3 weeks of daily training of 20 patterns per day.

An advantage of this procedure is that rats begin the first day of the sequence production training experiencing the entire pattern under exactly the same procedure that will be maintained throughout the acquisition phase. No pre-training on simpler patterns or under simpler forms of the procedure is necessary as is often the case in other sequential tasks involving patterns of this length and complexity (cf. Fountain, 1990). Even so, the transition from the 1-lever shaping procedure to the 8-lever sequence production task can be difficult for rats and their response rate in the first day of training is often quite slow. Early in acquisition, shaping is typically required and the number of pulses of BSR may need to be increased to maintain responding. A few rats simply fail to make the transition and have to be excluded from the study. However, most rats become completely independent within the first day or two of acquisition (20-50 patterns) and their sequence production rate increases rapidly over the first few days of training. To make training more manageable during the first few days, we often break the "Day 1" block of training into several days of fewer patterns. For example, if daily training should consist of 20 patterns, we may train the equivalent "Day 1" block over three days of 5, 5, and 10 patterns, then train 20 patterns per day from Day 2 onward.

Considerations in Constructing Serial Patterns

Our past research has indicated several factors to consider in constructing sequential patterns for rats so as to avoid potential biases or artifacts. Although rats will learn almost any pattern of responses under the sequence production procedure, patterns that are highly structured are easier to learn than repeating pseudorandom patterns. Past research has shown that the number of simple rules that are required to describe the serial pattern, rather than pattern length or other factors, is the best predictor of the difficulty of the pattern (Fountain and Rowan, 1995a).

Rats also appear to be sensitive to the distance they are required to travel between levers from trial to trial such that learning responses farther away seems to be more difficult than learning responses on adjacent levers, so equating this factor across trials within patterns is advisable if relative trial-by-trial acquisition rates are of interest. Similarly, equating this factor between patterns is important if comparing acquisition rates between pattern groups is critical.

Rats seem to use whatever cues are available to facilitate learning in this task; one particularly salient cue appears to be unused levers or those with nearby salient cues. For example, our original studies with a sequence production method used a horizontal array of levers along one long wall of an oblong operant chamber, but our results were affected by rats' tendency to use end walls adjacent to levers at each end of the array as cues for responses on those levers (Fountain, 1990). The circular array was adopted to remove those cues. We have since observed that rats are sensitive to the presence of any levers in the chamber they are not required to press and can use those as cues to guide responses in their vicinity, so we typically create patterns so that all levers are used in the course of any pattern the rats must learn.

Transfer and Probe Procedures

Our recent work has shown that transfer procedures and probe patterns can be very efficient and informative procedures for characterizing the psychological and neural processes that underlie rats' behavior in sequential learning tasks (cf. Fountain, 2006). Rats can easily be trained on a single pattern for 20 to 50 pattern repetitions per day during acquisition until a high criterion is met, then they can be transferred to another pattern in a transfer phase for one or more days. This approach allows detailed scrutiny of the effects of pretraining in one pattern on learning of another over the course of acquisition of the second pattern.

Recently, we developed a more efficient approach modeled after probe tasks often associated with pigeon conditioning studies. In our probe procedure, rats are trained on a single pattern for 20 to 50 pattern repetitions per day during acquisition until a high criterion is met (no more than 10% errors on any pattern element within a day), then we increase the number of pattern repetitions each day if necessary to accommodate the number of probes we wish to introduce. Next, we begin a 10-day probe phase where we introduce probe patterns randomly interspersed with blocks of 5 training patterns within daily sessions. Rats receive one of each type of probe pattern each day; the order of presentation of probe patterns is randomized. We thus obtain data for 10 probe trials for each of several probe patterns for each 10-day probe phase. Multiple probe phases can be conducted; between probe phases, rats are returned to normal training for a minimum of 3 days to assure that they still meet criterion performance before going to the next probe phase. This method allows us to present patterns with as few or as many features changed as we wish so that we can determine the factors that control performance and, in the case of pharmacological or lesion studies, the psychological processes that are compromised by psychobiological manipulations. Fountain (2006) provides detailed examples of this approach.

Variations on the Sequence Production Procedure for Studies Involving Other Species, Psychopharmacology, and Brain Lesions

Several situations call for a sequence production method that avoids using BSR for one or more reasons. For example, studies with mice or other species may be impractical if they involve implanting electrodes for purposes of reinforcement. Another example is lesion studies that would be difficult or impossible to conduct because the manipulations interfere with BSR or are impractical with the BSR electrode present. Yet another example is developmental studies that would be compromised by electrode implantation. For these situations, we have developed a variation on our standard sequence production paradigm that involves a nosepoke response reinforced by water. We have used this procedure with rats and mice (Fountain, 2006; Fountain, Krauchunas, and Rowan, 1999). The procedure has the disadvantages that animals must be water deprived and that daily training is severely constrained in terms of the number of pattern presentations that are possible per day. However, it has the advantage of not requiring surgical implantation of BSR electrodes.

The Sequence Production Procedure with Nosepoke for Water Reinforcement

As shown in Figure 3, the nosepoke apparatus is an analogue of the BSR apparatus in that the test chamber used is also octagonal in shape and composed of clear Plexiglas walls with a floor of hardware cloth. The nosepoke chamber for rats has identical dimensions to the BSR chamber, whereas the nosepoke chamber for mice is half the diameter and height of the rat chamber, with 7.5 cm wide and 15 cm tall walls and approximately 20 cm between parallel walls. Centered on each wall is a nosepoke receptacle made of a PVC pipe end cap with an indicator light mounted in the back. This receptacle also contains a small line to deliver a 0.025 ml water droplet into the bottom of the receptacle from a syringe reservoir and solenoid on each wall. Nosepoke responses into the receptacles are detected by infrared emitter/detector pairs mounted in holes on opposite sides of the receptacles. Experiments are controlled from an adjoining room by a microcomputer and interface.

The nosepoke procedure is an analogue of the BSR procedure. At the beginning of each trial, all 8 indicator lights are illuminated in the 8 nosepoke receptacles. If the rat makes a correct nosepoke choice, a water droplet is immediately administered and all indicator lights are extinguished for the next ITI. For incorrect choices, all indicator lights but the correct one are extinguished and the rat must locate the correct receptacle with the illuminated indicator light and respond correctly; after the correct response, a water droplet is immediately administered and the remaining indicator light is extinguished for the next ITI. On each trial, the receptacle chosen and the latency to the first response are recorded. Rats learn to perform sequences of responses that involve choosing the 8 receptacles in the proper serial patterns.

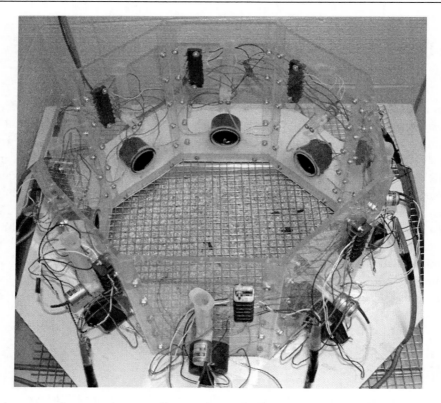

Figure 3. An octagonal operant chamber equipped with a nosepoke receptacle on each wall to form a circular array. Rats nosepoke for water reinforcement for correct responses.

Advantages and Disadvantages of the BSR Versus Water Reinforcement Procedures

The principal disadvantage of the BSR procedure is the need to implant BSR electrodes in all rats whereas the principal disadvantage of the water reinforcement procedure is the severe limitation imposed on training and testing by satiation to the water reinforcer. The number of pattern repetitions per day that rats and mice can complete in the nosepoke procedure will depend on the species, the length of the pattern, and other factors such as effects of drug exposure on thirst and satiation in pharmacological studies, but typically rats can be trained or tested on no more than ten 24-element patterns per day. This limitation effectively doubles or triples acquisition times and precludes the kinds of probe studies that have proven to be so useful in the BSR procedure for an analytical approach to characterizing the processes involved in rat sequential learning. On the other hand, not having to implant electrodes and instead using water reinforcement simplifies the sequence production procedure sufficiently that it should make the procedure more generally accessible to animal learning and cognition researchers. The water reinforcement procedure also allows researchers to do lesion studies, drug studies, and developmental studies that are impossible or impractical when BSR is involved.

An Analogue of Our Sequence Production Procedure for Studies of Human Serial Pattern Learning

We have also developed an analogue of the rat sequence production procedure to examine the correspondence between human and animal sequential learning. Fountain and Rowan (1995a) compared rats' and humans' performance on similar variants of the original task. The human variation of this task required college students to learn to produce a response sequence on a computer. Subjects first read a simple set of instructions that was presented on the computer screen. They were informed that they would see eight circles on the screen and that they were to use an arrow (cursor) key to move a smaller circular cursor to the circle of their choice. They should then press the spacebar to choose the circle. The instructions required the participants to locate and use the right and left arrow keys and the space bar before the experiment began. Subjects were then informed that they would be given feedback as to the correctness of their choice. They were told not to be concerned if they made errors, to guess when necessary, and to follow instructions in the box at the top of the screen if they forgot what to do. At the beginning of the testing session, eight circles (13 mm in diameter) appeared on the screen along with a message in the help box at the top of the screen instructing the participant to make a choice. The circles were equally spaced in a circular arrangement (opposite circles were 104 mm apart). Subjects moved the cursor to one of the circles and selected it by pressing the space bar. If the subject selected the correct circle, then "CORRECT" was displayed on the center of the computer screen during the ITI. If the subject selected an incorrect circle, the correct one remained displayed, and the other incorrect circles were removed. The subject was then instructed to choose the correct circle.

Both rats and humans were trained using their respective sequence production procedures to learn the same set of patterns. They learned either completely hierarchical patterns or linear patterns created from the hierarchical patterns with elements rearranged so as to maintain the same pairwise associations found in the hierarchical patterns but with the overall pattern structure disrupted. Three experiments compared rats' and humans' learning of patterns with increasing hierarchical complexity. Experiment 1 compared rats' and humans' performance in learning either a pattern which could be expressed with two rules and had perfect structure or the same pattern elements rearranged so that the simple structure was disrupted. Pairwise associations between the elements were the same in the two patterns. Experiment 2 examined the effects of disrupting the structure in a pattern whose structure could be described by three rules; Experiment 3 examined this phenomenon in a hierarchical pattern described by four nested rules. Pattern difficulty and the error profiles generated by humans and rats were parallel indicating that rats were using similar cognitive strategies to those humans employed to learn these patterns (Fountain and Rowan, 1995a). More generally, these types of studies with analogous sequence production procedures can be very useful for establishing bridges between human and nonhuman animal cognitive research and between human and animal research on the neurobiology of cognitive processes, particularly those processes that contribute to the organization of complex, intelligent behavior through time.

Sequence Production Paradigms and the Study of the Psychological and Neural Mechanisms of Cognition

Sequence production paradigms are powerful tools for studying the psychological and neural process that underlie the organization of sequential behavior. In our lab, they have been used to study a variety of psychological processes that contribute to the structure of ongoing behavior, including hierarchical and linear rule learning (Fountain, 1990; Fountain and Rowan, 1995a), phrasing and its effects on cognitive chunking (Fountain and Rowan, 1995b), phrasing as discrimination learning (Fountain et al., 2000; Stempowski et al., 1999), species differences in response to pattern structure and phrasing (Fountain, Krauchunas, et al., 1999), cognitive "sorting" of interleaved patterns driven by subpattern structure (Fountain, Rowan, and Benson, Jr., 1999; Fountain and Benson, Jr., 2006), the role of discrimination learning in sequence production (Fountain, 1990; Fountain and Rowan, 1995a; Fountain et al., 2000; Stempowski et al., 1999), and the role of multiple concurrent cognitive process in sequential behavior (Fountain, 2006; Fountain and Benson, Jr., 2006; Fountain and Rowan, 1995a; Fountain et al., 2002).

Procedures for studying sequence production in humans have also become popular tools for examining and characterizing the effects of pharmacological manipulations and brain dysfunction on complex cognitive processes (cf. Hartman et al., 1989; Knopman and Nissen, 1991; Reber, 1989; Willingham, 1998; Willingham et al., 1989). We have applied the same approach to examine the effects of drugs, toxic chemicals (e.g., Fountain, Raffaele, and Annau, 1986), and brain lesions on neurobehavioral systems involved in organizing sequential behavior.

Recently, the sequence production paradigm has been used to examine and characterize long-lasting cognitive deficits resulting from adolescent exposure to nicotine and other psychoactive drugs. This work employs a rat adolescent drug exposure protocol that has been used to characterize the effects of adolescent drug exposure on a broad range of biological and behavioral processes including genetic expression, apoptosis (programmed cell death), synaptogenesis, cell replication, receptor expression in neurotransmitter systems, and the functional programming of simple behavioral responses. Animal adolescent exposure protocols have been used to study the effects of a variety of drugs including nicotine, alcohol, and cocaine, to name but three common drugs threats for adolescents (Kelley and Rowan, 2004; Kelley and Middaugh, 1999; Sircar and Sircar, 2005). One particularly important link to sequential learning research is that early exposure to nicotine in mice, using this exposure procedure, has demonstrated alterations in serotonergic, dopaminergic, noradrenergic, and, most importantly, cholinergic systems (Kelley and Middaugh, 1999; Trauth, Seidler, McCook, and Slotkin, 1999). What the sequence production paradigm brings to the table is a rat cognition paradigm tightly modeled after paradigms for studying high-level cognitive functions in humans. Initial studies show that our paradigm detects cognitive dysfunction in adult rats that over a month earlier received adolescent exposure to nicotine. To our knowledge, this is the first evidence that long-term, low-level adolescent nicotine exposure significantly impairs higher cognitive functioning in adulthood. Numerous studies have established adolescence as a critical developmental period during which unique pharmacological sensitivity is exhibited. This line of research promises to extend our understanding of both the development of higher cognitive processes and the neurobiological basis of these processes in the rat brain.

Our recent work has shown that sequential learning is likely subserved by at least three dissociable brain and behavioral systems that are recruited concurrently in sequential learning tasks (Fountain, 2006). When rats learn serial patterns with phrasing cues and a violation element, learning about chunk boundary elements is impaired under physiological manipulations such as the NMDA receptor antagonist, MK-801 (Fountain and Rowan, 2000), the anticholinergic drug, atropine, and hippocampal lesions, but not by medial frontal cortex lesions. In addition, learning about violation elements in serial patterns is profoundly impaired by MK-801 and atropine, but not by hippocampal lesions or medial frontal cortex lesions. Learning about within-chunk elements is resistant to disruption by all these manipulations and may reflect learning by internal representations of motor or cognitive rules. The sequence production paradigm is a rich and flexible methodology for studying the complex interactions of the multiple psychological and neural processes that mediate the organization of sequential behavior.

REFERENCES

Botvinick, M. and Plaut, D. C. (2004). Doing without schema hierarchies: A recurrent connectionist approach to normal and impaired routine sequential action. *Psychological Review, 111*, 395-429.

Capaldi, E. J., Verry, D. R., Nawrocki, T. M., and Miller, D. J. (1984). Serial learning, interitem associations, phrasing cues, interference, overshadowing, chunking, memory, and extinction. *Animal Learning and Behavior, 12,* 7-20.

Chen, S., Swartz, K. B., and Terrace, H. S. (1997). Knowledge of the ordinal position of list items in rhesus monkeys. *Psychological Science, 8,* 80-86.

Fountain, S. B. (1990). Rule abstraction, item memory, and chunking in rat serial-pattern tracking. *Journal of Experimental Psychology: Animal Behavior Processes, 16,* 96-105.

Fountain, S. B. (2006). The structure of sequential behavior. In E.A.Wasserman and T. R. Zentall (Eds.), *Comparative Cognition: Experimental Explorations of Animal Intelligence* (pp. 439-458). Oxford: Oxford University Press.

Fountain, S. B., Benson, A. M., and Wallace, D. G. (2000). Number, but not rhythmicity, of temporal cues determines phrasing effects in rat serial-pattern learning. *Learning and Motivation, 31,* 301-322.

Fountain, S. B. and Benson, D. M., Jr. (2006). Chunking, rule learning, and multiple item memory in rat interleaved serial pattern learning. *Learning and Motivation, 37,* 95-112.

Fountain, S. B., Henne, D. R., and Hulse, S. H. (1984). Phrasing cues and hierarchical organization in serial pattern learning by rats. *Journal of Experimental Psychology: Animal Behavior Processes, 10,* 30-45.

Fountain, S. B., Krauchunas, S. M., and Rowan, J. D. (1999). Serial-pattern learning in mice: Pattern structure and phrasing. *Psychological Record, 49,* 173-192.

Fountain, S. B., Raffaele, K. C., and Annau, Z. (1986). Behavioral consequences of intraperitoneal carbon monoxide administration in rats. *Toxicology and Applied Pharmacology, 83,* 546-555.

Fountain, S. B. and Rowan, J. D. (1995a). Coding of hierarchical versus linear pattern structure in rats and humans. *Journal of Experimental Psychology: Animal Behavior Processes, 21,* 187-202.

Fountain, S. B. and Rowan, J. D. (1995b). Sensitivity to violations of "run" and "trill" structures in rat serial-pattern learning. *Journal of Experimental Psychology: Animal Behavior Processes, 21,* 78-81.

Fountain, S. B. and Rowan, J. D. (2000). Differential impairments of rat serial-pattern learning and retention induced by MK-801, an NMDA receptor antagonist. *Psychobiology, 28,* 32-44.

Fountain, S. B., Rowan, J. D., and Benson, D. M., Jr. (1999). Rule learning in rats: Serial tracking in interleaved patterns. *Animal Cognition, 2,* 41-54.

Fountain, S. B., Wallace, D. G., and Rowan, J. D. (2002). The organization of sequential behavior. In S. B. Fountain, M. Bunsey, J. H. Danks, and M. K. McBeath (Eds.), *Animal Cognition and Sequential Behavior: Behavioral, Biological, and Computational Perspectives* (pp. 115-150). Boston, MA: Kluwer Academic.

Harris, E. H. and Washburn, D. A. (2005). Macaques' (Macaca mulatta) use of numerical cues in maze trials. *Animal Cognition, 8,* 190-199.

Hartman, M., Knopman, D. S., and Nissen, M. J. (1989). Implicit learning of new verbal associations. *Journal of Experimental Psychology: Learning, Memory, and Cognition, 15,* 1070-1082.

Keele, S. W., Ivry, R., Mayr, U., Hazeltine, E., and Heuer, H. (2003). The cognitive and neural architecture of sequence representation. *Psychological Review, 110,* 316-339.

Kelley, B. M. and Middaugh, L. D. (1999). Periadolescent nicotine exposure reduces cocaine reward in adult mice. *Journal of Addictive Diseases, 18,* 27-39.

Kelley, B. M. and Rowan, J. D. (2004). Long-term, low-level adolescent nicotine exposure produces dose-dependent changes in cocaine sensitivity and reward in adult mice. *International Journal of Developmental Neuroscience, 22,* 339-348.

Kesner, R. P. (2002). Neural mediation of memory for time: Role of the hippocampus and medial prefrontal cortex. In S. B. Fountain, M. Bunsey, J. H. Danks, and M. K. McBeath (Eds.), *Animal Cognition and Sequential Behavior: Behavioral, Biological, and Computational Perspectives* (pp. 201-226). Boston, MA: Kluwer Academic.

Knopman, D. and Nissen, M. J. (1991). Procedural learning is impaired in Huntington's disease: Evidence from the serial reaction time task. *Neuropsychologia, 29,* 245-254.

McGonigle, B. and Chalmers, M. (2002). The growth of cognitive structure in monkeys and men. In S. B. Fountain, M. Bunsey, J. H. Danks, and M. K. McBeath (Eds.), *Animal Cognition and Sequential Behavior: Behavioral, Biological, and Computational Perspectives* (pp. 269-314). Boston, MA: Kluwer Academic.

Palmer, C. and Pfordresher, P. Q. (2003). Incremental planning in sequence production. *Psychological Review, 110,* 683-712.

Reber, A. S. (1989). Implicit learning and tacit knowledge. *Journal of Experimental Psychology: General, 118,* 219-235.

Restle, F. (1970). Theory of serial pattern learning: Structural trees. *Psychological Review, 77,* 481-495.

Restle, F. (1973). Serial pattern learning: Higher order transitions. *Journal of Experimental Psychology, 99,* 61-69.

Restle, F. and Brown, E. R. (1970a). Serial pattern learning. *Journal of Experimental Psychology, 83*, 120-125.

Restle, F. and Brown, E. R. (1970b). Serial pattern learning: Pretraining of runs and trills. *Psychonomic Science, 19*, 321-322.

Rowan, J. D., Fountain, S. B., Kundey, S. M. A., and Miner, C. L. (2001). A multiple species approach to sequential learning: Are you a man or a mouse? *Behavior Research Methods and Instrumentation, 31*, 435-439.

Sands, S. F. and Wright, A. A. (1980). Serial probe recognition performance by a rhesus monkey and a human with 10- and 20-item lists. *Journal of Experimental Psychology: Animal Behavior Processes, 6*, 386-396.

Sands, S. F. and Wright, A. A. (1982). Monkey and human pictorial memory scanning. *Science, 216*, 1333-1334.

Sircar, R. and Sircar, D. (2005). Adolescent rats exposed to repeated ethanol treatment show lingering behavioral impairments. *Alcoholism, Clinical and Experimental Research, 29*, 1402-1410.

Stempowski, N. K., Carman, H. M., and Fountain, S. B. (1999). Temporal phrasing and overshadowing in rat serial-pattern learning. *Learning and Motivation, 30*, 74-100.

Sun, R. (2000). Introduction to sequence learning. In R. Sun and C. L. Giles (Eds.), *Sequence learning: Paradigms, algorithms, and applications* (pp. 1-10). New York: Springer.

Terrace, H. S. (2005). The simultaneous chain: A new approach to serial learning. *Trends in Cognitive Sciences, 9*, 202-210.

Terrace, H. S. and McGonigle, B. (1994). Memory and representation of serial order by children, monkeys, and pigeons. *Current Directions in Psychological Science, 3*, 180-185.

Trauth, J. A., Seidler, F. J., McCook, E. C., and Slotkin, T. A. (1999). Adolescent nicotine exposure causes persistent upregulation of nicotinic cholinergic receptors in rat brain regions. *Brain Research, 851*, 9-19.

Treichler, F. R., Raghanti, M. A., and Van Tilburg, D. N. (2003). Linking of serially ordered lists by macaque monkeys (*Macaca mulatta*): List position influences. *Journal of Experimental Psychology: Animal Behavior Processes, 29*, 211-221.

Willingham, D. B., Nissen, M. J., and Bullemer, P. (1989). On the development of procedural knowledge. *Journal of Experimental Psychology: Learning, Memory, and Cognition, 15*, 1047-1060.

Willingham, D. B. (1998). A neuropsychological theory of motor skill learning. *Psychological Review, 105*, 558-584.

In: Tasks and Techniques: A Sampling of the Methodologies...
Editor: Matthew J. Anderson, pp. 261-265

ISBN 1-60021-126-7
© 2006 Nova Science Publishers, Inc.

Chapter 21

MIRROR SELF-RECOGNITION: RESEARCH DESIGN AND METHODOLOGY

Gordon G. Gallup, Jr. [*]

State University of New York at Albany, Albany, NY 12222

ABSTRACT

A variety of claims have been made about the ability of different species to recognize themselves in mirrors. Many of these claims, however, are based on intuitive, subjective, impressionistic data rather than rigorous, experimental evidence. The purpose of this chapter is to describe some of the techniques that can be used to provide definitive evidence for an organism's capacity to correctly decipher mirrored information about itself.

INTRODUCTION

In its most rudimentary sense, self-awareness means that you can become the object of your own attention. As a consequence, organisms that are self-aware are in a position to 1) become aware of their own existence, 2) use their experience to make inferences about comparable experiences in others, and 3) begin to think about themselves in relation to past, present, and future events (Gallup, 1998). One objective way to determine if an organism is self-aware is to confront it with its own reflection in a mirror. Mirrors represent an explicit test of this capacity for the simple reason that when confronted with your reflection, you have (wittingly or not) become the object of your own attention. Mirrors enable organisms to see themselves as they are seen by others. In front of a mirror you are an audience to your own behavior. So the question of self-awareness becomes one of trying to determine whether different species are capable of recognizing themselves in mirrors.

[*] Address correspondence to: Gordon G. Gallup, Jr. Department of Psychology, State University of New York at Albany, Albany, New York 12222, Phone: 518-442-4852, Fax: 518-442-4867, E-Mail: gallup@albany.edu

In contrast with humans, most species react to themselves in mirrors as though they were seeing other animals and, even after periods of extended exposure, engage in a variety of species typical social responses directed toward the reflection (see Gallup, 1968). In contemplating this apparent discontinuity, it occurred to me a number of years ago that it might be a consequence of differential experience with mirrors. While mirrors are a common, everyday feature of the human environment, naturally occurring mirrors are infrequently encountered by most species. So I decided to give a group of chimpanzees the benefit of extended exposure to mirrors.

METHODS

The Initial Paradigm

In the original experiment (Gallup, 1970), four preadolescent chimpanzees that had been maintained in social groups, were placed in individual cages all by themselves in separate rooms. Positioned in front of each cage and out of reach, was a full length mirror. Each chimpanzee was given eight hours of mirror exposure each day for a total of 10 days, and their behavior was monitored through a hole in the wall for a period of time every morning and afternoon. As is true for most species, the chimpanzees reacted toward the mirror initially as though they were seeing another chimpanzee, and they all engaged in a variety of species typical social responses directed toward the image.

After the first couple of days these social or other-directed responses to the mirror began to subside, and were replaced on the third day by the emergence of patterns of self-directed behavior. That is, rather than continue to respond to the mirror as such, they began to use the mirror to respond to themselves. They used the reflection to examine and manipulate parts of their bodies they had never seen before, such as looking at the inside of their mouths, making faces at the mirror, inspecting their genitals, and grooming areas they could not otherwise see. We also kept records of the amount of time they spent looking at themselves in the mirror, and once these patterns of self-directed responding appeared their interest in the reflection began to wane.

I was convinced on the basis of these observations that the chimpanzees had learned to recognize themselves in mirrors; i.e., they had come to realize that their behavior was the source of the behavior being depicted in the mirror. However, to move beyond my subjective impressions of what had transpired, I undertook to develop a more rigorous, unobtrusive, experimental test of mirror self-recognition. After the tenth day of mirror exposure, each chimpanzee was completely anesthetized and removed from the cage. While the animal was unconscious I applied a bright red, odorless, nonirritating, alcohol soluble dye to the uppermost portion of an eyebrow ridge and the top half of the opposite ear. The chimpanzee was then returned to its cage and allowed to recover in the absence of the mirror.

There are three special properties to this procedure. First, since the animals were under deep anesthesia when the marks were placed on their faces, they had no information about the application of these marks. Second, the dye was carefully chosen so that once it dried there would be no telltale tactile or olfactory cues. Finally, the marks were strategically applied to predetermined points on the chimpanzees' faces so that they could not be seen without a mirror.

Once the animals had completely recovered from the effects of anesthesia they were fed and given water. We then recorded the number of times they touched the facial marks for 30 minutes in the absence of the mirror to establish a baseline of contact with these marks. There was only one animal that touched a mark on its face during the baseline period, and that only happened once. The mirror was then brought back into the room as an explicit test of self-recognition, and upon seeing themselves with strange red facial marks the chimpanzees attempted to reach up and touch these marks on their faces while intently watching themselves in the mirror. In addition to touching and inspecting these marks that could only be seen in the mirror, the amount of time spent viewing the mirror increased, and several chimpanzees also looked at and smelled their fingers after contacting these marks.

The use of the pre-exposure baseline period serves as a control procedure that can be used to demonstrate that the mark-directed responses seen on the test trial were in fact conditional upon seeing themselves in mirrors. As another control condition, several comparable chimpanzees without the benefit of prior mirror exposure were also anesthetized and marked. Once they recovered from anesthesia and saw themselves in the mirror for the first time, none of the control animals located the marks on their faces. Nor did any of these mirror naïve animals show signs of self-directed behavior, and they all acted as though they were seeing another chimpanzee. These control data demonstrate that the mark-directed responses shown by the other chimpanzees were 1) dependent upon prior exposure to mirrors, 2) not an artifact of anesthesia, and 3) not a consequence of any confounding residual cues left by the dye.

Other Methodological Considerations

It may not always be possible or practical to anesthetize animals for purpose of conducting the mark test. Sham marking, if properly conducted, represents a viable alternative to anesthetization (see Gallup, Povinelli, Suarez, Anderson, Lethmate, and Menzel, 1995). This involves the repeated application of an uncolored solution (typically alcohol) to the facial features that you want to mark. Once the animal habituates to the application of these sham marks (i.e., fails to respond or touch the area that the colorless solution is applied), it can then be marked with the same solution containing the dye. It is important, however, to distract the animal during the marking procedure so it will not see you apply the marking material (e.g., red dye dissolved in alcohol) to its face.

In preparing animals for the mark test it is also important to minimize any prior exposure to the marks. The mark test is predicated on mark salience and among chimpanzees there is evidence for rapid habituation to such marks; i.e., once they discover that the marks are inconsequential they lose interest in the marks (see Povinelli, Gallup, Eddy, Bierschwale, Engstrom, Perilloux, and Toxopeus, 1997). Therefore, animals should only be given the mark test once, and care should be taken before testing to minimize their exposure to other animals that have been marked.

Many primate species avoid eye contact with one another and show gaze aversion, which may minimize exposure to their own image in a mirror (Gallup, Wallnau, and Suarez, 1980). Anderson and Roeder (1989) developed a clever solution to this problem. By positioning a pair of mirrors together at an angle of 60 degrees, the animal can still see itself in the mirror but it cannot make direct eye contact with the image. The use of this technique, however, has not led to mirror self-recognition is species that typically fail the mark test (see Gallup, Anderson, and Shillito, 2002).   *why?*

DISCUSSION

In the process of trying to resolve one apparent evolutionary discontinuity (the difference between the way humans and animals use mirrors), I appear to have run up against another. Many different primates and other mammalian species have been tested for self-recognition (see Gallup et al., 2002). However, using different variations of the methodology detailed above, only three species have show compelling, reproduceable evidence of mirror self-recognition: chimpanzees, orangutans, and humans. While the clear implication of these findings is that the precursor to great apes and humans was self-aware, it is interesting to note that the distribution of this trait among these species is different (see Gallup, 1997). Although the methods used to test human children are not as rigorous (Gallup, 1994), infants begin to show evidence of self-recognition at about 18-24 months of age. By comparison, the onset of this capacity in chimpanzees is developmentally delayed. Chimpanzees do not typically show self-recognition until they are about seven years old (Povinelli, Rulf, Landau, and Bierschwale, 1993). However, once the trait appears among chimpanzees, it remains surprisingly stable over time. In a recent longitudinal study spanning a period of eight years, the majority of the chimpanzees that tested positively for self-recognition initially, continued to show robust evidence of self-recognition eight years later, in spite of the fact that they received no explicit exposure to mirrors during the interim (de Veer, Gallup, Theall, van den Bos, and Povinelli, 2003).

While it is true that not all chimpanzees recognize themselves in mirrors (e.g., Povinelli et al., 1993), not all humans recognize themselves in mirrors either. Prior to about 2 years of age, infants react to mirrors as though they were seeing other babies, and mentally retarded people, autistic children, patients with damage to the frontal cortex, people with advanced senility, and those suffering from certain forms of mental illness, such as schizophrenia, often fail to show self-recognition (for a review of this literature see Gallup, Anderson, and Platek, 2003).

REFERENCES

Anderson, J. R., and Roeder, J. (1989). Responses of capuchin monkeys (Cebus paella) to different conditions of mirror-image stimulation. *Primates, 30,* 581-587.

Gallup, G. G., Jr. (1968). Mirror-image stimulation. *Psychological Bulletin, 70,* 782-793.

Gallup, G. G., Jr. (1970). Chimpanzees: Self-recognition. *Science, 167,* 341-343.

Gallup, G. G., Jr. (1994). Self-recognition: Research strategies and experimental design. In S. Parker, R. Mitchell, and M. Boccia (Eds.), *Self-Awareness in Animals and Humans.* Cambridge University Press. Pp. 35-50.

Gallup, G. G., Jr. (1997). On the rise and fall of self-conception in primates. In J. Snodgrass and R. Thompson (Eds.), *The Self Across Psychology: Self-Recognition, Self Awareness, and the Self-Concept. Annals of the New York Academy of Sciences,* 818, 73-82.

Gallup, G. G., Jr. (1998). Self-awareness and the evolution of social intelligence. *Behavioural Processes, 42,* 239-247.

Gallup, G. G., Jr., Wallnau, L. B., and Suarez, S. D. (1980). Failure to findself-recognition in mother-infant and infant-infant rhesus monkey pairs. *Folia Primatologica, 33,* 210-219.

Gallup, G. G., Jr., Povinelli, D. J., Suarez, S. D., Anderson, J. R., Lethmate, J., and Menzel, E. W. (1995). Further reflections on self-recognition in primates. *Animal Behaviour, 50,* 1525-1532.

Gallup, G. G., Jr., Anderson, J. R., and Shillito, D. J. (2002). The mirror test. In M. Bekoff, C. Allen, and G. Burghardt (Eds.), *The Cognitive Animal.* MIT Press. Pp. 325-333.

Gallup, G. G., Jr., Anderson, J. R., and Platek, S. M. (2003). Self-awareness, social intelligence, and schizophrenia. In T. Kircher and A. David (Eds.), *The Self in Neuroscience and Psychiatry.* Cambridge University Press. Pp. 147-165.

Povinelli, D. J., Rulf, A. R., Landau, K. R., and Bierschwale, D. T. (1993). Self-recognition in chimpanzees (Pan troglodytes): distribution, ontogeny, and patterns of emergence. *Journal of Comparative Psychology, 107,* 347-372.

Povinelli, D. J., Gallup, G. G., Jr., Eddy, T. J., Bierschwale, D. T., Engstrom, M. C., Perilloux, H. K., and Toxopeus, I. B. (1997). Chimpanzees recognize themselves in mirrors. *Animal Behaviour, 53,* 1083-1088.

de Veer, M. W., Gallup, G. G., Jr., Theall, L. A., van den Bos, R., and Povinelli, D. J. (2003). An 8-year longitudinal study of mirror self-recognition in chimpanzees (Pan troglodytes). *Neuropsychologia, 41,* 229-234.

INDEX

D

E

M

Q

R

S

T